MW01630428

NEGOTIATING AND DRAFTING SPORTS VENUE AGREEMENTS

Second Edition

Peter A. Carfagna
Visiting Lecturer in Sports Law
Harvard Law School

AMERICAN CASEBOOK SERIES®

444 Cedar Street, Suite 700
St. Paul, MN 55101
1-877-888-1330

Printed in the United States of America

ISBN: 978-1-63460-348-5

Acknowledgments

I would first like to thank Staci Herr and her colleagues at West Academic for their continuing support in helping me publish my Second Edition of this Book. In so doing, West Academic has now allowed me to update all 3 of my Sports Law Books with a 2nd Edition, which can serve as a strong foundational triad for any law school embarking upon, or seeking to enhance, its Sports Law and Marketing Curriculum, as I have done at Harvard Law School since I first began visiting there in 2007.

I would next like to thank all of my Research and Teaching Assistants at Harvard (and at the other law schools where I visit) for helping me compile the 2nd Edition's many Study Guides and New "Template" Sports Venue-related Agreements, as well as a New Chapter on the Purchase and Sale of a Sports Franchise. Special thanks goes out to Ricky Volante (and his colleagues at Sixth City Sports and Entertainment), who also works with me at Magis, LLC—as well as my most recent Research Assistants at Harvard, Mario Cuttone and Marissa Lambert.

These significant enhancements to my Book should help make this 2nd Edition even more user-friendly and interactive as a Drafting Course Book—not only for Law School Professors and Students, but also for Sports Law Practitioners.

I therefore hope that you will enjoy using this 2nd Edition of my Drafting Course Book both in the classroom and in practice, to refine your contract-drafting skills. In that regard, as I often hear from my students at Harvard and at other law schools where I teach from this Book, the negotiating and drafting exercises contained herein "transcend" Sports Law, because each exercise challenges the Reader to produce Exemplar Clauses and Agreements that are "execution ready and litigation proof."

In closing, I hope that you, too, will accept and respond favorably to this challenge to use this Book to help make each of your next-drafted Sports Venue Agreements "letter perfect," as you prepare to submit them for signature to your Professor and/or Client.

PETER A. CARFAGNA
Visiting Lecturer on Sports Law
Harvard Law School (2007–Present)

Acknowledgements

Summary of Contents

Table of Contents

NEGOTIATING AND DRAFTING SPORTS VENUE AGREEMENTS

Second Edition

Introduction

This book is the third book in my series of "Sports and the Law" books, designed to complement the other two.[1] Having previously discussed the evolution of America's three major sports leagues in "Sports and the Law: Examining the Legal Evolution of America's Three Major Leagues" and athlete representation in "Representing the Professional Athlete," this book focuses on drafting sophisticated contractual documents for a sports venue owner/operator in the Sports Law world. In particular, rather than negotiating and drafting only particular clauses or the "material terms" of an agreement, a legal memorandum, or brief, as is done in the other two books, this book challenges students to negotiate and draft the entire agreement from beginning to end.

As such, this third book "completes the circle" begun by the other two, thus equipping the reader to be a "three-tool attorney," able to represent (1) a professional sports team ("Sports and the Law: Examining the Legal Evolution of America's Three Major Leagues"); (2) a professional athlete ("Representing the Professional Athlete"); and now, based on this book, and (3) the owner/operator of a sports venue.

The venue-related agreements that will be negotiated and drafted in this book will include a lease agreement between a municipality that is constructing a new stadium/arena and the owner/operator of a team that will play in the new venue (see Chapter 2). It will also require the drafting of a "naming rights" agreement for such a venue (see Chapter 3), as well as a companion "presenting sponsorship" agreement (see Chapter 4). Additional categories of sponsorship for the owner of the team (or venue) will also be explored, including media rights agreements (see Chapter 5), food and beverage rights agreements (see Chapter 6), the medical and financial services categories (see Chapters 7 and 8, respectively), sponsorships by state-operated entities (see Chapter 9), and lastly, a new chapter will explore asset purchase agreements, specifically the sales of franchises (see Chapter 10).

By drafting these agreements in seriatim fashion, students will learn how "exclusivity" will have to be offered in the foundational sponsorship agreement categories, which, in turn, will limit the "benefits" that will remain available to be offered in the remaining

---

1 SPORTS AND THE LAW: EXAMINING THE LEGAL EVOLUTION OF AMERICA'S THREE "MAJOR LEAGUES," 2D EDITION (West Academic 2011), A SUPPLEMENT TO SPORTS AND THE LAW: EXAMINING THE LEGAL EVOLUTION OF AMERICA'S THREE "MAJOR LEAGUES" (West Academic 2016), and REPRESENTING THE PROFESSIONAL ATHLETE, 2D EDITION (West Academic 2013).

categories of sponsorship. Students will also learn how to draft non-exclusive category sponsorships for smaller dollar amounts, by offering "softer" in-kind incentives to such sponsors including, for example, a variety of on-field and off-field corporate entertainment opportunities for the sponsor and its employees/clients. Also, the coordination of all such sponsorships with the team's print/multimedia advertising, as well as with the broadcasts of the team's games, will be examined. ("Exemplar" Student Group responses for each Chapter's drafting exercise are set forth in the Teacher's Manual that accompanies this book.)

In general, this book will strive to create an environment in which the students will be required to function as if they were members of a major sports agency's legal department or a law firm that specializes in sports law. Students will have the opportunity to explore and experiment with negotiating strategies as well, since there is rarely one "right answer" in most situations. In so doing, this book will better prepare students both for externship opportunities while in school and sports-related employment post-graduation by allowing them to master the skills related to negotiating, drafting, and analyzing the various moving parts of complicated sports venue-related agreements.

For more in-depth information relating to the topics discussed throughout this book, please further read A Supplement to "Negotiating and Drafting Sports Venue Agreements," by Peter A. Carfagna. The supplement is a compilation of Study Guides, which provide specialized information relating to negotiating and drafting sports venue agreements, and a look at non-traditional revenue events, such as celebrity softball games and concert agreements, that sports venues can utilize to maximize year-round revenues.

For professors teaching Sports Law courses with this book, a Course Overview Presentation and exemplar assignments for each assignment can be found in A Teaching Manual to "Negotiating and Drafting Sports Venue Agreements," by Peter A. Carfagna.

For up-to-date information related to the topics discussed throughout this book, please periodically review the following publications: Sports Litigation Alert, Sports Law Blog, Sports Agent Blog, SportsBusiness Journal, and Sports Sponsorship Insider. It is additionally recommended to become a member of the Sports Lawyers Association.

Links to certain footnotes throughout this text can be found in the course syllabus provided by the instructor.

Appendix B should be read in its entirety, as it provides necessary in-depth information for law students and practitioners alike.

Chapter 1

BOILERPLATE CONTRACTING CLAUSES

This chapter introduces and outlines several essential "boilerplate" clauses to be used across all types of agreements and in all of the hypotheticals throughout this book. When going through the drafting hypotheticals in the chapters that follow, students should refer back to this chapter to ensure that they do not miss essential clauses or elements of clauses presented here.

Contracts relating to the sports industry are often unique, particularly because most are subject to rules implemented by the governing bodies of the sports league. Such contracts, however, will usually still contain so-called "boilerplate" provisions. Although these clauses are often thought to be less meaningful parts of the contract because they do not contain the heart of the deal terms, the opposite is true—boilerplate provisions are so fundamental that lawyers include them in most contracts.

Boilerplate provisions include those designating the location and forum in which a dispute arising under the contract will be resolved, whether the parties must submit the dispute to an alternative dispute resolution process prior to or in lieu of litigation, the law that will govern the dispute, the effect of the invalidation of a portion of the contract, who has the right to amend the contract, whether the contract has third party beneficiaries, and the like. For instance, the terms set forth in the confidentiality and survival paragraphs may be critically important when a team terminates an agreement with one sponsor and seeks another sponsor in the same product or service category; indeed, the team does not want prospective sponsors to know the price paid by the original sponsor. If the terms of the deal are confidential, then neither the team nor the former sponsor can legally divulge the sponsorship fee paid, and provided that the confidentiality clause survives the termination of the original sponsorship agreement, its provisions will continue to bind the parties. Without survival, confidentiality would last only until the termination of the agreement, and the team would be unable to keep a prospective sponsor from discovering the amount of the past fee.

Boilerplate clauses should not remain identical across agreements; they should be altered to fit the specific contractual relationship. Termination and Remedies clauses, for example, will vary dramatically across agreements; in a sponsorship agreement, a breach like nonpayment will give rise to termination rights, whereas it might not in a lease agreement. Furthermore, remedies will include the right to injunctive relief in some cases, but not in others. These distinctions are essential to the agreements; having a right to seek an injunction is a very powerful equitable remedy that can be an important way for a party to enforce its rights in certain agreements, such as a lease agreement in which the city seeks to stop a team from playing in another venue.

Perhaps most important to keep in mind when tailoring standard clauses, as well as the other clauses of any sports-related agreement, are the preexisting limitations on the team's rights. The teams are generally members of larger leagues and are subject to league rules, regulations, and standards. League constitutions, bylaws, and other rules and regulations promulgated by the leagues may limit the amount of indebtedness that a team may take on, who can hold an ownership interest in the team, and the types of sponsors that the team can engage.

The following section discusses clauses common to most contracts, and, where appropriate, the ways in which these boilerplate provisions may be altered to reflect the unique aspects of the sports industry.

A. DEFINITION AND SCOPE OF THE DEAL

Definitions[1]

Although short and simple agreements usually define terms in context, parties often include a separate section listing all defined terms in longer agreements like in lease agreements or purchase and sale agreements. This enables the parties to refer to complex concepts repeatedly without explaining a concept each time it is addressed. This also enables lawyers to change material terms by altering only the definition, rather than modifying the concept each time it appears in the agreement. Often the parties' names will be defined terms, which allows parties to indicate which portion of their entity or which persons associated with their entity intend to be bound by the

---

1 For more information on the building blocks of deal documents, including use of definition, *see* Peter Carfagna, An Introduction to Agreement Structure, Recitals, and Definitions Study Guide, Appendix B: A SUPPLEMENT TO "NEGOTIATING AND DRAFTING SPORTS VENUE AGREEMENTS" (2016).

agreement. Other agreements incorporated by reference may also be important defined terms.

The critical defined terms will differ from deal to deal. For a lease agreement, the definition of the "Stadium Premises," or an equivalent term, will dictate which areas the lessor and lessee own, operate, and maintain. In a sponsorship agreement, the category for which the sponsor obtains "exclusivity" is perhaps the most important definition, and the most hotly debated deal point, within the agreement. A broadly defined category gives the sponsor greater freedom to exclude its competitors and to require the team to use a variety of its product or services, whereas a narrowly defined category may give the team the ability to economically exploit a larger number of categories.

If a team grants Coca-Cola exclusivity within a category defined as "All Beverages" without further defining the term "beverages," for example, the team probably could not contract with a different company to provide beer or other alcoholic beverages. Terms not otherwise defined in the agreement often take on their standard meaning outside the context of the agreement, so "All Beverages" would be understood to include all drinks. Thus if the team grants to Coca-Cola the "All Beverages" category, without a definition of the type beverages the parties intend to both include and exclude, it is likely that Coca-Cola could then claim that under the plain meaning of the agreement, it alone owns the right to advertise and sell all drinks, both alcoholic and nonalcoholic, in conjunction with the team and at the venue.

Pouring rights are the right of a beverage company, the pouring rights sponsor, to sell its beverages (or have them sold) in a given facility. Exclusive pouring rights ensure that the pouring rights sponsor is the only company, within its defined category of exclusivity, whose products will be sold, or "poured," in the venue. Under normal circumstances, either the team or the team's landlord owns the pouring rights of the facility. In the situation above, in which Coca-Cola has exclusivity for "All Beverages," Coca-Cola would effectively own, or at least have leased, all of the pouring rights for the facility. Coca-Cola, rather than the team itself, therefore, would likely have the right to sell the pouring rights for alcohol, instead of the team. If, however, the team sold Coca-Cola the exclusive rights to a more narrowly defined category like "Nonalcoholic Beverages," then the team would still have the freedom to contract with a different sponsor for exclusivity and pouring rights in an alcoholic beverages category.

In many sponsorship agreements, the definitions of "Competitor" and "Competitor Products" will be as important as that of their category. The defined "Competitor" and "Competitor Products" terms allow the parties to draft exclusivity from two perspectives: first, from the perspective of what is allowed under the agreement (that is, the definition of the Sponsor's "Products" within the "Category"); and second, from the perspective of what is disallowed (that is, the definition of "Competitor Products"). These and many other definitions can make enormous differences in terms of the scope of the contract. The definitions section is, therefore, a key tool (arguably the most important tool) for drafting a "litigation proof, execution ready" contract.

Term

Every contract has a term, even if the contract is perpetual and merely contains a list of termination events. Defining the length of the term will dictate, or be a function of, other portions of the contract, including payment, termination events, renewals, and obligations of the parties upon termination. The term can be a single length of time or a series of time periods with renewal options. Which party is given the option to renew the agreement for a period of time is often a key issue in negotiating the contract. For example, in a stadium lease, the city will likely want a longer term, but the team will prefer to have a shorter term with a team option to renew, or even better, several options to renew for shorter periods each time.[2]

Any time parties negotiate for one-sided renewal options (that is, renewal options that may be exercised at the sole prerogative of one, but not both, of the parties), the important question of "opting in" versus "opting out" arises. Most parties negotiating for a renewal option would prefer it to be opt-in; they would prefer the renewal to occur only if the party explicitly so elects. The party granting the renewal option, in contrast, might prefer an opt-out renewal provision under which the contract would renew automatically at the end of each term unless the party with the option elected not to renew within a specified notice period. The notice period is also a key negotiation point for the parties when negotiating options. In a lease agreement, the landlord wants enough notice to have time to find another tenant when a current tenant departs, whereas the tenant wants to have more time to consider its options before renewing or terminating the lease.

The Term clause of a contract may also provide a party with any combination of a right of first negotiation, first refusal, or exclusive

---

2 *See* "Term" Section of Levi's Stadium Naming Rights Agreement.

negotiation. The right of first negotiation requires the parties to engage in bona fide and good faith negotiations to renew the contractual relationship before either party seeks to go elsewhere. Typically, a first negotiation right will specify the window in which the parties must commence negotiations, which usually begins before the term of the current agreement expires. If such a right exists, the parties may only seek to find a deal with a different entity if the parties cannot reach an agreement during the first negotiation window after a bona fide and good faith attempt to do so.[3]

The right of first refusal, on the other hand, requires one party to allow the other to match or top any competing offer and win the deal. In a sports sponsorship deal, the right of first refusal would give the existing sponsor the right to match a competing offer from another sponsor and retain its sponsorship relationship with the team. As with a first negotiation right, the agreement should provide a window in which the parties should present and respond to such an offer, typically before the expiration of the current agreement. Once the window for first refusal ends, the team would no longer have an obligation to present competing offers to the existing sponsor nor afford it a right to match the offer to retain the sponsorship.

The right of exclusive negotiation requires the parties to negotiate only with each other for the period of time specified in the exclusive negotiation section. Often exclusive negotiation will be coupled with the right of first negotiation to ensure that during the window of first negotiation, the parties are negotiating only with each other.

The rights of first negotiation, first refusal, and exclusive negotiation can be included in an agreement either together or separately. When together, the windows of time for each right usually run consecutively. For example, a naming rights sponsor can contract for an exclusive right of first negotiation and a right of first refusal so that as the naming rights agreement is set to expire, the team is required to negotiate with the existing sponsor first to renew the relationship. If the parties fail to reach an agreement during the first negotiation window, the team could then negotiate with other potential naming rights sponsors but would have to return to the current sponsor to give it the opportunity to match the best offer. If the existing sponsor chooses to match, the team would then be bound to sign a new naming rights agreement with the existing sponsor.

3 *See* "Right of First Negotiation" Provision in Levi's Stadium Naming Rights Agreement.

Payment

The contents of any agreement will depend significantly upon payment terms, including costs associated with reaching the initial agreement. For instance, the number of representations and warranties that a party wants will depend upon the amount of risk that it is willing to undertake; the more representations and warranties that one party secures from the other, the fewer surprises there are likely to be after the agreement is signed. Completing the due diligence required for those representations and warranties is costly, however, so this section will be in part a reflection of the price that the parties are willing to pay in exchange for a few lingering uncertainties. The representations and warranties will also affect the cost of any indemnification provision that the parties are willing to provide because more indemnities can yield more unplanned future costs.

In a sponsorship agreement, the exclusivity category is likely to be the most expensive representation and warranty that the sponsor will buy. The team must weigh the desire to achieve a large sponsorship fee against how far it is willing to go in its representations and warranties. To determine the amount to which the team should be willing to agree, the team will need to look ahead and try to predict the options that it will have if it chooses each potential course of action. For example, selling the naming rights to a stadium for $100 million seems like a great deal for the team and clearly preferable to a deal selling them for $10 million. If, however, the $100 million deal includes a broad category of exclusivity for the sponsor and an enormous advertising package, the team may find this option inferior. This would be the case, for example, if the inventory given to the naming rights sponsor would be worth more than the $100 million offered by that sponsor, if later sold to multiple sponsors. Thus, with any agreement, payment should take into consideration the benefits offered, and if payment is determined first, benefits should be adjusted accordingly.

Intellectual Property

With any contract, the issue of the parties' intellectual property, including any intellectual property created under the agreement, must be decided. In many contractual relationships, one party is given a limited right to use the other party's intellectual property, such as a trademark. It is important, however, that the agreement clearly states when and how each party may use the other's intellectual property and who owns the intellectual property. In a sponsorship agreement between a team and a sponsor, for example, the sponsor will want to use the team logo in its advertisements, and the team may want to use the sponsor's logos in the team's venue. The team and sponsor, in allowing the use of their logos, must protect them by both retaining ownership and monitoring and controlling their use.[4]

In some relationships, a joint logo will be created to indicate and advertise the relationship. In such a case, the parties must decide who creates it, who owns it, how each side may or must use it, who has the obligation to pursue infringers, and what happens to the logo when the relationship ends. The Red Sox, for instance, do not want to share ownership of their logo with Lumber Liquidators, the official flooring provider of the Red Sox that paid to use the Red Sox logo in its ads. Teams also want to prevent any situation in which a company makes unauthorized use of certain identifiable characteristics of teams for less-than-honorable purposes.

To give an example, in 2009, Anheuser-Busch rolled out a marketing campaign targeting college campuses, home to binge drinking and underage drinkers, using its new "Fan Cans,"—beer cans decorated in the colors of the local college sports team and used in conjunction with slogans like "Show your true colors with Bud Light" and "... made for game day."[5] Such a practice can negatively impact the reputation of the teams, which is just one of the reasons why so many of the universities targeted by the "Fan Cans" campaign requested that Anheuser-Busch discontinue the campaign in their region.[6]

In any intellectual property provision in a contract with a sports team, the team has to be sure that it grants only rights that it actually has. Some of the intellectual property used by the teams belongs to the league, and the team must be very careful to license only what it owns. In addition, the league may limit the team's ability to license its intellectual property, and any contract in which the team grants a license to its intellectual property must adhere to those limits.

---

4 For more information on Intellectual Property Rights, *see* Peter Carfagna, Appendix B: An Introduction to Naming Rights Agreements and Intellectual Property Rights Study Guide, A SUPPLEMENT TO "NEGOTIATING AND DRAFTING SPORTS VENUE AGREEMENTS" (2016).

5 *See* John Fogg, "FIRST DOWN: Budweiser's shady ad campaign," *WASH. TIMES*, Sept. 5, 2009.

6 *Id.*

B. BREACH AND END-GAME PROVISIONS[7]

Insurance/Indemnification

Indemnification clauses allow the parties to prearrange which party will bear the costs of which liabilities. As such, indemnification provisions should indicate the liabilities for which each party will indemnify. A stadium lease agreement, for example, may have a two-part indemnification provision: one in which the city indemnifies the team for liabilities arising from the quality or fixtures of the facility, and another in which the team indemnifies the city for liabilities arising from the actions of the team.

Indemnification provisions are often necessary as suits for injuries caused within a sports venue often name both the team and the city as defendants. To take an example from fiction, in the classic film *The Fortune Cookie*,[8] Jack Lemmon's character, a CBS cameraman on the sidelines of a Cleveland Browns game, is run over by a player and trips over a tarp on the sidelines. His sleazy lawyer brother-in-law, played by Walter Matthau, convinces him to file a suit against the city, the team, and CBS.[9] If CBS's contract with the team lacked an indemnification provision, CBS could find itself paying for an injury proximately caused by the actions of a player on the team and the facility's negligence in failing to move the tarp.

An indemnification provision will often indicate not only who is indemnifying whom, but also what the indemnification involves. Indemnification frequently requires the indemnifying party to pay for the litigation and conduct it on behalf of the indemnified party. In some instances, the indemnified party will be given some control over decisions, including whether to settle. To ensure that a party has this right, the indemnification clause must clearly state it.

Also common in indemnification provisions is a basket or a deductible, which effectively prevents a party from bothering the other party for immaterial breaches of the agreement. This limits a party's right to indemnification. With both a basket and a deductible, the parties agree to an amount at which the aggregate value of breaches becomes material enough to trigger indemnification. With a basket, when this threshold is reached, the breaching party becomes liable for the full amount of damages. With a deductible, in contrast, the breaching party owes only the amount of damages over

---

7 For further discussion on breach and end-game provisions *see* Peter Carfagna, Appendix B: Breach Termination and Remedies, A SUPPLEMENT TO "NEGOTIATING AND DRAFTING SPORTS VENUE AGREEMENTS" (2016).

8 THE FORTUNE COOKIE (United Artists 1966).

9 *Id.*

the value of the threshold. The inclusion of a mini-basket is also possible, which prevents certain minor claims, such as individual claims below $5,000, from counting toward the basket or deductible.

Deductibles, baskets, and mini-baskets place a floor on indemnification obligations, but it is also possible to cap indemnification obligations at a specific amount or percentage of the value of the total deal. To ensure that indemnification provisions will have teeth, parties often require each other to carry insurance to cover possible indemnification obligations and expenses. In some cases, the failure to carry insurance may even rise to the level of a material breach by the uninsured party. Further discussion of indemnification will be addressed in later chapters, including Chapter 3.

Force Majeure

The force majeure clause of a contract tries to define the seemingly indefinable; it addresses what happens if an unforeseeable event occurs that precludes one or both parties from performing their obligations under an agreement. Essential to this clause is the definition of a "force majeure event." Examples of force majeure events include fires, floods, acts of God, insurrections, invasions, and strikes.[10]

In addition to listing force majeure events, the force majeure clause sets forth the obligations of the parties in the case of such an event. In many cases, the party suffering from the force majeure event will be obligated to notify the other party of its inability to perform and provide a reason for the nonperformance. After notice, the agreement may be suspended, relieving both parties of their obligations thereunder until the force majeure event ceases or until it becomes clear that the parties cannot recover from the force majeure event. For instance, if a flood destroys a stadium, the lease may be terminated, rather than suspended.

In the event that a suspension occurs, the parties may negotiate for an extension on the term of the agreement equal to the amount of time for which the agreement was suspended. In some cases, a party may wish to negotiate for a termination right upon the occurrence of a force majeure event. The party suffering from the force majeure event will strongly oppose a termination right, however, because such an event is by definition beyond the party's control. In sports-related agreements, player strikes or owner lockouts may also constitute

10 For an example of a Force Majeure Definition *see* "Definitions" Section of Levi's Stadium Naming Rights Agreement.

force majeure events. Further discussion of Force Majeure clauses will be addressed in later chapters, including Chapter 2.

Termination

The termination clause of a contract sets forth the events that allow one or both parties to terminate the agreement. The expiration of the term and the renewal terms can be included in this section because they are termination events. Further, in some instances, one party may get the right to terminate the agreement. Termination rights are usually tied to the concept of a material breach of the agreement by the other party. If this is the case, it will be necessary to define what constitutes a breach by either party and how a breach rises to the level of materiality. For instance, failure to pay rent may be a breach of a lease agreement. In many cases, the tenant would have the opportunity to cure the breach within a given time period before the breach is deemed material enough for the landlord to terminate the lease and evict the tenant.

The occurrence of a material adverse change (MAC) to either party could also constitute a termination event and grant either party the right to terminate.[11] The termination clause, therefore, will likely include an opportunity to give notice and cure in the event of a breach. If the breaching party does not cure within a specified time period after receiving notice, then the breach may reach the level of materiality required to give rise to a termination right for the non-breaching party. The league commissioner's censure of an owner or removal of that owner from the team may also give certain termination rights to the co-owners. These rights may pertain to both the partnership agreement and other agreements among the owners.

In addition to laying out the situations in which a party may terminate, a contract should indicate the rights and obligations of the parties upon termination. For instance, in a sponsorship agreement, the bearing of the costs of signage removal from a facility will often be addressed in the Termination or Post-Termination Rights and Obligations clause of the sponsorship agreement. Further discussion of Post-Termination Rights and Obligations will be addressed in later chapters, including Chapter 3.

Remedies/Limit of Liability

Two common types of remedies are available upon breach of an agreement: equitable remedies and monetary remedies. Equitable remedies include injunctions and specific performance, and monetary remedies consist of various types of damages, including actual,

[11] For further discussion of MACs, please *see* Chapter 3.

consequential, incidental, and punitive damages. The remedies provision of any contract needs to indicate which remedies are available to which parties, and sometimes for which types of breach. In many cases, equitable remedies will not be available to either party or will be available to only one party.

In a stadium lease agreement, for example, the city may obtain the right to seek an injunction enjoining the team from playing at another venue during the term of the lease, but the team is unlikely to be able to seek either an injunction or specific performance to ensure that the city performs its obligations under the lease. For monetary damages, the parties will often be limited to actual damages, and even those damages may be capped.

The parties may choose to limit liability in all situations or only in specific situations. The parties may want uncapped damages in the case of a knowing or intentional breach. If a party is able to show that a limitation of liability clause does not apply to the situation at hand and that uncapped damages are available, the non-breaching party has the leverage to either seek the damages or to negotiate a favorable settlement.

Assignment[12]

Many agreements in sports last for a number of years, if not decades. Although the agreements endure, the parties do not always remain static; companies merge, are bought, or become financially unable to continue to pay a sponsorship fee, and teams change venues, ownership, or even cities. An assignment provision allows the parties to indicate whether or not a party can assign their rights and obligations under the agreement to another party. A sponsor might want to assign an agreement if it can no longer afford to pay for it, or if another entity buys or merges with the ownership entity. In many cases, assignment by the sponsor will be allowed, so long as the team has approval rights.

Drafting a satisfactory assignment provision is more difficult when the team wants to assign its rights and obligations under the agreement, unless the assignment is pursuant only to a change in ownership, because it is rare that a comparable entity replaces a team that leaves a venue or a city. For example, if a sponsor pays a large Naming Rights Fee annually to an arena that houses both an NBA and an NHL franchise, then when one team leaves, the value of those naming rights decreases. Even if a Lacrosse team replaces the

---

[12] Further discussion of assignment provisions will be made in Chapters 3 and 4; *see also* Peter Carfagna, Appendix B: Assignment and Anti-Assignment, A SUPPLEMENT TO "NEGOTIATING AND DRAFTING SPORTS VENUE AGREEMENTS" (2016).

lost team, the value of those naming rights will still decrease. Like all other provisions in a sports contract, any assignment provision must be subordinate to conflicting provisions in league documents, including the league constitution, bylaws, and other agreements.

In any assignment provision, approval rights will play a large role because both parties want to have control over the parties with whom they maintain a contractual relationship. Whenever any party has approval rights, the contract should specify the standard of approval: Is the approval subject to a "reasonableness" standard? Should it be in the "sole discretion" or the "sole reasonable discretion" of the party with approval rights? In addition, the parties should address whether approval rights are opt-in or opt-out; that is, whether approval or disapproval is assumed unless the party indicates otherwise. The provision should also address when the party waiting for approval can assume approval or disapproval if it has not heard from the party with approval rights.

Governing Law/Dispute Resolution

Often the parties to an agreement want to preselect the manner in which any potential disputes will be resolved as litigation is costly, time consuming, and detrimental to the parties' reputations. As a result, confidential arbitration has become the preferred method of dispute resolution in contract disputes—it is cheaper, more expedient, and less injurious to the reputations of the parties than litigation. Some agreements may also include a mediation clause, allowing non-urgent disputes to attempt to be resolved through mediation first. If mediation fails, then the parties would arbitrate. Even if the contract does not permit litigation, the dispute resolution clause may also include a forum selection clause and a choice of law provision, which indicates the law that will govern the agreement.

C. MISCELLANEOUS CLAUSES

Confidentiality

Maintaining confidentiality is not always important to the parties, but one party often wants certain provisions of the agreement to remain confidential. A confidentiality clause, therefore, can indicate whether all or a part of the agreement is confidential and with whom parties may share information about the agreement.

Survival

It is common for rights and obligations provided within a contract to terminate when the contract terminates. This is not always ideal; the parties may want certain provisions, such as the intellectual property clause, the confidentiality clause, and any indemnification provisions, to remain effective even after the relationship terminates.

Integration

The integration clause is usually a one-line statement; for example: "This Agreement constitutes the entire agreement between the parties hereto with respect to the transactions contemplated hereby and may not be modified or changed except by a written instrument executed by each of the parties." Parties do not always want an integration clause; for example, parties with an ongoing and amicable relationship may want the freedom to make oral amendments or additional promises that bind them. Often, however, it is essential that only the provisions of the agreement, not any oral assertions made in negotiations or in any other forum, bind the parties. This assures both parties that only terms that each has agreed to in writing will be enforceable; difficult-to-prove and costly-to-litigate oral modifications will not.

It is important to note, however, that the inclusion of an integration clause highlights the need for very careful drafting. If the agreement seems facially unambiguous, parol evidence rules will often prohibit the admission of extrinsic evidence to prove the parties' intent, even if the seemingly "clear" interpretation sharply contrasts with the intent of the parties at the time of drafting.

Waiver

A waiver provision is a very short, but very powerful, clause in a contract. The waiver provision addresses whether the failure by a party to exercise a right created by an agreement will constitute a waiver of that right in future situations. For example, if the team has a right to interest on late payments of a sponsorship fee but accepts the principal amount without demanding interest on the first late payment, the team may have waived its right to ever receive interest on late payments, unless a waiver clause indicates otherwise. Waiver provisions commonly state simply that the failure by either party to exercise a right under the agreement does not constitute a waiver of that right in the future. A waiver provision will thus indicate whether waiver of rights may be implied by actions or whether a waiver must be express.

Severability

Like the integration clause, the severability clause often consists of just one line, such as the following: "If any portion of this Agreement shall be unenforceable, it shall not affect the enforceability of the remainder of the Agreement." This clause ensures that the unenforceability of any one portion of the contract does not invalidate the entire agreement.

* * * *

In every contract, it will be essential for the parties to define and outline the scope of the deal, address breach and end-game situations, and tie up as many loose ends as possible. In sports, the three types of boilerplate clauses listed above should appear in every sponsorship agreement, and some should appear in stadium lease agreements as well. Most of this book addresses various types of team sponsorship agreements, but because these sponsorships have elements of in-facility rights and obligations, the book begins with a chapter on the stadium lease agreement.

It is important to begin with the lease because it will, in many cases, define and limit the rights that the team will have with respect to the sponsorships that it will sign in the future. For example, the lease agreement will determine whether the team or the landlord owns the naming rights of the facility and, as such, the right to choose whether or not to sell a sponsorship. Each contract signed by a sports team will limit what the team has the right do, beginning with its franchise agreement with the league and continuing into its lease and sponsorship agreements. The stadium lease is a logical first step—the stadium gives the team a place to play before it begins to outfit the facility with sponsorship inventory.

Chapter 2

STADIUM LEASE AGREEMENTS

When fans think of sports teams, the facilities in which these teams play naturally come to mind. Some facilities, such as Fenway Park and Wrigley Field, are perhaps as identifiable as the teams themselves. But behind these partnerships between teams and facilities lie complex stadium lease agreements, which cover in great detail the precise relationship between the team and the facility. Stadium lease agreements represent some of the most complicated and contested agreements in the sports industry because they often involve the city. Indeed, lease agreements allocate responsibilities for stadium maintenance between the team and the city, and cities often try to secure the team's residence in the stadium with a "non-relocation" clause. The agreement also includes terms specifying the length of the lease, the means of terminating the lease, the manner of the team's payment for facility use, how the team and the owner of the facility split income generated from the facility, and the team's covered uses of the facility. In recent years, the manner of financing of the facility—essentially, whether public funds will be utilized in developing and maintaining the stadium—has become one of the more polarizing issues in negotiating stadium lease agreements. As sources of public funding for the construction of new stadiums have dwindled, team owners have had to issue personal guarantees in building new facilities.[1]

A. TERM OF LEASE

Cities traditionally have been the main source of funding for stadiums, mainly through the use of taxpayer-subsidized bond financings.[2] With the increase in sophistication of stadium facilities, costs of stadium construction, and competition for government funds, however, statutorily created entities have replaced cities and

---

1 *See* "The Conflict Between Private and Public Funding For Stadiums," *AOL*, Aug. 31, 2015, available at: http://www.aol.com/article/2015/08/31/the-conflict-between-private-and-public-funding-for-stadiums/21229466/.

2 *See* "Yankees, Mets Receive Additional Tax-Exempt Bond Financing," *SPORTS BUSINESS DAILY*, Jan. 19, 2009; *see also* Aaron Kuriloff & Darrell Preston, "In Stadium Building Spree, U.S. Taxpayers Lose $4 Billion," *BLOOMBERG BUSINESS*, Sept. 5, 2012, available at: http://www.bloomberg.com/news/articles/2012-09-05/in-stadium-building-spree-u-s-taxpayers-lose-4-billion.

counties as the primary sources of stadium funding. The owner of the stadium, whether a city, county, or specially created municipal authority, will usually seek a long fixed term of 20 to 30 years to "lock in" the sports team to the city and stadium. The city will need to carefully construct the term provisions so that the term length equals or exceeds the period necessary for the team to repay the bonds required for the stadium financing. The city will not want to agree to a "finance retirement" provision, which would enable the team to exit the facility upon payment of the debt incurred in connection with the stadium. If forced to agree to such a provision, the city should extract other value from the team, such as an increased percentage return on the debt. The city should seek multiple sequential options to renew the term of the lease for periods of five to ten years but will likely have to cede control of the options to the team. Although the city may have to give the team control over the extension options, the city should classify them as "opt-out" options, such that the default course will be an automatic extension of the lease term.[3] If the team opts out of the lease after the fixed term, the city should require a significant advance notice period, such as 180 days, from the team because the city will need to find a new tenant for its facility.

The team will likely seek a short lease term of 10 to 20 years to give itself more opportunities, greater leverage, and the freedom to move if it finds the city or facility unsatisfactory. As mentioned above, the team will fight hard for control over the options to extend the lease—it will want the option to extend a favorable lease to block another franchise from competing for the facility. The team will prefer many short renewal terms to a few long renewal terms, even if the cumulative option years are equivalent; each option represents an opportunity for the team to seek out other facility leases in different cities or extract additional concessions from the city. The team will insist that it has the sole and exclusive ability to exercise these options, but it will likely accept opt-out provisions despite its preference for opt-in provisions. Although the team will seek a shorter notice requirement in choosing to exercise its renewal options, it will likely understand the city's concerns about finding a replacement tenant and will ultimately agree upon a reasonable notice provision. The team will push for a "finance retirement" provision under which it can pay down the remaining debt on the lease and terminate the lease ahead of the anticipated term. The city will resist such a payment schedule unless the team pays a substantial premium. The team may also want an early termination option, but the city probably will not agree to this.

---

3 *See* "Term" Section in "Levi's Stadium Rights Agreement."

The zone of potential agreement (ZOPA) between the city and the team likely will be a term of 20 to 30 years, which should be long enough for the city to pay off the bonds and short enough to provide the team with enough flexibility to seek other options if the lease is unsatisfactory.[4] The $1.3 billion MetLife Stadium, home of the New York Giants and New York Jets, falls within this range, with a term length of 25 years. If all of the options are exercised, however, the term could last up to 97 years.[5] The team will likely be granted 2 to 4 renewal options in the form of opt-out options, for 5 to 10 years each, which must be exercised in writing prior to the expiration of the current term. The notice provision for exercising these options will likely be between 90 and 180 days before the expiration of the term. Depending upon the team's adamancy and what it is willing to give up in exchange, the lease may have a "financing retirement" provision. The provision will likely provide a moderate to substantial return on capital for the city (between one and ten percent above return on capital) before the team will be allowed to terminate the lease early. The city is unlikely to give the team a blanket early termination option.

B. TERMINATION OF LEASE

Either party may want to terminate the lease agreement for a variety of reasons, including a change in control or bankruptcy of one party, a material breach by a party, or frustration of the essential purpose of the agreement by a third party. Breaches of the lease agreement, including default on rental payments, can become so severe that termination of the lease is the most equitable option, but a default rarely results in lease termination. Only after all other remedies have been exhausted and the most serious breaches remain unmitigated will a party seek to terminate a lease agreement. As described above, the city would like to prevent the team from terminating the lease for any reason. The city has invested significant political and financial capital in constructing the facility and does not want the team to leave the facility early. On the other hand, the team will want the ability to terminate the lease at any time.

The ZOPA will likely be an agreement with a very limited termination clause. Termination will likely be permitted only in limited circumstances, after the breaching party is afforded multiple opportunities to cure a material breach and efforts to resolve the dispute through mediation or arbitration have failed. A debt retirement provision in the agreement might allow the team to terminate the lease early, but such a provision will be very costly for

---

4 *See* "Agreement of Lease—City of Eastlake and Cascia LLC."

5 *See* "Meadowlands Stadium," *SPORTS ILLUSTRATED*, Dec. 20, 2006.

the team to pursue and is unlikely to be exercisable early in the lease term.

C. RENT

Although rent provisions in lease agreements can become quite complex, most rent formulas derive from one or more of the three basic types of rent arrangements: fixed rent (per game or annual), flexible rent (based on ticket sales or some other metric), or a combination of the two. Some leases may take an unconventional approach and base rent upon operating expenses for the facility instead of revenue generated by the team; the former is less likely to fluctuate than the latter. A rent-per-game payment schedule is a common form of a fixed rent arrangement, but flexible rent schedules typically have a predefined floor and ceiling to ensure that the eventual rent payment is within a reasonable range. For example, the San Antonio Spurs pay rent per game, with the rate increasing from preseason games to regular season games to postseason games.[6] Similarly, the Houston Astros pay a fixed rent and retain the right to all stadium revenues during their home games.[7]

The city will seek a high floor on rent through a large fixed annual rent base. If the agreement contains a flexible component, the high fixed base will protect the city if game attendance is low. This stable source of income will ensure that the debt is paid in a low-risk manner. The city, however, will also want some upside if game attendance is high and may seek a percentage of ticket sales or concessions.[8] Ideally, the city would like to have a "greater of" provision under which it has the option to choose either the fixed or the flexible rent, depending upon which happens to be higher during a given year. This would represent a low-risk, high-reward strategy for the city.

The team will attempt to minimize its rent payment to the city in the fashion of the Indiana Pacers, who pay an annual rent of $1.[9] The team's preference between fixed and flexible rent payment schedules will depend upon its projected revenues. If the team produces high

---

6 San Antonio Spurs Lease Agreement *in* Martin J. Greenberg, THE STADIUM GAME 216 (2d Ed. 2001). This additional text provides exemplar clauses, and is cited throughout this book.

7 Houston Astros Lease Agreement *in* Martin J. Greenberg, THE STADIUM GAME 215 (2d Ed. 2001).

8 *See* Leila Atassi "FirstEnergy Stadium Lease Dissected—the costs and benefits of owning the home of the Cleveland Browns," *CLEVELAND.com*, Nov. 22, 2013, available at: http://www.cleveland.com/cityhall/index.ssf/2013/11/firstenergy_stadium_lease_diss.html.

9 Indiana Pacers Lease Agreement *in* Martin J. Greenberg, THE STADIUM GAME 226 (2d Ed. 2001).

revenue, like the Boston Red Sox, it will prefer a flat fee. If, however, the team produces smaller revenues, like the Pittsburgh Pirates, it will prefer a flexible rent schedule, which would keep its payments in line with its attendance. In a flexible rent arrangement, just as the city will push hard for a rent floor, the team will insist upon a rent ceiling to ensure that its rent does not become unreasonable with increased attendance or revenue. The Cleveland Indians use a flexible rent arrangement, with the progressive rate based upon the number of attendees at home games.[10]

The ZOPA will likely involve a mutually beneficial arrangement, including a fixed rent component as the base, with a flexible rent element to give the city an upside if the team does well and to protect the team if it does not.[11]

This will also involve a settlement on a "greater of" or "lesser of" rent provision with a reasonable rent floor and ceiling to protect both the city and the team. If the team gives the city a "greater of" provision, it will likely receive a declining flexible rate in exchange, such that its rent per person declines as the number of attendees increases (e.g., $1 for each of the first million attendees, $0.80 for each of the next million attendees, etc.). The flexible rent component may be determined by a variety of measures of team success, such as gate receipts, concession sales, or advertising revenue. The rent cap sought by the team may also benefit the city if it prevents the team from exercising a finance retirement condition and terminating the lease.

D. USES

Use provisions give the team both the right and the obligation to play its home games at the facility. In addition to home games, the team will seek use of various parts of the facility, such as its offices and clubhouse, throughout the year. The amount of exclusivity and control granted to the team is the most critical issue within these provisions. Very few leases grant the team absolute exclusivity because there is too much revenue to be gained from non-team-related sources when the team does not have home games. The current trend is to grant the team predominant access to the facility during its season of play, with some input into non-team-related events during the team's season.[12]

---

10 Cleveland Indians Lease Agreement *in* Martin J. Greenberg, THE STADIUM GAME 224 (2d Ed. 2001).

11 *See* Article 6 of San Francisco 49ers "Stadium Lease Agreement."

12 *See* Section 6.1 of "Agreement of Lease—City of Eastlake and Cascia LLC."

The city will want to use the facility to host its own events throughout the year, which do not involve the team. It will also seek to reserve for itself a prime luxury suite and a number of club seats for all events in the facility, including team events. The team will want to have its game dates take precedence over all other events, but on non-game dates, the city will seek final authority over the scheduling and use of the facility. The city will likely resist any attempt by the team to gain approval over city events not involving the team. The city will also seek to control the parking facilities throughout the year, including during team events, to capture revenue.[13]

The team will insist upon absolute priority for use of the facility during its games and other team events. This will also include a demand for exclusive use of certain portions of the facility throughout the year, such as the dugouts, locker rooms, team offices, and training facilities, even during city events. In addition to the playing of games, the team will also be concerned about its rights to usage of club/restaurant facilities, general offices, concessions areas, and potential advertising areas. The team will want a specific buffer zone before and after its games and other team events, likely 24 or 48 hours, so that the non-team events do not damage the quality of the playing field or other elements of the facility utilized during team events.

The team will want written assurances that parking facilities will be adequately staffed and of a certain quality during all team events. The team will want full control over a specially designed VIP lot created for the team's benefit to ensure that its premium customers are treated in a first-class manner. The team may also want to secure exclusive use of the stadium, but must comply with the "essential facility" doctrine in doing so.[14] The team will seek to obtain a covenant that no other sports organizations, especially those in the same professional sport, will be able to use the facility. To preserve field and facility quality, the team will also want to limit the ability of other sports teams or events to use the stadium.

The ZOPA will likely involve the city giving the team exclusive use of the facility during its home games and other team events, with its games given top scheduling priority. The team will likely receive seasonal exclusivity, to the extent that it does not have to share the stadium with a professional team playing a different sport. If it does have to share the stadium with a team from a different sport, the parties will likely agree that the postseason games of either team will

---

[13] *See* Article 7 of "Agreement of Lease—City of Eastlake and Cascia LLC."

[14] For more information on the Essential Facility Doctrine, *see* Essential Facility Doctrine Study Guide in Appendix B.

take precedence over the regular season games of the other team. No conflicting events will be allowed at the facility on team game days. This is in line with the modern trend of the city maintaining control over the use of the facility but granting the team plenty of input into and advance notice of non-team-related events. This represents a change from earlier leases, which gave teams nearly exclusive control or a right of first refusal for specific dates.

Certain team areas, such as its offices and clubhouse, will be given to the team throughout the year. The parties can agree to work together in scheduling their non-traditional revenue-generating events, and the city and the team will agree to mutually acceptable dates for events. Both will have reasonable veto power. The city will likely grant the team at least a 24-hour cushion around its home games to restore the playing field to first-class condition. The team will likely give the city use of a luxury suite during a portion of its home games and a group of club seats for each home game.

Both sides will likely agree to allow the city to control and staff the general parking facilities, with the exception of the team's VIP parking lot, over which the team will have exclusive control and staffing authority. The city must construct such a lot, but the team must pay a large portion of the construction costs and staff the lot with city employees at regular city wages during all team events. The parties must also agree upon a suitable seating structure and scoreboard setup to accommodate different uses of the facility to avoid a dispute similar to that between the Cincinnati Reds and Cincinnati Bengals.[15]

The parties may also wish to insert an individual and corporate morals clause, under which each party must ensure that it does not bring disrepute upon the other party or the facility itself. Courts have limited the ability of teams to seek sports exclusivity via the "essential facilities" doctrine, so the parties will likely agree upon exclusivity for the team only to the extent that other professional teams of the same sport will be prohibited from using the facility.[16]

E. REVENUES

The sports facility explosion of the 1990s and 2000s can be attributed largely to the development of new revenue sources, such as luxury

---

15 *See Cincinnati Bengals, Inc. v. Cincinnati,* 567 N.E.2d 284 (1989) (holding that the Cincinnati Reds could not obstruct the view of Cincinnati Bengals fans by installing a new auxiliary scoreboard).

16 *See Fishman v. Estate of Wirtz,* 807 F.2d 520 (7th Cir.1986) (holding that Chicago Stadium had to negotiate with the Chicago Bulls); Hecht v. Pro-Football, Inc., 570 F.2d 982, 985–86 (D.C. Cir.1977) (holding that the Washington Redskins' exclusive lease of RFK Stadium presented a triable issue of violation of antitrust laws).

boxes, club seats, personal seat licenses, and stadium naming rights.[17] As team owners sought to capture revenue from these streams, cities were forced to build new stadiums to keep teams from looking elsewhere when their current leases expired. Additionally, league officials wanted to capture as much of this local revenue as possible, so cities that constructed new facilities were rewarded with marquee events like All-Star games and Super Bowls. Luxury box revenues have become a critical source of revenue for all sports franchises, perhaps second to only television revenues. New facilities are often constructed solely to increase the revenue generated from high-end streams, such as luxury boxes and club seats. The $1.15 billion, 3 million square-foot AT&T Stadium is a recent example of this trend; it boasts the capacity to hold more fans than have ever witnessed a live professional football game.[18] These fans must pay for amenities like a $40 million state-of-the-art video board, evidenced by the Dallas Cowboys having the highest average ticket prices in the NFL.[19]

The city will seek to keep the naming rights of the facility so that it can capture this source of revenue for itself. The city will also seek a share of the concessions revenue from team events and will argue that it deserves to retain all concessions, merchandise, and other revenue from non-team-related events. In particular, the city will seek to keep all of the advertising revenue from its events. The city will insist upon some level of approval over signage within the facility and an even greater level of approval over any signage that reaches the general public outside of the facility. The team will likely want a state-of-the-art video board, so the city will request a large contribution from the team towards its construction. In terms of advertising on the video board, the city will want a certain amount of time dedicated to public service announcements and other city-generated content during team events. The city will also seek to retain all revenues from parking facilities, especially if it staffs and controls such facilities.

The team will attempt to obtain the facility naming rights from the city, sell them, and keep all of the proceeds. The team will argue that it is much more capable of selling these rights and maximizing revenue. The team will also seek to retain most of the concessions and other revenues generated from all team events, including

[17] *See* Frank A. Mayer III, "Stadium Financing: Where We Are, How We Got There, and Where We Are Going," *VILLINOVA SPORTS & ENT. L.J. 2–5 (2005)* (discussing possible revenues a new stadium can generate).

[18] *See* "Stadiums of Pro Football: AT&T Stadium," available at: http://www.stadiumsofprofootball.com/nfc/AT&TStadium.htm.

[19] *Id.*

merchandise and ticket sales revenue. The team will attempt to maximize the advertising revenue it can generate during team events and will therefore limit the time allocated to the city during these events. The team will also look to earn revenue from the sale of club seats, luxury suites, and personal seat licenses ("PSLs"), and to prevent the city from dictating their pricing. The team will insist upon retaining all revenues from the VIP parking lot and will be responsible for staffing and controlling this lot.[20]

The ZOPA will likely involve the team buying the naming rights for the facility from the city. These rights might include not only the stadium itself, but also the playing field and entryways into the stadium. This will be a mutually beneficial arrangement; municipalities are increasingly moving towards selling stadium naming rights to corporate entities, as opposed to naming the stadium after a county, team, or notable individual. The city and team will likely agree upon each party retaining the concessions, merchandise, ticket sales, and other revenues from its own events, subject to any flexible rent conditions in the lease. The team, however, may give the city a small percentage (perhaps five percent) of its concessions revenue from team events because of the city's role in constructing and maintaining the concessions facilities. Each party will probably retain the rights and advertising revenue from its own events, with the exception of some permanent year-round advertising, which the parties will likely split.

The parties will split program and publication advertising revenue. The city will likely bear the burden of constructing new signage and maintaining existing signage in the facility, and the team will contribute to a capital repairs and expenditures fund (CRIF) or similar account to cover a small portion of the costs. The right to advertise on the scoreboard will belong to the party whose event is taking place in the facility on a given date, subject to reasonable constraints upon disparaging or otherwise harmful advertising. The team will probably agree to a small financial contribution to construct a state-of-the-art video scoreboard and may even offer to finance the entire construction in exchange for retaining all of the revenue associated with its use.

The team will likely retain most or all of the revenue from the sale of club seats, luxury suites, and personal seat licenses, subject to any contributions to the city that a flexible rent provision requires. Locking in this revenue over a period of years is beneficial to both

20 *See e.g.*, David Kaplan, "Big sponsorships, seat license sales allow 49ers to refinance early," *SPORTS BUSINESS DAILY*, May 13, 2013, available at: http://www.sportsbusinessdaily.com/Journal/Issues/2013/05/13/Finance/49ers-refi.aspx.

parties; it protects the city and the team from poor attendance in future years. Although this revenue is typically allocated based on a flat percentage, some agreements feature scaled percentages; the percentage varies based upon ticket sales. Club seats will typically be leased on an annual basis with terms of one to ten years. Personal seat licenses are similar, but they create a property right and can be transferred to a third-party buyer. The costs and terms of personal seat licenses are key issues.

Additionally, the parties may want to limit the transferability of the personal seat license, which would enable them to generate new revenue from the license after a certain time period. Luxury suites usually will be leased for a term of years, from one to ten or more years, with a few suites reserved for individual game rentals. As such, luxury suites entail their own lease agreements that contain many of the provisions discussed here, including rent, events of default, termination, maintenance, and the like, as discussed in the first chapter. The city will likely retain the revenue generated by general parking facilities, and the team will receive the revenue from the VIP lot.[21]

F. REPAIRS AND MAINTENANCE

Operating expense provisions in a stadium lease agreement usually include clauses dealing with cleaning costs, utility costs, staffing, insurance, and repairs and maintenance. Many agreements also address capital expenditures. The division of these costs between the city and the team vary widely and depend upon the particular agreement, but in general, the more exclusive a team's use of a facility, the more costs it will have to bear. Usually both the city and the team must carry various levels of insurance coverage.

The city must take responsibility for repairs and maintenance of the facility, but will insist upon reasonableness requirements pertaining to the time it has to remedy maintenance issues and the overall facility condition. The team will seek a guarantee that the facility will be kept in first-class or excellent condition, but the city will likely concede only to keep the facility in good condition. The city will also seek a substantial contribution to the CRIF from the team throughout the lease term. The city must contribute to this fund as well and will draw from this fund in making repairs and improvements to the facility. The team will probably desire state-of-the-art concessions equipment, so the city will request that the team

---

[21] *See* Article 8 *Revenues* in "Agreement of Lease—City of Eastlake and Cascia LLC."

contribute a portion of the costs associated with building and maintaining this equipment.

The team will likely insist that the city be responsible for repairs and maintenance of the facility but will argue for a self-help option through which it can make necessary repairs to the facility if the city does not do so. Under this option, the team could fix certain problems with the facility on its own timetable and bill the city for the repairs.

The team will want a representation from the city that requires the facility to be kept in a first-class condition, using language such as "suitable for professional sports." The playing field must be kept in excellent condition, so the team will seek self-help authority over its maintenance. The team will seek to minimize its contribution to the CRIF, especially any contribution early in the lease, because the team will expect the city to have the facility in excellent condition at the start of the lease. The team will want state-of-the-art concessions equipment but will argue that its financial contribution to such equipment should be minimal; it will want a state-of-the-art facility at the beginning of the lease, and any initial contribution should count towards its overall contribution to the CRIF.[22]

The ZOPA will likely involve the city accepting responsibility for handling the maintenance and repair of the facility. The team may have a limited self-help remedy, which will be subject to a reasonableness condition, a cost limit, and will be limited to specific types of repairs, such as the maintenance of the playing field. The floor on the representation from the city for facility condition will probably be "good condition," and the ceiling will be "excellent condition and suitable for professional sports." The parties will likely agree on a reasonable annual team contribution to the CRIF, with most of the payment coming later in the lease and possibly based upon a percentage of the total building cost. The city may have a cap upon overall liability; indeed, the city sought and received a spending cap of $611 million in the Washington Nationals' new lease.[23]

In terms of the concessions equipment, the parties will likely agree upon the team contributing a reasonable amount to the construction of state-of-the-art concessions equipment. Any such contribution will count towards the team's overall contribution to the CRIF. The parties will likely agree to split the utility bill; the more exclusive the team's use of the facility, the larger portion of the utility bill it will

---

22 *See* Leila Attasi, "FirstEnergy Stadium Lease: Bad Deal for Cleveland or Better than Most?", *CLEVELAND.com*, Nov. 29, 2013, available at: http://www.cleveland.com/cityhall/index.ssf/2013/11/firstenergy_stadium_lease_bad.html.

23 *See* David Nakamura, "Council Forges Deal on Stadium," *WASH. POST*, Feb. 8, 2006.

have to pay. The parties will each carry insurance to protect against damage to the facility or team equipment, potentially "all risk" insurance coverage of up to $1 million. Mirroring the current trend, the responsibility for most cost overruns in repairs and maintenance will shift to the team.

G. EVENTS OF DEFAULT

Default provisions specify which acts and omissions by either the city or the team violate the terms and conditions of the agreement. Events of default, which place a party in breach of the agreement and potentially afford the other party remedies, must be divided into curable and incurable breaches. If the default is curable, which usually means that the breach is insignificant, the parties will need to provide details regarding how the default might be cured, including the notice required and the time period available for cure. Typical curable defaults include failure to pay rent when due, violation of an exclusivity provision, failure to perform repairs and maintenance, and other similar temporary failures. If the default is incurable, which usually applies to material breaches of the agreement, the parties will need to specify the consequences of that default, such as an immediate termination. Typical incurable defaults include initiating bankruptcy proceedings, failure to fulfill material obligations, covenants, or agreements under the lease, abandonment of operations without the other party's consent, and failure to pay rent for an extended period of time.

The city will likely agree that the team's failure to pay rent will constitute a curable breach for a reasonable time period, after which the team would be in default. The city will seek to exclude from the agreement any language giving it a duty to mitigate damages; it will be difficult to find comparable alternative revenue sources on such short notice. The city will insist that if the team moves or plays its home games outside of the facility, the team will be in default.

The city will want the team to cover the costs of obtaining all necessary permits and approvals. The team will require the city to deliver all permits and approvals for use of the facility, particularly those associated with exterior signage, including freeway signage, in a timely fashion. The team will also insist that a failure to make repairs within a specified time period, particularly after notice by the team, will trigger city default. This time period will help the team to determine when it can exercise a self-help remedy and make the repairs itself. The team will be concerned about the quality of the playing surface in particular, so it will want specific language guaranteeing the first-class condition of the playing surface and the ability to use self-help remedies. Additionally, the team will seek language that makes the failure to comply with the agreed upon maintenance program a breach and default event by the city.

The team would also like to place a duty to mitigate damages from team breaches upon the city to limit the team's liability. The team will want to limit its liability to monetary damages, thereby keeping the city from pursuing injunctive relief or specific performance, which could force the team to play in the facility.

The ZOPA will likely involve the city representing and warranting that it will obtain all necessary permits and approvals, particularly for exterior signage, and the team will contribute some portion of the costs of these processes. The team will likely buy this inventory from the city on a back-to-back basis so that it can sell advertising spaces to sponsors, including the naming rights sponsor. The parties will likely agree that the team's failure to pay rent is a curable breach that can become an event of default after a certain period of time. The city will likely have a duty to act reasonably in mitigating damages, but the city's recovery will be limited to monetary damages from the team, rather than an injunction or specific performance. The city will force the team to accept a high liquidated damages clause so that it will be very costly for the team to breach the agreement and play its home games elsewhere. The team and the city will work together to generate a list of preapproved contractors to perform regular facility maintenance.[24]

H. FORCE MAJEURE

A force majeure provision protects the parties when part of an agreement cannot be performed due to causes beyond the control of the parties. This can include natural disasters, such as floods, earthquakes, and hurricanes, as well as labor disputes and civil disturbances. Events commonly listed in force majeure provisions include war, fires, floods, earthquakes, riots, terrorism, epidemics, governmental action, and acts of God. The clause sometimes includes labor disputes, such as strikes or lockouts, and may employ a catchall phrase, such as "any act beyond the reasonable control of the parties."

The city will seek to narrow the force majeure clause, but will keep it broad enough to cover any events that might prevent the city from performing its lease obligations. The city will also want to add any time lost due to force majeure to the lease term, but other options include an excuse of performance, a right of termination, or equitable adjustment. Both the city and the team will want to receive adequate written notice in the event that either side claims a force majeure

---

24 *See* Article 18 *Events of Default* in "Agreement of Lease—City of Eastlake and Cascia LLC."

event. The team will want a broader force majeure provision that includes sport-specific events, such as lockouts or strikes, and may also want a provision relating to insolvency or financial hardship, which would allow the team to suspend its lease obligations. The team will prefer not to have a term extension to make up for time lost due to a force majeure event but will likely accept such a clause as fair and reasonable. The team will also likely agree with the city upon reciprocal written notice provisions requiring each party to notify the other of a force majeure event within a given time period.

The ZOPA will likely include a standard force majeure provision containing the typical list of natural disasters and other events beyond the reasonable control of the parties, with the addition of lockouts and strikes. The team will likely acquiesce to the term extension. Both parties will want prompt written notice, likely within ten days of the invoking party's recognition of the force majeure event, so the parties should easily agree upon this mutual provision. The parties should ensure that each side's rights and obligations are explicitly specified.[25]

I. NO RELOCATION/NO MOVE

Teams may seek to move from their existing stadium for a variety of reasons, including stadium deterioration, decreased fan support, financial losses, and attractive lease opportunities elsewhere. Sports teams wishing to relocate are subject to league constitutions and bylaws, which can prevent a team from moving into a new market but usually cannot prevent a team from moving to a new facility within the same market. To enhance their protection, cities have inserted no relocation/no move clauses in stadium leases, which impose an exorbitant financial penalty on a team for leaving a facility in advance of the term expiration. Some cities have also provided for a right of first refusal before a team attempts to move or relocate.

The city will seek to keep the team in the facility for perpetuity, or at least for the length of the term. The city will push strongly for the ability to seek injunctive relief should the team seek to move during the term. The city will also want plenty of advance notice if the team attempts to relocate or move. By using language such as "irreparable harm," the city will seek to bolster its legal position should the team threaten to leave the facility prior to the expiration of the term. The addition of this language may not always protect the city, however.[26]

---

25 *See* Article 18, Section 5 of Exhibit 1 in Appendix A.

26 *See Indianapolis Colts v. Mayor of Baltimore*, 733 F.2d 484 (7th Cir.1984) (Baltimore Colts); Greg Johns, "Schultz withdraws lawsuit seeking Sonics' return," *SEATTLE POST-INTELLIGENCER*, Aug. 29, 2008 (Seattle SuperSonics). *Also see* In re Dewey Ranch Hockey, 414 B.R. 577 (D. Ariz. 2009) (Phoenix Coyotes).

In terms of ownership changes, the city may want to use one of several options to ensure that the team stays in the facility. These options include a designated first option to buy the team or a local buyer option. The team will desire great flexibility to relocate as it pleases. To facilitate this, the team would likely offer to pay reasonable liquidated damages to free itself from the lease. The team will argue that the city does not have any rights to interfere with any potential ownership change because it will not affect the team's obligations to the city under the lease. The team will also push for an attendance guarantee clause, either forcing the city to pay for any shortfalls in attendance or permitting early lease termination.

The ZOPA will likely involve an acknowledgement that because the league rules regarding relocation already apply to the team, the city is fairly protected, and the team probably will not relocate during the term. The city will not be able to keep the team beyond the lease term regardless. The contract will likely include a liquidated damages clause for relocation, but the fee will be exorbitant if the team chooses to move before the end of the lease term. Although liquidated damages provisions are often prohibitively expensive, their cost may decrease over time as the lease nears the end of its term. A liquidated damages provision combined with a no relocation/no move provision will effectively give the city the option to choose whether to force the team to stay in the current facility or accept a large payout for allowing the team to leave.

Liquidated damages provisions were effective in preventing the Phoenix Coyotes from leaving Glendale, Arizona.[27] Similarly, the Seattle SuperSonics were allowed to become the Oklahoma City Thunder after new ownership paid Seattle $45 million to get out of its existing lease (the total reached $75 million—an additional $30 million was paid because Seattle was not given a replacement team within five years).[28] The team probably will not have to pay any penalty fees to the city upon a sale or transfer of ownership of the team, assuming that the new ownership intends to honor the terms of the lease agreement. Courts have rewarded cities for their creativity in fashioning these no relocation and no move clauses.[29] A local buyer option may be inserted into the agreement, under which local buyers must be solicited before an out-of-town buyer can

---

27 *See In re Dewey Ranch Hockey*, 414 B.R. 577.

28 *See* "SuperSonics, Seattle reach last-minute settlement," *ESPN.com*, July 3, 2008, *available at* http://sports.espn.go.com/nba/news/story?id=3471503.

29 *See Metropolitan Sports Facilities Comm'n v. Minnesota Twins*, 638 N.W.2d 214 (Minn. Ct. App. 2002) (holding that money could not compensate the public for intangible damages if the team breached its promise to play its games at the facility; the unique lease of the publicly financed stadium made the city dependent upon concession and merchandising revenue, instead of a fixed rent payment).

purchase the team. An attendance guarantee clause will likely be difficult to get into the agreement unless the parties can agree upon a low threshold.

J. REMEDIES

The city and the team will likely agree upon a remedies clause that affects each side reciprocally. When a party breaches the agreement, the non-breaching party must notify the breaching party immediately upon noticing the breach. Certain minor breaches, if left uncured for a designated period, will give rise to only a nominal damages fee. All disputes over incurable or uncured material breaches will first be submitted to confidential mediation, followed by confidential and binding arbitration, if mediation fails to resolve the dispute. Alternative dispute resolution is becoming more prevalent in the sports industry because of both the specialized nature of contracts within the industry, and the enormous costs, unpredictability, and time contributions associated with litigation. Furthermore, arbitration protects the confidentiality interests of the parties and allows parties to participate in the selection of some or all of the neutral decision makers. One common approach allows each party to select one arbitrator, and the two selected arbitrators then decide upon the third arbitrator. The parties may also pursue an approach similar to a jury selection; through which each side proposes potential arbitrators and has a limited number of vetoes over the other party's selections. Disputes over the overall liability of either party, likely to be in the millions, are almost always subject to such a process.[30]

Generally, the parties will agree to use the rules of the American Arbitration Association, with the dispute heard and decided in its closest local branch office. To limit costs of this process, the parties will likely agree to rules limiting discovery and the calling of witnesses. The city would prefer to have injunctive relief as an option, but the team will likely insist upon the dispute resolution process described above. The team prefers to pay liquidated damages in lieu of permitting the city to invoke injunctive relief or specific performance. A liquidated damages clause must be carefully drafted to ensure that the amount is the reasonable approximation of predicted damages agreed to both parties or the court could decide to exclude the clause as a penalty for breach of contract. Conversely, the team will want to have the option of seeking injunctive relief against the city to enforce the maintenance and repairs clause. The team, however, will likely be forced to accept its self-help remedies because

30 *See* "Council Forges Deal on Stadium," *supra* note 23.

the city will resist granting any injunctive relief or specific performance rights to the team.

Under this system, the team will be able to use its self-help remedies on repairs after a given time period, and the team may deduct the reasonable costs of these repairs from its rent payments to the city. The parties will likely want to avoid the courts, which can be both costly and unpredictable. They will, however, preserve legal recourse if procedural errors occur in mediation or arbitration or if the dispute is non-arbitrable. Equitable relief may not be available in the courts despite the language of the agreement; courts will prefer to grant monetary damages wherever possible and allow equitable relief only where monetary damages are inadequate. The parties will also have to decide between using the American Rule or British Rule for the costs of dispute resolution. Under the American Rule, each party bears its own costs but may recover attorneys' fees and other costs in exceptional cases. If the action lacks merit or is maintained in bad faith, the parties can agree to allow the party acting in good faith to recover all of its costs from the bad faith actor.

HYPOTHETICAL EXERCISE

Negotiating and Drafting a Lease Agreement Between a City/County/Statutorily-Created Authority and a Professional Sports Franchise

A. Imagine that the Boston Red Sox have abandoned Fenway Park and are negotiating the lease agreement between the team and the City of Boston for the new stadium, built for the team, constructed using public bonds that mature in 30 years. This is the only stadium of its kind in the area (given that the TD Garden is indoors and Gillette Stadium is in Foxboro).

1. The new state-of-the-art ballpark has club seats and luxury suites, and the team also plans on selling personal seat licenses.

2. In addition, the new stadium has traditional stationary signage, including signage on the scoreboard, on the outfield wall panels, visible from the Massachusetts Turnpike, at the Entry/Exit Gates, at first base, at third base, and in the bleacher area; video board advertising; and program/publication advertising.

3. In addition to traditional concessions areas, the stadium has a "higher end" restaurant.

4. Finally, the ballpark has limited space available for executive offices.

B. How you would negotiate and draft the following clauses:

1. <u>Term</u>

a. How long will the initial term be? Will it be a set period of years, or will the initial term last as long as any bonds used to finance the stadium are outstanding?

b. Will the parties have the option to extend the term? If so, what will the length of each extension be, and how many such extensions will each party have? Is there a notification period for the extensions? What is the consequence of failure to notify? Is there an automatic renewal provision? Are there any other conditions to renewal?

2. <u>Termination of Lease</u>

a. Can the Red Sox or the City terminate the lease prior to the end of the initial term or any renewed terms, under certain conditions?

b. Consider the ZOPAs discussed in Chapter 2.

3. <u>Rent</u>

a. What rental structure will the parties adopt? Consider the various permutations possible, and how each might benefit your client (e.g. fixed rent, adjustable rent, rent per game, minimum payments, or a floor and a cap). For example:

1. The Houston Astros pay a fixed rent and retain the right to all stadium revenues.

2. Similarly, the Cincinnati Bengals pay a fixed rate for 9 years of the lease, after which no rental payments are due.

3. By contrast, the San Antonio Spurs pay rent per game. The rate increases from preseason games to regular season games to post-season games.

A. Consider the potential disputes that might arise from such a structure in the event of a strike or lockout.

4. The Cleveland Indians pay rent at a progressive rate based upon the number of attendees.

4. <u>Uses</u>

a. How will the City and the Red Sox share the use of the stadium?

b. Consider the uses that the Team might require, such as playing of games, operation of club/restaurant facilities, general offices, sale of concessions, and sale of advertising.

c. What, if any, will be the limits to the City's use? How will the parties ensure that there are no conflicting events on game days? Consider the grant of approval rights to the Team for City-sponsored events.

d. When delineating the uses to which each party is entitled, consider the Steelers-Dolphins "Mud Bowl" in 2007[31] and the dispute between the Cincinnati Reds and the Bengals.[32]

5. Revenues

a. *Club Seats, Luxury Suites, and PSLs:* How might revenues from the sale/license of club seats, luxury suits, and personal seat licenses be divided, as part of the payments from the Lessee to the Lessor?

1. Will the City retain any rights to approve the prices of these items?

b. *Naming Rights:* Which party will retain the right to name the stadium or sell the naming rights to the stadium over the term of the lease?

c. *Advertising:* Which party has the right to sell and display all advertising in the Ballpark and on the Premises? Program and publication advertising? Which party bears the cost of constructing new signage and maintaining existing signage?

1. Also consider who has the right to advertise on the scoreboard during the various events held in the Ballpark, and how the revenues will be divided.

6. Repairs and Maintenance

a. Divide the responsibilities for repairs and maintenance between the Lessee and Lessor.

b. When describing the responsibilities, consider which adjectives you will use to describe the condition of the premises. Some terms you might use are "first-class condition," "first-class condition

---

31 "Mud Pitt: Poor Field Conditions Mar 'MNF' Tilt," *SPORTSBUSINESS DAILY*, Nov. 27, 2007.

32 "Disobedient Marge Takes a Schott at Bengals New Stadium," *SPORTSBUSINESS DAILY*, Feb. 26, 1996.

suitable for Professional Baseball Games," ". . . as necessary to keep the premises in a neat, clean, sanitary and safe condition," etc.

c. Consider how these responsibilities for "Repairs and Maintenance" correspond with the "Uses" negotiated/drafted.

7. Events of Default

a. Distinguish between curable and incurable events of default.

b. If the default is "curable," provide details as to how the default might be cured (e.g. the notice required and the time period available for cure). Typical curable defaults include failure to pay rent when due, failure to perform repairs and maintenance, and other similar "temporary" failures.

c. If the default is "incurable," explain the consequences thereof. Typical incurable defaults include failure to fulfill obligations, covenants, or agreements under the lease; abandonment of operations without the Lessor's consent; and the failure to pay rent for an extended period of time.

d. Synchronize "Events of Default" with "Remedies," described below.

8. Force Majeure

a. Define the scope of a "force majeure" event, the notice required to trigger a "force majeure" (e.g. written notice within a certain period of time), and the type of relief available (e.g. excuse or extension, excuse of performance, suspension of performance, right of termination, or equitable adjustment).

b. When creating your definition, you may want to address what would happen in the event of a strike or lockout.

9. No Relocation/No Move

a. How might the City ensure that the Red Sox stay in the city? Consider the importance of this clause, given the Seattle Supersonics move to Oklahoma City and the Baltimore Colts move to Indianapolis. Does this constitute "irreparable harm"? Should the team explicitly acknowledge it as such in the lease?

b. What notice provisions might the Lessor require prior to the lessee's move?

c. Consider the use of a liquidated damages provision as a deterrent. The parties may consider de-escalating the magnitude of the damages over time.

d. You might want to use alternate methods to ensure the team stays in the city, though ownership changes. For instance, consider the use of (a.) a designated first option to buy the team, (b.) a local buyer option, (c.) a team option to purchase the stadium, or (d.) some other creative mechanism you create.

10. Remedies

a. Which defaults or breaches give rise to which remedies?

b. Consider the use of mediation and arbitration for certain breaches or as the exclusive remedy. For what might the parties seek to preserve recourse to courts?

c. Which party will pay for costs? Consider the use of the "American Rule" or the "British Rule."

Please see the "Exemplar" Student Group response in the Teacher's Manual that accompanies this book.

Chapter 3

NAMING RIGHTS AGREEMENTS

Naming rights agreements are typically the most profitable and most prominent of the sponsorship deals that any team will sign for its venue. As a result, it is typically the first sponsorship contract any team will want to sign upon acquiring a new facility.[1] Though it is not necessary to sign the naming rights sponsor first, it is often practical to do so because the team will more than likely give the best benefit package to the naming rights sponsor, including the best signage, advertising space, and other promotional options. The size of the benefit package will reflect the price the sponsor is willing to pay—to enable the team to lure a large naming rights sponsor, the team should offer the choice of as much inventory as possible.[2] For example, if a team first signs a bank to an exclusive financial services sponsorship, it will no longer be able to solicit a naming rights sponsor from any other financial institution, significantly limiting its pool of potential naming rights sponsors.[3]

In Chapter 2, this book discussed which party to a lease agreement would have the rights to sell the naming rights to the park. In our example, it was the team that ended up with the right to sell the naming rights, and the team had to pay a hefty price to be in that position. There are several benefits to the team selling the naming rights, as opposed to the city, most importantly that the team already has relationships and contacts within the realm of sponsorships and endorsements, and has the staff and expertise necessary to immediately begin to work out a naming rights deal. As a result, this chapter will assume that the Naming Rights Agreement is being

1 *See* Brian Hall. "U.S. Bank Awarded Naming Rights to New Vikings' Stadium," *FOX SPORTS*, June 15, 2015, available at: http://www.foxsports.com/north/story/u-s-bank-awarded-naming-rights-to-new-minnesota-vikings-nfl-stadium-061515.

2 The overall value and popularity of the franchise may affect the total value of the Naming Rights Agreement too. For the value of each MLB team, *see* "The Business of Baseball: MLB Team Values," *FORBES*, available at: http://www.forbes.com/mlb-valuations/list/.

3 For more information on Naming Rights Agreements, *see* Peter Carfagna, An Introduction to Naming Rights Agreements and Intellectual Property Study Guide, A SUPPLEMENT TO "NEGOTIATING AND DRAFTING SPORTS VENUE AGREEMENTS" (2016).

negotiated between a team and a sponsor, as opposed to a city or other entity and a sponsor.[4]

As with any other sponsorship deal, the Naming Rights Agreement will need to address the scope and definition of the deal, the end-game provisions, and all the miscellaneous clauses that accompany such an agreement.[5] For the Naming Rights Agreement, the most important scope and definitional clauses are the Grant of Naming Rights, Term and Payment, Naming Rights Benefits, Logo/Change of Logo, and Service Mark and Trademark Grant of Rights, or the Intellectual Property clause. These clauses will lay out the extent of what the parties are agreeing to, including the actual naming rights and benefits. These benefits will include any potential joint projects the parties will undertake as a part of the relationship, such as a joint logo to be used in publicity or advertising. Beyond the scope of a naming rights deal, the parties need to address the end-game possibilities, which include the situations in which the parties may need to alter the existing nature of their relationship. Should the sponsor change its name, for example, such a change will likely necessitate the change of either the name of the facility, or some of the signage and advertisements present at the facility, including the team's promotional materials.

Though not expressly addressed in this chapter, the miscellaneous clauses in Chapter 1 will, in most cases, also be necessary within a completed Naming Rights Agreement, unless the parties negotiate for, and agree to, something different.

A. GRANT OF NAMING RIGHTS

The grant of naming rights is the first and most important of the rights the sponsor is paying for—after all this is a Naming Rights Agreement! By the time the parties sit down to the table, they know they are negotiating for a grant of naming rights. The Grant clause, however, is more than just a simple phrase granting the sponsor the

---

[4] For more information on negotiation principles, *see* Peter Carfagna, Appendix B: Negotiating Contracts: Basic Principles and Strategies Study Guide, A SUPPLEMENT TO "NEGOTIATING AND DRAFTING SPORTS VENUE AGREEMENTS" (2016).

[5] Though this chapter will focus almost exclusively on whole-facility naming rights, it is also possible to sell naming rights to only parts of the facility. For example, the luxury automobile manufacturer Audi has a naming rights deal for the "Audi Club," a VIP space for season ticket holders with a club membership open pre and post-games at Wrigley Field. *See* Danny Ecker, "Cubs rev up Audi sponsorship with new naming rights deal," *CRAIN'S CHICAGO BUS.*, March 26, 2015). The scope of any grant of naming rights should be reflected expressly in the deal, and if a team wants to be able to sell naming rights to part of the facility as well as the whole, as with Wrigley Field, then it should expressly reserve that right in the Grant of Naming Rights section.

right to name the facility. The next question this clause needs to address is what the name of the facility will be.[6]

The name of the facility will affect the reputations of both the team and the sponsor; thus it is important that both sides agree on the prospective name for the facility.[7] Often this is as simple as the sponsor naming the park after itself. AT&T Park, home of the San Francisco Giants,[8] and American Airlines Center, home of the Dallas Mavericks and the Dallas Stars, are examples of this naming practice. The name of the facility could also be the trade name of the sponsor, as with Levi's Stadium, home of the San Francisco 49ers,[9] and Citi Field, home of the New York Mets.[10] Sometimes, the sponsor might even want to name the park after one of its best-selling products, in order to be more recognizable and more effective as an

---

[6] Usually names are signed on for long periods of time, and these are the naming rights this chapter discusses, but while searching for larger naming rights sponsors, teams have been known to be creative as in Boston in 2004, where the owner of the Garden auctioned one-day naming rights on eBay. These rights were sold 30 different times and netted the owners a little over $150,000. For two days during this period the facility was actually known as "The Yankees S**k Center". Despite the allowed creativity in some of the names, the owners still retained the right to disapprove of the naming proposals, rejecting an offer to call it the Derek Jeter Center. *See* "Quirkiest Stadium Naming Rights Deals: TD Garden," *BUSINESS WEEK* No. 21 of 26, available at: http://images.businessweek.com/ss/09/10/1027_quirkiest_stadium_naming_rights_deals/21.htm.

[7] Companies must also be selective of the teams they choose to endorse. In 2014, FedEx shareholders attempted to block the company from purchasing the naming rights to the Washington Redskins' stadium as they believed the company would suffer "reputational damage" from associating themselves with the controversial team. *See* Mike Florio, "SEC blocks FedEx Shareholder vote on naming-rights deal," *PRO FOOTBALL TALK*, July 16, 2014, available at: http://profootballtalk.nbcsports.com/2014/07/16/sec-blocks-fedex-shareholder-vote-on-naming-rights-deal/.

[8] AT&T Park, so named in 2006, used to be SBC Park, which used to be PacBell Park until SBC Communications acquired PacBell in 2003. The naming rights deal is for $2.1 million annually and lasts until 2024. *See* "It's official: SBC Park becomes AT&T March 1/S.F. Giants will be playing ball on field's second name change since opening in 2000," *SFGATE.com*, available at: http://www.sfgate.com/business/article/It-s-official-SBC-Park-becomes-AT-T-March-1-2542007.php.

[9] Levi's Stadium is named for Levi Strauss & Co. Jeans and these naming rights are worth approximately $11 million per season to the 49ers for this twenty-year naming rights deal beginning in 2014. The only team in the NFL to have a bigger naming rights deal is the New York Giants/Jets receiving $16 million per year from MetLife Insurance for MetLife Stadium. *See* Louis Bien, "49ers' Levi's Stadium the 3rd-biggest naming rights deal in American Sports," *SB NATION*, May 8, 2013, available at: http://www.sbnation.com/nfl/2013/5/8/4313344/49ers-levis-stadium-biggest-naming-rights-contracts.

[10] Citi Field is named for Citigroup Inc., which purchased the naming rights in 2006 for $20 million annually for 20 years. Construction on Citi Field was completed in 2009 to replace the Mets' former home Shea Stadium. As one of the most expensive naming rights deals ever made, the Citi Field naming rights deal became rife with controversy when Citigroup suffered in the economic crisis beginning in 2008, prompting a government bailout of over $45 billion. *See* Egan, Matt. "CitiField: A $400M Catch-22 for Citigroup," *FOX BUSINESS*, November 26, 2008.

advertisement for the sponsor.[11] If the Naming Rights Sponsor is a person or a family, the family name will usually be the choice for the name of the facility.[12] In any of these cases, it is important for the Team that the name not have any negative connotations or connotations that are inconsistent with the nature of the game.[13] Baseball, for example, considers itself a family-friendly sport; thus a baseball team would need to make sure that its ballpark name reflects, or at least doesn't impair the perception of the park as a family-friendly atmosphere. For example, if a video game company were the naming rights sponsor and they wanted to name the park after one of their most violent, but best-selling, games, the team would absolutely want the right to veto such a name choice.

The grant section should thus reflect both the sponsor's desire to freely name the facility, and the team's desire to have some veto power over proposed names. By the time the agreement is done, there will likely be a name already decided on, and this name will be explicit in the Agreement. There may be a situation, however, where the parties will not have agreed to a specific name by the time of signing; thus the Grant clause might need to reflect the procedure the parties will utilize to come to later agreement on the name of the facility.[14]

Also within the grant section is the all-important decision of the type and scope of the category the team will grant the sponsor as part of the naming rights deal. Usually, the naming rights sponsor will have exclusivity within its category, though there could be a situation where a sponsor would rather pay less and give up the right to exclusivity. In Chapter 1, we discussed the category of exclusivity for a sponsor in the context of the definitions section of an agreement. The category can be defined anywhere in the agreement, including in this Grant section, though the authors recommend defining it in the definitions section to keep it prominent and easily accessible. It is

---

[11] Busch Stadium, home of the St. Louis Cardinals, is one such stadium where the naming rights owner, Anheuser-Busch, named the field after one of its products.

[12] In the current climate where some naming rights deals are for tens of millions of dollars annually over more than one decade, a family or individual would have to be both very rich and very motivated to outbid corporate sponsors for naming rights to a major league facility.

[13] The Metro Sports Authority in Nashville Tennessee, for example, has limited approval rights over proposed names for the facility at which the Nashville Predators play. Such disapproval rights is limited only to names that are vulgar in nature. This limited right of disapproval was clearly not needed when it signed the five year naming rights deal with Bridgestone in February 2010 for the Sommet Center to become Bridgestone Arena. *See* Michael Long. "Bridgestone Extends Naming Rights of Nashville Area," *SPORTSPRO MEDIA*, Dec. 16, 2011, available at: http://www.sportspromedia.com/news/bridgestone_extends_naming_rights_of_nashville_arena.

[14] *See* Section 2(E) "Grant: Naming Rights" in Exhibit 2 in Appendix A.

critically important that the category is carefully defined somewhere in the agreement.

Every category represents income, or at least the potential for income, to the team. Thus the narrower the category granted to individual sponsors, the more inventory the team has to sell. If the Naming Rights Sponsor is a beer company, for example, there are several versions of the category that the team can grant, including: Beverages, Beer, and Alcoholic Beverages, to name a few. For illustration purposes, take a look at the result if the team grants a beer company each of these three categories individually.

If the team grants the sponsor "beverages," then the team cannot sign a soft drink sponsor, like Pepsi or Coca-Cola. In order to have soft drinks provided in the park, as they are beverages, it would have to be the Sponsor that provides them. This would mean that the category of soft drink is now inventory of the Sponsor beer company instead of the team; thus it would be the sponsor who recognized the benefits of a third-party soft drink pouring rights deal. Furthermore, unless the team contracted with the Sponsor for it, the team would have no input or control over the type or quality of soft drinks that would be provided by the third party with whom the Sponsor contracts. The Sponsor could make a lot of money selling the rights to No-Name Cola, but it might hurt the team in the end.

The category of "beer," on the other hand, is the narrowest of the three examples. The Sponsor, which is a beer company, would have exclusivity within its category, which is the goal, and the team would retain the other beverage categories to sell.

"Alcoholic Beverages" as a category is broader than just Beer, but significantly narrower than the whole Beverage category. If the beer company also makes other kinds of alcohol, it might prefer this category because it has a chance to sell its lesser-known products, wine for example, to a captive audience. Depending on the quality of such other products, the team may not want to allow the Sponsor to be the only seller of higher-end, and more expensive, alcoholic beverages such as wine. The team can protect against this by either granting the narrower category, or carving out exceptions for specific products or locations within the facility. For example, the team may allow the Sponsor exclusivity within the Alcoholic Beverage category but carve out an exception that the team can sell any type of wine or hard liquor on the club level and in the suites. Either method can be an acceptable compromise.[15]

---

15 For an example of an exclusivity provision, *see* Section 4(a) "Exclusivity and Certain Other Rights: Category Exclusivity" in Levi's Stadium Naming Rights Agreement.

In addition to the grant of rights under this section, it is important for the team to include a reservation of rights, or at least a very specific limitation of the granted rights. Specifically, it is worthwhile for the team to be expressly clear that the grant of rights is subject to previous grants made by the league to which the team belongs. This is especially important if the venue houses NBA and/or NHL teams, as those leagues control a good amount of possible advertising inventory. In addition, it may be necessary to expressly subordinate the rights granted in a naming rights agreement to any pertinent league contracts, constitutions, and bylaws.[16]

B. TERM AND PAYMENT

The term of the naming rights agreement needs to reflect both the desire of the sponsor to get a long term, and the desire of the team to be able to sell the naming rights several times over. Both parties have to consider the costs of creating and removing signage as well as the creation of the publication materials that will identify the facility by name. It is not in the best interests of either party to have to bear these one-time costs at frequent intervals; the term of the agreement will thus need to take these costs into consideration as well. Who will bear the costs at the end of the term will be part of the "Actions at the End of Term" clause, but the decision reached by the parties for that clause will affect the term to which they agree.

Though the team wishes to get a shorter term so that, upon expiration of the term, the team may resell the rights, the team is most likely going to be willing to sign on to a longer agreement if the price is right. The team will not, however, sign up for a term that extends beyond its lease term. Doing so would likely have the effect of limiting the team's freedom at the end of its lease term, and, if public, the information that their naming rights deal lasts longer could greatly decrease the team's bargaining power in its future negotiations with its landlord.

The sponsor will want a longer term, provided that such a term fits with its long-term business plans.[17] In general, naming rights deals present a host of issues to be considered by the sponsor, including whether the company will be able to sustain the cost of such a deal in the long term. In good years, many companies do not foresee a future

---

[16] *See e.g.* "Arena Naming Rights Agreement" between Kiel Center Partners and Savvis Communications Corporation for the naming rights to the home of the St. Louis Blues available at: Ian S. Blackshaw, SPORTS MARKETING AGREEMENTS: LEGAL, FISCAL AND PRACTICAL ASPECTS 179 (Oct. 20, 2011).

[17] For a list of the 10 most lucrative American stadium naming-rights agreements, *see* Louis Bien, "49ers' Levi's Stadium the 3rd-biggest naming rights deals in American Sports," *SB NATION*, May 8, 2013, available at: http://www.sbnation.com/nfl/2013/5/8/4313344/49ers-levis-stadium-biggest-naming-rights-contracts.

where they can no longer afford the annual naming rights fees, but this is a distinct reality for many companies, especially if the country experiences an economic crisis of the proportions found in 2008–2010.[18]

The Term provision of a naming rights agreement can also provide for a renewal option for another period of time. It may be in the interests of both parties to include an option to renew to be exercised during some window before expiration of the agreement. Chapter 1 discussed the many options for renewals and first negotiation or first refusal that the parties may want to include in a Naming Rights Agreement, either in a term clause or elsewhere in the agreement.

This clause must also provide for the payment amount and payment schedule throughout the Term. As with any other sponsorship agreement, the payment amount will depend on the benefits conferred and the length of the agreement. The payment schedule, however, may be determined by other factors. In some cases, the team has bought the naming rights off of the landlord and has a certain amount of time to pay the landlord for those rights. Thus, the team will want to assure that the payment schedule under the naming rights agreement at least covers the payments the team owes to the landlord for the use of the naming rights. The amount of money the naming rights are worth will also depend on the team or teams that play at the facility, the location of the facility, the quality of the facility, and the history of the facility name. For a facility that has had several name changes, the naming rights will be less valuable because many people have ceased to refer to the facility by its official name.[19] A facility for a team that is not very successful will command a lower naming rights price, as will a facility in a rural or out of the way area, and an old facility that is in poor condition.[20]

In terms of actual numbers, the naming rights fees have been as little as $620,000 annually, as was the case with the Jacksonville Jaguars until 2007, and as high as Citigroup's $20 million annual fee for the naming rights to Citi Field over the course of a twenty year period.[21]

---

18 *See* "Pols want new name for Mets home: Citi/Taxpayer Field," *USA TODAY*, Nov. 26, 2008.

19 *See* Rovell, Darren, "Are Naming Rights Deals a Good Buy?", *CNBC SPORTS BUSINESS*. January 20, 2010.

20 For an example of a Naming Rights Term provision, *see* Levi's Stadium Naming Rights Agreement.

21 Nancy Kercheval & Eben Novy-Williams, "MetLife Signs 25-Year Deal to Put Name on Giants, Jets Home," *BLOOMBERG BUSINESS*, Aug. 23, 2011, available at: http://www.bloomberg.com/news/articles/2011-08-23/metlife-sets-25-year-naming-rights-deal-for-jets-giants-new-jersey-stadium.

C. NAMING RIGHTS BENEFITS

Naming rights benefits can be many and of any variety. The sponsor enjoys these benefits in return for the payment of the naming rights fee. As mentioned above, one significant benefit is the category of exclusivity in which the sponsor becomes the "exclusive" and "official" provider for the team and the facility. Beyond the category, however, a naming rights agreement must include a signage and advertising package along with other miscellaneous benefits.[22]

As the naming rights sponsor will name the facility, there will at the very least be a large sign over the entrance with the name of the facility on it. Beyond this, the naming rights sponsor will want additional signage. Additional signage can be on the scoreboards or video boards, at the entrance turnstiles, at the concession and souvenir stands, elsewhere on the signage boards, the list continues. Beyond signage, the naming rights sponsor is likely to want advertising. This can be on tickets, in the programs, on the concession stand equipment and inventory, on the radio and television broadcasts, and even on the video board during the games.

Other benefits include luxury suites and club seats. A naming rights sponsor is very likely to want a suite of its own, in a good position in the facility, as well as a number of club seats. These could then be enjoyed by members of the corporation, or be used by the sponsor for business purposes such as entertaining clients. How many and which luxury suites and club seats the sponsor will get will depend on the price they pay and the willingness of the team to grant them, instead of reserving them for sale to other customers. Additionally, the team may be willing to allow the sponsor the use of the facility for corporate events for some amount of time in each year, provided such use doesn't interfere with the operation of the team. Should the parties wish to negotiate for any such benefits, they too must be laid out in this section.

D. JOINT LOGO/CHANGE OF JOINT LOGO

In addition to the existing corporate logos and marks of the parties, in a Naming Rights relationship it may be in the interests of both parties to create a joint logo that identifies them and their relationship. If the parties so decide, they must resolve which party will create the logo, how much approval the other party will have over

---

[22] For an example of possible naming rights benefits, *see* Alicia Jessop, "Levi's Gains Value Beyond Naming Rights In Its Partnership With The San Francisco 49ers" *FORBES*, Oct. 19, 2014, available at: http://www.forbes.com/sites/aliciajessop/2014/10/19/levis-gains-value-beyond-naming-rights-in-its-partnership-with-the-san-francisco-49ers/.

its final form, who will bear the costs associated with creation, how and where the logo will be used after its creation, who will bear the costs of such uses, who owns the logo, who has the obligation to pursue infringement of the logo, who will own the logo upon the expiration of the term of the agreement, who may use the logo after the expiration, what uses the logo may be put to throughout its life, what happens if one party wishes to alter the joint logo, who performs the alterations, and who pays for any alterations.[23] This is not an exhaustive list, but it certainly brings up many points that should be considered.

In addition, the parties should consider the possibility that the logo would need to be changed, perhaps pursuant to a change in control or change of name. As both parties would always prefer to not bear the costs of such a change, it makes sense for the costs of changing the logo to be borne by the party that forced the change and this might be the ZOPA for both parties in such a situation.

E. SERVICE MARK AND TRADEMARK GRANT OF RIGHTS

The naming rights sponsor is likely to want some of its advertising benefits to be achieved through the placement of its marks throughout the facility, and through use of the team marks in its external advertisements. After all, the sponsor will wish to claim its category of exclusivity in advertisements outside the facility as well as in. Thus, an important part of any sponsorship agreement is the clause that addresses the use of marks.[24]

This section will likely allow limited use of the parties' marks by the other party. Such use may be subject to approval rights or not, depending on the deal that is struck. Furthermore, the situation must be addressed in which one party changes their marks. In such a situation, will the other party still be able, or obligated to use it? How soon must the change go into effect? What if programs had already been printed using the past marks, do those have to be thrown out and new ones created? These are important situations to address in an agreement, and must be addressed early in order to avoid any future conflict or confusion. As with any intellectual property provision, the parties should be sure to be clear as to ownership and the scope of any license granted in order to avoid confusion surrounding any of the parties' intellectual property.

---

23 *See* Section 3(d) "Grant of Naming Rights: Stadium Logo: Signage, displays and other collateral" in Levi's Stadium Naming Rights Agreement.

24 *See* Section 3(b) "Grant of Naming Rights: Official Designation and Right to Use Image of Stadium" in Levi's Stadium Naming Rights Agreement.

F. TERMINATION

In any termination clause, it is important to define any material breach that gives rise to termination rights. In a naming rights agreement, there are several breaches that the parties may want to give rise to termination rights. For the team, continuing non-payment of the naming rights fee is a key example of a breach that can and should be a termination event. For the sponsor, certain force majeure events (such as those resulting in considerable damage to the facility) and any team relocation are obvious examples of events that could trigger a sponsor's termination right. In addition, material adverse changes (MACs) to either party can result in either bilateral or unilateral termination rights. If there is a MAC to the sponsor's business, the sponsor may want out because it is no longer economically feasible to perform under the agreement or because the company as it now exists does not benefit from this type of advertising.[25] The team may want out because the sponsor is no longer the type or quality of sponsor the team originally negotiated with and the team no longer wants to associate with the sponsor. If the Team suffers a MAC, there is little chance it will want to get out of its naming rights deal, but the sponsor will likely want the right to terminate.[26] If the sponsor has such a right it can either terminate and cut its losses, or use that right as leverage to negotiate a better deal with the team.

It is especially beneficial to be specific as to which breaches render the agreement terminable and which do not; failure to do so can result in serious disagreements as to the existence of a termination event such that the parties end up with a long and expensive dispute to resolve.

Beyond the termination events, are the post-termination rights of the parties, including rights to the paid and unpaid portions of the naming rights fee. The team would obviously like to be able to not only keep all the monies paid under the agreement, but would also like some rights to future payments as well, especially if the termination event comes from a material breach by the sponsor. The sponsor, on the other hand, would prefer to retain not only unpaid portions of the naming rights fee, but also some portions of the fee already paid, especially if the termination is the result of a team breach. The parties may also have obligations post-termination that may or may not be the same as those they would have had if the

---

[25] *See* Section 2(b) "Term: Special Termination Right of Naming Rights Sponsor" in Levi's Stadium Naming Rights Agreement.

[26] *See* Section 2(c) "Term: Special Termination Right of the SCSA" in Levi's Stadium Naming Rights Agreement.

agreement had expired instead of being terminated. Other clauses in the Naming Rights Agreement such as Actions at the End of Term, Limit of Liability, and other damages clauses will all address end of term rights and obligations, which either will or will not also be applicable in a termination situation. Whether or not termination, or specific situations of termination, will alter the other procedures for the end of term should be addressed in this section, even if it is only to reference the other clauses where such altered rights and obligations are set forth. For example, it may be that upon expiration the parties will jointly bear the costs of removing the sponsor's signage at the facility, however, in a situation where one party materially breaches the agreement, and the other party terminates, the breaching party will be responsible for all the costs of the removal. While all of this information will be addressed in the Actions at the End of Term section, the Termination clause may want to be specific as to which sections control the post-termination relationship.

Termination clauses must also address the procedure the parties must follow when there has been a breach. This may include notice and an opportunity to cure, as discussed in Chapter 1 of this book.

G. ACTIONS AT THE END OF TERM

At the end of a naming rights relationship any physical evidence of the past affiliation between the parties will need to be removed from the facility, the parties' advertising materials and any other place the relationship is publicly displayed. This means that changes will need to be made, including signage that will need to be covered or removed, advertising materials that will need to be replaced, and commercials that will cease to run as they are. In this clause, responsibility for these actions needs to be allotted between the two parties. The parties should decide who will be responsible for making the changes, the time frame in which the changes need to be made, which party will bear the costs of the changes, who owns the removed signage, any intellectual property associated therewith, and any other issues relating to the alterations that are made at the end of term.

As mentioned in the section above on termination, this clause will also want to address how the responsibilities of the parties at the end of their relationship will change if the agreement is terminated prior to expiration, if the responsibilities alter at all. To do this, it may be worthwhile to begin with the expiration rights and obligations but to qualify it with language such as "except as provided below in Sections . . ." or "unless otherwise provided in this Agreement, the Parties rights and obligations at the end of Term are . . . ". Then, other sub clauses can address any situation in which the parties feel that allocation of rights and obligations at the end of term should be different from the standard practice.

H. INSURANCE AND INDEMNIFICATION

In any contract, the parties are likely to require an indemnification clause to shift any liability onto the other party, often the party with more control over the cause of liability. If the sponsor is a food or beverage company, for example, the team will no doubt require the sponsor to indemnify the team for any liability arising from a poor quality of product or defective packaging. Furthermore, if the agreement requires the sponsor to maintain a specific level of quality, which should be included in the agreement, the team will want the sponsor to also indemnify it for any breach of such a quality provision. In turn, the sponsor will want the team to indemnify it against liabilities arising from team actions or omissions as well as team breaches. For example, if the naming rights sponsor is a beer company and someone at the facility slips on a puddle of beer and is injured, the sponsor would likely want to be indemnified against liability for such an injury because team personnel should have cleaned up the puddle of beer.

Insurance provisions are often as important as the indemnification provisions, in some cases, because the only way a party will be able to effectively indemnify the other is if they carry insurance for that purpose. An indemnification provision does no good for the indemnified party if the indemnitor is judgment proof. In such a situation, the indemnitee would have to bear the costs of the litigation without a hope of recovery from the indemnitor. In many cases, the parties will have to cross indemnify each other, and will have to carry liability insurance for that purpose. Failure to carry the insurance will often be a breach, or even a material breach, of the agreement.

Any indemnification clause should also include the procedure followed to seek indemnification from the other party in a given situation, and the rights and obligations of the parties in responding to complaints and conducting the litigation or other dispute resolution process. The indemnitee's rights to approve and participate in the process will also need to be delineated in this section.[27]

[27] For examples of Insurance and Indemnification provisions, *see* Art. 11 and Art. 12 in Exhibit 3 in Appendix A.

I. ASSIGNMENT/NAME CHANGES

In any long-term agreement, the parties may change and develop into new entities. Teams and sponsors can be acquired and moved, both can change their names, and many intervening factors can change the priorities of the parties as time goes on. The "Assignment/Name Changes" clause should lay out what happens in these situations. If the sponsor is acquired, can it assign the agreement to its new parent company? Can the sponsor assign the agreement for another reason? Does the team have approval over assignments? If the sponsor changes its name, can it change the name of the facility? If the team moves, can it assign the agreement to a new occupant? All of these questions, as well as the procedure for changes or assignments, should be addressed in this clause.

It is often the case that if the sponsor's name changes so too will the name of the facility. For example, in 2009 TD Banknorth re-branded itself as TD Bank in New England, and in July what had been TD Banknorth Garden in Boston, home of the Bruins and Celtics, became TD Garden.[28] Though the specifics were not released, both Delaware North Companies, owners of the Garden and the Boston Bruins, and TD Bank had to decide on or approve the new name and which party would cover the costs associated with removing the old name and putting up the new.[29]

J. LIMIT OF LIABILITY

A limit of liability clause will discuss the type, and often amount, of damages the parties will be entitled to under the agreement. This clause will often include a cap on damages. For certain breaches of the agreement, the parties will want to limit their liability, and this clause will lay out the situations in which liability will or will not be limited and what the limit of liability is in terms of the type and amount of damages. In many cases, damages will be capped only for breaches that do not rise to the level of knowing or intentional breaches. For knowing and intentional breaches, damages are often uncapped. This is obviously to prevent a party from choosing to breach if it is more efficient for them to do so.

Damages can be actual, consequential, incidental, and punitive. In a limitation of liability clause, it is important for the parties to choose which combination of types of damages the parties will be entitled to under different breach situations. The parties must keep in mind

---

28 *See* Delaware North Companies press release: "TD Banknorth Garden Announces Its New Name," April 15, 2009.

29 *Id.*

that the damages should always be reasonable for the situation, or a court will not uphold them.

HYPOTHETICAL EXERCISE

Negotiating and Drafting a Naming Rights Agreement Between a Sponsor and a Professional Sports Franchise

Imagine that the Boston Red Sox have finalized their lease agreement from the previous chapter. Now, to raise revenues, to maintain and keep the stadium up to date, and to pay higher salaries and signing bonuses, the Red Sox have entered into negotiations to sell the "naming rights" of the stadium.

The company who is most interested in acquiring the naming rights is Anheuser-Busch InBev. The now world's largest beer company, after its recent acquisition of Anheuser-Busch, is the maker of popular beers such as Budweiser, Stella Artois, and Beck's, and has a strong global presence. Though the company already has the naming rights over Busch Field—the stadium on the campus of the College of William and Mary—it is eager to be the naming rights sponsor of a professional baseball franchise. Anheuser-Busch InBev hopes that the naming rights over the new Red Sox' stadium will not only give it advertising opportunities and exposure, but that it will be able to create goodwill in the United States, get exclusive pouring rights to alcoholic beverages at the stadium, and sky boxes/luxury suites.

Assume that the company is "recession resistant," given that sales of alcohol increase during economic downturns, and therefore unlikely to go bankrupt. The company is casually considering acquiring/merging with other companies, if a lucrative opportunity arises, given that the prices of competitor companies might be artificially depressed.

Further assume that the company, whose name is a mouthful, is open to creative titles for the stadium, using the company or its products.

Students should split into two groups, with one representing Anheuser-Busch InBev and one representing the Red Sox. After discussing how they would negotiate and draft the clauses and exhibits of a Naming Rights Agreement in their subgroups, students should come together to begin to negotiate the following clauses:

1. Grant of Naming Rights

   Establish the grant of the naming rights from the Red Sox to Anheuser-Busch InBev. Be specific as to what is being granted, for example, the rights to which facility. Explain what rights, if any, are reserved by the Red Sox. Consider whether there should be any limits on the Company's ability to sponsor other stadiums or venues. Consider also whether the Company have "category exclusivity" with respect to certain aspects of stadium advertising. Be careful when defining the category, and the limits on the Red Sox to pursue Company competitors as advertisers/sponsors.

   In the biggest beer deal in history, Anheuser-Busch InBev bought its main rival SABMiller for $104 billion, resulting in a brewery capable of sales topping $55 billion per year. Consider how this purchase has further defined this already ultra-important category. The Red Sox have fewer leverage options to secure another alcoholic beverage partner as a result.

2. Term and Payment

Consider the section on Term and Payment above and that the price of a naming rights agreement is a function of (1.) the number of events held at a venue, (2.) the types of events, (3.) the presence of the corporate entity in the area, and (4.) the composition of the naming rights package.

3. Exhibit A—Naming Rights Benefits

Detail the list of benefits or inventory that the Company will receive in connection with the Agreement. These may include, for example:

- Signage, both inside and outside the stadium; and logo placement on napkins, team letterhead, trashcans, employee uniforms, etc.;
- Inclusion in promotional materials or newsletters;
- Mention in television and radio broadcasts, as well as in-game announcements;
- Access to the stadium for a certain number of days each year for Company events;
- Logo/name on tickets to Red Sox games and all stadium events;
- Use of the season-ticket holder mailing list;
- Luxury suites/club seats;
- Division, Championship, and World Series tickets;
- Appearances by players (and the level of efforts the Red Sox must use to ensure such appearances);
- The right of the Company to call itself "The Official Beverage Provider of the Red Sox" for a certain number of years; or
- Company-specific benefits (e.g. FirstEnergy's agreement with the Cleveland Browns as the official energy provider of FirstEnergy Stadium).

When compiling the list, consider how the team will preserve certain other rights for additional sponsors with the purpose of maximizing total revenues.

4. Logo/Change of Logo

Consider the Logo/Change of Logo section of this chapter, in particular:

- Consider which party will bear the responsibility and expenses for creating the new joint logo.
- Include what approval rights over the logo each party will have.
- Be specific as to what uses the logo will be put to and whether the parties have approval rights over the other party's uses.
  - Suggested uses include: use on or in signs, posters, etc., use in printed material, and use in spoken, written and visual advertising.
- Define the ownership interest in the new logo including who owns the goodwill in the mark.
- Consider "quality control" requirements on behalf of the Red Sox or the Company in order to continue the use of the other party's marks.
- Be sure to include who will have the responsibility/discretion to pursue infringers or potential infringers.

5. <u>Exhibit B</u>—Service Mark and Trademark Grant of Rights Agreement

Establish a reciprocal grant between the Company and the Red Sox of their intellectual property. Consider whether approval will be required before either party makes use of the other party's intellectual property and, if so, what the standard of approval is. Standards of approval can be "not to be unreasonably withheld," or "in [the party's] sole discretion."

6. <u>Termination</u>

Make use of the section in this chapter on termination. Consider whether the following will constitute termination events: failure to use the logo according to the limits you agreed upon, failure to get the requisite approval, failure to perform material terms of the agreement, a change of control at Anheuser-Busch InBev, a change at the Company that would result in a material adverse change, the effect of the team losing its franchise, an extended labor dispute, a relocation, non-payment, a breach of covenants, bankruptcy, insolvency, and force majeure events.

Once you have agreed upon the various termination scenarios, consider the remedies available, if any, or are all claims waived. Keep in mind the Limit of Liability clause you will also be drafting.

7. <u>Actions at the End of the Term</u>

When writing this clause, be sure that the parties have addressed what will happen with the joint intellectual property created including any time limit within which the Red Sox and the

Company have to stop using the joint intellectual property or the intellectual property of the other party.

Be sure to allocate who is responsible for making the changes to the signage and other materials, and who will bear the costs.

8. Insurance and Indemnification

Consider whether the parties want to indemnify one another for infringement, unfair competition by third parties, the cost, expense and steps necessary to file applications to obtain trademarks or trade names, the pursuit of infringers, and negligent, reckless, or willful conduct.

To support these indemnities, the parties might require each other to carry insurance. Consider what amount of insurance each party should require from the other.

9. Assignment/Name Changes

In negotiating and drafting this clause, consider whether the Parties will require approval for a transfer or assignment of the rights under the agreement, should ownership of either party change. What rights will the parties be able to transfer/assign, either with or without approval from the other party?

Consider also what will happen in the event that the Company decides to change its name prior to the termination of the agreement?

10. Limit of Liability

When drafting this portion of the agreement, consider how it interacts with the "Indemnity." Will the limitation of liability exclude claims for indemnity, or not? What is the cap on the limit? Are the parties able to recoup consequential/incidental damages in the event of breach? What about punitive damages?

For guidance, please see the "Exemplar" Student Group response in the Teacher's Manual that accompanies this book.[30]

[30] For more information on Naming Rights Agreements and the involvement of intellectual property, *see* Peter Carfagna, Appendix B: An Introduction to Naming Rights Agreements and Intellectual Property, A SUPPLEMENT TO "NEGOTIATING AND DRAFTING SPORTS VENUE AGREEMENTS" (2016).

Chapter 4

PRESENTING SPONSORSHIP AGREEMENTS

Presenting Sponsorship Agreements are very similar to Naming Rights Agreements in the amount of money they can command and the type of sponsorship inventory they include. The manner in which these two agreements interact, however, is very complex, as is how these two agreements interact with any other existing sponsorship agreement. The naming rights package is most likely to be the most valuable and most prominent sponsorship package in the team's or the facilities' inventory. From the perspective of signage and advertising, the naming rights sponsor will have the greatest sponsorship package. However, the presenting sponsor will want as much, or nearly as much, inventory as was given to the naming rights sponsor.

Part of what a team is selling to the presenting sponsor is a signature phrase, which can go something like: "Team Baseball Presented By. . . ". The importance of the signature phrase lies in its uses in television, radio and other new media broadcasts, as well as in locations throughout the park. In addition to the presentation signature phrase, the presenting sponsor will typically get a category of exclusivity and a corresponding benefits package. The category of exclusivity allows the presenting sponsor to also call itself the "official" or "exclusive" provider to the team within the category.

Sometimes, instead of sponsoring the entire team, sponsors elect to become the presenting sponsors of a part of the facility or a specific event. For example, at Dodger Stadium part of the stands were turned into a beach-themed area known as "Bleacher Beach," which is presented by Bud Light as of July 2009.[1] Presenting sponsorships can also be sold for specific events or regular days of the week. Similarly, in 2009, Chipotle became the presenting sponsor of

1 *See* "Anheuser-Busch's Bud Light named presenting sponsor of 'Bleacher Beach,' " *LOS ANGELES DODGERS: PRESS RELEASE*, July 24, 2009, available at: http://losangeles.dodgers.mlb.com/news/press_releases/press_release.jsp?ymd=20090724&content_id=6031740&vkey=pr_la&fext=.jsp&c_id=la.

"Chipotle Student Nights" and the "Chipotle T-Shirt Toss" at Boston Bruins hockey games as part of a larger sponsorship deal.[2]

In addition to specific events, sponsors can present parts of the season. For example, in 2015, Chinese smartphone maker ZTE signed an agreement to be the presenting sponsor of the first Chinese New Year Celebration for the Cleveland Cavaliers at Quicken Loans Arena taking place February 2016.[3] ZTE will also be the presenting sponsor of the "Bulls-Eye View" for the Chicago Bulls at the United Center, announcing a three-year agreement for the series of exclusive, behind-the-scenes content that will only appear on Bulls.com.[4] As with other sponsorship deals, the parties to any type of presenting sponsorship begin by negotiating the sponsorship benefits and the other aspects that define and limit the deal.[5]

A. SPONSOR BENEFITS[6]

Presenting sponsorship benefits are often similar, but pared down versions of the naming rights benefits. Of course, the presenting sponsor cannot have the same benefits as the naming rights sponsor, nor should the presenting sponsor be given as many or as valuable benefits as the naming rights sponsor considering the presenting sponsor is less prominent than the naming rights sponsor. The presenting sponsor will, however, always want as many benefits as possible for as little money as possible. Considering the presenting fee, the team will give as many benefits beyond the sponsorship category as possible without providing more inventory. This allows the team to reserve sponsorship benefit inventory to sell to other sponsors.

It is critical for the team not to allow any presenting sponsorship benefits to overlap with benefits given in other sponsorship packages.

---

2 *See* "Bruins and Chipotle Mexican Grill Announce Multi-year Partnership Agreement," *BOSTON BRUINS: NEWS*, Nov. 11, 2009, available at: http://bruins.nhl.com/club/news.htm?id=505682.

3 *See* "ZTE Becomes Smartphone Partner of the Cleveland Cavaliers," *CLEVELAND CAVALIERS: PRESS RELEASE*, Oct. 27, 2015, available at: http://www.nba.com/cavaliers/releases/zte-partnership-151027.

4 *See* "ZTE Becomes the Official Smartphone of the Chicago Bulls," *CHICAGO BULLS: PRESS RELEASE*, Oct. 27, 2015, available at: http://www.nba.com/bulls/news/partnerships/zte-becomes-official-smartphone-chicago-bulls.

5 For example, the 2015 49ers and Esurance presenting sponsorship joint logo created for the 2015 season for the "Faithful 49" fan engagement program. *See* "49ers Launch Faithful 49 Fan Program." *SAN FRANCISCO 49ERS: PRESS RELEASE*, June 17, 2014, available at: http://www.49ers.com/news/article-2/49ers-Launch-Faithful-49-Fan-Program/67a09352-e566-4be2-8866-c7a27fb77683.

6 For more information on what to include in the presenting sponsorship package, *see* Peter Carfagna, Appendix B: Presenting Sponsorship Agreements: What to Include in the Sponsorship Package Study Guide, A SUPPLEMENT TO "NEGOTIATING AND DRAFTING SPORTS VENUE AGREEMENTS" (2016).

That is, the team cannot sell to any sponsor what it has already sold. The specific benefits given to each and every sponsor must be carefully memorialized and described in the contracts so that the team can go back and be sure of exactly what it has already promised. If a team gives a naming rights sponsor all the advertising space on the stadium turnstiles, then the presenting sponsor cannot buy advertising space on those turnstiles.

In addition to not reselling what the team has already sold, the team must also be careful not to sell what the league has already sold. This is especially important in presenting sponsorships because a key sponsorship benefit is the obligation of the broadcasters to use the signature phrase in live broadcasts. Keep in mind that often, national broadcasting contracts are signed not by teams, but by the leagues, and the team may or may not be able to influence the number of "mentions" of the signature phrase in the national broadcast. Teams do sign local broadcasting contracts, however, so they will likely be able to offer a fair amount of presenting sponsor "mentions," as well as advertising space in local broadcasts.

The biggest sponsor benefit is the category of exclusivity, which will be discussed further in the exclusivity section of this chapter below. Along with the category comes the advertising package. The team is most concerned that the sponsor only gets as much inventory as makes sense given the type of sponsorship and the money the presenting sponsor will be paying. To preserve the relationship with the naming rights sponsor, the team will also want to ensure that no individual sponsor gets more inventory than the naming rights sponsor. The presenting sponsor however, wants to be sure it is grouped with the top tier sponsors, like the naming rights sponsor, and thus is likely to be willing to spend a bit more money on the presenting fee so as to maximize its exposure at the park.

One way the sponsor can maximize its exposure is through creative, "experiential" marketing strategies, both within and outside the facility. Within the facility, a presenting sponsor can offer promotional events, including being featured on specific days or during specific games and offering deals or coupons for its products. Alternatively, for every home run hit by the home team, a select group of fans could receive a product that the presenting sponsor sells, such as pizza or ice cream. The presenting sponsor could set up a target above the outfield in a baseball stadium and say that for every team home run ball that hits the target, the sponsor will give out a coupon to every guest at the stadium, or in a hockey arena, offer some prize or benefit to ticketed fans for every hat trick by the home team. Sponsors can also set up shop in the facility in the form of a restaurant, if the category is appropriate, sharing control over the restaurant and the profits with the team. Or a sponsor can put areas of the stadium to other uses, as in AT&T Park in San Francisco where giant Coca-Cola bottle structures house the Coca-Cola Superslides as part of the Coca-Cola Fan Lot.[7] These promotions will also benefit the team because they have the potential to bring in more fans.

Other key benefits the presenting sponsor would want are (a) the right to make use of the facility for corporate events from time to time and (b) the right to bring in team personnel for corporate events. The team would like to limit the number of times the sponsor can do either of these things and would like to determine, in its sole discretion, which days the sponsor gets in the facility and which personnel the sponsor gets for its events. The sponsor, of course, wants to be able to maximize flexibility of which days to have its events and wants to choose which team personnel to have at its events. The sponsor may want to have these events as often as possible, while the team may want to limit the number of times it is required to provide personnel or services to its sponsors. One possible ZOPA for the parties is that the sponsor would get one day a year inside the facility, provided it is either in the off-season or will occur a few days before or after a game. To maintain control of the facility schedule, the team would probably have approval over the final date decided on. As for player appearances, a possible ZOPA is to allow one to three members of the team personnel to appear for the sponsor's event on up to two or three occasions from a list of pre-selected players and coaches to be updated annually.

Additionally, the presenting sponsor will likely want a luxury suite, though it won't necessarily need to be in the best location, and a number of club seats. The team will likely be willing to give somewhat on these issues, though it might limit tickets to the regular season only and offer the sponsor the right to purchase the same seats or suites at a discount for postseason games. For the suites, the team will want to keep the sponsor to one suite, ideally for only a partial season, regulate how the suite is used, and give one of the less well-located suites so as to preserve the best suites for ticket sales.

B. PAYMENT SCHEDULE AND TERM[8]

For many sports teams, the off-season is a time of strained financial circumstances. For that very reason, many teams want to schedule

---

[7] The Coca-Cola Fan Lot has five attractions including the Coca-Cola Superslides, a Giant Baseball Glove, Little Giants Park, Fantasy Photo booth, and a Make Your Own Lou Seal Workshop. *See* "AT&T Park: Ballpark Attractions," available at: http://giants.mlb.com/sf/ballpark/attractions.jsp.

[8] For more information on how to structure an agreement, *see* Peter Carfagna, Appendix B: An Introduction to Agreement Structure, Recitals and Definitions Study

the receipt of their sponsorship fees in the off-season. Alternatively, the team might want to have biannual payments and can schedule one in-season and one off-season. Considering the time value of money, both parties will seek to remain in possession of the fee for as long as possible. As a result, the ZOPA for the parties may be between one and two payments a year of the sponsorship fee for the term of the agreement.

Presentation rights agreements are often multi-year, though not necessarily as many years as a naming rights sponsorship. As with any other sponsorship agreement, the term will depend on the amount of the total presenting fee. The parties to a presenting sponsorship agreement can agree to a short or a long term and any number of renewal terms at the option of one or both parties. In any case, the team will likely not want the term of the presenting sponsorship to exceed that of the naming rights sponsorship, and it will certainly want to keep the term under the length of the stadium lease agreement, so as to maintain its freedom with regards to renegotiating with its landlord.

C. EXCLUSIVITY

Like any sponsor, the category of exclusivity for the presenting sponsor will pertain to its product. If it is Coca-Cola or Coors, it will be a beverage category, and may include a pouring rights agreement;[9] if it is a bank, it will be a financial services category;[10] and if it is a food company, it will be a category of food for which the team grants exclusivity. In all situations, the sponsor wants the category to be worded broadly and to include complimentary products (provided it does not have to pay too much) and conversely, the team wants the category worded narrowly. For the two parties, the ZOPA will be some middle ground that has the category including all of the sponsor's primary products, but will specifically exclude products the sponsor does not make. In some cases, the sponsors are enormous corporations, with many affiliated entities that create all sorts of products. In many cases, the category will not encompass all the products made by the sponsor and its affiliates, but will encompass the main products for which the company is known and for which the company wants to secure the category.

In addition, the sponsor will want to decide if it wants the exclusivity to pertain to just advertising within the facility and in conjunction

Guide, A SUPPLEMENT TO "NEGOTIATING AND DRAFTING SPORTS VENUE AGREEMENTS" (2016).

9 Pouring Rights Agreements will be discussed in more detail in Chapter 6.

10 Financial Services Agreements will be discussed in more detail in Chapter 8.

with the team, or if it also wants the exclusive right to sell its products within the facility. If the company is a food, beverage, apparel, or financial service company, for example, it is realistic to suppose that it wants to be the only one of its type selling products from the category at the venue. If the company is a flooring provider, a car company or a company that makes other products that people do not use in a sports venue, it is less likely that the sponsor will also want to pay for the right to sell in the venue. In such a situation, the company would still want to be the exclusive company in the category, but the exclusivity would not produce in-facility sales. The sponsor could, however, ask to use the team's marks at the sponsor's point of sale locations.

For the team, the agreement must not overlap with any pre-existing league or team sponsorship agreement or violate any league rule. In addition, the team needs to think ahead to the other categories it has to sell to second tier sponsors. While the team should be willing to sell a big category to the presenting sponsor, it will not want to broaden the category in such a way that takes another piece of inventory off the table for future sponsorships.

As the team signs more sponsorship agreements, the sponsors will be wary about the categories it agrees to due to the dangers of an overlap that the team may have missed in its due diligence. As a result, the presenting sponsor and others will require the team to represent and warrant that it has the right to sell the exclusive rights to the categories it is selling as they are defined in the agreements. Furthermore, the sponsor will want a series of remedies in case it is later discovered that part of the inventory sold was not in fact the team's to sell. Realistically the sponsor would not be able to demand rescission of an earlier overlapping deal, but they could ask for either monetary damages and, if the overlap is large, the right to terminate its sponsorship agreement with the team. The danger of having to pay damages and of possibly losing a sponsor is just one of the many reasons the team needs to keep very close track of the definitions of the various sponsorship categories it sells. The team thus needs to be very careful that its representations and warranties are accurate in every sponsorship agreement.

D. INTELLECTUAL PROPERTY

As with any other sponsorship agreement, a presenting sponsorship agreement will need to have a formidable intellectual property clause. In the previous chapters, this book has discussed several issues that such a clause needs to address including ownership, scope of licenses, approval rights, and joint logo options. In addition to all of the previously mentioned intellectual property concerns, the creative marketing strategies used as a part of any presentation rights agreement will require the parties to address additional disposition of intellectual property rights.

If the parties elect to pursue a sort of joint venture, for example if the sponsor creates a team-themed product or promotion, there will be additional intellectual property created and the parties will need to allot the intellectual property rights between themselves. This will encompass the rights to the product itself, which may include copyrights, patents, and/or trade secrets, the rights to any trademarks used in promoting the product, and any other rights created as a result of the relationship and the joint product. As with other intellectual property, the parties will also need to decide who has the obligation to pursue infringers, who will control litigation over possible infringement and what happens at the end of the sponsorship relationship.

E. ASSIGNMENT/ANTI-ASSIGNMENT

Assignment clauses are critical parts of agreements between two unique parties. Especially from the perspective of the sponsor, it is important to address assignability of the agreement, since it is negotiating with a specific and unique team. Any assignment (or anti-assignment) clause will interact very closely with the covenants of both parties. Covenants create a right to the party who is the promisee, and an assignment is a transfer of those rights to a third party. For example, when a sponsor covenants to pay a team the sponsorship fee, the team can usually assign the receipt of the fee to someone else. In this example, the team is the "assignor," the new recipient of the payments is the "assignee," and the sponsor is the "non-assigning party." Once the team assigns its payment rights, it no longer has a right to payment. That right belongs to the third party, who can enforce the sponsor's duty to perform. Interestingly, if either party assigns its rights under the agreement without also delegating its obligations, the assignor would still have the obligation to perform all of its representations, warranties, and covenants after assignment, while the assignee would get all the benefits.

Under the arrangement described above, the third party has no duty to perform in favor of the sponsor, as the team did not delegate its performance, or obligations at the time of the assignment. A party officially delegates its performance only when it appoints someone else to perform in its place. The party who delegates its performance is the "delegating party," the party to whom it delegates its performance is the "delegate," and the other party is the "non-delegating party." After delegation occurs, the performance refers not only to duties, but also to conditions. Not all duties are delegable, specifically those that are personal in nature or require unique skills.

Anti-assignment provisions bar a party from assigning its rights under a contract. Such clauses exist to prevent assignments that would materially change the non-assigning party's duties or materially increase its risks. Parties will often include them with anti-delegation provisions but it is difficult to render them effective. The Uniform Commercial Code (UCC) renders ineffective any anti-assignment provisions for agreements subject to the UCC. If the UCC is inapplicable, a court might still invalidate the provision because of the view that such provisions restrain commerce. If the prohibition only extends to "the assignment of the agreement," however, a court is likely to instead interpret the provision as an anti-delegation provision, which are generally enforceable.[11] To create an anti-assignment provision that renders an assignment void, a drafter must take away not only the right to assign, but also the power to assign. To do this, the contract must prohibit the assignment of rights under the contract and declare that any assignment is void.

Below are some sample assignment clauses:

> Neither party shall assign or otherwise transfer any of its rights, interests or obligations under this Agreement to a third party [without the prior written consent of the other party] [which shall not be unreasonably withheld, conditioned or delayed].

> Neither this Agreement nor any rights or obligations hereunder may be assigned or transferred by either party to any other person or entity, voluntarily or by operation of the law, without the advance written consent of the other party; provided, however, that Sponsor may assign this Agreement to an affiliate. If Sponsor makes such an assignment, it shall remain liable for all payment obligations to Team hereunder.

> This Agreement shall be binding upon and inure to the benefit of each party's respective successors and lawful assigns; provided, however, that Sponsor may not assign (by operation or law or otherwise) this Agreement, in whole or in part, without the prior written approval of Team. For purposes of the foregoing, an assignment shall be deemed to include, without limitation, a merger of Sponsor with another party, whether or not Sponsor is the surviving entity, or the acquisition of direct or indirect control of

[11] Restatement (Second) of Contracts, § 322(1).

> management through one or a series of transactions. Any attempted assignment by Sponsor in violation of this Section shall be void and shall entitle Team to terminate this Agreement immediately upon written notice to Sponsor.

The options for approval in the various assignment clauses can be essential to such clauses and the amount of discretion the parties can provide for that approval can be heavily negotiated aspects of the agreement.

Finally, it is important to understand the meaning of "successors and lawful assigns." The general understanding is that with this language, there is a need for an express delegation in the event of assignment, binding the assignee to perform as though it is also a delegate. Depending on state law, sometimes an assignment does not bind an assignee merely because of the presence of a "successor and assigns" provision and sometimes it does. Drafters should thus check the law in the state whose law governs the contract, through a valid selection clause or otherwise, the contract if they choose to include this language.

The parties to a presenting sponsorship agreement will feel very strongly about assignment provisions. The Sponsor will very likely want the right to assign the agreement and delegate all its rights in any situation, including a change in control or even a simple sale of the agreement to dump it if it is no longer economically beneficial to the sponsor. The team, on the other hand, does not want to end up in a sponsorship relationship with a party with whom it did not negotiate and who might be undesirable from the team's perspective, may damage the team's brand, or disturb the symbiotic relationship with other sponsors. To protect the team, the parties can negotiate for an anti-assignment clause, or an assignment clause that gives the team approval rights. If the team has approval rights in its sole discretion, then the team will have extra leverage to possibly even renegotiate the agreement in exchange for its approval of the proposed assignment. The team has similar leverage in the anti-assignment situation; however, if it intends to use it, the team should be sure to include a waiver provision in the agreement so as not to lose the value of the anti-assignment provision in future situations.

The parties will feel differently about team assignment than they do about sponsor assignment. For the part of the sponsor, it is less important if the team wants to assign its rights in the agreement to another party but extremely important that the team be unable to delegate its duties. Just as the team does not want to end up in a sponsorship relationship with an undesired party, the sponsor does not want to end up presenting a completely different team. If neither party envisions making an assignment or delegation, the simplest solution is to require approval by the other party on all future assignments. The specific standard of approval will also need to be determined in these negotiations.

F. TERMINATION[12]

As with any termination provision, the parties to a presenting sponsorship should begin by defining breach and its various levels, such as material or immaterial. In addition, the parties may want to consider whether a dramatic change in the reputation or business of the other party should be a material breach, giving rise to a termination right. For example, if the sponsor is publicly outed for using child labor or some other illegal or disfavored business practice, the team might want to terminate. Similarly, if the team were discovered to be cheating in some way, e.g. the trainers are all encouraging the players to use illegal performance enhancers or disturbing the equipment used during the game, or if the players were caught doing something wrong or distasteful, maybe the sponsor would want to be able to terminate.

Beyond breaches giving rise to termination events, the parties should also consider whether some force majeure events will count as termination events or not. If so, the parties must determine if there would be a window in which the parties required notice, but continue to perform in order to allow the other party to mitigate the potential damages. Bankruptcy is one situation that the parties might or might not characterize as a force majeure event and the parties might want to address what happens to the Presentation Rights Agreement if one party files for bankruptcy. Of course, if the sponsor has filed for bankruptcy, it is not as important financially that it get to terminate the agreement, though reputationally being able to terminate might shore up some of the damage caused by the bankruptcy. For the sponsor, it would be better to be able to suspend or terminate the agreement before complete insolvency, to terminate at the point where the company determines that continuing the relationship would be financially impossible. Of course, the team does not want the sponsor to be able to unilaterally decide to terminate the Agreement just because it no longer wants to pay. The parties will have to work out a ZOPA that allows the sponsor to terminate the agreement if it needs to do so to avoid bankruptcy, which may be through assignment, and allows the team to police such a right—so

[12] For more information on breach, termination, and remedies, *see* Peter Carfagna, Appendix B, Breach, Termination, and Remedies Study Guide, A SUPPLEMENT TO "NEGOTIATING AND DRAFTING SPORTS VENUE AGREEMENTS" (2016).

that it is only used in legitimate circumstances and that the team is adequately protected from and compensated for this situation.

G. POST-EXPIRATION/POST-TERMINATION RIGHTS

After deciding what events will be termination events and what the procedure for termination must be, the parties should determine what rights and obligations they will have in the event of each type of termination. This should include determining how long the parties have to perform their obligations such as selling off jointly produced products, ceasing advertising campaigns that capitalize on the relationship between the parties, and removing sponsorship signage.

In most situations, the parties may decide the rights and obligations of the parties will be to share the costs of dismantling the relationship while each party takes on the obligation of about half of the actions required to complete the dismantling. There may be some situations, however where the parties want to allocate costs and obligations differently. For example, if the termination happens because one party suffers significant reputational harm, then the party with the tarnished reputation may have to bear a higher percentage of costs in addition to any damages it may owe.

In addition to the costs and actions to dismantle the relationship, the parties will want to address the possible damages that could be owed in different termination or expiration situations as well as any surviving indemnification obligations. If the parties agree to a limitation of liability clause, they may also want to expressly exclude certain termination events from that limit of liability, such that the breaching party would owe uncapped damages.

HYPOTHETICAL EXERCISE

Negotiating and Drafting Presenting Sponsorship Agreements Between Sponsors and Professional Sports Franchises

Assume that the Red Sox are now seeking sponsors to advertise in their new stadium. The Red Sox hope that the presenting sponsorship will be a highly lucrative revenue stream for the team, as it seeks to establish an intimate, high-profile sponsorship relationship beyond the stadium naming rights sponsor and earn additional monies to improve the team's future. Assume that Edy's Ice Cream is seeking to secure the presenting sponsorship, and is especially interested in creating a creatively named Red Sox brand of ice cream, selling Edy's ice cream at the stadium, and holding fan ice cream eating contests at the stadium.

Consider the boundaries to the potential rights/assets that the Presenting Sponsor can obtain through the Agreement. The parties will need to avoid impinging upon the rights/property of the Naming Rights Sponsor. Consider what kinds of rights the Red Sox will want to reserve for additional, lower-level sponsors down the road. These considerations must be balanced with Edy's desire to get a "fair" return on its investment, distinguishing itself from "second-tier" sponsors and establishing its special association with the Red Sox in the local community.

Students should split into Groups of four, with one group representing the Presenting Sponsor, Edy's, and one group representing the Red Sox franchise. Each subgroup should consider how they would negotiate and draft the following clauses:

1. Sponsor Benefits

Consider signage, promotional activities within the stadium, advertising and publications, appearances by team personnel at sponsor events, promotional activities outside the stadium, exposure and mention during broadcasts, whether the sponsor will be featured on specific game nights or days, and what benefits would come along with an Edy's Friday night game—for example, tickets, suites, etc. Be sure to look back at what the team gave the Naming Rights Sponsor to be sure that it doesn't offer more inventory or already sold inventory to Edy's.

2. Payment Schedule and Term

Negotiate the term of the Presenting Sponsorship Agreement and the schedule for which Sponsor payments should arrive.

3. Exclusivity

Consider what exclusivity (if any) Edy's will seek within its particular category and with regard to the various benefits it receives from the Red Sox. Think about what rights and degree of flexibility the Franchise wishes to reserve for its marketing to other Sponsors. Specifically, the parties will be interested in defining the "category" in a way that is as broad as possible for Edy's, and as narrow as possible for the Red Sox—all the while keeping in mind what "category exclusivity" has already been "sold" to InBev. The Red Sox will have to give a "representation and warranty" that it is authorized to sell the "categories" and "benefits" in question. In return, Edy's will want a remedy if its exclusivity and/or "benefits" are "invaded" by other contracts into which the Red Sox might have already entered or will enter into, as it extends its sponsorship agreements throughout the rest of the stadium.

4. Intellectual Property

Include a provision addressing any IP issues, such as ownership and the right/obligation to pursue infringers that might arise from, e.g., the inclusion of the Sponsor's logo on the Red Sox website or from the creation of a Red Sox flavored ice cream.

5. Assignment

Consider whether the presenting sponsor should be able to assign any of its rights under the Agreement.

6. Termination

In your discussions, begin by specifying what amounts to "breach" of the agreement, and the various levels of breach. Be sure to determine what will happen in the event of a strike or lockout. You should address what the effect will be of any reputational harm to the Sponsor or the Franchise. What will be the effect of bankruptcy?

7. Post-Expiration/Post-Termination Rights

In the event the Agreement expires or terminates, how long will the parties have, and which party will be responsible, for selling off jointly produced products and exhausting promotional materials? Consider the time limit for such sell off.

After 15 to 20 minutes of preliminary preparation, during which each party should outline its interests and identify its "must haves," "nice to haves," and "throw-aways," Groups should convene and engage in clause-by-clause negotiation of the presentation rights provisions above.

"Exemplar" Student Group responses are set forth, as usual, in the Teacher's Manual that accompanies this book.

Chapter 5

MEDIA RIGHTS AGREEMENTS[1]

Media Rights Agreements are typically dual-purpose agreements. First, they serve as service agreements in which broadcasters agree to provide broadcasting services to the team. Second, they provide sponsorship benefits similar to, but often smaller than, the naming and presenting rights sponsorship agreements, with the broadcaster as the sponsor. As a dual-purpose agreement, the media rights or broadcast agreement will need to address all the rights, duties, and obligations of the service relationship along with the sponsorship relationship.

Broadcasting agreements can be a large source of revenue for teams and leagues. At the college level alone, broadcasting deals are millions of dollars each, if not billions.[2] The NFL makes between five and six billion dollars a year from its broadcasting contracts alone.[3] Broadcasting deals can be so important to teams and leagues that they will consider altering their entire business strategies in order to achieve the best possible broadcasting deal.[4]

---

1 For more information on Media and Broadcasting Rights Agreements, *see* Peter Carfagna, Appendix B: Media and Broadcasting Rights Agreements: The Nexus of Intellectual Property, Antitrust, and Administrative Law Study Guide, A SUPPLEMENT TO "NEGOTIATING AND DRAFTING SPORTS VENUE AGREEMENTS" (2016).

2 For example, in 2011, the Pac 12's announced a television contract with ESPN and Fox network worth $3 billion over 12 years ($250 million per year), which is the largest right package for a college sports league. *See* "Pac-10 Signs Record 12-Year, $3 Billion TV Deal With ESPN, Fox." *BLOOMBERG BUSINESS*. May 4, 2011. In 2011 the NFL signed a broadcasting deal with ESPN to cover Monday Night Football through 2021 for about $1.9 billion per year. *See* "ESPN Extends Deal with N.F.L. for $15 Billion," *NEW YORK TIMES*, September 8, 2011, available at: http://www.nytimes.com/2011/09/09/sports/football/espn-extends-deal-with-nfl-for-15-billion. html? _r=0.

3 Comments of George Attalah, Assistant Executive Director, External Affairs NFLPA, *see* The Second Annual Sports Law Symposium: Labor Uncertainty in Sports: Operating in the Shadow of Upcoming Collective Bargaining Negotiations, Harvard Law School, March 26, 2010.

4 For example, the Pac 10 expanded to become the Pac 12, thereby paving the groundwork to negotiate the largest right package for a college sports league. *See* "Pac-10 to change name to Pac-12," *ASSOCIATED PRESS*, July 28, 2010, available at: http://espn.go.com/college-sports/news/story?id=5414966.

Sports broadcasting agreements cover all different broadcast media, including radio, television, Internet and mobile device media.[5] For example, the 2009 SEC broadcasting deal with ESPN extends SEC college football and basketball coverage to mobile devices.[6] Beyond the different media available as inventory to teams and leagues, the leagues also have the ability to sign multiple different deals for broadcast rights in different markets.[7] To create additional revenue, leagues also create broadcasting deals with multiple broadcasters for different events. For example, the MLB is broadcast on both Fox and TBS, but TBS retains the rights to air one LCS, two Division Series, one Wild Card game and afternoon games on the final 13 Sundays of the regular season; while Fox retains the rights to the World Series, the All-Star Game, one LCS, two Division Series, one Wild Card game and double the previous amount of regular season national window games.[8]

Thus, any broadcasting agreement needs a detailed "Scope of the Broadcast" section to address the type of medium the broadcaster will use, the locations it is allowed to broadcast to, and the inventory of games that the agreement will cover. Another essential, yet sometimes difficult to negotiate, section of the agreement is the term, as teams in different situations with regards to performance and attendance will have vastly different earning potentials over both the long and short term.

A. TERM

The length of term desired by the parties to a broadcasting or media rights agreement will depend on many factors, including the past success of the team, the breadth of the fan base, and the potential

---

[5] For example, the Big 10 has a deal with ESPN and ABC for television broadcasting and a separate deal with Sirius XM Radio to broadcast football and men's basketball games.

[6] *See* Humes, Mike. "ESPN and Mid-American Conference Extend Exclusive, Multi-Platform Agreement through 2026–27," *ESPN MEDIA ZONE*, Aug. 19, 2014, available at: http://espnmediazone.com/us/press-releases/2014/08/espn-and-mid-american-conference-extend-exclusive-multi-platform-agreement-through-2026-27/.

[7] For example, the NFL has sold the broadcast rights for the AFC to CBS through 2022, while also having sold the right to broadcast NFL games in Europe to ESPN. *See* "NFL Renews Television Deals," *ESPN*, Dec. 14, 2011, available at: http://espn.go.com/nfl/story/_/id/7353238/nfl-re-ups-tv-pacts-expand-thursday-schedule; and "ESPN America Enters Deal with the National Football League to Broadcast NFL Games in Europe," *SATELLITE TELEVISION NEWS*, Sept. 4, 2009. In addition, the NHL, in 2015, signed a groundbreaking digital media rights partnership with Major League Baseball Advance Media (MLBAM). *See also* "Commissioners Bettman, Manfred Announce Historic Media Rights Partnership Between NHL, MLBAM," *NHL PRESS RELEASE*, Aug. 4, 2015, available at: http://www.nhl.com/ice/news.htm?id=776247.

[8] *See* Newman, Mark. "MLB Reaches Eight-Year TV Agreement with Fox, Turner," *MLB PRESS RELEASE*, Oct. 2, 2012, available at: http://m.mlb.com/news/article/39362362/.

future performance of the team. To the broadcaster, aside from the market in which the team plays, team performance is likely the biggest predictor of the value of a broadcast agreement. If the team is performing well and is poised to continue to do so, then the broadcaster is going to value the broadcast agreement more highly, as it will likely bring in more viewers, and thus more advertising revenue and ratings. If the team is performing poorly, and does not look to be poised for a better future, the broadcaster will value the agreement less. If the agreement is valuable to the broadcaster over a longer term, the broadcaster will want to negotiate for an agreement with a longer term.

A longer term may also be desirable to the team, unless it believes that the current deal is going to be less valuable in the coming years than what an alternate agreement would be. For example, for a team that renegotiates its broadcasting contract in a slump year, the team will likely want a shorter term because it predicts that the price it gets in an agreement signed during a slump will be inadequate once, or if, the team bounces back. The broadcaster, however, will want a longer-term contract in a slump year, especially if it feels that the team will rebound shortly, because it can negotiate more favorable terms that will then become more profitable when the team's performance improves. In fact, in most cases the broadcaster will want a longer-term contract unless the team looks poised to perform worse in the foreseeable future.[9]

Both parties have to account for the risk that performance will continue to be poor, or become worse, over the term of the agreement. The level of uncertainty surrounding performance, which can be compounded by the possibility of a labor stoppage, will have a large effect on the term desired by both parties. The broadcaster will not want to be tied into an agreement to broadcast all of the team's games if the team plays poorly, and if it does not play at all, the broadcaster may want the freedom to sign another deal. This may be the case if the team is hurt by league blackout rules, discussed later in the chapter. During leaner years, the team will wish to retain a broadcaster it signed while possessing greater bargaining strength, or more simply, during previously successful years. Thus, it is likely that the broadcaster will want a termination right if performance falls below a certain level, while the team would not want that at all. In addition, the broadcaster might want a termination right in the event of a labor stoppage, while the team will probably prefer a suspension of term and reinstatement at the end of the stoppage. Either way, the party that bears the most risk, either risk of poor

9 For example, if a team is poised to presently win, but has an aging roster or salary cap issues, which could lead to diminished performance in coming years.

performance for the broadcaster or risk of being in a leaner broadcasting contract when the team's performance rebounds, will want to enact contractual structures that diminish said risk.

The importance of the projected future performance of the team on the term of the broadcast agreement can be mitigated or exacerbated by the loyalty of the team's fan base. That is, the future performance will be even more determinative of the term of a broadcasting contract in cities where the fans are more casual. In contrast, for teams with "die hard" fans who support the team even in bad years, performance will be less important to the value of the team's media rights because those die-hard fans will tune in no matter how poorly their team is performing. The loyalty of the fan base weakens the need to connect the term of the broadcasting agreement to projected future performance, but it does not eliminate it. For example, Notre Dame football enjoys a wide range of popularity, even in years in which performance is mediocre. As a result of this broad fan base, and despite the Irish having finished in the top ten only three times between 1992 and 2009, Notre Dame still holds a long-term NBC Sports broadcasting deal with a flat sponsorship fee not based on shifts in ratings over the term of the contract.[10] In most cases, however, the parties, especially the broadcaster, will want to look at how the team is poised to perform in the coming years before negotiating for a multi-year deal, and may want to tie term and projected performance together in its negotiation strategy.

Anytime parties are relying on future projections, there is a measure of uncertainty they have to account for. Thus, it may be beneficial to both parties facing an uncertain future of team performance to begin with a short trial term and provide for successive renewal periods, provided that both parties perform within a certain range. The parties may also choose to sign an agreement with a short term, and instead of offering renewals, choose to include exclusive rights of first negotiation and/or first refusal. These options are more suited to situations in which a team is looking to perform differently in the coming years than it currently does or has in the past. With teams that show a more consistent performance, or consistent viewership despite performance, longer broadcasting agreements would seem to be the better option.

---

[10] *See* "NBC's Notre Dame Deal Extended," *THE ASSOCIATED PRESS*, April 18, 2013, available at: http://espn.go.com/college-football/story/_/id/9186897/nbc-extends-notre-dame-fighting-irish-football-deal-2025.

B. RIGHTS, DUTIES, AND OBLIGATIONS OF BROADCASTER

A media rights agreement is more than a sponsorship agreement—it is also a service agreement. As such, the agreement should lay out more than the grant of a sponsorship category and the benefits that accompany it; the agreement should also define the scope and quality of the services that the Broadcaster will be providing to the team.

Scope of the Broadcast

Perhaps the first aspect of the broadcast that should be covered in this section is the medium in which the broadcaster will operate. Traditional media include television and radio,[11] but with the prevalence of Internet use, teams and leagues are signing broadcast agreements to broadcast games, interviews or other team coverage through online media as well.[12] In addition, with the emergence of smart phones and mp3 players, teams, leagues and broadcasters are making information and footage available through mobile applications and podcasts.

The scope of the broadcast section should also address what games the broadcaster will cover, where and how the broadcaster will cover the games, and what will happen if there is a programming conflict. First, the parties have to decide which games the broadcaster will cover. In many cases, the national broadcasting rights will have already been sold to a broadcaster by the league, and, as such, the team has a limited inventory of what it can offer the local broadcaster. Often this limitation comes in the form of blocking off some games to which the league has already sold the exclusive rights. For the games the broadcaster may air, it may still be limited by league rules.[13] The team needs to be aware of what locations it has the right to sell the broadcasting rights to, so that it sells the right to broadcast team games to as much of that area as possible.

Generally, the team wants the broadcast to be available in as many places as possible, provided such availability does not violate any

---

11 Though television is a traditional medium for sports, television itself is going through constant innovation. For example, Rogers Communications announced it would broadcast every Tornto Blue Jays game and 20 "marquee" NHL games in 4K, while the NFL and FIFA World Cup have made minimal strides to offer original content in 4K. *See* De Vynck, Gerrit. "Rogers Plans Sports Broadcasting in High-Quality 4K Resolution," *BLOOMBERG BUSINESS*, Oct. 5, 2015, available at: http://www.bloomberg.com/news/articles/2015-10-05/rogers-plans-sports-broadcasting-in-high-quality-4k-resolution.

12 For example, Yahoo! offered the first global NFL webcast, which reportedly cost Yahoo! at least $20 million. *See* "Behind the Scenes of the Internet's First Football Game." *WIRED MAGAZINE*. October 28, 2015.

13 Discussion of blackout rules will come later in the chapter.

league rules. For example, from 1973 to 2014, the NFL had a blackout rule, wherein a game would not be broadcast in the home team's local market unless the stadium was sold out for the game 72 hours before, but this policy was suspended for the 2015 season.[14] This meant that, prior to 2015, any NFL broadcasting contract would have to allow for the possibility of a local blackout. In addition, MLB's blackout rules extend even to MLB.tv and Extra Innings, their subscription-based services, such that local games are automatically blocked to local viewers regardless of whether the local team is playing at home or away. In 2015, 15 teams in the MLB announced they would lift streaming blackouts for FOX broadcasts.[15] This means that in negotiating local broadcasting contracts, MLB teams do not need to worry that live coverage of their games will be made available through MLB.tv in competition with the deal they are trying to sign. The teams have to keep in mind, however, that those games become available online, as an archived game, 90 minutes after each game to MLB.tv Premium subscribers; thus, if the league rules allow the team to sell archival rights to local broadcasters, those broadcasters will not have exclusive archival rights.[16]

The scope of the broadcast also includes how the coverage of team games will be formatted and who will be hired for that purpose. For the team, it is important that there be as much coverage of games and news as possible, including pre-game and post-game segments that break down team play and air team news. The length of the pre and post-game segments should be decided as well as what happens to the length of the post-game segment, if anything, should the game run over the allotted time.

It is also very important to the team that the reporters covering the games and news are knowledgeable and likable by the fan base. As a result, the parties should work out a procedure and criteria for selecting reporters and a method by which the team can approve or disapprove of the choices. Such a procedure may include a trial period in which the team can observe the quality of reporting and then veto any reporter that the team does not like.

Additionally, the parties will need to work out a pre-emption procedure in case there are any conflicts between team events and other network programming. For example, if the broadcaster also broadcasts another local sport, there may be times when the games overlap. Ideally, the broadcaster would not cover another sport with

---

[14] *See* Patra, Kevin. "NFL Suspends Local Blackout Policy for 2015." *NFL.com*. March 23, 2015.

[15] *See* "Report: Local Streaming Coming to 15 MLB Markets Next Season." *CBS SPORTS*. August 17, 2015.

[16] Archival rights will be discussed further in the next section.

the same season so the chance of overlap is relatively small.[17] Often, overlap happens when the post-season of one sport conflicts with the pre-season or regular season of the other. Oftentimes, the post-season games are more important to air, because of the nature of the postseason excitement and its relative importance over individual pre-season or regular season games. Sometimes, however, the regular season game of one sport is a big rivalry game and has the potential to draw a significantly larger viewership than even the post-season game of another sport, thus the broadcaster will want to preempt the post-season game for the rivalry game.

In some cases, the broadcaster will come to the team with a pre-existing broadcast agreement with another team, in another sport, that requires the broadcaster to cover all of those games. If that is the case, the team may not be able to force the broadcaster to preempt the other team's programming in their favor. Thus the team should be very careful when negotiating the broadcast agreement to look at the issue of programming preemption, see where it might happen, work out a system by which the parties will address whether the team gets preempted, and then they must decide what happens to the preempted game. In some cases the broadcaster will be able to air the game on a secondary channel.[18] In other cases, the broadcaster will have to air the game at a later date or time to make up for the preemption. If aired at a later time, the team will want to have some control over what time, since it does not necessarily want its game aired directly following the conflicting program, which may be in the middle of the night. Preemption becomes especially necessary when seasons overlap—for example, the start of the NFL season overlaps with the post-season in baseball.

Simulcasting, Archiving, Website, and Availability Post-Game

In addition to live and pre-empted live broadcasts, the parties will need to address the issues of creating simulcasts and archives, and where, and to whom, this footage will be available. Simulcasting occurs when the broadcast is available simultaneously on more than one medium. Traditionally this meant over both radio and television, but it can also mean over television and the Internet. It may be that the team wants the broadcaster to make the broadcast available simultaneously on a website, so fans who are not within the radius of

---

17 For example, hockey and basketball have significant scheduling overlap, and ideally would not be covered by the same broadcaster, unless that broadcaster has several channels on which to offer coverage.

18 For example ESPN has ESPN2, ESPNW, ESPN Classic and others and NESN has NESNPlus.

the broadcast can still enjoy the games.[19] If the broadcaster makes a simulcast available online, the next question is, "on whose website?" Ideally, the broadcaster wants the simulcast to be on its website, and the team wants it on the team's website. Both sides, if the broadcast is simulcast on the other party's site, will want their site to link directly to that simulcast. In addition to the location of the simulcast, the parties will have to determine who will have access to it and whether the viewers will have to pay for such access.

Once the parties have determined if there is going to be a simulcast, where it will be and who has access to it, they will then need to address the issue of archiving the broadcast from the individual games. Generally, the broadcaster will perform the archiving, but then the questions of who owns the archived footage, who has access to it, and how it will be used arise. Questions of ownership and uses will be addressed in the Ownership Of and Rights To the Broadcast section below, and for consistency, will most likely be only referenced, and not set forth, in this section of the agreement.

Both parties may want archived footage to be available to users who want to watch the game after it is aired, so the agreement can also provide for such availability to online users for a certain period of time.[20] Beyond availability online, the broadcaster might want to re-air some of the archived footage as part of a compilation or simply re-show a game on a slow day, thus the parties should specify the process by which the parties approve such uses. How this process works will be determined in part by the ownership of the copyright to the broadcasts, whether the owner will grant a license to the other party and the scope of such a license.[21]

Equipment and Technical Support

The broadcaster is in the business of creating and airing its broadcasts whereas the team is not; thus, the broadcaster will likely be the provider of the equipment and technical support needed to create the broadcast.[22] The team will often contribute in some way,

---

19 If the parties wish to do this, it is important that they do not run afoul of the league's blackout rules and any other conflicting league agreements.

20 Keep in mind that often the leagues have archival rights to the games as well and so if league rules allow for the team to offer archival rights to local broadcasters, these rights will not be exclusive. *See* MLB.TV discussed in the Scope of the Broadcast section.

21 These aspects can be referenced here, but should be covered completely in the Ownership of and Rights to the Broadcast section of the agreement.

22 The expertise of the service provider is essential when contracting for the services. For example, the NBA uses Turner, through Turner Digital Basketball Services, Inc., to operate NBA TV and NBA.com so as to benefit from Turner's expertise in digital work. *See* Lombardo, John & John Ourand. "NBA, Turner Sports

usually by providing the location in the facility used to create the broadcast, as well as the utilities required to operate the equipment.[23] The team may require a certain level of equipment to be used—for example, high definition cameras so that the games can be broadcast in high definition to those that have such channels and televisions. Similarly, the team may require the broadcaster's technical support to meet certain standards; often this would be a time limit by which problems need to be fixed. Obviously, if the broadcaster is having sound or picture problems during the game, the team will want them resolved immediately as opposed to allowing a longer time frame.

Quality of Broadcast

The requirement of a certain quality of equipment and technical support covered above helps to force the creation of a higher quality of broadcast, but, in addition, the team will want to explicitly require the broadcaster to create "high quality" or the "highest quality" broadcasts. Quality, in this sense, is about more than just picture and sound quality, but is also about the talent of the reporters and announcers used, the quality of their coverage, and the absence of anything that could offend viewers, like colorful language or public scandals.[24]

In light of the possible damage caused by announcers that are either indiscreet or intemperate, the parties may consider requiring the broadcaster to include morals clauses for its announcers in their employment contracts. A Morals Clause is a clause in a contract that penalizes a party if they act in the specific ways that are discouraged by the clause. Such specific actions can range from the commission of, or conviction for, a crime, or the simple act of making use of strong language in public. An announcer-friendly morals clause would penalize, usually by firing, the announcer only if they are convicted of a felony, which is a very low moral standard since it would allow the announcer to retain his employment while participating in all sorts of other bad acts as long as he does not get convicted of a felony. A team, however, will likely require the morals clause to be

Deliver First Live Game in Virtual Reality For Fans." *NBA: PRESS RELEASE.* October 27, 2015.

23 The team's obligations will be addressed later in this Chapter.

24 Recent scandals include ESPN firing Bill Simmons, who was fired after calling Commissioner Goodell a "liar" on the Dan Patrick Show, a non-ESPN property, "Bill Simmons Will Not Appear Again On ESPN Platforms, Including Grantland," *SPORTS ILLUSTRATED.* May 15, 2015, and CBS's Greg Anthony was suspended indefinitely for soliciting a prostitute, who was subsequently reinstated to announce Summer League games, *see* Deitsch, Richard, "Exclusive: Turner Sports Reinstates Broadcaster Greg Anthony," *SPORTS ILLUSTRATED*, July 3, 2015.

significantly more employer and team friendly, giving the broadcaster the right to terminate the employment of an announcer for less serious moral problems, including public scandals and on air gaffes. In addition to requiring the broadcaster to include an announcer morals clause in its employment agreements, the team will likely want the right to force the broadcaster to exercise its termination rights arising out of an announcer breach of the morals clause, in certain situations.

The parties should also decide whether they will include a non-disparagement clause—penalizing the announcers for speaking negatively about the team or its personnel. In addition, the parties will want to work out an indemnification provision that covers a breach of any non-disparagement clause and any other offenses, including morals clause violations, which occur during the broadcast. For example, this could include the uttering of obscenities or clear intoxication of one of the personalities featured.[25] In most cases, the parties will want to cross-indemnify each other for this purpose, with the broadcaster indemnifying the team for offenses occurring through the fault of the broadcaster, including any gaffes by broadcasting personnel, and the team indemnifying the broadcaster for offenses caused by the team or its personnel, such as coaches and players who may be featured on the broadcast.

Promotion of the Team and Team Sponsors

The team, when signing the broadcaster, will also require the announcers to mention and promote, during the broadcast, some of the team sponsors along with the team itself.[26] These mentions will be artifacts of the sponsorship agreements signed by the team and its other sponsors, reflecting some inventory and/or benefit the team has given those other sponsors. For example, the team will likely have offered the naming and presenting sponsors a certain number of mentions of its sponsorship or of the venue name as part of that sponsorship deal, and it is necessary for the team to make good on those promises by building the required mentions into its deal with the broadcaster, since the broadcaster will be performing that obligation.[27] Thus, it is important for the parties to be specific and

---

[25] Such problems have been highlighted in two sports films: SEMI-PRO and MAJOR LEAGUE.

[26] For example, during Fox Sports Ohio's coverage of Cleveland Indians games, color commentator Rick Manning chooses the "McDonald's I'm Loving It" play of the game.

[27] Sometimes as well it is not the mere number of mentions of sponsors of events that is important but the effectiveness of the mentions they get. For example, for the 2010 NBA All-Star Game, Turner Sports came up with a plan to both continue to market the game on sports related channels and websites, and to increase

build into the agreement the broadcaster's obligation to promote the team and its sponsors in such a way that the team will honor all its pre-existing broadcast-related obligations to sponsors, as well as providing for the addition of future sponsors to the broadcast.

In some rare situations, the team, or the league, when signing a broadcasting agreement, will actually give the broadcaster the right to sell some of the team or league's sponsorship inventory. For example, CBS "owns and sells the NCAA's marketing and sponsorship rights as part of its broadcast agreement."[28] Thus, it is CBS who finds and signs sponsors for the NCAA.

Category of Exclusivity

The broadcaster is a sponsor as well as a service provider to the team; thus in many cases, it will have a broadcasting-related category of exclusivity. Keeping in mind what broadcasting rights the league may have sold, the parties can formulate a category for the local broadcaster that does not infringe upon the rights of any league broadcasters. This category may be that the broadcaster is the official local broadcaster, or the "flagship" station for the team. Often, the exclusivity will mean that the broadcaster will have the exclusive right to broadcast team games in its medium, which can be television, radio, or other media, within the region decided upon by the parties in the "Scope of the Broadcast" section. If the team wants to reserve the right to sell broadcasting rights to other broadcasters in other markets, it should consider doing so explicitly so that there is no confusion as to what rights the team still owns and can sell to another broadcaster.

Advertising and Signage Package

As with any sponsorship agreement, the media rights agreement will give the sponsor, in this case the broadcaster, an advertising and signage package within the team's facility. This package will be significantly smaller than the package given to a top tier sponsor like a naming or presenting sponsor. The parties will also need to address how the broadcaster may advertise, in terms of whether it may advertise its affiliates as well as itself. As with any sponsorship, in-facility signage can be had on all sorts of surfaces including signage boards and temporary advertising on video boards. The advertising package can also include space in the program for events and possibly some space on the team's website. In addition to an in-facility signage

dramatically the number of spots on non-sports-based broadcast and cable networks compared to the 2009 All-Star Game.

28 Crupi, Anthony. "March Madness is 95% Sold Out Across TV, Online Inventory" *ADVERTISING AGE*. March 10, 2015.

and advertising package, the parties will allocate the commercial airtime during broadcasts between the two of them such that each party can sell broadcast advertising space for their respective allotments of ad space. The parties may choose not to split the advertising airtime, but whether they do or not, the broadcaster will still be obligated to run ads for the team's top tier sponsors.

In-Facility Perks

The broadcaster will need a space within the facility from which to make its broadcast as well as access to other areas of the facility as a part of its press rights and obligations. In addition, the broadcaster might want a luxury suite and some club seats for corporate use. The team will likely not want to give away a suite, especially since the broadcaster will have its own broadcasting space with an excellent view of the games as part of its provision of services. In addition, the broadcaster will require access to the facility for the purposes of broadcasting the games and for maintaining its in-facility equipment, thus the team will need to provide not only all required press credentials for the broadcaster's personnel to be allowed in the facility during games, but also an access card, or equivalent device, for certain areas of the building on off days.

Creative Marketing Strategies

The broadcaster might want to run additional marketing campaigns around its involvement with the team, including, perhaps, an announcer for a day competition or something similar. If the broadcaster wants to run such a promotion, it can provide for it in this agreement. In addition, the broadcaster might want to do giveaways or other promotions before the games and this section will address the rights, duties, and obligations of the parties in such a scenario. In addition to running promotions in the facility, the broadcaster may wish to make use of the facility parking lot or a nearby venue for events taking place on off nights, before the facility is open, or during away games.[29]

C. RIGHTS, DUTIES, AND OBLIGATIONS OF TEAM

In many cases, this section and its subsections will mirror the section above relating to the broadcaster's rights, duties, and obligations. Broadcaster rights are often duties to the team and broadcaster duties are often rights of the team. It is worthwhile, however, to

---

[29] For example, the broadcaster may run a promotion at a local sports bar where fans can watch the game together while the broadcaster offers a raffle or contest of some sort.

reference the rights and obligations that arise from the earlier section in this later one so that it is clear that the team has assumed the obligations it gave as rights to the broadcaster.

Broadcasting Team and Approval Rights

In the "Scope of the Broadcast" section above, it is necessary to address the broadcasting team that would be covering the games and doing the pre and post-game shows. In this section, the parties should consider reiterating the rights and obligations of the team in the process of choosing and approving the individuals, in its sole or reasonable discretion or some permutation thereof, hired to do the broadcast. If the parties choose not to reiterate, it is at least necessary that the parties reference the above section so that there is an effective "bring down," or confirmation that the section applies here as well, of the team's rights and obligations into this section, solidifying it as a team obligation as well as a right of the broadcaster.

Commercial Inventory and Use of the Broadcast

In the Advertising and Signage Package section above, the chapter discussed the allocation of the commercial inventory between the parties. This allocation should be confirmed here, or if the parties so desire, can be introduced here and referenced above. It will be the duty of the broadcaster to air the team's sponsors' advertisements as well as to mention various sponsors during the broadcast. If the broadcaster fails to make these mentions or air these advertisements, the team may face liability from its sponsors. The team should have the right to shift this liability onto the broadcaster vis-à-vis an indemnification provision that can be addressed in this section or in a larger indemnification section.

In addition to commercial airtime, the team will want the right to use the broadcast in its own promotions and on its website. The team may further want to be able to grant to a sponsor the right to use a clip of the broadcast in the sponsor's advertisements. If the team is to have either of these rights, they should be addressed or referenced here, and then addressed in the Ownership of and Rights to the Broadcast section.

Advertising, Promotion, and Category of Exclusivity

The team should use this section to acknowledge the obligations it has with regards to the advertising and promotion it will provide to the broadcaster. These should directly mirror the rights of the broadcaster. For ease and consistency, this can be accomplished by referencing the section above in which the team provides those rights to the broadcaster. In addition, the team should explicitly acknowledge the category it has granted to the broadcaster and agree to refer to the broadcaster as the exclusive provider in the category if necessary.

Non-Traditional Revenue

For all of the promotions the broadcaster wishes to run as part of its creative marketing strategies, the parties will need to decide what role the team will play both as provider and beneficiary of the events. It will be important for the parties to allocate their responsibilities for these events as well as the allocation of risk and reward. As some of the promotions will take place in or around the facility, the question of liability will arise. As the team has likely indemnified the landlord for liabilities proximately caused by team negligence, the team will have to address whether it wants to continue to have all this liability even for broadcaster-sponsored events. Thus the parties should allocate the risks and liabilities for these promotional events as well as the obligations of the parties to provide necessary equipment or prizes. In addition, the allocation of revenue between the parties should be addressed.

Access to the Facility and Personnel

For the purpose of creating a high quality and informational broadcast, the team will want to provide the broadcaster access to team personnel, including players, coaches, managers, and trainers, for interviews and spots on the pre and post-game shows. The team will, however, want to limit such access to what is feasible for the personnel and what will not take away from necessary time preparing for the games. As a result, the team should promise personnel in a limited capacity and have the option to switch out who will be available if, for some reason, the promised person is unavailable. This may mean that the team asks the head coach to be available for a brief press conference a few hours prior to every game and that the broadcaster will have access to one of the assistant coaches midway through the game for an update on the coaching advice given up to that point. Players will likely not be available until after the game, though brief interviews between play periods might be an option. The parties should lay out the specifics of which personnel will be available and when, within this section of the agreement, as an obligation of the team, or above, as a right of the broadcaster.

Effectiveness

As a quality control mechanism, the parties should work out a way to measure the effectiveness of the broadcast. Often, this measure will be in the form of ratings. The broadcaster will have already obligated itself to create a high quality broadcast as part of its rights, duties, and obligations, but beyond that representation, the parties will likely want an objective measurement to determine if the quality is inferior or superior. The team will not want to be stuck in a media rights agreement if the quality of the broadcast is sub-standard and ineffective, thus the effectiveness measurement can be useful for providing a threshold at which the broadcaster must improve or risk termination. The parties may also use the measure of effectiveness as an incentive for the broadcaster. For example the broadcaster can pay a certain amount if it keeps ratings within a certain range and if ratings improve above the rage, the annual fee for the following year can be decreased. Of course, if the broadcaster slips below the range of ratings the team will want a termination right or at least a right to a higher annual broadcasting fee.

D. OWNERSHIP OF AND RIGHTS TO THE BROADCAST

Though the broadcaster creates the footage, the team will want to either own it and control the uses of the broadcaster, or have a broad license to use it and restrict the broadcaster's uses. Thus, as with any other intellectual property, the parties will need to decide who owns the broadcast. It is possible that ownership will not remain static, perhaps shifting from the broadcaster during the term to the team after expiration. The team wants to have ownership of the broadcast to control its uses, especially after the contractual relationship between the parties is over, so that it can control all uses of the footage and have it for the team's own archival purposes.

Along with ownership, the parties will need to decide if the owner will grant the other party a license to make use of the broadcasts and the scope of that license. For example, the parties will need to decide if the licensee will be able to transform the broadcast into other media like podcasts or video montages, etc. The parties should be specific as to what uses are acceptable for both the owner and the licensee. For example, during the term, the team is probably willing to agree to the broadcaster using a clip of game footage to advertise itself, but would not like the broadcaster to be able to use the footage in conjunction with another sponsor or event.

The parties should also decide who will be responsible for stopping the "piracy" of any broadcasts and who will be responsible for pursuing those infringers. It is important that any license to the broadcast granted to a party be well defined with approved uses, or explicitly lay out methods of getting approval in cases where the licensee seeks to use the broadcast. The license may also be perpetual, or have a termination date after which the licensee may not make use of the broadcast except for maybe internal or archival purposes.

E. GRANT OF RIGHT TO USE NAME AND LOGO

A grant of rights to use the other party's name and logo clause should exist if the parties covenant to promote one another in the "Rights, Duties, and Obligations" sections. If the parties have so agreed, they should draft a supplementary grant of right to use name and logo in order to lay out the scope of the grant, the length of the grant and any approval or disapproval process that the parties must engage in before making use of the others' name and logo. In addition, this section should make clear that the grant of the right to use does not transfer any ownership rights or privileges and that each party maintain ownership of its intellectual property.

The broadcaster will very likely want to use the team's name and logo for self-promotion and the team should agree to this as long as it has some approval rights over the proposed uses. For the team, it is not as important to identify the broadcaster with the team except for informational purposes in telling fans where they can catch the games. Thus, this section will likely be a "give" for the team and a "get" for the broadcaster.

F. REPRESENTATIONS AND WARRANTIES

In every contract, there will be a section on representations and warranties where both parties make statements about themselves, their status with regard to important aspects of the agreement, and any actions they have agreed to take. Examples of representations and warranties might be as follows: authorization and authority to enter into the transaction, possession of necessary licenses and government approvals, absence of conflicting agreements or other third party rights, absence of pending litigation on the issues raised in the agreement, and the absence of a material adverse change, or MAC, on either party. In addition, both parties will have to represent that they are in compliance with all applicable laws and regulations. For the broadcaster, this means being in compliance with all Federal Communications Commission (FCC) rules and for a team or a league, the deal needs to be in compliance with the Sports Broadcasting Act.

The Sports Broadcasting Act allows the major leagues to sign broadcasting agreements without violating the antitrust laws.[30] Before the passage of the act in 1961, it was considered a violation of the antitrust laws for the league to sign broadcasting deals because it was, in effect, acting on behalf of all the teams combined.[31] The Sports Broadcasting Act also allows for the major leagues to sell a television package to a network or networks, which is what most of the leagues now do.[32] Traditionally, the Act has also been interpreted to include the blackout rules used by leagues like the NFL.[33] Previously, the league could black out a local game if it was not sold out. Beyond that, the blackout rules could also black out competing out-of-market games when the local team was playing. It could even block professional games from being broadcast on Fridays and Saturdays thus competing with high school and NCAA sports. This being said, the NCAA does not share the protections afforded by the Act and as a result, it has not been able to sell broadcasting packages for its larger league.[34]

The result of selling broadcasting packages to television networks has been that often fans lose the ability to watch all of the games they want to see without having to pay.[35] The blackout rules, for example, benefit the teams at the expense of some fans by limiting the choice of programming available to fans. The FCC is currently attempting to address this problem of choice across all programming by opening up the cable industry to independent programmers and rival services.[36] In addition, FCC rulings are opening up certain markets to more broadcast options—for example, by forcing Comcast, which has a monopoly on local sports in Philadelphia, to sell this content to competitors like satellite television.[37]

In addition to a representation and warranty that the deal is in compliance with all applicable laws and regulations, the parties will want representations from each other that the agreement does not

---

30 15 U.S.C. §§ 1291–1295.

31 *United States v. National Football League*, 116 F.Supp. 319 (E.D. Pa.1953).

32 15 U.S.C. §§ 1291–1295.

33 The NFL Blackout Rule was suspended by the owners for the 2015 season, as discussed in the scope section above.

34 *See Board of Regents of University of Oklahoma v. National Collegiate Athletic Ass'n*, 546 F.Supp. 1276 (W.D.Okla. 1982). These rights are instead sold by the individual conferences of the NCAA.

35 The NFL is the only sports league that televises every game in local markets on free, over-the-air television. *See* "NFL suspends local blackout policy for 2015."

36 In September 2014, the FCC repealed its sport blackout rules. *Id.*

37 This would allow other providers such as satellite to request to carry the Comcast coverage and, if denied, file an official complaint with the FCC. *See* MacDonald, Tom. "FCC ruling opens local sports broadcast to competition," *WHYY NEWS AND INFORMATION*. January 1, 2010.

conflict with any existing and binding agreements or other authorities over the party entering into it. In sports sponsorships, it is always important to be aware of potential conflicting agreements and third party rights because the teams and leagues sign away so much sponsorship inventory in such very detailed categories that it is easy to overlook what has already been sold. The sponsor will demand a representation from the team that the inventory leased to the sponsor in this agreement has not been sold and cannot be claimed by another party and is thus not the subject of any existing or impending litigation. In addition, the parties may require an indemnification provision in case any litigation does arise because of alleged infringement third party rights as a result of this agreement.

HYPOTHETICAL EXERCISE

Negotiating and Drafting Media Rights Agreements Between Media Entities and Professional Sports Franchises

A. Assume that the Los Angeles Clippers, who recently learned that ESPN Radio 710 would not be renewing their broadcasting contract for next year, are looking for a new radio broadcasting outlet.[38] Further assume that the new radio broadcaster will have the ability to broadcast all 82 regular-season games, any playoff games, as well as pre-and post-game coverage and preseason games. The Clippers are looking for a radio broadcasting outlet with a strong presence in the marketplace and for a dynamic broadcasting team. In the provision of the broadcasting agreement that addresses advertising sales, the Clippers must ensure they do not violate, nor do they permit the radio broadcaster to violate, their category exclusivity deal with their Naming Rights Sponsor, Staples, and their top-tier sponsor, JetBlue. The team is interested in using the game broadcasts to create content on its own webpage. If the team does a deal with FOXSPORTS, as it is contemplating, it would like to negotiate a deal with all FOX affiliates in Southern California. This will enable the Clippers to "outflank" the Lakers, who stole ESPN from the Clippers.

---

[38] The team currently has a television broadcast deal with local cable channel KTLA. KTLA can broadcast games that are not nationally broadcast pursuant to the following deals:

1. ABC: Sunday Afternoon Game; NBA Finals until 2025,
2. TNT: Thursday night doubleheader; All-Star Game; Eastern Conference Finals until 2025,
3. ESPN: Wednesday night game and Friday night doubleheader; Western Conference Finals until 2025; and
4. NBA TV: Saturday, Monday, and Tuesday night games until 2025.

B. FOXSPORTS Radio is interested in finalizing a broadcasting agreement for the games, especially because the Clippers have one of the most talented rosters in the NBA, and therefore the team is expected to draw much interest next year. FOXSPORTS is also interested in garnering advertising space in the Staples Center, selling on-air advertising during Clippers' games, and having exclusive interviews with the players and coaches. Further assume that FOXSPORTS is interested in airing the broadcasts online at its website, so as to increase traffic to its website. (For the purposes of this negotiation, assume that the NBA already owns satellite rights and does not need to go out and acquire these rights.)

C. Students should split into Groups of four, with two members representing FOXSPORTS Radio and two members representing the Clippers.

D. Copies of a media rights agreement between a media outlet and a professional sports franchise will be distributed to the groups, with the most critical/challenging clauses redacted for ultimate resolution and drafting by the groups.

E. How you would negotiate and draft the following clauses:

1. Term

a. Do the Clippers/FOXSPORTS want a long-term deal, or a one-year deal? How does the fact that the Clippers are poised for a continued increase in their fan base (although this is not guaranteed) affect the term duration?

b. Consider how the language you draft will account for flexibility in response to scheduling changes.

c. At the end of the term, will the Team/Radio outlet have any options for extension/renewal? If so, what is the notice window? Will FOXSPORTS have a right of first refusal/first negotiation?

2. Rights, Duties, and Obligations of FOXSPORTS Radio

a. What will the scope of the radio broadcast be?

b. Will the game be "simulcast" on the internet? On whose website? Who has the right to "archive" these broadcasts? Will they be available to users after the game?

c. Who will be responsible for purchasing and maintaining equipment and providing technical support?

d. Is there a level of quality that the Clippers will demand for the broadcast?

e. Is FOXSPORTS obligated to promote the Clippers, JetBlue, or Staples? If so, how frequently?

f. How long will the pre-and post-game segments be?

g. What Staples Center advertising will FOXSPORTS have under this agreement? Consider the use of ribbon boards, signs, advertisements on tickets and in game books, scoreboard announcements, video boards, etc.

h. Will FOXSPORTS get access to a luxury suite, VIP treatment, or complimentary tickets?

i. Can FOXSPORTS hold its own fan giveaways and contests from time to time before, during or after Clippers' games? What about the ability to set up a booth in the parking lot or a stand to sell radios in the Staples Center?

j. What, if any, in stadium signage will FOX receive? Can FOX also advertise its "affiliated companies," including FOX television and its movie divisions, or will it be limited to its radio affiliates?

3. Rights, Duties, and Obligations for the Los Angeles Clippers

a. Will the Clippers or FOXSPORTS put together the "broadcasting team"? Will the party who does not put the team together have approval rights?

b. How much of the commercial inventory during the game will the team have the right to sell, and how much will it give to FOXSPORTS? Are there any restrictions on whom FOXSPORTS can sell the advertising time? Consider a restriction on the Clippers from selling radio inventory to FOX competitors. Will it be a material breach if the Clippers do so?

1. The following comprises the available inventory: 15 minutes pre-and post-game; and four minutes per quarter. Thus, the total amount of inventory is 66 minutes. The rate card calls for $20 per minute for pre-and post-game sports, and $40+ per minute for in-game spots.

2. Who must compensate an advertiser who "calls in" if an advertisement is cut short or

botched by a negligent broadcaster, and the advertiser complains?

c. Do the Clippers have the obligation to promote FOXSPORTS radio during the game, at the Staples Center, in its promotional materials, etc.?

d. Will the Clippers grant FOXSPORTS the recognition of "flagship station"?

e. Are the Clippers obligated to provide access to or interviews with players and coaches? Will the players, coach, or mascot make an appearance at FOXSPORTS events?

f. Will the Clippers generate non-traditional revenue for on-site pre-and post-game radio broadcasts sponsored by FOX? Consider a special deal for "Thirsty Thursdays" and "Family Sundaes."

g. Will the Clippers demand a "measure of effectiveness" of the switch from ESPN to FOX, to show an improvement (or not) in ratings and thereby adjust the rights fees FOX will have to pay during the contract term?

4. Ownership of and Rights to the Broadcast

a. Who will own the audio recording of the broadcast?

b. Will the owner grant the other party a license to use the broadcasts? What will the scope of such license be?

c. Will the parties be able to transform the broadcast into other media, e.g. podcasts?

d. Who will be responsible for stopping the "piracy" of any broadcasts?

e. Who will indemnify whom if there is defamation, obscenity, or some other offense during the broadcast? What if a player or coach utters such things? What if the broadcaster is intoxicated (e.g. Semi-Pro/Major League)?

f. Is there an anti-disparagement clause whereby the broadcasters cannot bad mouth the Clippers, coaches, owners, etc.?

5. Grant of Right to Use Name and Logo

a. If the parties covenant to promote one another in the "Rights, Duties, and Obligations" sections, draft a supplementary grant of right to use name and logo.

6. Representations and Warranties

   a. Draft a set of representations and warranties from each side to the other.

   b. Examples of representations and warranties might be: authority to enter into the transaction, possession of necessary licenses and government approvals, and, as in the Mets litigation, absence of conflicting agreements or other third party rights.

F. After 15 to 20 minutes of preliminary preparation, during which each party should outline its interests and identify its "must haves," "nice to haves," and "throw-aways," Groups should convene and engage in clause-by-clause negotiation of the media rights provisions above.

Please see the Teacher's Manual for an "Exemplar" Student Group response to this Hypothetical.

Chapter 6

FOOD AND BEVERAGE RIGHTS AGREEMENTS

A. POURING AND CONCESSION RIGHTS

Pouring and Concession Rights Agreements can be some of the most complicated agreements to negotiate because of the variety of different third parties who are affected by each such agreement.[1] The first significant decision the team will face in this area is whether to handle concessions in-house, or to outsource the provision of these services to a dedicated provider such as the often-used Delaware North. If outsourcing concessions, the team may end up with a different primary concessionaire and primary beverage provider, so it will be imperative for the team to structure its contracts with each so as to ensure that they will work together for the benefit of the team. The joint venture between the Dallas Cowboys, New York Yankees, and IMG is one example of innovative branding in the concessions area, as Legends Hospitality Management will offer not only concessions services, but also personal seat licensing, premium seating and suite sales, and merchandise services.[2]

The concessionaire will seek to gain exclusive rights to be the official concessionaire and official supplier of the team for any item in a broadly defined category, so that it can advertise itself as the official provider of the team for each of its products.[3] Retaining as large a portion as possible of its product sales within the stadium will be a priority for the concessionaire. The concessionaire will also seek to maximize its distribution channels, and will want exclusive rights to distribute its products within the stadium and on property owned by the team adjacent to the stadium, such as RavensWalk—a

1 In some cases, the league may have already sold part of the category. For example, the NFL has an agreement for an official NFL beer. Since 2011, Anheuser-Busch's Bud Light has been the official beer. In 2015, the agreement was extended through the 2022 Super Bowl for $1.4b, a 15% increase over the previous six-year agreement. *See* Mickle, Tripp, "AB InBev Extends Bud Light's NFL Sponsorship." *THE WALL STREET JOURNAL*. Nov. 4, 2015.

2 *See* "Cowboys, Yankees join IMG in college sports marketing venture," *USA TODAY*, Oct. 6, 2009.

3 *See* "Beverage Battle: Venue Pouring Rights for '08," *SPORTS BUSINESS DAILY*, April 16, 2008.

partnership between the Baltimore Ravens and Aramark that allows for the sale of products outside of the stadium at substantially discounted prices.[4] It will be important to the concessionaire to receive advertising throughout the stadium and to be able to sell its beverages at all concession stands and restaurants within the stadium complex. The concessionaire will also want the right to approve any third parties who are granted the right to provide specialty food or beverages to the stadium or arena.

The concessionaire may also want to hold special events for fans and create distinctive dining areas in the stadium. Having the team purchase its entire inventory of products within the category from the concessionaire for use by players and office staff seems to be logical. The concessionaire will seek the ability to change its inventory of products throughout the season and to control which products are distributed at certain locations throughout the stadium. Logo placement on all containers in which its products are sold at the stadium will be important to the concessionaire. The concessionaire, who likely has expertise in producing such containers, will seek to gain control of the design and production of the containers. It will be vital to the concessionaire that the team has enough signage within the stadium to direct fans to concession areas, as well as enough staffing at concession areas and enough vendors roaming throughout the stadium.

The concessionaire will also ask the team to install state-of-the-art concessions equipment to facilitate the sale of its products, such as the wireless ordering systems that have been utilized by the San Francisco Giants and Seattle Mariners.[5] Controlling the pricing of the products, particularly in terms of being able to offer promotions and discounts during the season, will be a top priority of the concessionaire. If the concessionaire is to provide products for use by the team's players, it will want to prevent the players from consuming any competitor products. The concessionaire may be interested in creating a specifically themed restaurant within the stadium to gain publicity, attract fans, and sell its products. Because of the team's expertise in stadium development, requiring the team to design, build, and maintain such a space seems to make sense. The concessionaire will seek to retain a majority of the revenues generated from this specifically themed facility.

While the team may want to only grant non-exclusive rights to the concessionaire to items in the category, it will likely acknowledge

---

[4] *See* "Commissions and Pricing," *SPORTS BUSINESS JOURNAL*, January 29, 2009.

[5] *See* "In Line for a Change," *SPORTS BUSINESS JOURNAL*, April 14, 2008.

that its efforts should be concentrated on limiting the scope of the category itself. The team will also want as large a commission as possible on the sale of the concessionaire's products. The team will need to be cognizant of its other sponsorships in categories such as alcoholic beverages, ice cream, etc., such that it does not violate a prior agreement or foreclose its ability to enter into a future agreement or provision of these products. The NBA's decision to reverse its ban on hard liquor advertising in order to open up new revenue streams underscores the need to preserve this category of sponsorship in any pouring rights agreement.[6] The team will want to limit the concessionaire's exclusive distribution channels, perhaps agreeing to exclusivity within the stadium, but seeking to allow competing products in areas adjacent to or around the stadium. The team will seek to carve out its restaurants, club seats, and luxury boxes from concessionaire exclusivity.[7]

The team will want to limit the ability of the concessionaire to constantly change its selection of products throughout the season, particularly in terms of introducing new products in the middle of the season. The team does not want its fans to be the trial audience for the concessionaire's new products, and would instead prefer to only have the concessionaire sell products that have proven to be popular and well received. The team will likely seek control over the determination of which products are sold at what parts of the stadium. The team will want to make sure that particular groups of fans (i.e., premium customers) are served certain types of products, and that there are an adequate variety of products conveniently accessible at all locations within the stadium, such as the Carolina Panthers have done with the "grab-and-go" concept.[8] The team, while acknowledging the concessionaire's interest in placing its logo on containers in which its products are sold within the stadium, will want final control over the design of such containers, so that it can place its own logos on such containers and sell additional space to other corporate partners. The team will seek to transfer a portion of the costs of producing such containers to the concessionaire, since its logo will be prominently featured on the containers. The team will also seek to preserve its right to design and manufacture containers for use in its premium facilities (restaurants, club seats, and luxury boxes), as the team will want to specifically cater its services to its high-end clientele.

---

6 *See* "NBA cans ban on liquor ads," *SPORTS BUSINESS JOURNAL*, January 19, 2009.

7 *See* STADIUM GAME, Martin Greenberg, p. 349.

8 *See* "Walk In and Take a Look Around," *SPORTS BUSINESS JOURNAL*, January 29, 2009.

The team will likely also be interested in creating state-of-the-art concessions areas, using the latest technology and maintaining a high level of quality control (as the Cleveland Indians have done), but will want the concessionaire to financially contribute to such a large undertaking, as the Anaheim Mighty Ducks and Colorado Rockies have done.[9] The team will want to ensure that the concessionaire provides products of the highest quality, in adequate quantities and varieties to satisfy the needs of its customers. This is similar to the Cleveland Indians incorporation of local restaurants in the Right Field District.[10] The team will want to have final control over the pricing of products sold within its stadium.[11] In its restaurants, club seats, and luxury boxes, the team will allow the concessionaire to sell its products, but will seek to have the ability to sell types of products that the concessionaire does not provide (i.e., sparkling water). The team will seek a large quantity of the concessionaire's products for use in its owner's suite, front office, and team locker rooms, but will also seek to allow its players to consume products not made by the concessionaire. The team will consent to the creation of a specifically themed restaurant for the concessionaire given the publicity benefits, but will ask the concessionaire to provide the products for the restaurant and seek a large share of the revenues from it. The team will want control over the size and location of the facility, and will need to staff the facility per its agreement with its concessionaires, and will possibly need to provide products from its other food and beverage sponsorship agreements within this restaurant.

The ZOPA will likely involve the team granting the concessionaire exclusivity within the category as the team's official concessionaire and supplier for such products, as Pepsi and Coca-Cola have demonstrated the importance of exclusivity in a category of sponsorship.[12] The category will likely be broad enough to encompass most, if not all, of the concessionaire's main products, but will likely carve out alcoholic drinks and desserts to be negotiated separately. The parties will agree on a revenue sharing system that will align the incentives of each to promote the sale of the concessionaire's products, through either a commission contract or management fee

---

9 *See* "Looking Outside for Quality Control," *SPORTS BUSINESS JOURNAL*, January 29, 2009; *see* "In Line for a Change;" *see* Greenberg, p. 351.

10 *See* "Cleveland Indians announce Great Lakes Brewing Co. and Dynomite Burgers will serve popular food at Progressive Field in 2015," *CLEVELAND INDIANS: PRESS RELEASE*, March 4, 2015.

11 *See* "Legends Sees Food/Retail Per Cap In Mid-$60s For WS Game Six," *SPORTS BUSINESS DAILY*, Nov. 10, 2009 (Yankees did not change their concessions prices from regular season to post-season). *See also* "Prices for Commemorative NBA Finals Concessions at Oracle Arena are Steep." *SPORTS ILLUSTRATED*. June 4, 2015 (Warriors gouging concessions stand prices for NBA Finals).

12 *See* "Beverage Battle: Venue Pouring Rights for '08."

arrangement, with the rate of commission in each category increasing once certain thresholds are reached.[13] There are a variety of revenue sharing arrangements between teams and concessionaires, with the Seattle Mariners and San Antonio Spurs at one end of the spectrum (retaining all game day concessions revenue), and the Milwaukee Bucks right in the middle of the spectrum (revenue split based on type of concession).[14]

In terms of distribution channels, the parties will likely agree on giving the concessionaire exclusivity within the stadium (minus the premium areas), and non-exclusive access to team-controlled areas adjacent to the stadium. The team and concessionaire will likely agree on jointly deciding the inventory of products available within the stadium prior to each season, so that there is minimal disruption during the season. The team will likely allow the concessionaire to introduce a small number of new products during the course of the season, but will in return get final control over the selection of locations for the distribution of specific products, which will be done with cooperation from the concessionaire. The Arizona Diamondbacks and Levy Restaurants have worked together to introduce several new items to their concessions stands, including the D-bat Dog, an 18-inch corndog stuffed with jalapeños and cheese, and the Churro Dog, a cinnamon churro inside a long john chocolate glazed donut with frozen yogurt, caramel and chocolate sauce.[15] The team and concessionaire will likely agree to give the team final control over the physical design of the containers, with the stipulation that the concessionaire's logo will be prominently featured on all such containers. The concessionaire, depending on its capabilities, may agree to provide the containers at a certain cost to the team. The concessionaire will likely allow the team to specifically design containers for its high-end clientele, provided it receives some visibility within these areas.

The team and the concessionaire will likely agree on using state-of-the-art concessions equipment, particularly in new stadiums and arenas, as have the San Francisco 49ers, with part of the costs potentially being covered by the concessionaire.[16] Quality control will also be important to both parties, as the team will want to ensure that none of the concessionaire's products are harmful to the public.

13 *See* Greenberg, p. 350–351.

14 *See* Seattle Mariners Lease Agreement; San Antonio Spurs Lease Agreement; Milwaukee Bucks Lease Agreement.

15 *See* Rovell, Darren. "Diamondbacks offer Churro Dog," *ESPN*. March 4, 2015. *See also* Chase Field, Arizona Diamondbacks: Dining and Concession.

16 *See* "Meet Levi's Stadium, the Most High-Tech Sports Venue Yet," *TIME*, Aug. 18, 2014.

The parties will likely agree to each use commercially reasonable efforts to promote the sale of the concessionaire's products in the facility, including the team providing adequate staffing of concession areas and the concessionaire providing products of the highest quality.[17] The team will likely be given final control over the pricing of the products sold in the stadium, which will be based on industry standards, with the concessionaire being able to hold various promotional events throughout the season.[18] The concessionaire will likely agree to provide the team with an assortment of products for use in its owner's suite, front office, and locker rooms, but will want any usage of competitor products by players to be done in a non-visible manner. Both parties will be interested in quality control, so they may potentially agree to hire a third-party industry expert to periodically evaluate the level of service and quality of the products, and split the cost of such a service. As the team will likely be responsible for designing, building, and maintaining the concessionaire-themed restaurant, it will also get control over the size, location, operations, and pricing of the facility. The concessionaire will be responsible for providing adequate quantities of its products for consumption in such a restaurant, and will likely be able to keep a substantial portion (up to 50%) of the revenue generated from sale of its products in the restaurant. Non-concessionaire products may potentially be sold in the restaurant, which the team will be responsible for providing and will keep all of the revenue from sale of these products.

B. ADVERTISING RIGHTS

The food and beverage providers whose products are sold in the arena will seek to gain the exclusive advertising rights for all products in the category, both with respect to advertising within the stadium and in connection with the team.[19] The providers will likely specifically seek some permanent advertising within the stadium and virtual advertising on the JumboTron, on a level consistent with other corporate partners at its spending level. The provider will also want guaranteed language ensuring that its signage is clearly visible to all fans at the stadium and is not obscured in any way throughout the term, despite potential renovations made to the stadium by the team. The provider will also seek approval rights over signage that appears near its advertising, so as to ensure that there is no conflicting

[17] *See* "In Line for a Change."

[18] *See* Detroit Tigers Lease Agreement.

[19] Recently, SABMiller and AB InBev announced a merger, upon SABMiller accepting an offer of $104 billion. *See* Colley, John. "Why beer drinkers lose in the SABMiller-AB InBev merger," *FORTUNE.com*, Oct. 15, 2015, available at: http://fortune.com/2015/10/15/sabmiller-ab-inbev-merger-beer-drinkers-lose/.

message nearby. The provider will want the team to pay for all the costs of erecting and dismantling the signage at the beginning and end of the term.

The team will want to protect the advertising rights of its other sponsors as well as its unsold categories, so it will want to carefully limit the grant of advertising rights given to the provider. The team will want to limit the amount of permanent and virtual signage it gives the provider and control its size and location, because this is very valuable inventory for the team. The team will want the provider to contribute to the costs of designing, erecting, and dismantling its signage at the beginning and end of the term.

The ZOPA will likely involve the team granting the provider exclusive advertising rights for all products within the category with respect to stadium advertising and advertising in connection with the team, but this grant of rights will be explicitly limited so as not to conflict with the team's existing sponsorship agreements. The ZOPA will likely involve the team granting the provider permanent and virtual signage rights consistent with other corporate partners at its spending level, with the team retaining control over the size, location, duration, and content of such advertising. The parties will likely work out a financial arrangement whereby the provider contributes some portion of the funds required to design and build the signage at the beginning of the term, but the team will likely be responsible for dismantling the signage at the end of the term.

C. SPONSORSHIP RIGHTS

The provider and/or concessionaire will seek to gain rights to host promotional events and giveaways throughout the course of the team's season, preferably on multiple occasions. The concessionaire will also want to be able to use the stadium for its own events throughout the course of the term. The concessionaire will seek advertising in team publications and communications with its fans, including print and digital communications. The concessionaire will also seek promotional mentions in the team's television and radio broadcasts of live game action. The concessionaire will want to receive a package of tickets to all of the team's home games for its promotional usage. This will likely consist of a limited number of season tickets, plus additional club and premium seats, which it can use to entertain its own clients and business associates.

The team will benefit from promotional events, but will want reasonable control over the dates selected for these events and the content of these promotions and giveaways. The team will want to limit the concessionaire's use of its stadium during its regular season.

The team will value its digital and print inventory, so it will be hesitant to give the concessionaire additional marketing opportunities unless the concessionaire is willing to pay for this exposure. The team will also want to limit the concessionaire's advertising across its television and radio networks, as it will highly value in-game advertising. The team will want to only give the concessionaire tickets consistent with its other agreements with sponsors of a similar level.

The likely ZOPA will involve multiple promotional events and giveaway nights for the provider or concessionaire, with the team having full approval rights over the dates selected and content of these promotions. Similarly, the team will likely give the provider a few dates on which it can use the stadium for its own events, with the nature of the event subject to the team's approval. The team will perhaps give the provider some advertising space in its game programs, but will likely charge them for additional advertising in its print and digital communications to its fans. The team will likely agree to some minimal level of in-game promotions for the provider across its television and radio broadcasts of game action. The team will likely also give them five to ten season tickets each season for its own use, with the ability to purchase similar tickets for any post-season games. The quality of the seats will be at the team's discretion and will depend upon the provider's level of sponsorship within the team's hierarchy of sponsorships. As both parties will be interested in promoting their partnership with each other, they will likely agree to a mutual grant of a limited license to use each other's name, trademarks, and logos on a royalty-free basis for the purpose of promoting the partnership, always subject to the other party's approval. The parties will likely want such reciprocal promotional rights beyond the stadium, to encompass the local market, so the grant may be valid within 75 miles of the stadium.

D. BREACH

The ZOPA will likely involve an agreement on a force majeure clause, which will temporarily relieve each party of their obligations under certain specified conditions. Typically included in such a clause will be acts of God, violence, natural disasters, labor stoppages, and other acts beyond the control of the parties. The parties will also agree on a breach system that classifies breaches into various categories, ascending in severity. It simply does not make sense to terminate the agreement over a minor violation, while a serious violation may frustrate the essential purposes of the agreement, so such a tiered system is in the interests of both parties. Typically, the non-breaching party will have to give written notice of an alleged breach to the other party, and will likely give that party an opportunity to cure the breach before remedies can be sought. A common structure may involve nominal damages for the lowest level of breach, liquidated damages and injunctive relief for a middle level breach, and damages, injunctive relief, and potentially termination for material breaches of the agreement. The class of breach may be based on the specific clause violated, the value of the breach, some materiality standard or some other determination agreed upon by the parties. The parties will likely stipulate that uncured breaches, after a reasonable period of time, will rise in severity of breach until they become material breaches. Intentional wrongdoing or willful misconduct in the course of a breach will likely cause the breach to rise to the highest level of severity, irrespective of the nature of the breach. If either party goes into bankruptcy or experiences a material change in control, the other party will likely want an option to terminate the agreement.[20] Similarly, if an act of government (such as a new regulation) frustrates the essential purpose of the agreement, the parties will likely want an option to terminate the agreement.

E. EXPIRATION AND TERMINATION

The concessionaire will not want the team to have an early termination option that can be exercised without a material breach of the agreement. The concessionaire will likely seek a right of first offer and right of first refusal or first negotiation to extend the agreement for a subsequent term. This will include a right to match any offers by competitors. The concessionaire will want the team to return all unsold products to the concessionaire if the agreement is allowed to expire.

The team will likely seek termination rights if at any time the concessionaire fails to perform its material obligations, or if it can pay some liquidated damages fee for early termination of the agreement. The team will likely acknowledge that termination because of breach of the agreement by the other party will be allowed only in very limited circumstances. The team will want to be able to solicit competitive offers for the sponsorship package given to the concessionaire, such that it can potentially secure a more lucrative corporate partnership for these rights. The team likely will want the

[20] In *Twin City Sportservice v. Charles O. Finley & Co.*, the Ninth Circuit found that the "follow the franchise" provision of the concession's agreement violated antitrust laws. *See* 512 F.2d 1264 (9th Cir.1975). After Finley bought the franchise and moved it to Oakland, he wanted to get out of the team's contract with its concessionaire. The court determined that the concession agreement was unreasonably restrictive because it prevented other concessionaires from dealing with the Athletics.

concessionaire to cease any promotional activity in conjunction with the team's marks upon termination of the agreement.

The ZOPA will likely involve termination rights only in very limited circumstances, and upon the occurrence of a material breach. The concessionaire will likely receive a right of first offer and right of first refusal or first negotiation for extension of the term of the agreement, provided that it is able to match the terms of any competitor making an offer for the same rights, though both sides must be careful of an antitrust violation in this respect.[21] Both the team and the concessionaire will likely want any concessionaire signage and advertising removed immediately if the concessionaire is not renewing its sponsorship beyond the expiration of the term. Each party will be prohibited from using the other's marks beyond the term of the agreement if there is not an extension of the term of the agreement.

F. DISPUTE RESOLUTION

As with a dispute resolution provision in any of the agreements discussed in this book, the parties will value quick and quiet resolution to their problems. The ZOPA will thus likely involve the parties agreeing to confidential mediation to resolve any dispute relating to the agreement. Both parties value confidentiality, minimization of costs, and efficiency in resolving disputes, so such a dispute resolution mechanism is preferable to the courts. If mediation cannot resolve the dispute, confidential binding arbitration will likely be pursued, as this is still preferable to the high costs and uncertainty involved in litigation, these clauses are discussed in further detail in Chapter 10 and Appendix B. While at times each side might prefer to have access to injunctive relief, such relief will likely only be available in highly limited circumstances, and perhaps only after mediation is attempted. Liquidated damages provisions for certain types of breaches may also enhance the efficiency of dispute resolution.

HYPOTHETICAL EXERCISE

Negotiating and Drafting a Food and Beverage Sponsorship Agreement Between a Food or Beverage Provider (Coca-Cola) and a Professional Sports Franchise (New York Jets)

A. The New York Jets are looking to partner with a company engaged in the food and beverage industry. The Jets hope that the relationship will not only earn additional monies from the sale of advertising and additional traditional sponsor benefits, but will also sell the "pouring rights" to the

[21] *See* Twin City Sportservice.

stadium. The Jets are interested in creating state-of-the-art concessions areas using the latest technology and in maintaining a high level of quality control.

B. Coca-Cola, after realizing how much of the market for sports-venue pouring rights it has lost to Pepsi over the last ten years, is very interested in reaching an agreement with the Jets. Coca-Cola seeks to advertise throughout the park and sell its beverages at all the concessions stands/restaurants. The soda company is also interested in holding special events for fans and creating distinctive dining areas in the stadium.

C. How you would negotiate and draft the following clauses:

1. Pouring and Concessions Rights

a. Create a grant of rights from the Jets to Coca-Cola. Will it be exclusive or non-exclusive? Will the Jets specify the containers in which the beverages must be sold?

b. Are there any covenants to promote the sale of the products? If so, what is the level of efforts? Try to draft a specific covenant that specifies the locations/methods of promotion.

c. To what areas will Coca-Cola's products have access?

d. How will the parties approach the creation and maintenance of Coca-Cola sponsored dining facilities?

e. What level of quality will the Jets require that Coca-Cola maintain? What specific approval rights will the Jets seek?

f. Will the agreement require the use of "state-of-the-art technologies" for dispensing the beverages?

2. Advertising Rights

a. Does Coca-Cola have exclusivity? If so, how will you define the category as to not interfere with the alcohol contract the Jets have?

b. Will Coca-Cola have approval rights of any new signage that appears near its signage?

c. Will the Jets have approval rights over Coca-Cola's advertisements?

d. What will the "advertising package" include? Describe any signage to be erected for the Sponsor, including whether it will remain permanent throughout the term of the agreement or be displayed on a temporary basis.

3. Sponsorship Rights

   a. Will there be any "giveaways," promotional nights, or title sponsorships associated with the Sponsor's relationship with the Team?

   b. Consider the Coca-Cola's presence in game programs and other printed materials, as well as in broadcasts and any coverage the Team may receive in the local community.

   c. Will the Sponsor obtain season tickets or a luxury suite for use at every game, or a block of games? What about post-season games?

   d. Which party has the burden of producing and paying the costs of material associated with the package of sponsorship benefits? Will the responsibilities be split?

   e. Specify Sponsor's "Official" status as it pertains separately to the Team and the stadium, if necessary.

4. Breach

   a. Specify what counts as a breach of the agreement for each party.

   b. Consider dividing the breaches into various classes.

5. Termination

   a. Outline the items that will trigger either party's right to terminate the agreement, as well as the financial and logistical consequences following such termination.

   b. Is there a period within which certain breaches may be cured?

   c. How will the parties divide up the responsibilities for dismantling the equipment/signage in the event of a breach or expiration of the contract?

Please see the Teacher's Manual for an "Exemplar" Student Group response to this Hypothetical.

Chapter 7

HEALTH/MEDICAL SERVICES PROVIDER AGREEMENTS

Sports teams looking to further establish ties within their local community have increasingly turned to health/medical services provider agreements to create goodwill within the community. Not only do teams want to promote athletic activity and healthy, active lifestyles, they also are looking to send positive messages to children about the importance of exercise and risks of heart disease. For instance, snack food maker Pirate Brands has partnered with David Wright to promote a healthy, active lifestyle for families and children through nutrition and exercise.[1] In particular, teams are looking to capitalize on health foods as an alternative to traditional concessions. The Seattle Mariners are one such team, with menus featuring an increased selection of fresh, local and healthy options, and a dedicated concession stand called "The Natural," which offers a variety of organic and vegetarian items, such as smoothies, vegan soup, and gluten-free snack bars.[2]

While the team may work with a health/medical services provider to promote such healthy alternatives, it must be careful not to disparage its traditional food, beverage, and alcohol concessionaires, which will form the bulk of its concessions revenue and concessions sponsorships. Health/medical services providers are eager to work with sports teams to attract wider attention to their own health care facilities and to promote awareness of health issues. These providers will typically help the team build goodwill in the community in return for a discounted sponsorship package and the ability to advertise itself as the official health/medical services provider of the team, which will generate plenty of positive publicity for the provider.

1 "David Wright, Star Third Basemen, Acquired By Pirates," *EUROINVESTOR*, April 1, 2010, available at: http://www.euroinvestor.co.uk/news/story.aspx?id=10974282&bw=20100401005635.

2 "A Whole New Ballgame For Chef Ethan Stowell," *CAPITOL HILL TIMES*, April 8, 2015, available at: http://www.capitolhilltimes.com/2015/04/a-whole-new-ballgame-for-chef-ethan-stowell/.

A. SPONSORSHIP PACKAGE BENEFITS

A hospital sponsor will want to be known as the "official healthcare facility of the team," or some permutation thereof, and use the team logo and other marks on its website and promotional materials, as this will greatly enhance its profile within the community.[3] The sponsor will also want the team to make all first referrals of its players to the hospital, such that the sponsor becomes the hospital of choice for the team. In addition, a sponsor will want the agreement to cover as broad a range of medical issues as possible, so that it can get as close as possible to being the exclusive first referral hospital for the team.

In addition to category and referrals, the hospital may seek to present a specifically themed activity area within the facility, such as a playground for children.[4] The hospital will want the area to be constructed by the team, at the team's expense, and will want the team to ensure that the area is compliant with all relevant safety regulations. To this end, the hospital will likely ask the team to maintain both casualty and liability insurance for use of the activity area. Additionally, the medical services provider may want to negotiate to operate a food cart serving specially designed health foods within the facility. The team should ensure this doesn't conflict with its agreements with the concessionaire or food or beverage providers. The hospital will also want signage throughout the facility directing fans to the food cart and introducing the nutritional items available.

In addition to special promotions and areas of the facility, the hospital will also want the standard advertising and signage package. Of course, for the sponsor, it will want a large signage package especially within the facility for promoting itself, its affiliation with the team, and its activity area. Both parties will want to be sure that such signage is not placed near those of other sponsors with conflicting messages, such as those advertising alcohol or tobacco.[5]

In terms of the actions of the team, the hospital will also want a non-disparagement clause to prevent team officials or players from

---

[3] "Sports Medicine; Sports Turnaround: The Team Doctors Now Pay the Team," *NEW YORK TIMES*, May 18, 2004, available at: http://www.nytimes.com/2004/05/18/sports/sports-medicine-sports-turnaround-the-team-doctors-now-pay-the-team.html?pagewanted=1.

[4] "Cleveland Indians Premier The Kids Clubhouse At Progressive Field May 6." *CLEVELAND INDIANS: PRESS RELEASE*. May 2, 2012. (University Hospitals Rainbow Babies & Children's Hospital presents "The Rookie Suite.")

[5] "5 Tips for Taking Your Kids to a Royals Game," June 24, 2014, available at: http://kansascity.citymomsblog.com/5-tips-for-taking-your-kids-to-a-royals-game/.

making negative comments about the hospital or its physicians in the event the players are treated there. When it comes to referrals, the team will have to be careful not to obligate players to use the hospital for their medical treatment. In many cases, like in the NBA, such an obligation would violate the Collective Bargaining Agreement and the Uniform Player Contract.[6] Rather, the team will seek to allow its players to use the hospital and physicians of their own choosing. The team will also want to limit the scope of the medical issues covered under this agreement, as it may want to use other hospitals for particular areas of medical care. The team will also seek to reserve the right to use other health care providers to undertake additional evaluations of its players or to provide any medical services, as per the league's Collective Bargaining Agreement and Uniform Player Contract.[7]

As the hospital is a community organization, it will be interested in exploring barter opportunities instead of financial payment for the benefits it receives under the agreement. The hospital may also seek to obtain tickets for patients to attend the team's games and to tour the team's offices and facility, as well as to have players come visit the hospital and its patients.[8]

The team will have different perspectives on the benefits it will grant to a hospital sponsor, especially when it means giving away sponsorship inventory at lower rates. For example, the team will want to limit the hospital's large signage within the facility, as this is highly valuable inventory, and will want approval over the content of all signage. In addition, the team may want to sign a non-exclusive agreement with one sponsor while retaining the ability to enter into agreements with other health care providers, without breaching any of the rights given to the hospital. Most importantly, the team will need to be able to monitor its sponsorship inventory and ensure that its grant of rights to the hospital does not conflict with any other sponsorship agreements it has, including potential hospital/health care companies that may sponsor its affiliated entities, such as its practice facility.

For the team, intellectual property issues will always be important, thus it will want reasonable approval rights over the use of the team

---

6 NBA Collective Bargaining Agreement, Article 2, § 2; NBA Uniform Player Contract, § 7(h).

7 NBA Collective Bargaining Agreement, Article 2, § 2; NBA Uniform Player Contract § 7(h).

8 "Nationwide Children's Hospital Patients Championed." *NASCAR: PRESS RELEASE*. Aug. 16, 2014.

logo and other marks on the hospital website. This will ensure that team marks are not used in ways that would weaken their protection.

As for the financials of creating the sponsorship relationship, the team will likely ask the hospital to contribute financially to the construction and maintenance of any activity area within the facility that the hospital wants to sponsor, especially if this facility will be relationship specific and thus less valuable to the team when used with any other sponsor. The team will also ask the hospital to provide staffing for the activity area, and to certify that its employees are of good moral character, do not have serious criminal records and are qualified. The team may also ask the sponsor to obtain insurance coverage for the operation of the activity area, since it would be sponsor employees staffing the area.

The team will want to ensure that the operation of the hospital's food cart does not violate any of its existing concessions agreements or foreclose any categories to be sold in the future. To this end, the team will want approval over any and all items sold at the food cart, in order to ensure that they meet quality standards and that they do not conflict with what is already being sold within the facility. This may involve limiting the signage given to the hospital for its food cart, and ensuring that such advertising does not violate any of the team's other concessions agreements in terms of advertising exclusivity. The team will also want the quality control over the products sold at the food cart to include indemnification from the sponsor against any damages associated with the consumption of products from the food cart. The team will also want the hospital to be responsible for all costs associated with the food cart and its associated signage.

The ZOPA between these two parties will likely result in giving the hospital sponsorship exclusivity and the designation as the "official healthcare facility of the team," with usage of the team's logo and other marks on all materials, subject to reasonable team approval. While the hospital may also get first referrals from the team in certain medical disciplines, it will not be the exclusive provider of medical services to the team, and the team's players will have the right to use a health care facility and physician of their choosing. The team will also likely retain the right to use a health care facility of its choosing for any medical service, despite the first referral commitment to the hospital.

In addition, the team will likely agree to construct a children's activity area for the hospital, such as the "Rookie Suite," and to certify that it complies with all applicable safety regulations, but will want the hospital to bear a portion of the costs for maintenance and continued safety compliance.[9] The hospital may end up being responsible for staffing the activity area, and will have to be responsible for the moral character and prior background of its employees working in the activity area. The team will probably be the best party to be responsible for maintaining appropriate levels of casualty and liability insurance coverage, but may request an indemnification from the sponsor for liabilities arriving from staff error.

In addition, the parties may agree to have the team's players in public service announcements promoting issues of community health. The Minnesota Twins and the Mayo Clinic have formed a mutually beneficial partnership allowing Mayo staff members to be at Target Field for every Twins home game this season. Mayo will increase its visibility at Twins games by having Mayo patients throw out the first pitch at some Twins games, through advertisements in Twins Magazine, and by getting Twins players to offer health tips during home games.[10]

Another benefit the team will be likely to grant is to allow the hospital a number of tickets for selected home games that can be used in order for patients to attend the team's games, similar to what the Houston Astros did with "Berkman's Bunch" or the Houston Texans with "Domanick's Zone."[11] The team will benefit from this publicity, and the patients will get a chance to interact with players and team employees before and after the game in "VIP" fashion. Partnering with the hospital in this way will give the team enormous public relations benefits, and the hospital will gain tremendous publicity and raise awareness of important community issues through its partnership with the team, so a barter agreement makes sense for both parties. The team and hospital may even agree on an equitable balance of benefits under this agreement, such that there will be no financial payment from the hospital to the team for this agreement (except where specifically indicated).

B. TEAM BENEFITS

If the team benefits can be as valuable as those belonging to the sponsor, then the sponsor may not have to pay the team in cash. One of the easiest things for the hospital to provide to the team is free or

---

9 *See* "Cleveland Indians Premier The Kids Clubhouse At Progressive Field May 6."

10 Mayo Clinic Sports Medicine Minnesota Collaborations: Minnesota Twins, available at: https://sportsmedicine.mayoclinic.org/collaborations/minnesota-twins.php.

11 "Houston Astros All-Star Lance Berkman Partners with the Methodist Hospital," *THE METHODIST HOSPITAL SYSTEM*, June 16, 2008.

partially compensated medical care. Ideally, for the sponsor, it will provide only basic medical services to the team at no charge and will still charge the team for surgeries and other expensive medical procedures. If the hospital agrees to an annual vaccine clinic at the team's offices, the hospital may provide the clinic but ask the team to pay for all its costs, including the medical supplies and staff required. In addition, the hospital will want any medical assistance area within the facility to be designed and maintained by the team, with the team paying all of the costs for the staffing and supplies required.

The team, on the other hand, may want the hospital to provide all free medical services within the scope of the agreement to all team employees and players. The team may also want the hospital to provide an annual clinic at its offices to ensure that all of its employees are properly vaccinated. The team will want the hospital to pay for the costs of this clinic.

Mirroring the benefit the team would give the hospital, the team too will want a non-disparagement clause to ensure that hospital staff and physicians do not make any negative remarks about the team or its players/employees. Similarly, confidentiality about the health status of players will be extremely important to the team and it will definitely want the benefit of an enhanced representation from the hospital that it and its entire staff will maintain confidentiality.

One great benefit the team will want is a medical assistance area within the stadium, to provide first aid and emergency care to fans. The team will want the hospital to provide the staffing and the equipment for the medical assistance area at its own cost, but realistically the team will need to help out with these costs. The team will want approval rights over the staffing decisions of the hospital with respect to the medical assistance area but will need the hospital to be responsible for all liability and claims arising out of care provided at the medical assistance area.

The team will also want to partner with the hospital to feature its players in television, radio, and billboard advertising promoting community health and interacting with hospital staff and patients.[12]

The ZOPA will likely be the hospital agreeing to provide free medical services within the scope of the category granted in the agreement to all team employees and players, with surgeries and other advanced medical procedures excluded from this clause. The team will likely receive a discount on these expensive medical services, but will have

---

[12] An increasing number of health care partnerships have focused not only on the team's health care needs, but also on promoting healthy lifestyles within the general community. *See* "Red Sox and Beth Israel Deaconess Medical Center," available at: http://www.bidmc.org/About-BIDMC/Red-Sox-BIDMC.aspx.

to pay out of pocket for them. In addition, the hospital will likely agree to run an annual vaccine clinic at the team's offices, provided that the team will pay for the costs of medical supplies and the costs of staffing such a clinic.

The team should receive a reciprocal non-disparagement clause from the hospital.

It is mutually beneficial for the parties to have a cross-branded medical assistance area in the facility. The team will likely be responsible for designing and constructing such an area while the hospital would staff and supervise it with reimbursements from the team for the costs of medical supplies. While the hospital will pay for the staffing of this area and be responsible for any liability arising from the medical assistance area, the team will likely have reasonable approval rights over the selection of staff for this area.

The parties will also likely agree on producing a few different television, radio, and billboard advertisements, as well as a few public service announcements, featuring the team's players and potentially hospital staff and patients.[13] The parties will probably have joint financial responsibility and joint creative control over these advertisements, and the team's players will be reasonably available and free of charge for the purpose of producing these advertisements, provided the team is able to under its league obligations.

C. CHANGES TO THE SPONSORSHIP PACKAGE

The ZOPA will likely involve the team agreeing to provide the hospital with all information reasonably related to the services it provides under the agreement and which could impact the hospital's rights under the agreement. The hospital will likely agree to do the same for the team in a reciprocal manner. In consideration of the hospital's role in the community, the team will likely offer to the hospital the benefits of any price reduction or discounts offered to other community or non-profit sponsors since the date of its agreement with the hospital. The hospital will likely have the ability to substitute similar services under the agreement, provided that it notifies the team in advance and that the substitute services are actually similar to the services that would otherwise be provided. Any changes to the sponsorship package may trigger payments from one party to the other, or else an adjustment of the bartered benefits under the agreement.

---

13 *See* Cleveland Clinic Ad Campaign, "Power of Today: Cleveland Clinic Salutes Cleveland Indians," available at: https://www.youtube.com/watch?v=-UNCfkX50XE.

D. EXCLUSIVITY

The hospital would like to be the exclusive provider of medical services to the team, but will likely have to settle for being the official provider. As the official provider the hospital will be the only hospital allowed to advertise in conjunction with the team and will be the only hospital that can run promotions or a first aid clinic at team events. The hospital will want the team to make all "first referrals" of players to the hospital.[14] The hospital will seek advertising exclusivity, in being the only health care facility (within the covered specialties) able to advertise within the stadium. The hospital will also want a right of first negotiation and first refusal at the expiration of the current agreement.

The team will, of course, be willing to grant that the hospital can call itself the "official" medical services provider of the team, but it will not grant the hospital the exclusive right to treat the players, as player choice in medical issues must be protected.[15] The team will also want to ideally be able to sell advertising inventory to health care providers outside of the scope of the agreement to be able to solicit offers for the covered categories shortly before the expiration of the agreement.

The ZOPA will likely be allowing the hospital to be the official medical services provider of the team, exclusive within the specialties covered by the agreement. The team will make all "first referrals" to the hospital, provided the hospital is qualified to address the problem the team is referring, but the players will ultimately be free to use any physician at the hospital or at any other medical facility.[16] In these categories, the hospital will have advertising exclusivity within the facility, but the team will be able to sell advertising to health care facilities that provide services solely outside of these categories. The parties will likely agree on a short, exclusive negotiation period for the hospital as the agreement is about to expire, followed by a short period in which the hospital may solicit outside offers without violating the hospital's exclusivity. The hospital may also get the right to match the terms of any potential competing agreement within the categories.

---

14 NBA Uniform Player Contract § 7(c).

15 Jeff Gewirtz, Executive Vice President, Business Affairs and Chief Legal Officer, Brooklyn Nets and Barclays Center, Interview at Great Lakes Sports and Entertainment Law Academy. *See* "Integris Health: Oklahoma City Thunder Official Health Care Provider," available at: http://integrisok.com/thunder.

16 "Sports Medicine; Sports Turnaround: The Team Doctors Now Pay the Team."

E. INTELLECTUAL PROPERTY

The parties will likely agree on a reciprocal limited right to use each other's logo and marks for the purpose of promoting the partnership between the team and the hospital. Each party will have the right to use the other party's marks in connection with any of the services it provides, subject to reasonable approval by the owner of the marks. Each party will also be prohibited from modifying the marks of the other party. Upon expiration or termination of the agreement, each party will lose its rights to use the other's party's logo and marks and will have to immediately cease and desist in any such use of the other party's marks.

Consider how the right to use each other's marks may differ in this sponsorship where the sponsor is a hospital instead of a large for-profit corporation.

F. DISPUTE RESOLUTION

The parties will likely agree on confidential mediation as the first dispute resolution mechanism for any claim or controversy arising under the agreement, with the costs to be jointly borne by the parties. Decision-making authority will rest with the parties, not the mediator, who will assist the parties in identifying issues, fostering joint problem-solving, and exploring settlement alternatives.

If mediation is unsuccessful, the parties will probably prefer to proceed to confidential, binding arbitration at the closest mutually convenient location of the American Arbitration Association (AAA), and in accordance with AAA rules as applied in the jurisdiction where the team is located, with the losing party paying for the costs of arbitration, which will be limited by rules on the scope of discovery and the taking of depositions. If the parties decide on arbitration instead of litigation, the arbitration decision should be confidential, binding, and enforceable in a court of competent jurisdiction. The parties might also consider pre-selecting an arbitrator with expertise in the sports industry. As all dispute resolution will be confidential, any breach of this confidentiality should also subject that party to damages.

HYPOTHETICAL EXERCISE

Negotiating and Drafting a Sponsorship Agreement Between a Medical Service Provider and a Professional Sports Franchise

A. Imagine that the Oklahoma City Thunder, seeking to establish ties with the Oklahoma City community, is looking to finalize a sponsorship agreement with St. Anthony Heart

Hospital. The team hopes that the relationship will create goodwill with the community.

1. Further, the team wants to avoid controversies such as the one that arose when Coca-Cola created a children's playground at AT&T Ballpark—complete with an 80 foot bottle of the soft drink—inciting opponents who claimed it was sending a poor message to children.

2. Instead, the Thunder hope to follow the lead of the Mariners' SafeCo. Field and create a play area for children emphasizing athletic activity and information for adults about the risks of heart disease.

3. The Thunder is also considering tapping into the new health food fad, and partnering with the hospital to provide nutrition information and healthy alternatives to the traditional concessions.

4. Nevertheless, it is important to the team not to portray the play area/foods in such a way that disparages its food, beverage and alcohol concessionaries, so as to preserve sponsorship opportunities, and it needs to preserve the exclusivity of its sponsorship agreement with INTEGRIS, the hospital sponsoring the team's practice facility.

B. St. Anthony Heart Hospital is interested in a sponsorship deal, complete with the playground and healthy food area described above, to attract wider attention to its state-of-the-art heart care and cancer center and to health issues.

1. The hospital is concerned about maintaining "creative control" over its signage, so as to preserve its accuracy, and about getting a heavily discounted rate for the sponsorship package.

2. The hospital is also hoping to be the "official" treatment center for the athletes, and to have its name mentioned in press releases regarding player injuries.

3. Further, St. Anthony would like to use the Thunder logo on its own website to promote the relationship and on the information pages of the doctors who treat the players.

C. Students should split into groups of four, with two members representing St. Anthony and two members representing the Thunder.

D. Copies of a sponsorship agreement between a Medical Services sponsor and a professional sports franchise have been distributed to the groups, with the most critical/challenging clauses redacted for ultimate resolution and drafting by the groups.

E. Negotiate and draft the following clauses:

1. <u>Sponsorship Package Benefits</u>

a. What (limited) items will the Hospital agree to pay for?

b. Who will bear the production costs of the playground and restaurant area? Who will have approval rights over such areas?

c. Where will the hospital signage be displayed? Are there any limitations on juxtaposition of signage with alcoholic beverage or other advertisements? Approval rights?

d. What print advertising will the hospital have? Can the hospital include information pamphlets?

e. Will the Hospital be the exclusive provider of medical services to the team? How will the parties carve out exceptions for players who refuse to be treated there? How will the parties deal with the specter that the exclusive deal might breach ethical bounds?

f. Will the team's medical assistance area, to give immediate help to injured fans, be staffed by St. Anthony employees? Who will pay for the first aid supplies and equipment in the medical assistance area? Who will select it?

g. Will the team covenant to have players/coaches appear at the hospital, creating a program similar to "Berkman's Bunch"?

h. What other benefits might the sponsor have, such as the right to have patients visit the field for a special VIP day?

i. Will the Hospital be able to sponsor any game days? If so, how many?

j. Consider in-game announcements/commercials on video board as well as time during Radio/TV broadcasts. Include designation of responsibility for writing and approval of advertising content.

2. <u>Changes to Sponsorship Package</u>

a. Will either of the parties retain a right to alter or substitute the benefits to be accrued pursuant to the Agreement? What limitations/procedures apply?

b. Think about a "price matching" provision, which guarantees the Sponsor the most favorable treatment that the Team has given to any sponsor.

3. Exclusivity

a. What kind of exclusivity, if any, will the Team grant to the Sponsor?

b. If it is anything less than full exclusivity, the parties may consider detailing the specific types of inventory that are available to other sponsors within the Sponsor's category.

c. How does the exclusivity provision interact with players' rights to seek medical treatment of their choice?

4. Intellectual Property

a. Delineate parties' rights in each other's marks, the permitted uses of the marks, and corresponding limitations.

b. Common limitations to consider are a prohibition on modification, a prohibition on taking actions that will undermine goodwill, a requirement to use the appropriate trade or service mark notice, and approval rights.

5. Dispute Resolution

a. Draft a dispute resolution clause for what to do in the event of breach or threatened breach of the agreement.

b. Consider using mediation/arbitration, determine how the mediator/arbitrator will be selected, and the notice provisions.

c. Include a confidentiality provision, to ensure that the Thunder and St. Anthony do not have the ability to air their grievances in public.

F. After 15 to 20 minutes of preliminary preparation, during which each party should outline its interests and identify its "must haves," "nice to haves," and "throw-aways," Groups should convene and engage in clause-by-clause negotiation of the medical service provider provisions above.

As usual, please see the Teacher's Manual for an "Exemplar" Student Group response to this Hypothetical.

Chapter 8

FINANCIAL SERVICES PROVIDER AGREEMENTS

Throughout this book, you have been learning about several different sponsorship and service agreements available to a sports team. A team can sell as many categories as it can create as long as it does not infringe on the categories of its other sponsors or the inventory owned by the league. With medical services, food and beverage, and broadcasting agreements, the team signs up sponsors who will also provide services to the team within and outside the facility. The same can be true of a financial services provider sponsorship. The team can draft a category for a financial institution that includes being the "official" bank of the team while also providing a category that renders the sponsor the exclusive sponsor within a defined financial services category. This will mean that only the sponsor of all banks can advertise in the facility and market itself using a relationship to the team. In addition, it will also mean that the financial services sponsor is the only bank that may place ATMs in the facility and offer bank promotions within the facility. It may also be possible that team personnel will choose to have accounts with the sponsor's bank. Drafters will need to be careful that if the category is exclusive, then the sponsor must actually provide the requisite financial services, like ATMs, within the facility. Thus a financial services agreement is another dual-purpose agreement that is both a sponsorship and a service agreement.

A financial services sponsorship alone can be rather small when compared to the other sponsorship deals signed by a team.[1] As a result, a financial services sponsor may want to pay for, and take

[1] Notice that large financial services sponsorships are often not limited solely to financial services, as with Citibank and Citi Field and TD Garden and TD Bank, which are both also whole-facility naming rights deals. In addition, financial services might desire a smaller piece of inventory that is still greater than a lone financial services sponsorship. For example, PNC Financial Services Group, in 2010, bought the naming rights to a club at Wrigley Field in Chicago, now the "PNC Club of Chicago," which is a 71-seat area of the mezzanine along the third baseline. *See* Muret, Don. "PNC Financial Inks Naming-Rights Deal For Club At Wrigley Field," *SPORTS BUSINESS JOURNAL*, March 8, 2010. Another example is the Barclays Center, home of the Brooklyn Nets and New York Islanders, sponsored by Barclays PLC. *See* "Ceremonial Groundbreaking for Barclays Center at Atlantic Yards in Brooklyn," *WALL STREET JOURNAL*, March 11, 2010.

some additional inventory so that its sponsorship can be more prominent than it would be by just having, for example, exclusive advertising rights and having ATMs scattered throughout a team's facility.[2] As such, the financial services sponsor may want to be the naming rights sponsor, sponsor a level or area of the facility, such as a restaurant, or may want to otherwise make its presence better known at the facility by taking on a larger sponsorship package. For the team, the financial services sponsor is often one of the wealthiest sponsors, so it is often worthwhile for the team to search for a financial services sponsor while it is looking to fill its top tier sponsorships. Thus the financial service provider agreement may be significantly more complicated for the team than just providing a financial services category and some related benefits.

A. SPONSORSHIP PACKAGE BENEFITS

As with any other sponsorship agreement, the parties will need to address the varied benefits that the sponsor may buy and the amount of each benefit they will get. Types of package benefits, as we have seen from other chapters, include: the category (which will be discussed more fully in the Exclusivity section), the advertising and signage package,[3] in-facility perks, creative marketing strategies, and rights to conduct or offer other cross promotional activities. If the financial services sponsor also wants to present an event or a night of play, or name an area of the facility, then the benefits of such a sponsorship package should increase dramatically especially in the area of the signage and advertising. Of course, any such augmentation of the sponsorship category will need to comply with all existing league restrictions and other team and league arrangements. For example, the pre-existing presenting sponsorship agreement may not allow for another sponsor to present any part of, or events at, the facility.

Of the potential sponsorship benefits, a financial services sponsor will most likely want to provide all of the ATMs in the facility and be

---

[2] For example, Capital One is a "corporate champion" of the NCAA, which represents the highest tier of sponsorship, joining AT&T and Coca-Cola. Furthermore, Capital One is the title sponsor of the Capital One Orange Bowl, as well as the official Credit Card and Banking partner of the College Football Playoffs. These deals provide Capital One a great deal of exposure during the NCAA tournament and the College Football Playoff. *See* "Corporate Sponsorships: Capital One," available at: https://www.capitalone.com/about/sponsorship/.

[3] For example, Key Bank's sponsorship relationship with the Cleveland Indians includes an advertising and signage package that includes "the logo displayed across four light tower poles along the first-base line visible from Key Tower, in-park ATMs, the creation of the KeyBank ATM 'Ask the Manager' Show, an expanded social media presence and inclusion as the presenting partner of the annual Tribe Fest." *See* Nobile, Jeremy. "KeyBank, Indians expand partnership," *CRAIN'S CLEVELAND BUSINESS*, March 15, 2015.

able to run in-facility banking promotions in which fans can open accounts and take care of other banking needs, and the bank can do game-day giveaways of fan items that are either team or cross-branded. Also in the cross-promotional area, the bank will likely want the right to produce team-themed checks and ATM cards for fans that are also customers of the bank. In addition, the bank will want some sort of option to provide financial services to the players and other team personnel. While the team cannot mandate which financial service the players and personnel use, they can certainly allow the sponsor the opportunity to present its financial services to the players and other team personnel.

In addition, the sponsor will likely want to be involved in team charity events and want to have team personnel, including players, at some corporate or public events run by the sponsor throughout the year. The overall goal of such a sponsorship from the perspective of the financial services sponsor is to create more business. In this vein, one of the most important benefits the bank may also ask for is the mailing list of the team's season ticket holders, luxury suite renters and holders of personal seat licenses.

For all the sponsorship package benefits, the parties will need to decide the rights and obligations of the parties. For example, which party is responsible for putting up the advertising and whether one party has approval rights over the advertising materials created by the other. In addition, any procedures required to perform the agreement should be completely set forth in this section. This means that if the parties want to have a joint marketing opportunity, like a promotional event, the procedures for choosing the date of a promotion, the type of promotion, the number of recurrences of the promotion, and the obligations and rights of both parties in carrying out the promotional event should all be discussed in this section.

B. TERM

As the team begins to sign its second and third tier sponsors, if any, the team will want to structure the term of these later agreements in such a way that complement the previously signed top tier sponsorship agreements, like naming and presenting agreements. This may mean that the team ensures that the term of the second tier sponsorship expires concurrently with the top tier one, so that if the team loses the top tier sponsor, it is in the perfect position to either offer the higher level sponsorship to the lower level sponsor for an increased fee or to seek out a new sponsor for the top tier sponsorship within the category granted the second tier sponsor. In some cases this will be as simple as offering a term of the exact period of years remaining on a top-tier sponsorship, where in others it will involve giving the team an early termination right or a negotiation right if the team loses a top tier sponsor. This can be especially important with financial service provider agreements because financial service providers are often excellent choices for naming and presenting sponsorships. If the team is limited in its search for a new naming rights sponsor by the fact that it has a lower level financial service provider agreement in place, it could dramatically affect the earning potential of that top-tier sponsorship for the team.

C. EXCLUSIVITY

The category of exclusivity given away in any second or third-tier sponsorship will depend largely on the categories already granted by both the team and the league. Generally, a team will not be signing a separate financial services sponsor if it already has a financial services sponsor acting in any other sponsorship, so the actual financial services category is usually either available exclusively, or not available at all.[4] But if the financial services sponsor is also going to be naming the facility or presenting areas of the facility, there may be other categories that have some potential overlap. For example, the presenting sponsor may have, in their presenting agreement, the exclusive right to present the entire facility. Read broadly, that would prevent the team from later signing a financial services sponsor who wants to present a part of the facility, for example an area where they have a small financial services center.

If, for some reason, there is already a financial services sponsor in a top-tier sponsorship, but its category somehow allows for the addition of another financial services company, then the secondary grant of exclusivity will have to be very carefully worded so as to not overlap with the category of the top-tier sponsor. This may mean that one sponsor is the "Official Bank of the Team," while the other has the "Official Credit Card of the Team" or something similar. Either way, when signing another sponsor in the same general category, a team needs to be aware that while such an addition may be allowed by the wording of the sponsorship agreements, the effect of signing the second sponsor will affect the relationship with the prior sponsor. Depending on the amount of cooperation required to maintain the relationship with the first sponsor, it may be extremely ill advised for the team to sign another sponsor and risk losing cooperation from the first.

---

[4] In some cases it may be possible for the team to sign both a local bank and a national bank without violating exclusivity. For the two to co-exist, the categories must be drawn very narrowly and likely must explicitly allow for the existence of the other type of bank so that the team doesn't risk litigation when signing on a second bank.

Other issues of exclusivity can come into play when more than one team shares a facility, especially if the team that owns the facility, or is the primary lessee, signs a financial services sponsor first. For example, Delaware North Companies, the owner of the Boston Bruins, owns the facility where both the Bruins and the Boston Celtics play.[5] In 2005, the Bruins signed a naming rights deal with TD Banknorth, now re-branded TD Bank, after having been otherwise partnered with Banknorth since 2003.[6] For the Boston Celtics, the naming of its venue by TD Banknorth likely had the practical effect of narrowing its pool of potential financial services sponsors to just one bank. Just about three months after the Bruins' deal with TD Banknorth was announced, the Celtics announced that TD Banknorth would also be the Official Bank of the Boston Celtics.[7] The fact that TD Banknorth had the naming rights to the facility would have made it extremely difficult, if not impossible, for the Celtics to sign a different bank to a sponsorship.

D. TERMINATION

Financial services sponsorships, especially those that are also larger sponsorship deals like naming or presenting sponsorships, are often of long duration. As with any deal with a long term, such as twenty years, termination events will be essential to spell out in the initial agreement. While the parties may not be able to see the relationship changing over the term, they should plan for the possibility that circumstances may change dramatically and in such a way that one or both parties might want to terminate the sponsorship relationship.

In times of economic turmoil, this is especially important because the sponsor may no longer have the money or the desire to pay its sponsorship fees. For example, during the recession beginning in 2008, many financial services companies received government money to continue operations. The ones that used some of that money to pay sports sponsorship fees received a lot of negative press as a result.[8] In such a situation, one or both of the parties might want to terminate the sponsorship relationship: the sponsor, because it doesn't want to

5 This facility is the Boston Garden, currently named TD Garden.

6 In 2003, the Bruins signed Banknorth as the Official Bank of the Boston Bruins and in 2005, the renamed TD Banknorth became their naming rights sponsor. *See* "Banknorth Named Official Bank of the Boston Bruins," *BUSINESS WIRE*. July 18, 2003; Horrow, Rick & Karla Swatek, "Quirkiest Stadium Naming Rights Deals: TD Garden," *BUSINESS WEEK* No. 21 of 26, available at: http://images.businessweek.com/ss/09/10/1027_quirkiest_stadium_naming_rights_deals/21.htm.

7 *See* "TD Banknorth named official bank of the Boston Celtics," *CELTICS PRESS RELEASE*, October 26, 2005. Available at: http://www.nba.com/celtics/news/TD_BANKNORTH_NAMED_OFFICIAL_BA-155052-25.html.

8 *See* Lefton, Terry. "The Lefton Report: Bank of America renews its big sponsorship with Yankees," *SPORTS BUSINESS JOURNAL*, Nov. 10, 2014.

be forced to pay the fee, or the team, because it doesn't want to face the uncertainty that they may not get any fee. It is also possible that one or both of the parties may not want to allow termination in such an event: the sponsor, because it wants to maintain the relationship and likes to have the excuse that it is bound by the agreement to justify its actions, or the team, because it wants to continue to earn the high sponsorship fee it was able to command when economic times were better.

As a result, the parties should be very specific about the situations in which they wish to allow termination rights and which situations will give rise to other potential remedies. For example, the team may want to keep the financial services sponsor in an economic downturn because the team can continue to demand the higher sponsorship fee negotiated for in a better economy, but the team may still want a termination right if the company becomes insolvent or suffers some other material adverse change (MAC). The team will certainly not want to become yet another unsecured creditor in bankruptcy and be unable to get out of the agreement and mitigate by signing up another sponsor during the process.

As a result, the team will want the termination section to include a termination right for a MAC to the sponsor. In addition, the sponsor may want to include a termination right if the team experiences a MAC, defined perhaps as some level of extremely poor performance or attendance. In either situation, the parties should define the MAC as clearly as they can if they wish to avoid litigation on the matter. The more vague the MAC clause, the more likely that the parties will end up in litigation if one attempts to invoke it for a termination right. In order to be specific about the MACs, the parties want to give rise to termination, and to catch any other potential MACs they may not be considering, it may be best to define MACs both by the specific and the general. This would mean that specific MACs contemplated would be listed, but also there would be some sort of a catchall phrase that would catch other MACs for a party to be able claim in other, unforeseen situations.

In addition to outlining the events that give rise to termination, the parties should be sure to indicate when in the timeline of such events the termination right comes into existence. For example, if the sponsor becomes insolvent, there will probably have been some warning signs that might, if drafted into this clause, give the team the right to terminate before the company actually files for bankruptcy. For example, the team may begin to worry that a payment will not get made and may want the right to demand some sort of adequate assurance from the company in the form of a lien on company property or a deposit into an escrow account for the purpose of protecting the team's interest in that money.[9]

Other potential termination events besides MACs should be considered as well and included in this section. In some cases, the sponsor or the team will want the ability to terminate if the sponsor is bought or merges with another company.[10] In such a situation, the agreement can allow for the sponsor to terminate the agreement by paying a termination fee.[11] Should the parties decide to include such an option to buy-out the remainder of the contract, they should set the price of the buyout in each year of the term, with the price decreasing as the remainder of the term does. In addition, the team may want to set a limit on the sponsor's ability to buy itself out of the deal, limiting its use to specific situations such as a change in control.

If the team foresees the possibility of finding a preferable financial services sponsor before the end of term, the team may also want an option to buy out the agreement and terminate early. The price of such a buyout option will be more difficult to determine because the team would be reimbursing the sponsor for the intangible benefits it would be losing as opposed to a tangible amount of money, as is the case for the team when losing the actual sponsorship fee. The sponsor will, of course, claim that the benefits it gets from the sponsorship deal is significantly more valuable than the amount of the remaining sponsorship fee and will want the team to pay a termination fee of whatever the difference would be between the sponsorship fee and the value to the company. Such a termination fee, as defined by the sponsor, would likely be far too onerous for any team to actually exercise the right, since the new sponsor would have to offer a

---

9 Such an adequate protection guarantee would likely have the effect of making the team into a secured creditor as opposed to an unsecured creditor. The team will almost always prefer a termination right, however, as this will make it easier for the team to recover its fee but will subject the team to difficult post-bankruptcy collection procedures. Additionally, this will likely result in a lengthy wait should the sponsor file for bankruptcy, at which point all collection attempts would be stayed by the bankruptcy court pending the resolution of the bankruptcy proceedings.

10 In some cases the sponsor might want the team to have a termination right if the sponsor is bought or merges as a protection against a hostile bid for the sponsor. If the team has a termination right upon a change of control of the sponsor, then a potential purchaser risks losing a fairly substantial asset upon purchase and will be more likely to work with both the sponsor and the team to ensure that the team will not exercise that right upon the merger or change in control.

11 For example, in 2004 when Fleet Bank merged with Bank of America, the bank paid a termination fee in order to be released from its naming rights deal with the Boston Bruins six years before the expiration of the agreement. *See* Horrow, Rick & Karla Swatek, "Quirkiest Stadium Naming Rights Deals: TD Garden," *BUSINESS WEEK* No. 21 of 26, available at: http://images.businessweek.com/ss/09/10/1027_quirkiest_stadium_naming_rights_deals/21.htm.

significantly better sponsorship fee to make it worthwhile to pay off the original sponsor.[12]

As with any other termination section, the termination procedure should be laid out along with the termination events. This can become especially necessary when the parties want the different termination events to have different termination procedures. The same is true when different termination events give rise to different, or non-existent, termination fees. It is often good to provide a termination fee provision for each and every termination event, even if a provision simply states that there will be no termination fee for a specific termination event. That way, it is clear to both parties which situations entitle them to fees and which do not.

In addition, the section should address the costs of terminating the relationship, and which parties will be responsible for bearing which costs. In this part, the team may want to be in charge of the dismantling of the advertising and signage, but may want to shift some of that cost onto the sponsor. If this is the case, the termination section should provide for how the team intends to bill the sponsor for those costs. As with other agreements, these provisions can be split into smaller clauses for termination and post-termination rights and obligations, but either way, it is important that the issues are addressed.

HYPOTHETICAL EXERCISE

A. Assume that the New York Mets, who already have CitiBank as their naming rights sponsor, are looking to ink a sponsorship deal with Chase Manhattan Bank. Further, the Mets assume, that if the CitiBank agreement is terminated, it can easily transition to give the advertising space to Chase Manhattan. Moreover, the Mets want to ensure that the contract gives the team an "out" in the event Chase Manhattan suffers severe financial or reputational harm.

B. Chase Manhattan Bank is interested in advertising and setting up a credit card application display area and a financial tips and advising center. The Bank also wants naming rights over the ticket information center, the fan information center, luxury suite level naming rights and signage, publication advertising, pocket schedule naming sponsorship, title sponsorship for a few games in the season, and to sponsor a reading and financial advice program. (Assume that the category exclusivity in the deal with Citi

---

[12] The new sponsor would have to offer an amount that is greater than the total cost of the termination fee plus the original sponsorship fee combined for it to be worthwhile to the team to switch sponsors.

permits the sale of these categories, so long as each time the field is referred to, it is called Citi Field.)

C. Students should split into groups of four, with two members representing the Mets and two members representing Chase Manhattan Bank.

D. How would you draft the following clauses:

1. <u>Sponsorship Package Benefits</u>

a. Create a sponsorship package that satisfies Chase Manhattan's interests, as outlined above.

b. Which party bears the responsibility to produce signage, logos, and other promotional inventory to be created pursuant to the Agreement? Will the other party retain a right of approval?

c. Who will bear the related expenses? Consider the leverage in this deal is different as compared with last chapter's agreement with a hospital.

d. Consider grant of "naming rights" to various Team inventory/areas of the Stadium. While the Stadium Naming Rights have already been dispensed, other Official Sponsors and the Team may find it mutually agreeable to associate the Sponsor's name with such features outlined above.

e. Address auxiliary issues such as the creation of any logos to promote the naming rights and in what places the logo and other references to the relationship will appear, e.g. signage, menus, and commercials.

f. What permanent signage will be erected within the stadium? Consider provision of temporary signage (e.g. only for designated/a minimum number of home games) in conjunction with offering of Sponsor services/consultation to visitors to the Stadium.

g. Will any "giveaways" be involved? At whose cost and storage?

h. Establish Sponsor's advertising presence in designated Team print materials, keeping in mind the relative values of "premium" spots, e.g. inside cover of game programs. Will the parties' relationship have a web presence?

i. Consider special promotional nights dedicated to the Sponsor. How many per year? What additional benefits will the Sponsor receive specific to those games? E.g. Radio/TV tie-ins, newspaper advertising, tickets, etc. How will dates be selected—what priority, if any, will be given to this Sponsor? Will the Sponsor be permitted to have a representative throw out the first pitch?

j. Who will create and maintain the kiosks to dispense credit card and bank account information?

2. Term

a. How long will the relationship last?

b. Will there be any options to renew/rights of first negotiation/rights of first refusal?

3. Exclusivity

a. Now that you have drafted other sponsorship agreements, consider how the grant of exclusivity is the same/differs in this deal.

b. What type of exclusivity will the Mets grant Chase Manhattan?

c. How does this relate to the grant of naming rights to Citi?

4. Termination

a. Assume that the Mets would like to end the relationship with Chase Manhattan if Chase Manhattan suffers a material adverse change. The Mets are not interested in dealing with the company through bankruptcy/insolvency, but rather would like to terminate the agreement at the first sign of serious trouble, so as to avoid having to chase down payments due under the agreement.

b. Chase Manhattan would like to preserve the deal and does not want the Mets to be able to walk away easily.

c. Draft a termination clause to reflect the Mets/Chase Manhattan's interests.

E. After 15 to 20 minutes of preliminary preparation, during which each Group should outline its interests and identify its "must haves," "nice to haves," and "throw-aways," Groups should convene and engage in clause-by-clause negotiation of the Financial Services Provider provisions above.

The Teacher's Manual contains the usual "Exemplar" Student Group response to this Hypothetical.

Chapter 9

SPONSORSHIP BY A STATE-OPERATED ENTITY

Sponsorship by a state-operated entity ("SOE") is not so very different from any other sponsorship. Like any private corporate sponsor, a state-operated entity can buy either small or large sponsorships, including presenting sponsorships, if the entity is willing to pay the price. However, the representatives of a state-operated entity have to think very carefully about how to justify the expenditure of possibly millions of dollars on a sports sponsorship.[1] Unlike corporate sponsors, the officers of state-operated entities do not have the same decision making freedom that many corporate executives do. While both corporations and state-operated entities have duties to shareholders or citizens, the accountability scheme is somewhat different between the two. Also unlike corporations, the leadership in a state-operated entity can often be changed with little warning and over a short period of time.[2] This means that a state-operated entity may be limited in the length of agreement it can reasonably sign with a team, in order to be able to justify smaller expenditures at more regular intervals. The team, in contrast, will usually want a longer term in a sponsorship agreement, especially because of the volatility of public leadership; the team wants to keep the sponsor from repudiating the deal if a shift in control occurs.

There are many government entities that often sponsor sports franchises. Common of these are military sponsors, public schools, especially NCAA universities, and publicly owned hospitals.[3] This chapter will, however, focus mostly on sponsorship of a team by a state lottery, as such a relationship raises interesting compliance issues for both parties. In addition to compliance with laws and

---

1 *See e.g.,* Darren Rovell, "Roger Goodell Offers to Return Money if Tributes Specifically Paid for by DOD," *ESPN.com*, Nov. 4, 2015, available at: http://espn.go.com/nfl/story/_/id/14051326/nfl-audit-teams-marketing-contracts-patriotism-tributes; *see also* Scott Malone & Jacqueline Tempera, "U.S. Drops Boston's Embattled Bid for Olympic Games," *REUTERS*, Jul. 27, 2015.

2 This is in contrast to the hierarchy of most large corporations which tend to have staggered boards so a change in control of the company often takes several years when attempted through proxy contests.

3 Health and Medical Services Provider Agreements are discussed in more detail in Chapter 7.

league rules, state-operated entities are also limited by their own operating rules and regulations, which affect the types of benefits they can accept from the team and the uses to which they may put the benefits they do get.[4]

Many of the existing sponsorships by state-operated entities are state lottery sponsorships.[5] The lottery is perhaps ideally suited, when compared with other state entities, to the type of agreement it can work out with a sports team. This is because despite the expenditure of money on the sponsorship fee, the marketing benefits it can attain through such a sponsorship can still generate a significant increase in net revenue.[6] For example, the Boston Bruins and Celtics have special Bruins and Celtics lottery tickets on sale throughout Boston and even in vending machines within TD Garden. In this way, the state-operated entity, the Massachusetts State Lottery, is just like any other sponsor, using signage, advertising, and cross-promotional opportunities to increase its business.

Unlike many other sponsors, however, a lottery is a gambling venture, and as such, the team may be limited in what sponsorship inventory it may provide by league rules and state and federal laws. It used to be that league rules prohibited signing sponsorships with gambling ventures at all. For example, in the 1990s, when legalized gambling entities became a brand new market for sponsors, the NFL remained opposed to affiliations between teams and gambling organizations and would not change its league rules to allow for such affiliations.[7] Other leagues made efforts to shift their rules so that legalized gambling entities could be included as sponsors, and, as a result, many sporting events now have casino and lottery ads throughout the venue and the broadcast.[8]

A. SPONSORSHIP BENEFITS

Perhaps the greatest benefit that a state-operated entity can get from a sports sponsorship is the right to cross-promote and thus devise

---

4 For example, any state lottery must abide by state and federal lottery advertising and gaming regulations, as well as internal procedures and guidelines. Such laws and rules include prohibiting state employees from taking personal benefits, such as club seats, as a result of their employment by the state.

5 For example, the Massachusetts State lottery is the presenting sponsor of the Boston Bruins and is a sponsor of the Boston Celtics. The NCAA, however, strongly discourages any type of gambling sponsorship, including lottery sponsorships.

6 *See* "A Good Bet: More Sponsorships on Behalf of State Lotteries," *IEG SPONSORSHIP REPORT*, June 20, 2011, available at: http://www.sponsorship.com/IEG/files/cf/cfcc7d9e-3107-43a3-ba41-a7f48b36e2ff.pdf.

7 *See* McKelvey, Stephen M. "U.S. Professional Sport Organization Policies Shift to Embrace Legalized Gambling Entities: A Roll of the Dice?," *14 J. LEGAL ASPECTS OF SPORT 23, 27* (Winter, 2004).

8 *Id.*

some creative marketing opportunities. Team-themed lottery tickets are an example of this.[9] In addition, the ability to run promotions in areas of the venue on game days can be very valuable to the sponsor. Thus, the discussion of sponsorship benefits will linger over the question of creative, cross-promotional opportunities. In these discussions, the team is going to have to make sure that it does not violate any league rules. For example, many of the sports leagues have rules about gambling, and while sponsorships by the lottery may not be prohibited, certain other cross-promotional activities may be—though at a league level, these restrictions have seemingly been relaxed given the affiliations with daily sports leagues, such as DraftKings and FanDuel.[10] The sponsor, on the other hand, has to be sure it is complying with all state laws and regulations that apply to it as a state-operated entity, as well as any that generally control the industry to which the entity belongs.[11] Thus the parties have to be very careful when designing creative joint promotional opportunities. They should be aware of the applicable laws and regulations and make sure that in drafting the sections on cross-promotions, they explicitly mandate compliance with laws and league rules and plan for any changes that may become necessary to remain in compliance. While the "Compliance with Laws" section of the agreement will cover all necessary legal compliance, any mandated guidelines for advertising either by the league or the state can be outlined here.

As with any other creative marketing strategy that the parties develop concurrently with the sponsorship deal, the details of such a strategy and all it entails should be included in the agreement. Though additional cross-promotional activities may develop later in the relationship, any of these that the parties contemplate at the time of signing should be explicitly laid out in writing, as much as possible. This will ensure less ambiguity about the parties' required performance, as the details of both parties' rights, duties, and obligations would be set forth in the agreement. If the parties worry about including such clauses in the overall sponsorship agreement, they may also draft a separate document, such as a schedule, and

---

9 Team-themed lottery tickets will often bear the team logo and possibly photographs of some team personnel. In addition, the prizes may be cash or other monetary prize or team merchandise such as game tickets or team merchandise. For example, see the new San Francisco 49ers lottery tickets.

10 In some cases the issue will relate to the potential participation of the individual players in the cross-promotional activities, as most leagues have bylaws relating to the gambling activities of the athletes. For more information on sports sponsorships of legalized gambling entities, *see* McKelvey, Stephen M. "U.S. Professional Sport Organization Policies Shift to Embrace Legalized Gambling Entities: A Roll of the Dice?," *14 J. LEGAL ASPECTS OF SPORT 23* (Winter, 2004).

11 These laws and regulations can cover just about anything, including requiring a lottery agency to verify that the purchasers of lottery tickets are eighteen or over.

execute it concurrently with the sponsorship agreement, providing they also incorporate it into the agreement by reference.

In addition to the creative marketing strategies, the state-operated entity will want a prominent signage and advertising package and other benefits. The level of sponsorship sold will affect the signage and advertising in the agreement. If the state-operated entity is to be a high level sponsor, such as a presenting sponsor, or if it will belong to a high tier of sponsorships, such as a title sponsorship tier, then the signage and advertising should be significantly larger than that provided to lower tier sponsors. Just as promotional opportunities may be limited by rules and laws, so too can these limit what the team can allow the sponsor to do with the advertising and signage package.[12]

Where the state-operated entity is often most limited, however, is in its ability to enjoy some of the in-facility perks often afforded to sports sponsors. As these in-facility perks can include luxury suites and club seats, which are benefits that are available to a limited number of persons, state personnel have to be careful that they do not use these benefits for personal gain.[13] It would be corruption for state employees to use their status as government officials, and the government's money, to basically buy themselves season tickets to sporting events. Any of that type of in-facility perk thus has to be used only for legitimate governmental purposes.[14] Compliance with such applicable ethical and legal standards of government officials may therefore play a part in the Agreement's covenants section.

B. COMPLIANCE WITH LAWS

The need to comply with all laws and regulations is important for any sponsorship deal, but the legal landscape can be even more difficult to navigate when dealing with a state-operated entity. This is

---

[12] McKelvey, Stephen M. "U.S. Professional Sport Organization Policies Shift to Embrace Legalized Gambling Entities: A Roll of the Dice?," *14 J. LEGAL ASPECTS OF SPORT 23, 29* (Winter, 2004).

> League rules[, however,] restrict teams from allowing live or replayed lottery drawings to be held within their venues, as well as live or replayed lottery drawings to be shown on its video scoreboards or on any other in-venue visual display or broadcast in its venues. The leagues have deemed such activity to be too closely and visibly inked to the actual lottery process, as opposed to the advertising and promotion of the [lottery] itself.

[13] This would mean that such perks would be ok to use if they served an important state function, like hosting an important visitor, for example, but shouldn't be used regularly by the head of the entity or the mayor of the town or any other state employee.

[14] This is yet another reason why the state lottery is such a good fit for sponsorships because the in-facility perks can be given away as prizes to the people who play the lottery, which is a completely legitimate business and government purpose for the state lottery.

because compliance is essential for the relationship to function, as state-operated entities are subject to special laws and regulations, strict internal governance rules, and often, complicated bureaucracies. In addition, certain state-operated entities are also subject to federal and state laws that restrict where and how they may advertise. Some laws even provide criminal penalties for third parties who violate these laws, including for broadcasters who run out-of-state lottery advertisements in the wrong states.

Legal restrictions are especially present for state lotteries, as they are gambling ventures. For example, lotteries are prohibited in some states. It is thus completely illegal for any lottery to advertise within such a state.[15] On the other hand, it is often the case that a state that has its own state lottery will not be able to prohibit advertisements for out-of-state lotteries within their own state. That is, there would be no restrictions on broadcasters' ability to run advertising for, or promote, legally authorized in-state and out-of-state lotteries if the state has its own lottery.[16]

Of course, part of compliance with laws is that the entity be legally authorized. To remain legally authorized, the state-operated entity must be in full compliance with all applicable laws. Part of this section of the contract will require compliance with all applicable laws. The state-operated entity and team will represent and warrant they are in compliance. Furthermore, both parties will covenant that they will continue to be in compliance with all applicable laws.

At this point it makes sense to include some of the key laws with which the parties must promise to remain in compliance. For a state lottery, it is essential that the lottery be in compliance with all gaming laws, including any restrictions on broadcasters, so that the team does not cause its broadcasters to violate these laws when performing some of the team's obligations to its lottery sponsor. Beyond gaming laws, both parties will require compliance with other laws, such as equal employment opportunities, unemployment compensation, and workers' compensation.

These third-party contracting regulations may be very difficult to keep track of. Many state and local businesses include competitive bidding requirements for potential contractors, to ensure the

15 *See* 18 U.S.C. 1304, 1307 47 C.F.R. § 73.1211(a). This statute prohibits broadcasters within a state with no state lottery from airing advertisements for, or otherwise promoting, out of state lotteries.

16 For more information on advertising guidelines for lotteries, *see e.g.*, ADVERTISING LAWS AND REGULATIONS HANDBOOK, prepared by Indiana Broadcasters Association in cooperation with Bingham McHale, LLP, Indianapolis and Shaw Pittman, LLP, Washington, D.C. (June, 2004). *Available at:* http://www.indianabroadcasters.org/docs/Advertising%20Guidelines.pdf.

government is not overspending taxpayers' money.[17] Additionally, diversity ventures such as promotion of "Women-Owned Business Entities" (WBE), "Minority-Owned Business Entities" (MBE), or "Disadvantaged Business Entities" (DBE) frequently make their way into government contracts as clauses requiring certain proportions of, or at the least commercially reasonable efforts to secure, goods and services from businesses typified by those definitions.[18] What makes a business qualify as such a diverse entity, too, may change based on the geographic location or the current legislature.[19]

Public contracting may also require stringent prerequisites to any work done by any contractual partners. Construction or other work done on a state-owned facility such as a sports stadium will likely need to be insured and bonded to certain minimum standards to help minimize risk or liability.[20] Other required covenants may include adherence to local, state, or federal guidelines regarding accessibility or nondiscrimination, such as the Americans with Disabilities Act or Title VII of the Civil Rights Act. Exhibit 1 once again exemplifies such requirements in § 16.2: Representations, Warranties, and Covenants and in § 18.21: Conflicts of Interest and Ethics Compliance. The state-operated entity will likely be authorized to have a contractual relationship only with an entity that is in compliance with all applicable laws. Thus, it is as important for the team to represent, warrant, and covenant its ongoing compliance with all applicable laws as it is for the state-operated entity to do so.

In addition, the team needs to remain in compliance with all league rules. The leagues all have rules when it comes to a team aligning itself with any sponsor, but especially someone like a lottery. For example, the team may not sign a sponsorship deal with lotteries that offer schemes based on the outcome of actual sporting events, except for dog and horse racing, or with government-run lotteries that incorporate the use of the scores, or point totals as part of its scheme.[21] Thus, the agreement must also contemplate all league rules, as well as potential future changes in the league rules.[22]

---

17 *See* Exhibit 1, § 12.3: Transactions with Affiliates.

18 *See* Exhibit 1, § 12.4: Subcontracts.

19 Nearly all 50 States have some sort of MBE/WBE/DBE requirements. For example legislation, see S.C. Code Ann. § 11-35-5240 or Section 1 Title 62 of the Pennsylvania Consolidated Statutes, Chapter 22.

20 *See* Exhibit 1, §§ 12.3 and 15.4, which contain examples of the kinds of language that might be required.

21 McKelvey, Stephen M. "U.S. Professional Sport Organization Policies Shift to Embrace Legalized Gambling Entities: A Roll of the Dice?," *14 J. LEGAL ASPECTS OF SPORT 23, 29* (Winter, 2004).

22 *See* Walt Bogandich, Joe Drape, & Jacqueline Williams, "Attorney General Tells DraftKings and FanDuel to Stop Taking Entries in New York," *THE NEW YORK*

C. TERMINATION

As with any termination provision, this section should lay out the termination events and the termination procedure. In this situation, the termination events, possibly defined through the language of material breaches, should be discussed and decided upon by the parties during the negotiations. For example, the parties will need to decide if the denial of state funds to the sponsor is a termination event.[23] In addition, the parties will need to decide if such a termination is a material breach by the sponsor. Obviously the sponsor would like to say that a failure to get state funding is inherently not its fault, but seeing as how the sponsor does have some control over the process, though not ultimate control of course, the team may want to hold the sponsor responsible for an early termination fee in such a situation. Irrespective of whether the fault is the sponsor's, the denial of state funds will likely mean a termination of the sponsorship agreement. The sponsor will demand the right to terminate if it is denied state funding, as it will mean at least a budget crunch and, further, may violate appropriation laws.

A failure to comply with all applicable laws will also likely be a breach,[24] though whether it is material or not will depend on the type of law and on how the parties want to treat individual laws. The parties may also want to address whether legal non-compliance will involve a monetary penalty that the party not in compliance would owe as damages to the other party.

The parties might also consider including some form of a morals provision in the agreement. This would serve to allow the parties to get out of the relationship if it turns out that one of the parties, or one of their key employees, has been a bad actor. As a representative body of the public, the state sponsor does not want to be tied to a team run by a person with a bad reputation, and the team may not want to be connected with a state entity where a key official turns out to be corrupt or otherwise undesirable. Such a morals clause could offer both parties termination rights, and thus help protect both their images. The morals standard will have to be carefully crafted and negotiated, however, and both parties will likely try to raise the standard for the other party while simultaneously lowering their own. Objective measurements of morality may be difficult. The parties should, however, do their best to stick to objective

---

TIMES, Nov. 10, 2015 (describing the recent shift in New York policy to categorize "fantasy sports" as illegal gambling).

23 *See* Exhibit 1, § 2.2: Limitations on Manager's Duties (limiting liability for Manager's non-performance if such is based on lack of/untimely funds from the SOE).

24 *See* "Compliance with Laws," *supra*.

measurements so that they do not find themselves in lengthy and costly litigation as soon as they try to test the morals clause.

In addition to working out what breaches of the agreement are material or not, and which give rise to termination events, the parties will need to work out whether or not the breaching party will have the opportunity to cure a breach. If so, the parties should mandate the length of time a breaching party has to cure and the remedies available to the other party for any breach whether cured or not. For example, a failure to pay the sponsorship fee will be a breach. The team may allow the sponsor the opportunity to cure by paying the fee, but it will also want a penalty for the fee being late, maybe in the form of interest. The parties should also consider the difficulties inherent in working with the bureaucracy of the state-operated entity, and whether the period in which the sponsor has to cure, should be adjusted to account for a particularly complicated bureaucratic process.

If the breach is material and incurable or uncured, it will likely also be a termination event. Some termination events will not be breaches, however, such as a material change in state law that affects the parties' relationship, which may or may not constitute a termination event. Obviously, if the state law prohibits the sponsor from being aligned with the team, then such a change would be a termination event. In other situations, such a change in law might trigger the type of situation parties often negotiate for in their discussion of contract term, that is, a first negotiation right, a right of first refusal and/or a right to match.

D. SPECIFIC LIMITATIONS

Confidentiality

One place where state-operated entities might not be able to promise compliance with standard contract terms is confidentiality. The proliferation of legislation regarding transparent or open governance may sometimes extend to legal contracts and advice regarding any projects at least partly funded by public monies.[25] Exhibit 1, § 18.1 exemplifies warning language to this effect. Drafters must therefore be cognizant of this risk when drafting and be prepared for the possibility that their specific terms as well as boilerplate or form clauses might become publicly available. In a sponsorship situation such as this, then, it might be prudent to draft more from scratch, or concede to using the contract form of the SOE as the basis of the Agreement.

---

25 *See* San Francisco Administrative Code § 67.

Indemnification

In many cases, indemnification by a public body or state-owned enterprise is void as against public policy.[26] Even where not strictly void, many governments will refuse to accept indemnification or "hold harmless" provisions because such clauses (i) are not covered under their insurance policies, (ii) because they would purport to bind the government indefinitely or for a length of time that would be inappropriate to bind the government based on the elected party's term of service, or (iii) because holding another party harmless would conflict with other duties to respond to allegations of wrongdoing. Agreements with entities with such limitations, then, should take this imbalance into consideration when drafting other clauses, such as the limitation of liability or provision of insurance clauses. Note the unequal indemnification clause in Article 14 of Exhibit 1: § 14.1 promises indemnification flowing from the Manager to the SOE, while § 14.2, which normally would contain a reciprocal clause, is left "Reserved."

Taxation and Sovereign Immunity

The type of state-operated entity at issue may implicate unusual situations involving taxation and sovereign immunity. Tax laws usually apply differently to governments than to for-profit entities or individuals, including a general removal of income tax.[27] Many state-affiliated hospitals, which are frequent sponsors of teams, are also tax exempt as charities as well as non-profit government affiliates. Tax exemptions may impact not only the SOE itself, but also the SOE's relationship with contractual parties, such as its ability to repay certain expenditures.

Similarly, local or municipal governments, which often also sponsor their local teams in some fashion, will be immune to many types of suits against them, based on sovereign immunity. The Limitation of Liability clause of Exhibit 1, § 14.5 specifically exempts any action by the SOE as a waiver of sovereign immunity beyond that to which the state has specifically agreed. Parties to a contract with an SOE should be similarly careful in the range of promises they make regarding liability, indemnification, and insurance.

---

26 *See* Colorado Constitution Article XI, §§ 1–2.

27 "Issues for Government Entities," *IRS*, June 4, 2015, available at: https://www.irs.gov/Government-Entities/Federal,-State-&-Local-Governments/Issues-for-Government-Entities; *see also* Clayton Gillette, "Fiscal Federalism and the Use of Municipal Bond Proceeds," 58 N.Y.U. L. REV. 1030.

E. FORCE MAJEURE

For the force majeure section of this sponsorship agreement, the parties need to consider whether a standard force majeure provision, as you have seen in earlier sponsorship agreements, is appropriate. The parties here will want to decide what events will constitute force majeure events and whether these will be limited to the standard list including "acts of God" and things like war and insurrection. In particular, the parties may decide that a delay in receiving state funding is a force majeure event, even if it is through no fault of the sponsor. Another example would be approval of any agreement by an oversight or governing body or by public referendum, if such measures are required by local law.

In addition to evaluating the force majeure events, the parties might consider altering the standard procedure of notification, possible cure, and the extension of the term of the agreement in light of the type of sponsor. For example, the extensive bureaucracy of a state-operated entity may make a short notice period impractical. This being said, if a force majeure event occurs that would normally cause the end of the agreement, such as a fire destroying the facility, the parties might want the option to terminate with a shorter notice period. The manner and recipient of the notice, too, must be carefully chosen when dealing with an entity whose members or governors could be removed from office with little notice.

In general, when inserting a force majeure clause into an agreement, it is essential for the parties to look at the scope of the standard clause and decide whether it is practical for the specific deal at hand. If it is not, it should be altered accordingly.

* * * *

The above clauses are just some of many in a sponsorship agreement with a state-operated entity. When working on the hypothetical below, students should be able to craft a full agreement including many of the other clauses discussed throughout this book.

HYPOTHETICAL EXERCISE

Negotiating and Drafting a Sponsorship Agreement Between a State-Operated Entity and a Professional Sports Franchise

A. Imagine that the New Jersey Devils are interested in selling a sponsorship package for the new Prudential Center to the New Jersey State Lottery. Given the state's proclivity towards and receptivity of gambling, the Devils believe that this could be a very lucrative sponsorship sale. Further, the Devils are willing to permit the Lottery to create special giveaways in the two restaurants on the mezzanine level, to sell lottery tickets at the venue, and to create a fantasy sports game platform to engage fans and promote the Lottery through an affiliation with the team's "mega player" (prizes will include game tickets, autographed merchandise, scratch off tickets and other prizes).

B. The New Jersey State Lottery is interested in creating a sponsorship partnership with the Devils. It must abide by state and federal lottery advertising and gaming regulations, and the following guidelines that it has established:

1. Games and advertising will reflect Lottery policy.

2. Lottery products will not be associated with tobacco, alcohol, or sexually oriented products.

3. The Lottery will not encourage people to gamble beyond their means.

4. The Lottery will promote responsible play by printing the Gambler's Anonymous telephone numbers on all of its products.

5. The Lottery will not associate itself with unlicensed or unregistered businesses.

6. The Lottery will not target minors in its advertising and will actively work to prohibit minors from playing.

7. Advertising campaigns will be focused on adults 25 and older statewide with a very broad reach and cost-efficiencies.

8. All print advertising will include the following information:

   a. Benefits Education and Institutions.

   b. The name and title of the Governor and Executive Director of the Lottery.

   c. www.state.nj.us/lottery.

   d. If you or someone you know has a gambling problem, call 1-800-GAMBLER.

C. Students should split into groups of four, with two members representing the State of New Jersey and two representing the Devils.

D. Copies of a sponsorship agreement between a state lottery and a professional sports franchise will be distributed to the groups, with the most critical/challenging clauses redacted for ultimate resolution and drafting by the groups.

E. How would you draft the following clauses:

1. Sponsorship Benefits

   a. Will the state lottery be an "official sponsor" of any events at the arena?

   b. Describe any exclusivity requirements that the lottery may demand from the Devils. Consider how drafting this provision is different, given that that there is only one state lottery, than in other sponsorship agreements drafted in past weeks.

   c. Who will be responsible for preparing the advertising copy, in accordance with the guidelines above? Will either party have approval rights?

   d. Who is responsible for the maintenance of signage? Which signage in the arena will the Lottery get? Will the Lottery also get mentioned in print and broadcasting? Will the parties' relationship have a web presence?

   e. Who will establish the games/giveaways at the arena?

   f. Consider providing for a procedure through which the sponsorship inventory may be altered by either party.

   g. Refer back to the previous agreements drafted to determine if other benefits ought to be included.

2. Compliance with Laws

   a. Given that the team is dealing with a regulated, state-operated entity, compliance is essential for the relationship to function.

   b. Draft a provision that states the parties' obligations to comply with the laws, and which laws, specifically, they have to comply with. For example, consider including laws relating not only to gaming but also to equal employment opportunity, unemployment compensation, workers' compensation, etc.

3. Termination

   a. Delineate the terms under which either party may terminate the agreement, e.g. material breach (and cure) or denial of state funding for the Lottery/failure to comply with laws, as well as the consequences thereto.

b. Consider the equivalent of a "morals clause," which assures the state Sponsor that it will not become associated with any unfavorable parties or conduct.

c. What is the effect of a material change in state law that affects the parties' relationship?

4. <u>Force Majeure</u>

a. Draft a clause that governs performance or existence of the contract in the event of Acts of God, etc. that interfere with the parties' duties under the Agreement.

b. Does the clause you drafted earlier in the semester fit this Agreement? How does it need to be tweaked and tailored?

F. After 15 to 20 minutes of preliminary preparation, during which each party should outline its interests and identify its "must haves," "nice to haves," and "throw-aways," Groups should convene and engage in clause-by-clause negotiation of the State-Operated Sponsorship provisions above.

G. Prepare to report out results after 30 to 40 minutes of group negotiation. Compare your own Group's resolutions with that of the other Groups, and reconvene to continue negotiating.

Per usual, the Teacher's Manual will set forth an "Exemplar" Student Group response to this Hypothetical.

Chapter 10

ASSET PURCHASE AGREEMENTS

Outside of player trades, the most widely discussed transactions in sports are sales of franchises. These deals are structured as asset purchases, meaning the buyer purchases a set of tangible assets, intangible assets, and liabilities that the seller owns.[1] The dollar amounts keep climbing, drawing interest from fans and venture capitalists alike. For example, Steve Ballmer purchased the Los Angeles Clippers for $2 billion in 2014, the highest price for a professional basketball team at the time.[2] But these deals happen much more frequently in the minor leagues, with recent sale prices rising over the past decade. In 2014, the Dayton Dragons fetched a sale price of $40 million—and the team is a lowly single-A minor league baseball affiliate. Turnover at the ownership level is higher, leading to far more purchase agreements of the franchises, and new investment groups are seizing the opportunities to turn around flailing teams, leverage new revenue streams, and seek a new home city for the franchise.[3] Because minor league teams do not have the same ardent fan base as their professional counterparts, it also becomes easier to move the teams should the owner see a better location for (or a city more receptive to publicly funding) a new state-of-the-art stadium. But at the same time, desirable locations are becoming scarcer as teams get moved and the market gets increasingly more saturated with expansion and minor-league teams.

Behind each of these deals is an arduous process of bidding, negotiating, and renegotiating. While price is perhaps the most important term, lawyers spend a great deal of time allocating legal risk through the indemnification package and the representations and warranties that the parties offer each other through the agreement. Often, attorneys will require a separate section of

---

1 Contrast this with an equity purchase, the simplest version of which has the buyer purchasing only the seller's stock.

2 *See* David Meeks & Brent Schrotenboer. "Clippers sale to Steve Ballmer finalized, NBA says," *USA TODAY*, Aug. 12, 2014, available at: http://www.usatoday.com/story/sports/nba/clippers/2014/08/12/los-angeles-clippers-sale-steve-ballmer-donald-sterling-nba/13952797/.

3 *See* Bruce Schoenfeld. "Minor league teams, but mighty big numbers as franchise values soar," *SPORTSBUSINESS JOURNAL*, Aug. 4, 2014, available at: http://www.sportsbusinessdaily.com/Journal/Issues/2014/08/04/Franchises/Minor-league-teams.aspx.

fundamental representations and will haggle over materiality qualifiers on the representations—and the definition of materiality itself. The agreement ensures the seller has the proper premises liability insurance in place and will conduct its business consistent with past practice until the time of the closing of the agreement. The parties will also hash out a dispute resolution processes clause and terms that will survive closing.

A. REPRESENTATIONS AND WARRANTIES

When selling an asset or set of assets, the seller will want the buyer to bear as much risk as possible. This usually means that the seller will want to "rep and warrant" as little as possible and take the position that the buyer should rely on its due diligence to make its decision to enter into the agreement. The seller will not mind warranting that it is a duly organized entity, that it has authorization to enter into the agreement, and that it has the rights to the asset and its associated intellectual property, such as trade names used by the Club. But the buyer will want to minimize a greater amount of its risk by forcing the seller to "rep" more. For example, the buyer will want to secure a rep from the seller that there is no litigation, existing or pending, against the seller or its business, except for what may be listed in a separate schedule attached to the agreement. The seller will respond by asking to place a knowledge qualifier in the term. That is, the seller wants to warrant only to what it actually knows as an entity. The buyer will respond by asking for a "constructive knowledge" qualifier, which usually means that if a certain set of individuals at a particular level of the hierarchy in the organization is aware of a litigation matter pending or about to be filed against the seller, it would need to be disclosed.

The buyer will also want to know that the seller is not party to any "material" or "significant" agreements except for what may be listed on a separate schedule. Often, the definition of "materiality" will be heavily negotiated, and the parties may even choose to leave the definition intentionally vague, subscribing to the "you know it when you see it" mindset (and preserving the ability to litigate over the term later). Other times, materiality will be defined in terms of a certain percentage of the agreement. Lastly, sometimes the parties will define it as an amount that would alter the behavior of a reasonably prudent buyer or seller.

Sometimes, the buyer will also make a list of fundamental representations. If these representations are not true at any point, even after the closing date, the buyer will want the ability to walk away from the deal. For example, if the seller does not actually have the rights to the assets it claims to have, no matter when the buyer discovers it, the buyer will not own what it believes to own, so it will want the full purchase price refunded.

The ZOPA will likely be an agreement that has the seller providing a more robust set of representations and warranties than the buyer. The buyer will want to be sure that it is getting exactly what it is paying for, so the seller typically will have to provide the representations and warranties listed above, as well as warrant that there is no pending litigation (subject to a knowledge qualifier), that its tax returns have been submitted on time and are materially correct, and that it has no employees outside of what is listed on a schedule. In turn, the buyer will represent that it is the entity it claims to be, that it is authorized to enter into the transaction, and that it is qualified to own and operate the Club under the rules of the relevant sports league organization.

B. INDEMNIFICATION

Indemnification is the "yang" to the representations' and warranties' "yin." The two provisions are often negotiated together because they can operate in inverse relationship to each other. For example, if the buyer asks for a more robust set of representations and warranties from the seller, the seller may allow it, but will then diminish the amount of recovery the buyer may seek in indemnification. The seller will also usually limit the total indemnification amount to a "cap"—usually a percentage of the purchase price or to the amount held in escrow, if the parties agree to withhold a certain percentage of the purchase price in escrow. Conversely, should the seller not budge on certain representations and warranties, the buyer will request a larger indemnification package. The parties will also haggle over how long the indemnification period lasts, looking at comparable deal studies to help determine what seems appropriate. The buyer will want a long indemnification period, while the seller will want as truncated a period as possible.

The parties will also argue over the type of indemnification triggers. For example, as described earlier in the text, the parties will have to choose whether to use a basket provision, which means that if claims, individually or in the aggregate, are underneath a designated amount (the "basket"), they will not be counted toward the overall indemnification award. If the parties choose to employ a basket, they must next decide whether it will be a "tipping basket" or a "deductible basket." To refresh, in a deductible basket, the buyer will receive only the amount in excess of the threshold. But in a tipping basket, once the amount exceeds the basket threshold, the indemnified party receives the entire amount. Clearly, the buyer would prefer a tipping basket, while the seller would prefer a deductible basket. The indemnification package will also cover third-party claims, providing a process for notice from the protected party to the indemnifying party requiring the indemnifying party to cover the claim, while also allowing the protected party to retain co-counsel in the matter.

The ZOPA will likely involve a medium-length indemnification period for the majority of the representations and warranties. However, with respect to fundamental representations and warranties, the buyer will most likely insist on the period extending further, if not indefinitely. The exact indemnification package, more so than other provisions, are more subject to each party's relative leverage. In all likelihood, the indemnification will be capped to some percentage of the agreement, with some sort of basket provision being implemented. Third-party claims will be covered, and the buyer will probably need to agree that it cannot bring any claims based on a breach or inaccuracy if the buyer had knowledge of such breach or inaccuracy prior to the closing date. Outside of injunctive relief, the parties will likely agree that the indemnification provision constitutes the exclusive remedy with respect to the purchase agreement.

C. CONDITIONS PRECEDENT TO CLOSING

Before the date of closing, both parties must satisfy a negotiated set of conditions. The obligations of a party are subject to the other party satisfying its conditions. Of course, the parties may stipulate that a party may unilaterally waive, modify, or extend one of the other party's obligations as necessary. Usually, the buyer will include a longer list of requests for the seller than the seller will for the buyer, so the seller must meet more conditions than the buyer. This balance is skewed in favor of the buyer because the buyer bears a large financial risk through the deal, so it will try to mitigate as much other risk as it can. The seller understands this and will likely agree to many of the buyer's terms, provided they are reasonable.

For example, the buyer will want to ensure that the seller's representations and warranties will be true not only on the day when made, but also on the date of closing—this is called "bringing down" the representations and warranties. The seller will likely want a materiality qualifier in this term, as it probably cannot guarantee complete accuracy, and it will not want to lose the deal over a small discrepancy, such as a broken window or an incorrect number of office supplies. The buyer will also want the seller to represent that no litigation is pending against it. Again, the seller will look to add both a materiality qualifier and a knowledge qualifier. The buyer will also want the seller to possess all the relevant league consents and to assert that no material adverse changes in its business have occurred between the date of the agreement and the date of closing. The buyer will also want to ensure that no destruction or damage has occurred to any asset covered by the agreement. Again, the buyer will want materiality qualifiers on these, if not a definition of material damage as damage above a certain dollar amount not covered by insurance.

The seller will want far less than the buyer. Just like the buyer, though, the seller will want to ensure that the buyer's representations and warranties are brought down at closing. The buyer should also obtain the relevant league approvals on its end and have secured proper financing to fulfill its financial obligations under the agreement. Both parties should also place its required amount in the escrow account to secure its respective obligations under the agreement. A reasonable ZOPA involves some combination of the terms mentioned in this section, with varying degrees of materiality and knowledge qualifiers depending on the parties' respective leverage.

D. DELIVERIES AT CLOSING

Provided that all of the pre-closing conditions are met, the parties shall close the agreement on a specified date. At the closing, each party delivers documents and instruments necessary to effectuate different parts of the agreement. For example, both the buyer and seller will need to bring the proper documents pertaining to the bill of sale, escrow agreement, and assignment of the team to the buyer. Each party will need to procure a certificate of compliance that its pre-closing representations and warranties are true, and a certificate of good standing issued by the state in which it operates as an entity.

Additionally, the buyer will be required to furnish to the seller the portion of the purchase price that is not held in escrow (if the parties have chosen to use an escrow account). The buyer will also require an impartial legal opinion regarding the seller's due authorization and its ability to perform its obligations under the agreement. While this portion of the agreement may skew slightly in favor of the buyer, the seller will likely agree to many of the buyer's proposed terms, and those articulated here are all well within the ZOPA.

E. CONDUCT OF BUSINESS PENDING CLOSING

The buyer will most likely want to require some sort of provision that seeks to control the seller in how it conducts its business between the signing date and the closing date. The buyer wants to ensure that the asset it agrees to purchase is as identical as possible to the one it receives at closing. The buyer will seek to restrict the ability of the seller to enter into new contracts with employees, suppliers, etc. It will also try to require the seller to help the buyer obtain the necessary consents and approvals from third parties to effectuate the deal. In turn, the seller will want to operate its business with minimal encumbrances.

The ZOPA will likely involve the seller agreeing to operate its business in a normal and ordinary course. Sometimes it will be required to not enter into any material new contracts without prior approval by the buyer. Likewise, the agreement may specify that the seller cannot enter into multi-year agreements without first consulting the buyer. The seller will also agree to continue operating its business in compliance with relevant city, state, and federal regulations and any league bylaws.

F. ARBITRATION/DISPUTE RESOLUTION

As discussed in the Lease Agreement chapter, alternative dispute resolution is becoming more prevalent in the sports industry and can help tame costs, unpredictability, and time that come with litigation.

The buyer and seller will likely agree on a dispute resolution process that treats both sides reciprocally. In order to avoid costly and protracted litigation, the parties will likely agree that any claim arising out of a dispute regarding the agreement will go through the designated process. That process can be mediation, mediation followed by arbitration, simultaneous mediation and arbitration, or arbitration alone. In most purchase agreements, the parties will usually agree to arbitration. Because of their prevalence and the fact that parties are familiar with them, they will likely agree to use the arbitration rules of the American Arbitration Association, with the dispute heard and decided in its closest local branch office. To cabin the costs of arbitration, the parties will likely agree to rules limiting discovery, number of depositions, and the calling of witnesses (leaving to the arbitrator discretion to allow appropriate additional discovery for good cause shown).

Naturally, each party would prefer to select the arbitrator, but they will both agree to a process that will give them both a say in determining who the third-party neutral is who hears their arbitration. Two methods predominate. First, each party could select one arbitrator, and the two selected arbitrators then decide upon the third arbitrator, to comprise an arbitration panel. Second, the parties may also create a list of acceptable arbitrators (or receive such a list from the AAA), and each side gets a set number of "strikes," or vetoes, until an arbitrator is selected. This approach is similar to a jury selection.

As stated above, one of the reasons the parties want to avoid litigation is to avoid dealing with a jury, and with it the potential for a wild damages award. So in order to further reduce liability uncertainty, the parties will usually stipulate that the arbitrator will only have the authority to award actual damages (and explicitly disclaim the arbitrator's authority to award punitive, consequential, and incidental damages). The arbitrator may still, however, usually award costs and attorneys' fees to one party at the arbitrator's discretion. Usually, this is limited to instances in which the cause of action lacks merit or is maintained in bad faith, and the good faith actor will be able to recover all of its costs from the bad faith actor.

Absent the arbitrator awarding costs, each party will agree to bear its own costs and split the necessary administrative fees to conduct the arbitration. To not infringe on the parties' rights outside of arbitration, the two sides usually will also stipulate that nothing within the arbitration clause shall prohibit either party from seeking equitable relief, such as an injunction or specific performance. In addition, the agreement will probably specify that certain minor breaches (that is, those beneath a certain dollar amount) will not be subject to arbitration. Instead, if they are left uncured for a designated period, such breaches will result in only a nominal fee award.

One of the more important advantages of arbitration is confidentiality. Given the larger confidentiality provisions in a buy-sell agreement, the parties will also want to keep nearly everything about the proceedings confidential, including the award. Generally, parties will be wary that if the award is made public, it will be used as a precedent against one or both of the parties in the future. Sometimes, even the existence of the arbitration proceeding is subject to the confidentiality provision. The parties will usually agree to keep the entire proceedings confidential.

G. SURVIVAL

As alluded to in the beginning chapter of this text, parties sometimes will want particular terms to remain effective, or survive, beyond the termination of the agreement. Oftentimes such a survival provision is as simple as one sentence articulating that specific provisions will survive termination or expiration. In an asset purchase agreement, the parties will likely want the indemnification and limitation of liability provisions to survive—the buyer because it wants as full of an indemnification package as it can get, and the seller because it will want the indemnification package to represent the totality of its potential future liability.

Both parties will also agree that any confidentiality provisions will survive the expiration of the agreement. The buyer will want a certain set of representations and warranties to extend past the agreement—likely the fundamental representations and warranties—and the seller will likely agree. Each of these provisions is likely to be within the parties' ZOPA.

H. MISCELLANEOUS

The asset purchase agreement is a complicated, and the above clauses represent only some of the most important clauses. There are two other prominent clauses in such an agreement. First, both parties should carry premises liability insurance, and the agreement should mandate such an arrangement. For more information on this clause, see the Premises Liability Study Guide, incorporated into Chapter 2 of this text. Second, each party will have covenants it must satisfy under the agreement. Usually, these covenants are prospective assurances, as opposed to representations and warranties, which are usually assurances of something contemporaneously with the agreement. Such covenants may include league approvals that occur after closing, additional funds required to be transferred between the parties, and the transfer of intellectual property ownership.

HYPOTHETICAL EXERCISE

Negotiating and Drafting a Buy-Sell Asset Purchase Agreement Between a Prospective Buyers' Group and the Current Owners of a Minor League Baseball Franchise

A. Imagine that the current owners of the Charlotte Knights have decided to sell their entire interest in the team and are negotiating the asset purchase agreement between the team and an ownership group led by Michael Jordan for the rights of ownership to the team.

B. How you would negotiate and draft the following clauses:

1. <u>Representations and Warranties</u>

   a. What will the buyer's representations and warranties consist of? How many? For how long will the buyer be required to ensure these are accurate?

   b. What will the seller's representations and warranties consist of? Will the buyer require a subset to be categorized as "Fundamental Representations and Warranties"? If so, which ones? For how long will the seller need to ensure its representations and warranties are accurate?

c. What sort of materiality and knowledge qualifiers will each side agree to in the other's representations and warranties?

2. Indemnification

a. How long will the indemnification period last? Will it be the same for all representations and warranties?

b. Will there be a cap on the amount that the indemnified party may seek? What will it be?

c. Will the agreement contain a basket provision? Tipping, or deductible?

d. Will third-party claims be covered? What rights will the indemnified party have vis-à-vis the indemnifying party in responding to such claims?

e. Is this indemnification package the exclusive and total remedy available to the indemnified parties? Is a party allowed to seek injunctive relief?

f. Will an indemnification award be netted against any insurance proceeds it receives under any policies it maintains?

g. Does the buyer's actual knowledge of a material breach or defect impact its ability to bring a claim? Constructive knowledge?

3. Conditions Precedent to Closing

a. What conditions must the seller satisfy before closing? Will it just need to assure the buyer its representations and warranties are still true on the date of closing? How true? Must it assert that no litigation is pending?

b. What sorts of changes in the seller's business will be acceptable to the buyer? How much damage, and to what assets, will the buyer be willing to bear?

c. What conditions must the buyer satisfy before closing? What sorts of consents must it procure? Must it also bring down its representations and warranties?

d. What sort of materiality and knowledge qualifiers will be used? On what terms?

4. Deliveries at Closing

a. What will the seller be responsible for delivering on the date of closing? The buyer?

b. Will the parties use an escrow account to hold a certain amount of the purchase price? What portion of the purchase price will the buyer be responsible for upon closing?

5. Conduct of Business Pending Closing

a. What sort of discretion will the buyer have with respect to operating its business in between signing and closing?

b. Consider what sort of contracts the seller may be allowed to enter into, if any, during the pre-closing period.

c. What, if any, role does the buyer have in running the business and the seller's business decisions before closing?

7. Arbitration/Dispute Resolution

a. Will the parties choose to use arbitration, mediation, both, or neither?

b. If the parties opt for arbitration, how will an arbitrator be selected? What rules will govern the arbitration proceedings?

c. What level of confidentiality will govern the arbitration proceedings?

d. What sort of notice will be deemed sufficient to serve on a party to the agreement?

e. How will costs be allocated? What sort of discretion does the arbitrator (or arbitral panel) have on the type of award? May the parties also seek injunctive relief even while arbitration is pending?

8. Survival

a. What provisions will survive termination/ expiration of the deal? Why?

Please see the "Exemplar" response in the Teacher's Manual that accompanies this book.

Conclusion

While this book has focused on the major agreements that a sports entity will be concerned with, it would be impossible to cover all the potential agreement possibilities. Agreements such as product merchandising, non-profit promotions (such as the NFL's breast cancer awareness campaign), and national broadcasting agreements are beyond the scope of this book because they may interrelate to agreements entered into by the league and/or by the players' unions themselves. However, the negotiating, drafting, and analyzing skills obtained from the areas of focus in this book can apply to any additional agreements the sports entity may enter into.

Additionally, these skills can be applied outside the "sports law" arena, because they are equally important to contract drafting in general. Throughout the entire negotiating and drafting process, it is of utmost importance to keep the client's priorities in focus, while remaining flexible enough to successfully negotiate an "execution ready, litigation proof" agreement where both parties walk away satisfied that their clients' most important strategic priorities have been accomplished.

For more specialized and in-depth information relating to the topics discussed in this book, please further read Appendix B, A Supplement to "Negotiating and Drafting Sports Venue Agreements," by Peter A. Carfagna.

For professors teaching Sports Law courses with this book, a Course Overview Presentation and exemplar assignments for each assignment can be found in A Teaching Manual to "Negotiating and Drafting Sports Venue Agreements," by Peter A. Carfagna.

For up-to-date information related to the topics discussed throughout this book, please periodically review the following publications: Sports Litigation Alert, Sports Law Blog, Sports Agent Blog, SportsBusiness Journal, and Sports Sponsorship Insider. It is additionally recommended to become a member of the Sports Lawyers Association.

Appendix A

SAMPLE SPORTS VENUE AGREEMENTS: (1) SPORTS FACILITIES MANAGEMENT AGREEMENT; (2) SPORTS VENUE MARKETING AGREEMENT; (3) SPORTS VENUE CONCESSIONS AGREEMENT

This book was written as if the students were drafting the various agreements addressed herein for the owner/operator of a sports venue. However, in some cases, the owner of the team or facility may choose to hire a third party to manage the facility, market the venue, or handle the concessions.

Attached are three examples of such agreements: (1) a sports venue facilities management agreement (Exhibit 1); (2) a sports venue marketing agreement (Exhibit 2); and (3) a sports venue concessions agreement (Exhibit 3).

Please use these Sample Agreements as "templates," only, from which individualized Agreements can be negotiated and drafted to satisfy your clients' major business objectives, while also making them as "litigation proof" as possible, per usual.

EXHIBIT 1

MANAGEMENT AGREEMENT

between

XYZ STATE-OPERATED ENTITY

and

MANAGEMENT COMPANY

Effective as of _______, 20___

TABLE OF CONTENTS

MANAGEMENT AGREEMENT

This Management Agreement (this "Agreement") is made as of the __ day of ___, 20__ ("Effective Date"), by and between XYZ State-Operated Entity in the State of ______, with an office located at ________________________________ ("XYZ"), and Management Company, LP, a ______ limited partnership, with an office located at ________________________________ ("Manager").

RECITALS

WHEREAS, XYZ Entity owns a multi-purpose sports and entertainment arena known as the _____________ Arena and an attached conference center known as the ____________ Center, located in [City, State] (collectively, the "Facility"); and

WHEREAS, XYZ desires to engage Manager to manage and operate the Facility on behalf and for the benefit of XYZ, and Manager desires to accept such engagement, pursuant to the terms and conditions contained herein; and

NOW THEREFORE, for and in consideration of the foregoing, the mutual covenants and promises hereinafter set forth and other good and valuable consideration, the receipt and sufficiency of which is hereby acknowledged, the parties, intending to be legally bound, hereby agree as follows:

ARTICLE I
DEFINITIONS

Section 1.1 Definitions. For purposes of this Agreement, the following terms have the meanings referred to in this Section:

Affiliate: A person or company that directly or indirectly, through one or more intermediaries, controls or is controlled by, or is under common control with, a specified person or company.

Agreement: The "Agreement" shall mean this Management Agreement, together with all exhibits attached hereto (each of which are incorporated herein as an integral part of this Agreement).

Capital Expenditures: All expenditures for building additions, alterations, repairs, or improvements and for purchases of additional or replacement furniture, machinery, or equipment, where the cost of such expenditure is greater than [$xxx] and the depreciable life of the applicable item, according to generally accepted accounting principles, is in excess of five (5) years.

Commercial Rights: Naming rights, pouring rights, advertising, sponsorships, the branding of food and beverage products for resale, premium seating (including suites, club seats and party suites), and memorial gifts at or with respect to the Facility and owned or controlled by XYZ; provided however that all of Manager's activities (if any) with respect to memorial gifts shall be developed and implemented under supervision and direction of the XYZ Designated Office.

Concession Agreements: Vendor, concessions and merchandising agreements, user/rental agreements, booking commitments, licenses, and all other contracts or agreements generating revenue for the Facility and entered into in the ordinary course of operating the Facility.

[Concessionaire] Concession Agreement: The Food and Beverage Agreement to be entered into by XYZ and [Concessionaire Service] L.P. ("Concessionaire"), under which Concessionaire will provide concessions and catering services at the Facility.

Consumer Price Index: The "Consumer Price Index" (or "CPI") for the local [City] area, as published by the United States Department of Labor, Bureau of Labor Statistics or such other successor or similar index.

[Disadvantaged Business Enterprise]: A business designated as a "DBE" by local, state, or federal ordinance, including "Minority-owned Business Enterprises" ("MBE"s) and "Women-owned Business Enterprises" ("WBE").

Effective Date: "Effective Date" shall have the meaning ascribed to such term in the opening paragraph of this Agreement.

Emergency Repair: The repair of a condition which, if not performed immediately, creates an imminent danger to persons or property and/or an unsafe condition at the Facility threatening persons or property.

Event Account: A separate interest-bearing account in the name of XYZ and under XYZ's Federal ID number in a local qualified public depository, to be designated by XYZ, where advance ticket sale revenue is to be deposited by Manager.

Event of Force Majeure: An act of God, fire, earthquake, hurricane, flood, riot, civil commotion, terrorist act, terrorist threat, storm, washout, wind, lightning, landslide, explosion, epidemic, inability to obtain materials or supplies, accident to machinery or equipment, any law, ordinance, rule, regulation, act of government or government instrumentality (whether federal, state or local) or order of any public or military authority stemming from (i) the existence of economic or energy controls, (ii) hostilities or war, (iii) a labor dispute which results in a strike or work stoppage affecting the

Facility or services described in this Agreement, or (iv) any other cause or occurrence outside the reasonable control of the party claiming an inability to perform and which by the exercise of due diligence could not be reasonably prevented or overcome, provided that such party shall not be required to accede to the demands of any strike or labor dispute.

Existing Contracts: Service Contracts, Concession Agreements, Marketing Agreements, ticketing agreements, and other agreements relating to the marketing and the day-to-day operation of the Facility existing as of the Effective Date, as set forth on Exhibit B attached hereto.

Facility: The "Facility" shall have the meaning ascribed to such term in the Recitals to this Agreement, and shall be deemed to include the entire arena complex, including but not limited to the arena, suites, locker rooms, meeting rooms, box office, common areas, lobby areas, executive and other offices, storage and utility facilities, as well as the entire conference center complex, including the conference pavilion, auxiliary gymnasium, office space, conference rooms, atrium, XYZ Lounge, and the entrances, ground, and sidewalks (excluding any parking areas) immediately surrounding the Facility and adjacent thereto.

Facility Booking Policy: The document to be developed by XYZ which shall contain detailed policies and procedures to be implemented by Manager in connection with scheduling events at the Facility.

FF & E: Furniture, fixtures, and equipment currently used or to be procured for use at the Facility.

Fixed Management Fee: The fixed monthly fee XYZ shall pay to Manager under this Agreement, as more fully described in Section 3.1 of this Agreement.

General Manager: The employee of Manager acting as the full-time on-site general manager of the Facility.

Incentive Benchmark: The term "Incentive Benchmark" shall have the meaning ascribed to such term in Section 3.2 of this Agreement.

Incentive Fee: The contingent fee XYZ shall pay to Manager under this Agreement, if earned, as more fully described in Section 3.2 below.

Laws: Federal, state, local, and municipal laws, statutes, rules, regulations, and ordinances.

Management-Level Employees: The General Manager, Assistant General Manager, Business Manager (or employees with different titles performing similar functions), and any department head employed by Manager to perform services at the Facility (including employees performing the functions of the Director of Operations, Director of Sales and Marketing, Director of Security, Finance Director and Event Manager).

Manager: The term "Manager" means the company so listed in the Recitals to this Agreement.

Manager Financial Information: All information kept or required to be kept by law regarding the financial status and performance of Manager for services provided to XYZ by Manager at the Facility.

Manager's Office Space: The office space at the Facility designated by XYZ for use by Manager.

[Marketing Company] Marketing Agreement: The Marketing and Media Rights Agreement to be entered into by XYZ and [Marketing Company] Marketing, Inc. ("[Marketing Company]"), under which Marketing Company, as agent for XYZ, will provide to XYZ certain marketing and media services as more particularly described therein.

Marketing Plan: A plan for the advertising and promotion of the Facility and Facility events, which plan will be developed and implemented in conjunction with the [Marketing Company] Marketing Agreement (as defined above), and which plan may contain but not be limited to the following elements: (i) market research, (ii) market position, (iii) marketing objectives, (iv) marketing strategies, (v) booking priorities, (vi) targeted events—local, regional, national, and international, (vii) targeted meetings, conventions and trade shows, (viii) industry advertising campaign, (ix) internal and external support staff, (x) advertising opportunities at the local, regional and national level, (xi) attendance at various trade shows, conventions and seminars, (xii) incentive formulas for multiple event presenters, (xiii) suite and club seat sales, (xiv) merchandising and retail, (xv) food and beverage, (xvi) a plan regarding national, regional and local public relations and media relations, (xvii) development of an in-house advertising agency, and (xviii) policies regarding the use of trade/barter.

Operating Account: A separate interest-bearing account in the name of XYZ and under XYZ's Federal ID number in a local qualified public depository, to be designated by XYZ, where Revenue is deposited and from which Operating Expenses are paid.

Operating Budget: A line item budget for the Facility that includes a projection of Revenues and Operating Expenses, presented on a monthly and annual basis.

Operating Expenses: Expenses incurred by Manager in connection with its operation, promotion, maintenance and management of the Facility, including but not limited to the following: (i) wages, salaries, employee benefits, and bonus costs of Manager's employees engaged in providing services at the Facility; provided however that wages, salaries, employee benefits, and bonuses of corporate office employees, including corporate office administrative, executive, and management officers, shall not qualify as Operating Expenses, (ii) cost of operating supplies, including general office supplies, (iii) advertising, marketing, group sales, and public relations costs, (iv) cleaning expenses, (v) data processing costs, (vi) the Fixed Management Fee, (vii) printing and stationary costs, (viii) postage and freight costs, provided however that express delivery or overnight courier charges of any type will qualify as Operating Expenses only if approved by XYZ in writing and in advance, (ix) equipment rental costs, (x) repairs that do not exceed _______ dollars ($xxx), maintenance, and equipment servicing, not including expenses relating to performing capital improvements or repairs; and provided however that repairs necessary as the result of the negligent or intentional acts or omissions of Manager or Manager's employees shall not qualify as Operating Expenses, (xi) security expenses, (xii) telephone and communication charges, (xiii) travel expenses of Manager's employees, (xiv) cost of employee uniforms and identification, (xv) exterminator, snow and trash removal costs, if applicable (xvi) computer, software, hardware, and training costs, (xvii) parking expenses related to Manager's marketing and ticket sales activities, provided that parking expenses for Manager's employees shall not qualify as an allowable parking expense, (xviii) utility expenses, (xix) office expenses, (xx) insurance costs, including but not limited to personal property, liability, and worker's compensation insurance, (xxi) commissions and all other fees payable to third parties, (xxii) costs incurred by Manager to settle or defend claims asserted against Manager arising out of its operations of the Facility, provided, however, that such costs shall qualify as Operating Expenses only if it is determined by a court of competent jurisdiction that such costs are not the result of negligent or intentional acts or omissions of Manager, (xxiii) costs incurred under Service Contracts and other agreements relating to Facility operations, (xxvi) Taxes (not including any income taxes of Manager), (xxv) Incentive Fee (if any), and (xxvi) Transition Costs. The term "Operating Expenses" does not include the following: (a) debt service on the Facility, (b) Capital Expenditures, (c) accounting expenses incurred by Manager including costs of producing financial reports, (d) Manager's corporate office management costs such as general management overhead, transportation of management personnel, and any other indirect management costs as related to this Agreement, (e) monies or other property, lost or stolen, either on or off XYZ premises, (f) inventory interest or carrying cost, (g) excessive overtime pay (limits to be determined in consultation with XYZ), (h) legal expenses, (i) relocation expenses of any of Manager's employees, (j) interest charges on any loans incurred by Manager, unless specifically authorized by XYZ, (k) modem/TI/internet charges and any extra telephone lines, (*l*) memberships in local or national groups of any type, (m) costs for any Manager employee to attend seminars or conferences of any type, unless specifically approved by XYZ, (n) travel expenses of all personnel who hold a position senior to General Manager, (o) Manager's personal use of the Facility, and (p) any expense not expressly identified in the Operating Budget and approved by XYZ except as otherwise provided herein.

Operating Year: Each twelve (12) month period during the Term, commencing on _______ and ending on _______ of the following year.

Operations Manual: The document to be developed by Manager which shall contain terms regarding the management and operation of the Facility, including detailed policies and procedures to be implemented in operating the Facility, as agreed upon by both XYZ and the Manager.

Other Facilities: _______ Hall, _______ Club, and _______ Center collectively.

Performance Reports: The reports prepared by Manager and provided to XYZ on an annual basis, which shall include, without limitation, financial information, facility information, staffing changes or issues, operational issues, and contributions made to the [XYZ fund].

Quality Operating Standard: means the standard of quality or performance with respect to the ongoing maintenance, operation and management provided at the following sports venue arenas: (i) the _______________ Center in [City, State], (ii) the _______________ Center in [City, State], (iii) the _______________ Center in [City, State], (iv) the _______________ Center in [City, State], (v) the _______________ Center in [City, State], and (vi) the _______________ Center in [City, State]. In the event that two (2) of the arenas referenced above shall be closed or shall permanently cease to host [Sport/Sports] Games or shall, as generally reputed within the arena industry, cease to be maintained and operated in accordance with the standards of service and quality generally accepted within the arena industry for first class arenas, then (a) such arena or arenas shall be deleted from the list set forth in the foregoing sentence and (b) XYZ and Manager shall agree upon the substitution of another arena or arenas to replace the deleted arena or arenas, with appropriate adjustments to reflect newer building and technology than that possessed by the Facility. In applying the Quality Operating Standard to maintenance, operation, management and customer service issues, due consideration shall be given to [City]'s unique competitive market conditions, climate, topography, and the age of the Facility.

Revenue: All revenues generated by Manager's operation of the Facility, including but not limited to event ticket proceeds income, rental and license fee income, merchandise income, gross food and beverage income, gross income from any sale of Commercial Rights, gross service income, equipment rental fees, box office income, and miscellaneous operating income, but shall not include event ticket proceeds held by Manager in trust for a third party and paid to such third party.

RFP #123456: The Request for Proposals for Management and Operation of the Facility and/or Concessions and Catering at the Facility and/or Marketing and Media Rights for XYZ, issued on ________, 20__.

Service Contracts: Agreements for services to be provided in connection with the operation of the Facility, including without limitation agreements for computer support services, purchasing services, engineering services, fuel, extermination, elevators, fire control panel and other safety equipment, snow removal, ticketing, web development and maintenance, general maintenance, telephone service, staffing personnel including guards, ushers and ticket takes, and other services which are deemed by Manager to be either necessary or useful in operating the Facility, subject to existing agreements for the provision of such services.

Standard Contract Provisions: The provisions set forth on Exhibit F hereto, which are required to be included in every contract entered into by Manager as agent for XYZ pursuant to this Agreement. The Standard Contract Provisions may be modified from time to time by XYZ if determined to be necessary by XYZ's legal counsel. Any contract entered into by Manager, as agent for XYZ pursuant to this Agreement, which does not contain the Standard Contract Provisions shall, at XYZ's option and in XYZ's sole discretion, be void *ab initio* and shall not be enforceable against XYZ.

Taxes: Any and all governmental assessments, franchise fees, excises, license and permit fees, levies, charges and taxes, of every kind and nature whatsoever, which at any time during the Term may be assessed, levied, or imposed on, or become due and payable out of or in respect of, (i) activities conducted on behalf of XYZ at the Facility, including without limitation the sale of concessions, the sale of tickets, and the performance of events (such as any applicable sales and/or admissions taxes, use taxes, excise taxes, occupancy taxes, employment taxes, and withholding taxes), or (ii) any payments received from any holders of a leasehold interest or license in or to the Facility, from any guests, or from any others using or occupying all or any part of the Facility.

Term: The term "Term" shall have the meaning ascribed to such term in Section 4.1 of this Agreement.

Transition Costs: The term "Transition Costs" shall have the meaning ascribed to such term in Section 7.1 of this Agreement.

XYZ: The term "XYZ" shall have the meaning ascribed to such term in the Recitals to this Agreement.

XYZ's Contract Administrator: The term "XYZ's Contract Administrator" shall mean XYZ's Assistant Vice President of Support Services or such other individual as XYZ's President, General Counsel, Vice President of Business Affairs and Finance, or Vice President of [Department] shall designate.

XYZ Police Dispatcher: The term "XYZ Police Dispatcher" shall mean the person who is employed by XYZ and is designated by XYZ as the police dispatcher for XYZ's property.

ARTICLE 2
SCOPE OF SERVICES

Section 2.1 Engagement.

(a) XYZ hereby engages Manager during the Term to act as the sole and exclusive manager and operator of the Facility, subject to and as more fully described in this Agreement and, in connection therewith, to perform the services described in Exhibit A attached hereto.

(b) Manager hereby accepts such engagement, and shall perform the services described herein, subject to the limitations expressly set forth in this Agreement and in the Operations Manual. In performing its duties hereunder, Manager shall maintain, operate and manage the Facility in accordance with the Quality Operating Standard.

(c) In addition to the services set forth on Exhibit A hereto, Manager shall use reasonable commercial efforts to assist XYZ in its booking of the Other Facilities with non-XYZ events, provided that Manager shall not be obligated to book any event in the Other Facilities that can be booked in the Facility instead. Any events booked in the Other Facilities shall be subject to the prior written approval of XYZ. Manager shall have no obligations with respect to the Other Facilities or any events booked at the Other Facilities (including any events booked by Manager at such facilities), other than as specifically stated in this paragraph. Appropriate costs associated with Manager's obligations under this paragraph shall not be considered Operating Expenses, but shall be reimbursed to Manager by XYZ.

Section 2.2 Limitations on Manager's Duties. Manager's obligations under this Agreement are contingent upon and subject to XYZ making available, in a timely fashion, the funds budgeted for and/or reasonably required by Manager to carry out such obligations during the Term. Manager shall not be considered to be in breach or default of this Agreement, and shall have no liability to XYZ or any other party, in the event Manager does not perform any of its obligations hereunder due to failure by XYZ to timely provide such funds.

ARTICLE 3
COMPENSATION

Section 3.1 Fixed Management Fee. [AMOUNTS TO BE DETERMINED] In consideration of Manager's performance of its services hereunder, XYZ shall pay Manager a Fixed Management Fee. Beginning on the Effective Date and continuing through the first (1st) Operating Year, the Fixed Management Fee shall be _______ dollars ($xxx) per month. Beginning in the second (2nd) Operating Year, the Fixed Management Fee shall be _______ dollars ($xxx) per month, plus the percentage increase in the Consumer Price Index over the previous twelve (12) month period (i.e., the difference, expressed as a percentage, between the value of the CPI published most recently prior to the commencement of the preceding Operating Year and the value of the CPI published most recently prior to the commencement of the Operating Year for which the CPI adjustment will apply); provided, the percentage increase during the Term hereof or any extension shall not exceed a total of _______ percent (x%). Beginning in the third (3rd) Operating Year, the Fixed Management Fee shall be increased over the Fixed Management Fee from the previous Operating Year in accordance with the percentage increase in the Consumer Price Index over the previous twelve (12) month period Year. The first monthly payment of the Fixed Management Fee shall be payable to Manager on or within ___ days after the Effective Date [XYZ NOT PERMITTED TO MAKE ADVANCE PAYMENTS], and shall be payable on the first (1st) day of each month thereafter (prorated as necessary for any partial months). Manager shall submit monthly invoices to XYZ and XYZ shall promptly remit payment to Manager for the Fixed Management Fee upon receipt of each monthly invoice.

(a) The parties acknowledge that their agreement to the amount of the Fixed Management Fee, as set forth above, is contingent upon XYZ engaging both Concessionaire to perform food and beverages services at the Facility, and Ticketing Company, L.P. ("Ticketing Company") to perform ticketing services at the Facility, on terms mutually acceptable to XYZ and such parties, for a term of at least [X] (x) years. In the event one of either Concessionaire or Ticketing Company (for reasons other than the decision of Concessionaire or Ticketing Company not to execute an agreement with XYZ that contains material terms of RFP #123456) is not engaged by XYZ to provide such services for such term, the Fixed Management Fee shall increase by _______ dollars ($xxx) per Operating Year, and in the event neither Concessionaire nor Ticketing Company (for reasons other than the decision by Concessionaire nor Ticketing Company not to execute an agreement with XYZ that contains material terms of RFP #123456) are engaged by XYZ to provide such services for such term, the Fixed Management Fee shall increase by _______ dollars ($xxx) per Operating Year.

Section 3.2 Incentive Fee. In addition to the Fixed Management Fee, Manager shall be entitled to receive an Incentive Fee each full or partial Operating Year of the Term, except that for the first (1st) Operating Year Manager shall only be entitled to an Incentive Fee pursuant to Section 3.2(b) hereinbelow. For the second (2nd) Operating Year and each full or partial Operating Year of the Term thereafter, the Incentive Fee shall be made up of both the two (2) components, listed below as follows:

(a) Bottom-Line Component. The Incentive Fee shall, in part, be equal to [X] (x%) of improvement over a mutually agreed net profit/loss number (the "Incentive Benchmark") for the Facility. The parties shall work together in good faith to develop the Incentive Benchmark, and shall use reasonable best efforts to establish such mutually agreed Incentive Benchmark no later than _______, 20__. Once established, the Incentive Benchmark shall remain unchanged throughout the Term. In the event that despite their best efforts, the parties are unable to agree on an Incentive Benchmark by _______, 20__, either party may submit such matter to a mutually agreed independent third party mediator. The mediator must be an individual with experience in the facility management industry. The cost of such mediator shall be shared 50/50 by the parties.

(b) [Sports] Ticket Sales Component. In addition to the Bottom Line Component of the Incentive Fee as described in 3.2(a) above, Manager shall also be entitled to earn as additional Incentive Fee _______ percent (x%) of any increase each Operating Year in annual gross ticket sales actually received by XYZ (as measured by annual gross ticket sale funds actually received) to XYZ's [sport(s)] games at the Facility over a benchmark of _______ dollars ($xxx).

The Incentive Fee shall be paid to Manager no later than ninety (90) days following the end of each Operating Year. The parties further agree that, in the event this Agreement is terminated, for any reason, prior to the end of an Operating Year, the Incentive Fee shall be prorated accordingly.

ARTICLE 4
TERM; TERMINATION

Section 4.1 Term. Unless sooner terminated, this Agreement shall be in force and effective from the Effective Date through _______, 20__ and any renewal thereafter (the "Term"). Unless this Agreement is terminated before its normal expiration date and/or in accordance with the provisions hereof, XYZ shall have ___ (x) consecutive options (individually an "Option" and collectively the "Options") to extend this Agreement for a period of ___ years per Option. XYZ shall exercise an Option by providing written notice to Manager within 120 days prior to the expiration of the then-current Term.

Section 4.2 Termination. This Agreement may be terminated:

(a) subject to Section 4.3(a) below, by XYZ upon ___ (x) days written notice to Manager in the event of a permanent closure of the Facility, the fact of which is certified by XYZ in writing to Manager,

(b) by either party upon thirty (30) days written notice, if the other party fails to perform or comply with any of the material terms, covenants, agreements or conditions hereof, and such failure is not cured during such thirty (30) day notification period, provided, however, if such failure cannot reasonably be cured within such thirty (30) day period, then a longer period of time shall be afforded to cure such breach, up to a total of ninety (90) days, provided that the party in default is diligently seeking a cure and the non-defaulting party is not irreparably harmed by the extension of the cure period, or

(c) by either party immediately by written notice upon the other party being judged bankrupt or insolvent, or if any receiver or trustee of all or any part of the business property of the other party shall be appointed and shall not be discharged within one hundred twenty (120) days after appointment, or if either party shall make an assignment of its property for the benefit of creditors or shall file a voluntary petition in bankruptcy or insolvency, or shall apply for bankruptcy under the bankruptcy or insolvency Laws now in force or hereinafter enacted, Federal, State or otherwise, or if such petition shall be filed against either party and shall not be dismissed within one hundred twenty (120) days after such filing.

Section 4.3 Effect of Termination.

(a) In the event this Agreement is terminated by XYZ pursuant to Section 4.2(a), or by either party pursuant to Section 18.5 or Section 18.19, XYZ shall: (i) pay to Manager, within thirty (30) after Manager's submission to XYZ of reasonable evidence as required hereinbelow, the fees, if any, which have accrued to Manager under this Agreement and prior to said termination and (ii) reimburse Manager for reasonable costs and expenses actually incurred by Manager in connection with the termination and/or assignment of Service Contracts, Concession Agreements, or other contracts or leases entered into by Manager pursuant to this Agreement; and provided however that such expenses shall not include: (i) severance pay for any of Manager's employees, (ii) relocation expenses for any of Manager's employees and (iii) any cost or expense not itemized in the then-current approved Operating Budget. XYZ's payment of such expenses will occur only after Manager has provided reasonable evidence of the incurrence of such expenses, and within thirty (30) days after XYZ's receipt of such evidence of incurred expenses. Except for the reimbursement of the above stated expenses, Manager shall have no other right or remedy, at law or in equity, against XYZ for a termination pursuant to Section 4.2(a).

(b) Upon termination or expiration of this Agreement for any reason, (i) Manager shall promptly discontinue the performance of all services hereunder, (ii) XYZ shall, within thirty (30) days from the date of such termination or expiration, pay Manager all fees due Manager up to the date of termination or expiration (subject to proration if the Term ends other than at the end of the Operating Year), (iii) Manager shall make available to XYZ copies of all data, electronic files, documents, procedures, reports, estimates, summaries, and other such information and materials with respect to the Facility as may have been accumulated by Manager in performing its obligations hereunder, whether completed or in process, and (iv) without any further action on part of Manager or XYZ, XYZ shall, or shall cause the successor Facility manager to, assume all obligations arising after the date of such termination or expiration, under any Service Contracts, Concession Agreements, booking commitments and any other Facility agreements entered into by Manager in furtherance of its duties hereunder. Any obligations of the parties to this Agreement that are specifically intended to survive expiration or termination of this Agreement shall survive expiration or termination hereof.

ARTICLE 5
OWNERSHIP; USE OF THE FACILITY

Section 5.1 Ownership of Facility, Data, Equipment and Materials. XYZ will at all times retain ownership of the Facility, including but not limited to real estate, technical equipment, furniture, displays, fixtures and similar property, including improvements made during the Term, at the Facility. Any data, equipment or materials furnished by XYZ to Manager or acquired by Manager as an Operating Expense shall remain the property of XYZ, and shall be returned to XYZ immediately after the termination of this Agreement. Notwithstanding the above, XYZ shall not have the right to use any third-party software licensed by Manager for general use by Manager at the Facility and other facilities managed by Manager, the licensing fee for which is proportionately allocated and charged to the Facility as an Operating Expense; such software may be retained by Manager upon expiration or termination hereof. Furthermore, XYZ recognizes that the Operations Manual to be developed and used by Manager hereunder is proprietary to Manager.

Manager and XYZ agree that the Operations Manual is not to be made available to the public and Manager regards the Operations Manual as containing trade secrets within the meaning of [State] Code Section _______. XYZ will use its best efforts not to disclose the Operations Manual to any third party without the prior written consent of Manager unless directed by an order issued by a court of competent jurisdiction or compelled to do so by Law.

Manager and XYZ agree that XYZ shall have the right to use and maintain copies of the Operations Manual after the expiration or termination of the Agreement, subject to continuing confidentiality as above promised. The parties further agree that upon termination or expiration of the Agreement, XYZ shall provide to Manager a written acknowledgement and undertaking of XYZ that the Operations Manual (i) constitutes trade secrets of Manager, (ii) is confidential, and will be treated as such, and (iii) will not be disclosed to any person without the prior written agreement of Manager or as directed by an order issued by a court of competent jurisdiction.

Section 5.2 <u>Right of Use by Manager</u>. XYZ hereby gives Manager the right and license to use the Facility, and Manager accepts such right of use, for the purpose of performing the services herein specified, including the operation and maintenance of all physical and mechanical facilities necessary for, and related to, the operation, maintenance and management of the Facility. XYZ shall: (i) select, in XYZ's sole discretion, and designate offices at the Facility for use by Manager ("Manager's Office Space"), which Manager's Office Space has been or will be viewed and deemed acceptable by Manager prior to the execution of this Agreement, and (ii) provide Manager with such office equipment as is reasonably necessary to enable Manager to perform its obligations under this Agreement.

Section 5.3 <u>Observance of Agreements</u>. XYZ agrees to pay, keep, observe and perform all payments, terms, covenants, conditions and obligations under any leases, bonds, debentures, loans and other financing and security agreements to which XYZ is bound in connection with its ownership of the Facility.

Section 5.4 <u>Use by XYZ</u>. Subject to availability and in accordance with the Facility Booking Policy, XYZ shall have the right to use the Facility or any part thereof rent-fee for meetings, seminars, training classes or other non-commercial uses, provided that XYZ shall reimburse Manager, within thirty (30) days after XYZ's receipt from Manager of an invoice there for, for deposit into the Operating Account, for any out-of-pocket expenses incurred by Manager (such as the cost of ushers, ticket-takers, set-up and take-down personnel, security expenses and other expenses) in connection with such use.

Such non-commercial use of the Facility by XYZ shall (i) not compete with or conflict with the dates previously booked by Manager for paying events, (ii) not consist of normally touring attractions (such as concerts and family shows), and (iii) be booked in advance upon reasonable notice to Manager pursuant to the Facilities' approved booking policies. Upon request of XYZ, Manager shall provide to XYZ a list of available dates for XYZ use of the Facility. To the extent that Manager has an opportunity to book a revenue-producing event on a date which is otherwise reserved for use by XYZ, Manager may propose alternative dates for XYZ's event, and XYZ shall use commercially reasonable efforts to reschedule its event to allow Manager to book the revenue-producing event. For purposes of calculating Manager's Incentive Fee, Manager shall receive a "paper" credit for an amount equal to the difference between the "lowest-offered" rate and the rate (if any) charged to XYZ for such use of the Facility.

Section 5.5 Access/Coordination.

(a) Access. Manager shall provide XYZ's Contract Administrator with full access to all areas in the Facility used by Manager in the performance of Manager's obligations hereunder. In cases of emergency, XYZ security and facilities maintenance personnel shall have the right to access all areas used by Manager in the performance of Manager's obligations hereunder. Manager acknowledges and agrees that all areas occupied by Manager at the Facility shall be subject to inspection by appropriate representatives of federal, state and local agencies.

(b) Coordination. Throughout the Term of this Agreement, XYZ's Contract Administrator shall coordinate Manager's occupancy and use of the Facility.

Section 5.6 Equipment List/Annual Inventory. A list of the equipment owned by XYZ, and maintained at the Facility, will be prepared by XYZ. Manager and XYZ agree to review said list of equipment within ninety (90) days of the Effective Date of this Agreement. Manager and XYZ shall, at least once during every Operating Year, review, revise and update the list of equipment in the manner set forth hereinabove. Manager agrees to provide to XYZ a list of any Manager-owned equipment at the Facility, if any, and to revise and update such list of Manager-owned equipment on an annual basis. Manager may not remove any XYZ and/or Manager owned equipment from the Facility without the prior written permission from XYZ.

Section 5.7 Final Inventory and Inspection of the Facility. Upon termination or expiration of this Agreement, XYZ and Manager shall jointly conduct a physical inventory of all equipment owned by XYZ. Discrepancies and repairs shall be corrected at Manager's sole expense and all replacements of damaged or lost equipment shall be of comparable quality with items in the then-current XYZ owned equipment inventory. Manager shall surrender the Facility and all equipment therein or thereon in as good a condition as at the start of the Agreement, except for ordinary wear and tear, loss or damage by fire, other perils covered by the applicable fire and extended coverage insurance policies, acts of God, and theft by persons other than the employees of Manager without negligence on the part of Manager or Manager's employees. Manager shall be responsible for the costs of any necessary cleaning and repairs.

Section 5.8 Safety. Manager shall take all reasonable precautions for the safety of, and to provide all reasonable protection to prevent damage, injury or loss to: (i) all employees of Manager and XYZ and all other persons who may be affected thereby; (ii) all the material, whether in storage on or off-site, under the care, custody, or control of Manager; and (iii) to the extent under Manager's care and control hereunder, all other property of XYZ, including without limitation, trees, shrubs, lawns, walks, pavements, roads, structures and utilities.

Manager shall not load any XYZ property including elevators, in a manner that may reasonably endanger the safety of personnel, XYZ employees, agents or third parties or cause damage to any structure, property or equipment.

Section 5.9 Security. Manager and all of Manager's employees shall comply with all XYZ rules and regulations governing access to and conduct on XYZ property. Manager shall furnish Manager's employees with identification required for entrance to or exit from the Facility during normal work hours. Manager shall return employee identification, keys and keycards to XYZ within one (1) day of: (i) separation of an employee from employment with Manager; and (ii) removal of an employee from the Facility at the request of XYZ. Manager shall be responsible for determining that all appropriate equipment and lights have been turned off and appropriate doors locked at the close of operation. Manager shall be responsible to provide security for the areas of the Facility under Manager's supervision during the scheduled hours of operation.

Section 5.10 Emergencies. Manager shall provide XYZ Police Dispatcher with the names and telephone numbers of three (3) Management-Level Employees who will be available at any time to call in case of emergencies. Manager agrees that at least one of the Management-Level Employees shall be available by telephone, twenty-four (24) hours a day, seven days a week, in the event of XYZ closings, fire or other emergencies. Manager's employees shall immediately activate the fire alarm closest to the location of a fire and immediately call XYZ's fire emergency number. Manager shall train all of Manager's employees to respond to fire, civil defense, bomb threats, and other emergencies based on procedures established by XYZ.

Section 5.11 Damages, Injury, Theft. Manager shall provide XYZ and XYZ Police Dispatcher prompt written notice of any fire or damage occurring at the Facility, and a copy of all notices received of any claim for bodily injury occurring within the Facility and/or the exterior perimeter of the Facility. If vandalism or theft occurs to Manager's machines, equipment or operations, it shall be the sole responsibility of Manager to insure, repair or replace damaged or stolen equipment at Manager's expense within forty-eight (48) hours. All vandalism shall be reported to XYZ through XYZ Police Dispatcher immediately upon discovery. XYZ shall not be responsible for any of Manager's internal losses or thefts and any such losses shall be borne solely by Manager out of its own funds.

ARTICLE 6
PERSONNEL

Section 6.1 Generally. All Facility staff and other personnel shall be engaged or hired by Manager, and shall be employees, agents or independent contractors of Manager (or an Affiliate thereof), and not of XYZ. Manager shall select, in its sole discretion but subject to XYZ's right to approve the Operating Budget, the number, function, qualifications, and compensation, including salary and benefits, of its employees and shall control the terms and conditions of employment (including without limitation termination thereof) relating to such employees. Manager agrees to use reasonable and prudent judgment in the selection and supervision of such personnel. Manager agrees that the conduct of its employees shall be governed by, and Manager's employees shall be required to comply with, XYZ's Policies and Procedures, the Operations Manual and Manager's employment manual. XYZ specifically agrees that Manager shall be entitled to pay its employees, as an Operating Expense, bonuses and benefits in accordance with Manager's then current employee manual, which may be modified by Manager from time to time in its sole discretion but subject to XYZ's right to approve the Operating Budget and provided however that such bonuses and benefits shall not include any severance pay or relocation expenses. A copy of Manager's current employee manual shall be provided to XYZ upon execution of this Agreement.

Section 6.2 General Manager.

(a) Personnel engaged by Manager will include a qualified individual with managerial experience in similar facilities to serve as the full-time, on-site General Manager of the Facility. Manager and XYZ acknowledge that [Xxxx Xxxx] has been selected by Manager and approved by XYZ as the initial General Manager hereunder. Hiring of any successor General Manager by Manager shall require prior written approval of XYZ, which approval shall not be unreasonably withheld; provided, however, in the event of a vacancy of the General Manager position, Manager may, upon notice to XYZ temporarily fill such position with an interim General Manager for up to ninety (90) days without the necessity of obtaining XYZ's approval. The General Manager will have general supervisory responsibility for the Manager and will be responsible for day-to-day operations of the Facility, supervision of employees, and management and coordination of all activities associated with events taking place at the Facility.

(b) In the event XYZ is or becomes dissatisfied with the General Manager for any reason, XYZ shall provide written notice to Manager of XYZ's dissatisfaction and Manager will meet with XYZ within three (3) days of Manager's receipt of such notice to discuss such matters, and thereafter Manager shall take those actions mutually agreed upon by Manager and XYZ to resolve XYZ's concerns with the General Manager.

(c) XYZ may at any time request the termination of the General Manager or request that Manager take disciplinary action against the General Manager. Upon any termination or removal of the General Manager, Manager shall immediately commence the process for selecting and hiring a new General Manager, who will be subject to the approval of XYZ as set forth in Section 6.2(a) hereinabove.

(d) In the event that Manager desires to remove or terminate the General Manager for any reason, subject to the terms of subparagraph (e) below, Manager shall first notify and discuss with XYZ the reasons for the desired action and the steps Manager will take to find and recruit a qualified successor General Manager.

(e) Manager specifically acknowledges the importance placed by XYZ on the continuity of the General Manager at the Facility and therefore Manager agrees that any General Manager hired for the Facility shall not be relocated by Manager to another Manager-owned facility, or to a corporate or administrative position with Manager, for a term of no less than twenty-four (24) months from the General Manager's start date at the Facility, unless otherwise agreed by Manager and XYZ.

Section 6.3 Staffing. Manager shall employ and maintain adequate staff to ensure excellent customer service and consistent, efficient operation of all services specified under the terms of this Agreement.

Section 6.4 Non-Solicitation/Non-Hiring. During the Term and for a period of one (1) year after the expiration, termination or non-renewal of this Agreement, without the prior written consent of the other party hereto, neither Manager (or any of Manager's Affiliates) nor XYZ (or any of XYZ's Affiliates) shall directly or indirectly solicit, hire or seek to hire any of the employees of Manager or XYZ, as applicable, in any capacity whatsoever nor induce or attempt to induce any such employees to leave their employ to work for Manager or XYZ, as applicable, or for any other person, firm, corporation or other business entity.

Section 6.5 Indemnification by Manager for Employment-Related Activities and Claims. Manager agrees to defend, indemnify and hold harmless XYZ and its officials, trustees, officers, employees, agents, successors, and assigns against any claims, cause of action, costs, expenses (including reasonable attorneys' fees) liabilities, or damages suffered by such parties arising directly out of claims by Manager's employees in connection with the Manager's employment-related activities and/or the employment relationship between Manager and any of Manager's employees, except to the extent such claims are directly attributable to a negligent or intentional act or omission of XYZ or XYZ's employees or officials.

ARTICLE 7
TRANSITION COSTS; OPERATING BUDGET

Section 7.1 Transition Costs. XYZ shall reimburse Manager for Manager's actual and reasonable costs incurred in connection with transitioning the management services for the Facility to Manager (the "Transition Costs"), in an amount not to exceed _______ ($xxx). It is understood that the Transition Costs will include reimbursement for the costs of relocating employees; recruitment and re-branding; computer/website set-up; and corporate travel. Manager shall, after incurring such costs, invoice XYZ for such costs together with reasonable back-up documentation evidencing the incurrence of such costs, and XYZ shall pay such invoice to Manager within 30 days of its receipt thereof.

Section 7.2 Establishment of Operating Budget. Attached hereto as Exhibit C is the existing Operating Budget for the first (1st) Operating Year, which Operating Budget the parties acknowledge was prepared by the prior Facility manager and was approved by XYZ. Manager shall, within ninety (90) days from the Effective Date, propose to XYZ modifications to such Operating Budget as desired by Manager. Such modifications shall be subject to the approval of XYZ, which approval shall not be unreasonably withheld or delayed; provided, however, the parties agree, at a minimum, that the Operating Budget for the first (1st) Operating Year shall be amended to take into account: (i) any changes in the Fixed Management Fee or staffing levels resulting from the transition of management of the Facilities to Manager; and (ii) the Transition Costs. Manager agrees that at least 120 days prior to the commencement of each subsequent Operating Year in respect of such year, it will prepare and submit to XYZ its proposed Operating Budget for such year. Each such Operating Budget shall include Manager's good faith projection of Revenues and Operating Expenses, presented on a monthly and annual basis, for the upcoming Operating Year. XYZ agrees to provide Manager with all information reasonably necessary to enable Manager to prepare each Operating Budget. XYZ acknowledges that notwithstanding the Manager's experience and expertise in relation to the operation of facilities similar to the Facility, the projections contained in each Operating Budget are estimates only, and are subject to and may be affected by changes in financial, economic and other conditions and circumstances beyond the Manager's control.

Section 7.3 Approval of Operating Budget. Each annual Operating Budget shall be subject to the review and approval of XYZ, which approval shall not be unreasonably withheld or delayed. In order for XYZ to fully evaluate and analyze such budgets or any other request by Manager relating to income and expenses, Manager agrees to provide to XYZ such reasonable financial information relating to the Facility as may be requested by XYZ from time to time. If extraordinary events occur during any Operating Year that could not reasonably be contemplated at the time the corresponding Operating Budget was prepared, Manager may submit an amendment to such budget for review and approval by XYZ (which approval shall not be unreasonably withheld or delayed). If XYZ fails to approve any annual Operating Budget (or any proposed amendment thereto) within _______ (x) business days of XYZ's receipt of such Operating Budget, XYZ shall promptly provide Manager the specific reasons therefore and its suggested modifications to Manager's proposed Operating Budget or amendment in order to make it acceptable to XYZ. The parties shall then engage in good faith discussions and use reasonable commercial efforts to attempt to resolve the matter to the mutual satisfaction of the parties, including, if applicable, negotiation of a mutually acceptable modification to the economic terms of this Agreement to enable the Manager to achieve the compensation contemplated by its proposed Operating Budget. If the parties are unable to finalize the Operating Budget for the upcoming Operating Year prior to the commencement of that Operating Year, the Operating Budget for the then-current Operating Year shall automatically be the previous Operating Year's Operating Budget until the parties finalize the new Operating Budget in accordance with the terms and conditions contained herein, provided that the new Operating Budget shall be retroactively effective as of the start of the current Operating Year.

Section 7.4 Adherence to Operating Budget. Manager shall use all reasonable efforts to manage and operate the Facility in accordance with the Operating Budget. Without the prior written consent of XYZ, Manager shall not exceed, commit or contract to expend any sums in excess of the aggregate amounts allowed in the Operating Budget or otherwise approved in writing by XYZ, except for (i) additional expenditures necessary to perform an Emergency Repair, in which event Manager shall notify XYZ prior to making such repair, (ii) increased costs resulting from the scheduling by Manager of additional revenue producing events or activities at the Facility not contemplated by the Operating Budget in effect for such Operating Year; (iii) expenses for services or utilities provided to the Facility by unaffiliated third parties, the cost of which is not within the reasonable control of Manager, such as the costs of utilities and insurance; and (iv) increased costs resulting from events scheduled pursuant to Section 5.4. Manager agrees to notify XYZ within 30 days of any significant change or variance in the bottom line net profit/loss number in the Operating Budget, and any material increase in total Facility expenses from that provided for in the Operating Budget.

ARTICLE 8
PROCEDURE FOR HANDLING INCOME

Section 8.1 Event Account. On or before the Effective Date of this Agreement, XYZ shall open an Event Account, at a qualified banking institution selected by XYZ in XYZ's sole discretion. Manager shall deposit as soon as practicable following receipt, in the Event Account, all revenue received from ticket sales and similar event-related revenues which Manager receives in contemplation of, or arising from, an event, pending completion of the event. Such monies will be held in escrow for the protection of ticket purchasers, XYZ and Manager, to provide a source of funds as required for payments to performers and for payments of direct incidental expenses in connection with the presentation of events that must be paid prior to or contemporaneously with such events. Promptly following completion of such events, Manager shall transfer all funds remaining in the Event Account, including any interest accrued thereon, into the Operating Account. Bank service charges, if any, on such account(s) shall be deducted from interest earned.

Section 8.2 Operating Account. On or before the Effective Date of this Agreement, XYZ shall open an Operating Account, at a qualified banking institution selected by XYZ in XYZ's sole discretion. Except as provided in Section 8.1, all Revenue derived from operation of the Facility shall be deposited by Manager into the Operating Account as soon as practicable upon receipt (but not less often than once each business day). The specific procedures (and authorized individuals) for making deposits to and withdrawals from such account shall be set forth in the Operations Manual, but the parties specifically agree that Manager shall have authority to sign checks and make withdrawals from such account, subject to the limitation contained in this Agreement, without needing to obtain the co-signature of a XYZ employee or representative; provided, however, that Manager shall not be permitted to sign checks or make withdrawals from the Operating Account to pay fees to Manager or any of Manager's Affiliates but Manager shall instead submit invoices to XYZ for fees due to Manager under the Agreement and fees due to Manager's Affiliates under their respective agreements with XYZ.

Section 8.3 Cash Control. Manager shall institute and maintain cash control procedures necessary for the responsible safekeeping, management and accounting for all funds handled by its employees and agents in accordance in accordance with Manager's Manual on Cash Control attached hereto as Exhibit E.

Section 8.4 Payment Default. Manager acknowledges that any default in payment of any of the sums due or payable hereunder will result in loss and additional expense to XYZ. Manager further agrees that such loss and additional expense is difficult and impractical to ascertain, and Manager agrees that in the event any amounts due and owing to XYZ hereunder are not paid or forwarded to XYZ within ninety (90) days of invoice and/or written notice, Manager shall pay XYZ a late fee equal to _______ percent (x%) of such amount.

ARTICLE 9
FUNDING

Section 9.1 Source of Funding. Manager shall pay all items of expense for the operation, maintenance, supervision and management of the Facility from the funds in the Operating Account, which Manager may access periodically for this purpose. The Operating Account shall be funded with amounts generated by operation of the Facility (as described in Article 8 above), or otherwise made available by XYZ. To ensure sufficient funds are available in the Operating Account, XYZ will deposit in the Operating Account, on (or within ___ days after) the Effective Date, the budgeted or otherwise approved expenses for the month beginning on the Effective Date. XYZ shall thereafter, on or before the 1st day of each succeeding month following the Effective Date, deposit (or allow to remain) in the Operating Account the budgeted or otherwise approved expenses for each such month. Any funds advanced by XYZ pursuant to this Section 9.1 shall be refunded to XYZ once sufficient funds are available in the Operating Account. Manager shall have no liability to XYZ or any third party in the event Manager is unable to perform its obligations hereunder, or under any third party contract entered into pursuant to the terms hereof, due to the fact that sufficient funds are not made available to Manager to pay such expenses in a timely manner.

Section 9.2 Advancement of Funds. Under no circumstances shall Manager be required to pay for or advance any of its own funds to pay for any Operating Expenses. In the event that, notwithstanding the foregoing, Manager agrees to advance its own funds to pay Operating Expenses, XYZ shall, upon Manager's fully documented request for reimbursement, reimburse Manager for the full amount of such advanced funds within thirty (30) days of XYZ's receipt of documentation therefore.

ARTICLE 10
FISCAL RESPONSIBILITY; REPORTING

Section 10.1 Records. Manager agrees to keep and maintain, at its office in the Facility, separate and independent records, in accordance with generally accepted accounting principles, devoted exclusively to its operations in connection with its management of the Facility. Such records (including books, ledgers, journals, and accounts) shall contain all entries reflecting the business operations of Manager under this Agreement and copies of such records shall be provided to XYZ upon termination or expiration of this Agreement (except for employee files which are deemed to be confidential to Manager and shall be Manager's property). Manager shall keep in a safe place for a period of five (5) years from the termination or expiration date of this Agreement all employee files, provided that the period of record retention described herein shall continue until the final disposition of any disputes, claims or litigation relating any employee that may be ongoing at the end of such time period. XYZ or its authorized agent shall have the right to audit and inspect such records (other than employee files) at any time during the Term, upon reasonable advance notice to Manager and during Manager's ordinary business hours. XYZ shall, at all times and at XYZ's expense, have the right to receive copies of any and all such records (other than employee files). Manager shall provide advance written notice to XYZ of Manager's intent to transfer any such records to an off-site location or facility.

Section 10.2 Monthly Financial Reports. Manager agrees to provide to XYZ, within _______ (___) days after the end of each month during the Term, financial reports for the Facility including a balance sheet, aging report on accounts receivable, statement of revenues and expenditures (budget to actual), back-up documentation related to all expenditures, and rolling forecasts for such month and year to date in accordance with generally accepted accounting principles. In addition, Manager agrees to provide to XYZ a summary of bookings for each such month, and separate cash receipts and disbursements reports for each event held at the Facility during such month. Additionally, Manager shall submit to XYZ, or shall cause the applicable public depository utilized by Manager to submit to XYZ, on a monthly basis, copies of all bank statements and reconciliation statements and reports concerning the Event Account and the Operating Account. Manager shall also submit to XYZ, within _______ (___) hours after every event, a flash report that contains the interim financial results of said event.

Section 10.3 Audit. Manager agrees to provide to XYZ, within one hundred twenty (120) days following the end of each Operating Year, a certified audit report on the accounts and records as kept by Manager for the Facility. Costs associated with obtaining such certified audit report shall not be an Operating Expense of the Facility. Such audit shall be performed by an external auditor approved in writing by XYZ, and shall be conducted in accordance with generally accepted auditing standards.

Manager agrees to cooperate in the conduct of all audits of Manager scheduled by XYZ, its agents, XYZ's Department of Audits, independent auditors, or government auditors or investigators. All audits of Manager by XYZ shall be conducted in a manner that does not unreasonably interfere with the conduct of Manager's business. If any such audit discloses a deficiency, Manager shall promptly pay

XYZ the amount of such deficiency, and, if such deficiency is in excess of $_______ [OR percentage], the Manager shall also pay the costs of the audit. If the audit discloses a deficiency on behalf of XYZ, XYZ shall promptly pay Manager the amount of such deficiency.

ARTICLE 11
CAPITAL IMPROVEMENTS

Section 11.1 Schedule of Capital Expenditures. Manager shall annually, at the time of submission of the annual Operating Budget to XYZ, provide to XYZ a schedule of proposed capital improvements to be made at the Facility, for the purpose of allowing XYZ to consider such projects and to prepare and update a long-range Capital Expenditure budget.

Section 11.2 Responsibility for Capital Expenditures. XYZ shall be solely responsible for all Capital Expenditures at the Facility; provided, however, XYZ shall be under no obligation to make any Capital Expenditures proposed by Manager, and provided further that Manager shall have no liability for any claims, costs or damages arising out of a failure by XYZ to make any Capital Expenditures. Notwithstanding the foregoing, Manager shall have the right (but not the obligation), upon notice to XYZ, to make Capital Expenditures at the Facility for Emergency Repairs. In such event, XYZ shall promptly reimburse Manager for the cost of such Capital Expenditure.

ARTICLE 12
FACILITY CONTRACTS; TRANSACTIONS WITH AFFILIATES

Section 12.1 Existing Contracts. XYZ shall provide to Manager, on or before the Effective Date, copies of all Existing Contracts, which Existing Contracts are listed on Exhibit B, attached hereto. Manager shall administer and assure compliance with such Existing Contracts.

Section 12.2 Execution of Contracts. In connection with all services provided by Manager pursuant to this Agreement, Manager shall have the full power and authority to seek and negotiate Service Contracts, Concession Agreements and other contracts related to the operation of the Facility to the extent that such contracts (i) do not include XYZ as a signatory; (ii) do not extend beyond the Term or any renewal of this Agreement; (iii) do not violate any provision of [State] law applicable to XYZ, including DBE/MBE/WBE ordinances; and (iv) include the Standard Contract Provisions. Any contract that extends beyond the Term or any renewal hereof must be executed and ratified in writing by XYZ. XYZ shall fully perform, or arrange for the performance of, all obligations of Manager pursuant to such contract in the event of the expiration or termination of this Agreement provided that (a) such contract has been duly executed by both parties, and (b) XYZ's legal counsel has reviewed and approved of the form of such contract. Manager shall also have the full power and authority to make all disbursements necessary to carry out its duties and obligations under this Agreement but only to the extent authorized hereunder.

Section 12.3 Transactions with Affiliates. In connection with its obligations hereunder relating to the purchase or procurement of services for the Facility (including without limitation web design services and graphic design services), Manager may purchase or procure such services, or otherwise transact business with, an Affiliate of Manager, provided that the prices charged and services rendered by such Affiliate are competitive with those obtainable from any unrelated parties rendering comparable services. Manager shall, at the request of XYZ, provide reasonable evidence establishing the competitive nature of such prices and services, including, if appropriate, competitive bids from other persons seeking to render such services at the Facility. In addition, Manager shall, at all times during the Term of this Agreement, when purchasing or procuring services or otherwise transacting business with Manager's Affiliate in connection with Manager's management of the Facility or otherwise in connection with Manager's responsibilities under this Agreement, conduct all interactions with Manager's Affiliate in an arm's length manner and as if Manager and its Affiliate were independent third parties.

Section 12.4 Subcontracts. Manager may not unilaterally subcontract for the performance of the services Manager is itself to provide under the terms of this Agreement. Manager may engage third party service providers to perform those services incidental to or in furtherance of the services Manager is to provide under this Agreement, with prior written approval of XYZ's Legal Counsel. All subcontractors must be approved in writing and in advance by XYZ's Legal Counsel. The form and content of all subcontracts must be approved by XYZ's Legal Counsel and all subcontracts must contain the Standard Contract Provisions.

Manager shall be responsible for ensuring all subcontractors comply with all applicable XYZ policies and procedures (including diversity initiatives) and Manager shall require all subcontractors to have and maintain Workers' Compensation Insurance for such subcontractor's employees, commercial liability insurance and automobile liability insurance covering such subcontractor's operations. Such liability insurance will be in limits of not less than

$1 million ($1,000,000) per occurrence for bodily injury and property damage and shall name XYZ as an additional insured.

All subcontracts for services must have the prior written approval of XYZ and all subcontracts should contain the following restrictions.

(a) Manager shall not enter into any subcontract which purports to bind XYZ or its respective officers or agents,

(b) Manager shall not execute any subcontract

(i) requiring XYZ to maintain any type of insurance other than for XYZ's benefit,

(ii) renewing or extending this Agreement beyond its initial Term or continuing this Agreement's benefits from term to term,

(iii) requiring or stating that the terms of the subcontract prevail over the terms of this Agreement in the event of conflict,

(iv) requiring XYZ to indemnify or hold harmless subcontractor for any act or omission,

(v) directly imposing interest, service or late payment charges on XYZ on payments not made within a certain time,

(vi) requiring the application of the law of any state other than [State] in interpreting or enforcing the subcontract,

(vii) requiring any total or partial compensation or payment for lost profit or liquidated damages by XYZ if the subcontract is terminated before its scheduled expiration date,

(viii) permitting unilateral modification this Agreement or the subcontract by the subcontractor

(ix) binding XYZ to any arbitration or to the decision of any arbitration board, commission, panel or other entity or binding XYZ to bargain with any labor union,

(x) obligating XYZ to pay directly any damages, costs of collection, or attorneys' fees,

(xi) granting the subcontractor a security interest in property of XYZ, or

(xii) requiring any direct payment by XYZ within a period of less than thirty (30) days after invoice, due date or demand.

All damage or loss occurring in the course of delivery, assembly, and placement of furnishings and other items caused in whole or in part by Manager or any subcontractor or by anyone for whom such acts any of them may be held liable, shall be remedied by Manager at Manager's expense and in a manner satisfactory to XYZ.

ARTICLE 13
AGREEMENT MONITORING AND GENERAL MANAGER

Section 13.1 Contract Administrator. Each party shall appoint a contract administrator who shall monitor such party's compliance with the terms of this Agreement. Manager's contract administrator shall be its General Manager at the Facility, unless Manager notifies XYZ of a substitute contract administrator in writing. XYZ's Contract Administrator shall be its [Vice President] or such other individual as XYZ's President, General Counsel, Vice President of Business Affairs and Finance, or Assistant Vice President shall designate. Any and all references in this Agreement requiring Manager or XYZ participation or approval shall mean the participation or approval of Manager's contract administrator or XYZ's contract administrator, as applicable.

Section 13.2 Performance Review Meetings. Manager's contract administrator and XYZ's contract administrator shall hold meetings on a regular basis to enable the parties to review regularly all aspects of the Agreement and to allow Manager to present to XYZ operational issues, financial results, and related matters. These meetings may, if mutually agreed by the parties, include Manager's contract administrator's direct supervisor (via telephone) and any other member of Manager's organization mutually agreed to by the parties. The parties further agree that the meetings described in this Section will be held, at a minimum, thirty (30) days after the Effective Date of this Agreement, sixty (60) days after the Effective Date of this Agreement, ninety (90) days after the Effective Date of this Agreement, and every ninety (90) days thereafter for the Term of this Agreement.

Section 13.3 Operational Reports. Manager shall submit to XYZ: (i) operational reports on a monthly basis, (ii) year-to-date operational reports on a quarterly basis, and (iii) Performance Reports on an annual basis. Such reports shall include, without limitation, financial information, facility information, staffing changes or issues, operational issues, and contributions made to XYZ.

ARTICLE 14
INDEMNIFICATION

Section 14.1 Indemnification by Manager. Manager agrees to defend, indemnify, and hold harmless XYZ and its officials, trustees, officers, employees, agents, successors, and assigns against any claims, causes of action, costs, expenses (including reasonable attorneys' fees) liabilities, or damages (collectively, "Losses") suffered by such parties, arising out of or in connection with any (a) negligent or intentional act or omission, or intentional misconduct, on the part of Manager or any of its employees or agents in the performance of its obligations under this Agreement, or (b) breach by Manager of any of its representations, covenants, or agreements made herein. Manager shall pay all attorneys' fees, damages, court costs, and other expenses arising out any aforementioned claims or causes of action and shall, at its own expense, satisfy and cause to be discharged any such judgments as may be obtained against XYZ or any of its officials, trustees, officers, employees, or agents.

Section 14.2 [Reserved]

Section 14.3 Conditions to Indemnification. With respect to each separate matter brought by any third party against which a party hereto ("Indemnitee") is indemnified by the other party ("Indemnitor") under this Article 14, the Indemnitor shall be responsible, at its sole cost and expense, for controlling, litigating, defending and/or otherwise attempting to resolve any proceeding, claim, or cause of action underlying such matter, and neither Indemnitor nor Indemnitee shall agree to any settlement without the other's prior written consent (which shall not be unreasonably withheld or delayed) and no suit for money damages against XYZ shall be compromised or settled without approval of XYZ Counsel. In any event, Indemnitor and Indemnitee shall in good faith cooperate with each other and their respective counsel with respect to all such actions or proceedings, at the Indemnitor's expense. With respect to each and every matter with respect to which any indemnification may be sought hereunder, upon receiving notice pertaining to such matter, Indemnitee shall promptly (and in no event more than twenty (20) days after any third party litigation is commenced asserting such claim) give reasonably detailed written notice to the Indemnitor of the nature of such matter and the amount demanded or claimed in connection therewith.

Section 14.4 Survival. The obligations of the parties contained in this Article 14 shall survive the termination or expiration of this Agreement.

Section 14.5 Liability/Limitation of Liability. XYZ, to the fullest extent permitted by [State] and the laws and decisions thereunder, shall be responsible for any and all personal injury and/or property damage (excluding attorneys' fees) which is directly attributable to the negligent acts of omissions of XYZ or its trustees, officers or employees while acting within the scope of their employment, as set forth in [State] Code Section _______. The parties hereby agree that nothing in this section or in this Agreement shall be construed or interpreted as a waiver of the sovereign immunity of XYZ beyond the waiver provided in [State] Section _______. Any liability of XYZ hereunder shall be limited to contract damages only. Notwithstanding anything to the contrary contained in this Agreement, in no event shall either party to this Agreement be obligated to indemnify the other party with respect to any indirect, incidental, or consequential damages or for lost profits, lost revenues, or damage to goodwill or reputation.

ARTICLE 15
INSURANCE

Section 15.1 Types and Amount of Coverage. Manager agrees to obtain insurance coverage in the manner and amounts as set forth in Exhibit D, attached hereto, and shall provide to XYZ promptly following the Effective Date certificates of insurance evidencing such coverage. Manager shall maintain such referenced insurance coverage at all times during the Term, and will not make any material modification or change from these specifications without the prior written approval of XYZ. Each insurance policy shall include a requirement that the insurer provide Manager and XYZ at least thirty (30) days written notice of cancellation or material change in the terms and provisions of the applicable policy. The cost of all such insurance shall be an Operating Expense.

Section 15.2 Rating; Additional Insureds. All insurance policies shall be issued by insurance companies rated no less than A VIII in the most recent "Bests" insurance guide, and licensed in [State] or as otherwise agreed in writing by the parties. All such policies shall be in such form and contain such provisions as are generally considered standard for the type of insurance involved. The commercial general liability policy, automobile liability insurance policy, liquor liability policy, and umbrella or excess liability policy to be obtained by Manager hereunder shall name XYZ as an additional insured. The workers compensation policy to be obtained by Manager hereunder shall contain a waiver of all rights of subrogation against XYZ. Manager shall require that all third-party service providers at the Facility, including without limitation third-party licensees, ushers, security personnel, and concessionaires, provide equivalent certificates of insurance evidencing insurance appropriate for the types of activities in which such third party service provider is engaged. If Manager subcontracts any of its obligations under this Agreement, Manager shall either: (a) cover all subcontractors under its policies of insurance, or (b) require each subcontractor not so covered to secure insurance that will protect against applicable hazards or risks of loss as and in the minimum amounts designated herein, and name Manager and XYZ as additional insureds.

Section 15.3 Mutual Waiver of Subrogation. Manager and XYZ agree to waive all rights of subrogation against each other to the extent that any loss is covered by Manager's or XYZ's respective insurance policies.

Section 15.4 Performance Bond. On or before the Effective Date of this Agreement, Manager will deliver to XYZ an executed standard performance bond from a surety licensed to do business in [State] in the amount of $_______. This Agreement shall not be deemed in effect unless and until the bond has been received by XYZ and XYZ has determined that said bond complies with the requirements of this section. The performance bond shall remain in effect throughout the term of this Agreement. The performance bond shall be for the purpose of guaranteeing the faithful performance by Manager of all its obligations under and pursuant to the terms of this Agreement. Upon XYZ's request, Manager will provide to XYZ all documentation related to the performance bond.

ARTICLE 16
REPRESENTATIONS, WARRANTIES AND COVENANTS

Section 16.1 Manager Representations and Warranties. Manager hereby represents, warrants, and covenants to XYZ as follows:

(a) that it has the full legal right, power, and authority to enter into this Agreement and to grant the rights and perform the obligations of Manager herein, and that no third-party consent or approval is required to grant such rights or perform such obligations hereunder;

(b) that this Agreement has been duly executed and delivered by Manager and constitutes a valid and binding obligation of Manager, enforceable in accordance with its terms, except as such enforceability may be limited by bankruptcy, insolvency, reorganization, or similar Laws affecting creditors' rights generally or by general equitable principles; and

(c) that Manager will comply with all Laws applicable to its management of the Facility, provided that Manager shall not be required to undertake any compliance activity, nor shall Manager have any liability under this Agreement therefor, if such activity requires any Capital Expenditure.

Section 16.2 XYZ Representations, Warranties, and Covenants. XYZ represents, warrants, and covenants to Manager as follows:

(a) that it has the full legal right, power, and authority to enter into this Agreement and to grant the rights and perform the obligations of XYZ herein, and that no other third-party consent or approval is required to grant such rights or perform such obligations hereunder;

(b) that this Agreement has been duly executed and delivered by XYZ and constitutes a valid and binding obligation of XYZ, enforceable in accordance with its terms, bankruptcy, insolvency, reorganization, or similar laws affecting creditors' rights generally or by general equitable principles; and

(c) that the Facility is, as of the Effective Date and to the best of XYZ's knowledge based upon representations obtained from the prior Facility manager, in compliance with all applicable Laws relating to the construction, use and operation of the Facility (including, without limitation, Title III of the American with Disabilities Act), and that there exist no structural defects or unsound operating conditions at the Facility.

ARTICLE 17
SCHOLARSHIP

Section 17.1 Generally. Manager agrees to fund annually, from its own account, two (2) separate scholarships of _______ dollars ($xxx) each that will be awarded to XYZ [Charity]. The terms governing the provision of such scholarships, including the criteria for determining the recipient of the scholarships and the eligibility requirements, shall be mutually agreed upon by the parties following the Effective Date and the scholarships shall be managed by XYZ.

ARTICLE 18
MISCELLANEOUS

Section 18.1 Confidentiality. Subject to the conditions set forth in this Section, all documents received by XYZ in connection with this Agreement shall be subject to [State] laws, including but not limited to [State] Code Chapter _______. Manager and XYZ agree that Manager's Financial Information is not made available to the public and Manager regards Manager Financial Information as trade secrets within the meaning of [State] Code Section _______. XYZ will use its reasonable best efforts not to disclose such Manager Financial Information to any third party without the prior written consent of Manager directed by an order issued by a court of competent jurisdiction or compelled to do so by Law. Manager agrees that it will not disclose to any outside party the amount of revenues paid to XYZ hereunder or under any other contracts, unless directed by an order issued by a court of competent jurisdiction or compelled to do so by Law.

To the extent that Manager Financial Information is requested at any time by XYZ pursuant to the terms of this Agreement, Manager agrees to provide such information and may condition the provision of such information on the written re-acknowledgement and undertaking of XYZ that such Manager Financial Information (i) constitutes trade secrets of Manager, (ii) is confidential, and will be treated as such, and (iii) will not be disclosed to any person without the prior written agreement of Manager or as directed by an order issued by a court of competent jurisdiction or by Law.

Section 18.2 <u>No Discrimination</u>. Manager agrees that it will not discriminate against any employee or applicant for employment for work under this Agreement because of race, religion, color, sex, disability, national origin, ancestry, physical handicap, or age, and will take affirmative steps to ensure that applicants are employed, and employees are treated during employment, without regard to race, religion, color, sex, disability, national origin, ancestry, physical handicap, or age.

Section 18.3 <u>Use of Facility Names and Logos</u>. Manager shall have the right to use throughout the Term (and permit others to use in furtherance of Manager's obligations hereunder), for no charge, the name and all logos of the Facility, on Manager's stationary, in its advertising of the Facility, and whenever conducting business of the Facility; provided, that Manager shall take all prudent and appropriate measures to protect the intellectual property rights of XYZ relating to such logos. Manager and XYZ agree that prior to Manager's initial use of XYZ's name, logos, or other identifying marks or property, Manager and XYZ shall confirm, in writing, XYZ's format and/or content requirements related to Manager use of said name, logos, marks, and other intellectual property. All intellectual property rights in any Facility logos developed by the Manager or XYZ shall be and at all times remain the sole and exclusive property of XYZ. Manager agrees to execute any documentation requested by

XYZ from time to time to establish, protect or convey any such intellectual property rights.

Section 18.4 Facility Advertisements. Manager shall, in all advertisements placed for the Facility or events at the Facility: (i) subordinate its brand and mark's to those of XYZ, and specifically to the _______ Center; and (ii) ensure that XYZ's format and/or content requirements related to use of XYZ's name, logos, marks, and other intellectual property are met. Manager agrees that Manager will not place advertisements for the Facility that do not comply with XYZ's format and content requirements, without prior written approval from XYZ.

Section 18.5 Force Majeure; Casualty Loss.

(a) Neither party shall be liable or responsible to the other party for any delay, loss, damage, failure or inability to perform under this Agreement due to an Event of Force Majeure, provided that the party claiming failure or inability to perform provides written notice to the other party within thirty (30) days of the date on which such party gains actual knowledge of such Event of Force Majeure. Notwithstanding the foregoing, in no event shall a party's failure to make payments due hereunder be excusable due to an Event of Force Majeure.

(b) In the event of damage or destruction to a material portion of the Facility by reason of fire, storm or other casualty loss that renders the Facility (or a material portion thereof) untenantable, XYZ shall use reasonable efforts to remedy such situation. If notwithstanding such efforts, such damage or destruction is expected to render the Facility (or a material portion thereof) untenantable for a period estimated by an architect selected by XYZ, of at least one hundred eighty (180) days from the date of such fire, storm or other casualty loss, either party may terminate this Agreement upon written notice to the other, provided that XYZ shall pay to Manager its costs of withdrawing from services hereunder, as described in Section 4.3(a) above.

Section 18.6 Assignment. Neither party may assign this Agreement without the prior written consent of the other, which consent shall not be unreasonably withheld or delayed. Any purported assignment in contravention of this Section shall be void. For purposes of this Section, the term "assignment" shall be deemed to include, but shall not be limited to the following, whether occurring at any one time or over a period of time through a series of transfers:

(i) the sale or transfer of all or substantially all of the assets of, or the sale, assignment or transfer of any issued or outstanding stock, partnership interests, membership interests or other ownership interests which results in a change in the control of Manager, or a change in control in any entity which directly or indirectly controls Manager; and (ii) the issuance of any additional stock, partnership interests, membership interests or other ownership interests, if the issuance of such additional stock, partnership interests, membership interests or other ownership interests will result in a change of the controlling ownership of any entity described in (i), above, as held by the shareholders, partners, members or other owners thereof when such corporation, partnership, limited liability company or other entity.

Section 18.7 Notices. All notices required or permitted to be given pursuant to this Agreement shall be in writing and delivered personally or sent by registered or certified mail, return receipt requested, or by generally recognized, prepaid, overnight air courier services, to the address and individual set forth below. All such notices to either party shall be deemed to have been provided when delivered, if delivered personally, three (3) days after mailed, if sent by registered or certified mail, or the next business day, if sent by generally recognized, prepaid, overnight air courier services.

If to XYZ:	If to Manager,
[Address]	[Address]
With a copy to:	With a copy to,
General Counsel	[Company]
[Address]	[Address]

The designation of the individuals to be so notified and the addresses of such parties set forth above may be changed from time to time by written notice to the other party in the manner set forth above.

Section 18.8 Severability. If a court of competent jurisdiction determines that any term of this Agreement is invalid or unenforceable to any extent under applicable law, the remainder of this Agreement (and the application of this Agreement to other circumstances) shall not be affected thereby, and each remaining term shall be valid and enforceable to the fullest extent permitted by law.

Section 18.9 Entire Agreement. This Agreement (including the exhibits attached hereto) contains the entire agreement between the parties with respect to the subject matter hereof, and supersedes and replaces all prior negotiations, correspondence, conversations, agreements, and understandings concerning the subject matter hereof. Accordingly, the parties agree that no deviation from the terms hereof shall be predicated upon any prior representations, agreements, or understandings, whether oral or written.

Section 18.10 Governing Law/Consent to Jurisdiction. The Agreement is entered into under and pursuant to, and is to be construed and enforceable in accordance with, the laws of the [State], without regard to its conflict of laws principles. The parties agree that any dispute arising out of or related to this Agreement shall be brought in the appropriate state or federal district court within [State]; provided however, that the parties first agree that in the event any dispute, claim or controversy of any kind or nature relating to this Agreement arises between the parties, the parties agree to meet and make a good faith effort to resolve the dispute. If the dispute is not resolved within thirty (30) days after the parties first met to the resolve the dispute, and either party wishes to pursue the dispute further, then the party seeking to pursue the dispute will refer the dispute to non-binding mediation under the Commercial Mediation Rules of the American Arbitration Association ("AAA"). In no event shall the mediation be initiated more than one (1) year after the date a party first gave written notification of the dispute to the other party. A single mediator engaged in the practice of law, who is knowledgeable about the facility management industry will conduct the mediation under the then-current rules of the AAA. The mediation will be held in [City, State]. Nothing herein is intended to prevent either party from seeking any other remedy available at law including seeking redress in a court of competent jurisdiction. This provision shall survive the termination of this Agreement indefinitely.

Section 18.11 Amendments. Neither this Agreement nor any of its terms may be changed or modified, waived, or terminated (unless as otherwise provided hereunder) except by an instrument in writing signed by an authorized representative of the party against whom the enforcement of the change, waiver, or termination is sought.

Section 18.12 Waiver; Remedies. No failure or delay by a party hereto to insist on the strict performance of any term of this Agreement, or to exercise any right or remedy consequent to a breach thereof, shall constitute a waiver of any breach or any subsequent breach of such term. No waiver of any breach hereunder shall affect or alter the remaining terms of this Agreement, but each and every term of this Agreement shall continue in full force and effect with respect to any other then existing or subsequent breach thereof. The remedies provided in this Agreement are cumulative and not exclusive of the remedies provided by law or in equity. Notwithstanding anything to the contrary contained in this Section, in no event shall either party to this Agreement be liable to the other party for any indirect, incidental or consequential damages or for lost profits, lost revenues or damage to goodwill or reputation.

Section 18.13 Relationship of Parties. Manager and XYZ acknowledge and agree that they are not joint venturers, partners, or joint owners with respect to the Facility, and nothing contained in this Agreement shall be construed as creating a partnership, joint venture or similar relationship between XYZ and Manager. In operating the Facility, entering into contracts, accepting reservations for use of the Facility, and conducting financial transactions for the Facility, Manager acts on behalf of and as agent for XYZ (but subject to the limitations on Manager's authority as set out in this Agreement), with the fiduciary duties required by law of a party acting in such capacity.

Section 18.14 Independent Contractor. As between Manager and XYZ, Manager shall be an independent contractor with respect to its employment of its employees and shall have full and exclusive responsibility for its employees. Manager shall accept full and exclusive liability for payment of any and all contributions or taxes for social security, unemployment benefits, workers' compensation, pensions and annuities now and hereafter imposed under any state or federal laws which are measured by wages, salaries and other remuneration paid to persons employed by Manager on work performed under this Agreement. Manager shall indemnify and hold harmless XYZ, its officers, and employees from any contributions, taxes and liability related to such payments arising out of Manager's employment relationship with Manager's current and former employees.

Section 18.15 Counterparts; Facsimile Signatures. This Agreement may be executed in counterparts, each of which shall constitute an original, and all of which together shall constitute one and the same document. This Agreement may be executed by the parties and transmitted by facsimile or electronic mail, and if so executed and transmitted, shall be effective as if the parties had delivered an executed original of this Agreement.

Section 18.16 Authority. Each party warrants and represents it has full right, power and authority to enter into this Agreement and make the covenants in this Agreement. The individuals executing and delivering this agreement have been duly authorized to do so and this Agreement is legally binding upon and enforceable against the parties hereto.

Section 18.17 Workers' Compensation. Manager certifies to XYZ that Manager shall provide workers' compensation for all of its employees during the Term of this Agreement.

Section 18.18 Interpretation. No provision of this Agreement shall be construed against or interpreted to the disadvantage of any party by any court or other governmental or judicial authority by reason of any party having or being deemed to have drafted such provision.

Section 18.19 [Reserved]

Section 18.20 [Campaign Contributions. IF APPLICABLE Manager hereby certifies that all applicable parties listed in Division _______ of [State] Code Section _______ are in full compliance with Divisions ______________ and ______________.]

Section 18.21 Conflicts of Interest and Ethics Compliance. No personnel of Manager or member of the governing body of any locality or other public official or employee of any such locality in which, or relating to which, the work under this Agreement is being carried out, and who exercises any functions or responsibilities in connection with the review or approval of this Agreement or carrying out of any such work, shall, prior to the completion of said work, voluntarily acquire any personal interest, direct or indirect, which is incompatible or in conflict with the discharge and fulfillment of his or her functions and responsibilities with respect to the carrying out of said work.

Any such person who acquires an incompatible or conflicting personal interest, on or after the effective date of this Agreement, or who involuntarily acquires any such incompatible or conflicting personal interest, shall immediately disclose his or her interest to XYZ in writing. Thereafter, he or she shall not participate in any action affecting the work under this Agreement, unless XYZ shall determine in its sole discretion that, in the light of the personal interest disclosed, his or her participation in any such action would not be contrary to the public interest.

Manager represents, warrants, and certifies that Manager and its employees engaged in the administration or performance of this Agreement are knowledgeable of and understand [State] Ethics and Conflicts of Interest Laws and Executive Order No. _______. In accordance with Executive Order No. _______, Manager represents, warrants, and certifies that Manager and its employees and subcontractors shall not engage in discrimination against any employee or applicant for employment because of race, color, creed, religion, sexual orientation, national origin, sex, age, disability or veteran status. Manager further represents, warrants, and certifies that neither Manager nor any of its employees will do any act that is inconsistent with such laws and Executive Order. The Governor's Executive Orders may be found by accessing the following website: [http://www. . .].

Section 18.22 Findings for Recovery. Manager warrants that it is not subject to an "unresolved" finding for recovery under [State] Code Section ___. If this warranty is found to be false, this Agreement shall, at XYZ's option and in XYZ's sole discretion, be void *ab initio* and Manager shall immediately repay to XYZ any funds paid under this Agreement.

REMAINDER OF PAGE INTENTIONALLY LEFT BLANK

IN WITNESS WHEREOF, each party hereto has caused this Management Agreement to be executed on behalf of such party by an authorized representative as of the date first set forth above.

XYZ ENTITY	MANAGEMENT COMPANY, L.P.
	By: Management, Inc., its general partner
By: ______________________	By: ______________________
Name:	Name:
Its:	Its:

EXHIBIT A
MANAGER DUTIES

Manager's obligations under the Agreement shall consist of the following obligations, all of which are subject to the terms hereof and the controls and restrictions in the Operations Manual:

(a) Manage all aspects of the Facility in accordance with the Operations Manual and the terms of this Agreement, including but not limited to managing purchasing, payroll, fire prevention, security, crowd control, routine repairs, preventative maintenance, janitorial services, promotions, advertising, energy conservation, security, box office, admission procedures, and general user services.

(b) Establish and adjust prices, rates and rate schedules for user, license, concessions, occupancy, and advertising agreements, and booking commitments for the Facility, provided that such the above-described activities shall be subject to prior review by and written approval from XYZ, and provided further that:

(i) Manager's advertising agreement activities shall be developed and implemented in conjunction with the Marketing Agreement;

(ii) [SPECIFIC LANGUAGE TO BE ADDED REGARDING TICKETS AND PRICING—TBD]; and

(iii) Manager shall schedule events in accordance with and at rates established by the Facility's Booking Policy, provided that Manager may deviate from the established rate schedule when entering into any such agreements if determined by Manager, using its reasonable business judgment, to be necessary or appropriate with respect to the specific situation.

(c) Procure, negotiate, execute, administer and assure compliance with Service Contracts, Concession Agreements, and other contracts related to the operation of the Facility.

(d) Require that all material vendors and licensees of the Facility execute vendor/license agreements containing standard indemnification and insurance obligations on the part of each such vendor/licensee.

(e) Provide a standard form advertising/sponsorship contract and a Facility license agreement for use at or with respect to the Facility. Manager shall submit such form agreements to XYZ for prior review and action, and the parties shall work together to finalize such forms. Once finalized, Manager shall use such forms in furtherance of its duties hereunder, and shall not materially deviate from the terms contained in such forms without obtaining the prior written approval of XYZ's General Counsel or Contract Administrator (which shall not be unreasonably withheld). Manager's sole responsibility with regard to providing legal advice or assistance hereunder shall be to provide such standard form contracts.

(f) Operate and maintain the Facility, including the equipment utilized in connection with its operation and any improvements made during the term of this Agreement, in the condition received, normal wear and tear excepted.

(g) Arrange for and otherwise book events at the Facility in accordance with a Facility Booking Policy, which is attached hereto as Exhibit G.

(h) Hire or otherwise engage, pay, supervise, and direct all personnel Manager deems necessary for the operation of the Facility in accordance with Article 6 of the Agreement, and conduct staff planning, retention and training programs as determined to be necessary by Manager in its sole discretion.

(i) Maintain detailed, accurate and complete records of all its operations, transactions, managerial, financial and other records of all its activities under this Agreement in accordance with generally accepted accounting principles, which records shall be made available to XYZ upon request, in accordance with Section 10.1 of the Agreement.

(j) Submit to XYZ in a timely manner financial and other reports detailing Manager's activities in connection with the Facility, as set forth in Section 10.2 of the Agreement.

(k) Prepare a proposed annual Operating Budget and submit such proposed budget to XYZ, both in accordance with Article 7 of the Agreement.

(*l*) Pay all Operating Expenses and other expenses incurred in connection with the operation, maintenance, supervision and management of the Facility from the Operating Account or with funds otherwise made available by XYZ.

(m) Secure, or assist XYZ (or any other third party, as applicable) to secure, all licenses and permits necessary for the operation and use of the Facility. XYZ shall cooperate in this process to the extent reasonably required. All costs associated with this process shall be Operating Expenses.

(n) Collect, deposit and hold in escrow in the Event Account any ticket sale revenues which it receives in the contemplation of or arising from an event pending the completion of the event, as more fully described in Section 8.1 of the Agreement.

(o) Collect in a timely manner and deposit in the Operating Account all Revenue, as more fully described in Section 8.2 of the Agreement.

(p) Subject to XYZ making available sufficient funds in a timely manner, pay all Taxes.

(q) Plan, prepare, implement, coordinate and supervise public relations and other promotional programs for the Facility.

(r) Prepare, maintain and implement on a regular basis, subject to XYZ's approval, a Marketing Plan for the Facility, provided however that such Marketing Plan shall be developed and implemented in conjunction with the Marketing Agreement.

(s) Oversee the sale of Commercial Rights at or in connection with the Facility, provided that the parties acknowledge Manager shall have no right or obligation to actually sell Commercial Rights at the Facility, as such right and obligation shall be held by a third party, and provided that Manager's oversight of the sale of Commercial Rights at or in connection with the Facility shall be implemented in conjunction with the Marketing.

(t) Oversee the sale of food and beverage at or in connection with the Facility, provided that the parties acknowledge Manager shall have no right or obligation to actually sell food and beverage at the Facility, as such right and obligation shall be held by Concessionaire Food Services, L.P., an Affiliate of Manager.

(u) On an annual basis, or upon request by XYZ, cause a written inventory to be taken of all furniture, fixtures, office equipment, supplies, tools and vehicles at the Facility, and deliver a written report of the foregoing to

XYZ. Manager shall document all major damage to, or loss in, such inventory during the Term as soon as such damage or loss is discovered by Manager, and Manager shall promptly notify XYZ of any such damage or loss.

(v) Purchase, on behalf of XYZ and with XYZ funds, and maintain during the Term, all materials, tools, machinery, equipment and supplies necessary for the operation of the Facility.

(w) As agent for XYZ, manage risk management and Facility insurance needs, as more fully described in Article 15 of the Agreement.

(x) Make and be responsible for routine and minor repairs, maintenance, preventative maintenance, and equipment servicing. Manager shall be responsible for ensuring that all repairs, replacements, and maintenance shall be of a quality and class at least equal to that of the item being repaired, replaced or maintained. Any replacement of an item in inventory, or any new item added to the inventory, which is paid for by XYZ, shall be deemed the property of XYZ.

(y) Cause such other acts and things to be done with respect to the Facility, as determined by Manager in its reasonable discretion, or as reasonably requested by XYZ and provided that such requests from XYZ shall be reasonably consistent with Manager's Duties as described herein, to be necessary for the management and operation of the Facility following the Effective Date.

EXHIBIT B
EXISTING CONTRACTS

[TO BE ATTACHED BY XYZ]

EXHIBIT C
OPERATING BUDGET (1ST OPERATING YEAR)

[TO BE ATTACHED BY XYZ]

EXHIBIT D
INSURANCE

- At all times during this Agreement, Manager shall:

  (a) maintain commercial general liability insurance, including products and completed operations, bodily injury and property damage liability, contractual liability, independent contractors' liability and personal and advertising injury liability against claims occurring on, in, or about the Facility, or otherwise arising under this Agreement;

  (b) maintain umbrella or excess liability insurance,

  (c) maintain commercial automobile liability insurance, including coverage for the operation of owned, leased, hired and non-owned vehicles;

  (d) maintain appropriate workers compensation and employer's liability insurance as shall be required by and be in conformance with the laws of the [State]; and

  (e) maintain professional liability insurance and self-insured employment practices liability coverage; and

  (f) maintain liquor liability insurance;

- Such liability insurance shall be maintained in the following minimum amounts throughout the Term:

Commercial General Liability

$1,000,000 per occurrence

$1,000,000 personal and advertising injury

$1,000,000 products-completed operations aggregate

Automobile Liability

$1,000,000 per accident (PI and PD combined single limit)

$1,000,000 uninsured/underinsured motorist

Umbrella or Excess Liability

$5,000,000 per occurrence and aggregate

Workers Compensation

Workers Compensation: Statutory

Employer's Liability: $100,000 each accident-bodily injury by accident

$500,000 policy limit-bodily injury by disease

$100,000 each employee-bodily injury by disease

Professional Liability/Errors & Omissions (Claims Made)

$1,000,000 each occurrence/aggregate

Policy is to include:

- **Entity Coverage**

Crime Insurance

Coverage on all on-site Manager employees. Limit: $500,000.00

Liquor Liability Insurance

$1,000,000 per occurrence and any bonding required by law

EXHIBIT E
MANUAL ON CASH CONTROL

EXHIBIT 2

MARKETING AND MEDIA RIGHTS AGREEMENT

between

XYZ ENTITY

and

ABCD SPORTS MARKETING, INC.

Dated as of _____, 20___

TABLE OF CONTENTS

MARKETING AND MEDIA RIGHTS AGREEMENT
BETWEEN
XYZ ENTITY
AND
ABCD SPORTS MARKETING, INC.

THIS MARKETING AND MEDIA RIGHTS AGREEMENT (this "Agreement") having an effective date of _______, 20__ (the "Effective Date") is hereby executed by and between XYZ ENTITY, with an office at _______, [City, State] ("XYZ") and ABCD SPORTS MARKETING, INC., a ______ corporation located _______, [City, State] ("ABCD").

WHEREAS, XYZ desires to arrange for broadcasts of certain of its sports events, including, without limitation, its [sport] games, as well as related coaches' shows; and

WHEREAS, XYZ desires to arrange for the publication and distribution of official game programs and other publications relative to its [sport/team]; and

WHEREAS, XYZ desires to secure the assistance of ABCD to negotiate [sport/market]-wide business-to-business agreements and to market and negotiate the sale of Naming Rights (defined below) in connection with various buildings and spaces of XYZ; and

WHEREAS, XYZ desires to arrange for certain sponsorship and promotional activities, including business-to-business opportunities, and desires to engage ABCD to sell, market and engage in such marketing and promotional activities upon the terms and conditions described herein; and

WHEREAS, ABCD has the broadcast, publication and production capabilities and other marketing expertise to provide the services desired by XYZ;

NOW, THEREFORE, in accordance with these recitals and in consideration of mutual promises and covenants recited hereafter, the parties agree as follows:

I. DEFINITIONS.

Whenever appearing in this Agreement, each of the following terms (whether capitalized or not) shall have the meanings ascribed herein:

A. "Allowable Costs" means all of the following items of expense to the extent directly related to the performance of this Agreement, in accordance with the Budget and pre-approved by XYZ: (i) all salaries and related expenses of any ABCD employee dedicated solely to the performance of this

Agreement; (ii) talent for the Productions and their reasonable travel expenses, expenses of Coaches' Shows, play-by-play, color, engineers, spotters and analysts; (iii) engineering at studio; (iv) studio rental, office rent and other occupancy costs; (v) mailings, postage, and printing; (vi) all personnel expenses utilized in the technical production of the Games and Productions; (vii) telephone(s); (viii) advertising and promotion (including, but not limited to, newspaper and other research for sponsor and listener interest); (ix) reasonable travel expenses for administrative, office and sales staff pertaining to this Agreement; (x) booth fees charged by non-[league/division] opponents; (xi) the cost of any market clearances purchased by ABCD to fulfill its commitments hereunder; (xii) the cost of insurance, indemnity bonds, letters of credit, or the like; (xv) all costs associated with the production, printing, vending and delivery of the Programs, Roster Cards and other publications; and (xvi) any other operational and direct administrative expense of ABCD incurred in furtherance of performing this Agreement.

B. "Blue Line Stage" means the final proofing stage before a Program has been printed.

C. "Broadcast(s)" means a broadcast, transmission, and/or exhibition by means of simultaneously interconnected or simultaneously operating audio devices, methods and improvements now known or hereafter developed, including, without limitation, all broadcasts, transmissions, and/or exhibitions included in customary feed patterns and/or any rebroadcasts via any means of radio, audio and/or digital transmission methods and improvements now known or hereafter developed, including, without limitation the Internet and any computer, wireless or on-line services.

D. "Budget" means the projection of income and expense mutually agreed to by ABCD and XYZ, which shall be attached to and become incorporated into this Agreement as <u>Exhibit A</u> as if rewritten herein. Neither party shall have the right to modify the Budget without the prior written consent of the other party.

E. "Change Pages" means those pages for a Program which shall change with each Program published for a particular Game.

F. "Coach(es)" means XYZ's head coach (and assistant coaches) for all [sport games].

G. "Coach's (or Coaches') Show(s)" means any television, radio, computer or internet shows produced by ABCD which primarily feature XYZ's head Coach for all [sport games].

H. "Conference(s)" means the League division or such other conference that XYZ may be a member during the Term of this Agreement.

I. "Contract Year" means that period of time from the Effective Date through _______, 20__ for the first "Contract Year" and thereafter each twelve month period from _______ through _______ during the initial Term and any renewal of this Agreement.

J. "Covered Activity" singularly and "Covered Activities" collectively, mean the corporate sponsorships, signage contracts, and Game sponsorship packages as described in Section II.G. below.

K. "Department" means that certain organizational division of XYZ which oversees and administers its [sport/games].

L. "Existing Corporate Sponsors" collectively mean those corporations which are currently sponsoring XYZ pursuant to an executed sponsorship agreement and which is identified on Exhibit B attached hereto and incorporated herein.

M. "Game(s)" means any XYZ [sport/games/matches/competitions]

N. "Gross Revenues" mean ABCD's (i) total receipts received from commercial or advertising time sales less reasonable unaffiliated agency fees, (ii) total receipts received from Covered Activities, less agency fees or commissions, (iii) the value (as mutually determined by ABCD and XYZ) of all merchandise, goods, or services received in payment or exchange for commercial or advertising time or business expense of ABCD, and (iv) any income other than advertising income or receipts from Covered Activities, i.e., station fees or booth fees from a non-Conference opponent, or station fees charged to stations for selected Games outside of the advertiser commitment.

O. “Marks” means the name, trademarks, service marks, logos, symbols and/or mascots owned by XYZ.

P. “Media Guide” means the descriptive team brochures used to promote XYZ’s [sport/games].

Q. “Naming Rights” means the non-exclusive right to negotiate and obtain agreements for the right to name Facilities or spaces on a [team/sport/market]-wide basis pursuant to Section II.E. below.

R. “Net Profits” means Gross Revenues minus Allowable Costs.

S. “Posters” means the posters published pursuant to this Agreement to promote XYZ’s [sport/games] and/or events.

T. “Productions” mean all forms of materials which are Broadcasts by ABCD pursuant to Section III below in furtherance of the purpose and intent of this Agreement.

U. “Programs” means the programs published pursuant to this Agreement for purchase at XYZ [sport/games].

V. “Publication” means Programs, Posters, Roster Cards, Schedule Cards, Media Guides and/or newsstand publications primarily relating to XYZ’s [sport/games], and any other written product such as calendars or magazines produced by ABCD pursuant to this Agreement with the prior approval and agreement of XYZ.

W. “Residual Royalties” mean ______ percent (x%) of Net Profits payable pursuant to sponsorship agreements executed during the Term of this Agreement and that were generated by ABCD and which remain in effect after the termination or expiration of this Agreement. Residual Royalties shall not include commissions earned by ABCD on Naming Rights pursuant to Section VII.C.

X. “Roster Cards” means any publication published and distributed by ABCD under this Agreement listing XYZ teams, statistics, and opposing teams for any particular competitive sport.

Y. “Royalties” mean the amounts due to ABCD by XYZ in exchange for ABCD’s performance of its obligations and responsibilities under this Agreement. After the first [$xxx] in Net Profits, which will be paid to XYZ, Royalties shall be equal to the following amounts: (i) after the first

[$xxx] is paid to XYZ, the next [$xxx] in Net Profits will be split [x]% to XYZ, [x]% to ABCD; (ii) thereafter, the next [$xxx] in Net Profits will be split [x]% to XYZ, [x]% to ABCD; and (iii) thereafter, any remaining Net Profits will be split [x]% to XYZ, [x]% to ABCD.

Z. "Schedule Cards" means cards published pursuant to this Agreement containing the season schedule of Games for one or more of XYZ's [sport/games].

AA. "Standard Contract Provisions" mean those provisions as determined by XYZ's legal counsel, in their sole discretion, which are required to be included in every contract entered into by ABCD as agent for XYZ pursuant to this Agreement. Any contract entered into by ABCD as agent for XYZ pursuant to this Agreement which does not contain the Standard Contract Provisions shall be void *ab initio* and shall not be enforceable against XYZ.

BB. "Standing Material" means pages which shall remain unchanged and shall appear in each Program published in a single season for the applicable XYZ sport.

CC. "Today's Game" means the section of a Program describing XYZ's current Game opponent.

II. **GRANT**. XYZ hereby grants ABCD the following rights to use and license the use of Marks during the Term hereof in conjunction with the following: (provided that any rights not granted herein shall be reserved to XYZ, including but not limited to XYZ's archives)

A. **Broadcast Rights**. Subject to Existing Corporate Sponsors and to any [League or Conference] restrictions provided by XYZ to ABCD in writing, XYZ hereby grants ABCD the exclusive worldwide rights to produce and distribute Broadcasts via television, radio, computer, Internet and similar types of transmission, in all languages, the following: (i) all play-by-play and commentary for regularly scheduled pre-season, regular season and post season [sport/games], and related Coaches' Shows: and (ii) all other mutually agreeable XYZ events, including, without limitation its _______________, should ABCD reasonably determine there is a profitable market for any such events. Subject to any [League and Conference] restrictions provided by XYZ to ABCD in writing, XYZ further grants ABCD an exclusive worldwide license to rebroadcast any or all Broadcasts or Productions produced by ABCD pursuant to this Agreement and, the exclusive worldwide rights to organize and administer a network of radio, computer and Internet markets for any such Broadcasts produced and distributed by ABCD hereunder, if ABCD reasonably determines there is a profitable market for any such network (the "Radio Network").

B. **Coaches' Shows**. Subject to the provisions and limitations of any agreements now or hereafter existing between XYZ and any of its Coaches, and any [LEAGUE] and Conference restrictions, XYZ grants ABCD the exclusive right to produce and distribute worldwide Broadcasts of Coaches' Shows for the [sport] via television, radio, computer, internet or similar types of transmissions in all languages.

C. **Publication Rights**. XYZ hereby grants ABCD the exclusive worldwide rights to produce, sell and distribute all official Programs, XYZ's Website related to [sport/games] or that part of XYZ's main Website related to [sport], other newsstand publications relating to XYZ's events including, without limitation, the following:

1. **Programs**. ABCD shall provide official Programs for XYZ's [sports games], except pre-season and post-season Games, in sufficient quantities to meet the demand for the respective Games. For each [sport] season during the Term hereof, ABCD will produce a mutually agreeable number of separate issues. The Game Programs to be published under a single cover will be agreed upon by ABCD and XYZ at a cover price to be mutually determined by XYZ and ABCD.

2. **Other Sports**. At ABCD's option, ABCD shall have the exclusive rights to provide official Programs or Roster Cards for other XYZ [sport] events in sufficient quantities to meet the demand for the respective Games, should ABCD reasonably determine there is a profitable market for the same. ABCD and XYZ will mutually agree on the Programs and/or Roster Cards to be published for such Games, the cover materials (if applicable), the number of issues of such Programs and/or Roster Cards, and all relating deadlines, before each of XYZ's seasons during the Term of this Agreement.

3. **Newsstand Publications; Posters**. ABCD shall have the exclusive worldwide rights to produce

and distribute commercially all XYZ [sport] team posters and all other mutually agreeable newsstand publications, including, without limitation, magazines, calendars, schedule cards and other publications relating to XYZ's [sport/games]. All such publications produced and distributed by ABCD under this paragraph shall be approved by XYZ before they are produced and distributed by ABCD, such approval not to be unreasonably withheld or delayed, and shall comply in all respects with applicable [LEAGUE] and FCC rules and regulations.

D. **Website Rights**. Subject to Existing Corporate Sponsors, XYZ hereby grants ABCD the exclusive rights to sell sponsorships and advertising on XYZ's [sport/team] website, _______. Such sponsorships and advertising will be subject to the approval of XYZ. XYZ agrees not to give any of the same or similar rights to anyone else with regard to the [sport/team]-related pages on XYZ's website and XYZ agrees not to develop any commercial aspects of said pages without ABCD prior written approval which shall not be unreasonably withheld, conditioned or delayed.

E. **Naming Rights**. XYZ hereby grants ABCD the non-exclusive right to seek, negotiate and obtain agreements for the sale of the Naming Rights to the Facilities and spaces on the XYZ [Building] including but not limited to:

1. The _______ Center;
2. The _______ Conference Center;
3. XYZ's _______ Club;
4. XYZ's _______ Center has Naming Rights opportunities for the following:
   (a) Ballroom;
   (b) Media Wall;
   (c) Meeting and Conference Rooms;
   (d) Lounge;
   (e) Atrium; and
   (f) Dining Room.

5. XYZ's ______ has Naming Rights opportunities for the following:

   (a) Center for ______;

   (b) ______ Center;

   (c) Atrium; and

   (d) Conference and Seminar Rooms.

6. XYZ's ______Center (completed in 20__) has Naming Rights opportunities for the following:

   (a) various fitness and recreation areas.

Notwithstanding the foregoing, XYZ reserves the right to (i) review and approve of all terms and conditions of any agreement relating to Naming Rights; and (ii) solicit and negotiate with individual donors for Naming Rights agreements with regard to any of XYZ's Facilities or spaces thereon and therein; provided that XYZ shall have the right to retain all revenues generated from Naming Rights agreement entered into without assistance of ABCD. Furthermore, any agreement for Naming Rights entered into by ABCD as agent for XYZ pursuant to this Section shall not be effective or enforceable against XYZ unless and until XYZ's Board has authorized such Naming Rights agreement.

F. **Business-to-Business Opportunities**. Except for those contracts to which XYZ is a party as identified on Exhibits B and C attached hereto and incorporated herein, XYZ hereby grants ABCD the exclusive third party right to identify and negotiate all [sport/market] wide business-to-business opportunities for XYZ. Nothing herein shall limit XYZ's right to pursue such [sport/market]-wide business-to-business opportunities; however, XYZ shall fully cooperate with ABCD to identify and establish [sport/market]-wide business-to-business relationships to fully maximize Net Profits under this Agreement. As Request for Proposals (RFP's) for various business services at XYZ are issued and come due, the Financial Office of XYZ will include as part of each RFP the opportunity for vendors to participate in advertising and sponsorship opportunities. This will allow ABCD an opportunity to provide bidders for XYZ business services with a package of marketing and media rights as part of their participation in the RFP. Notwithstanding anything herein to the contrary, XYZ shall have the sole right to accept and negotiate terms of any marketing and media rights agreements which are not granted to ABCD hereunder.

G. **Other Covered Activities**. XYZ hereby grants ABCD, the following exclusive worldwide ancillary rights and privileges to the following Covered Activities:

1. **Corporate Sponsorships**. ABCD shall have the exclusive right to organize, develop and market a corporate sponsor program for XYZ's [sport/games]; provided however, that such grant of exclusive rights under this subsection 1 shall not prevent XYZ from granting certain rights to [Management Company], L.P. or any successor manager under a certain Management Agreement dated _______, 20__. Such marketing, merchandising, advertising, promotional and sponsorship rights shall include, but are not limited to, the following: (i) radio Broadcasting advertising rights; (ii) television telecast advertising rights for television Coaches' Shows; (iii) computer on-line service, CD Rom and/or other Internet and wireless or interactive media rights; and (iv) other rights relating to sponsorships, promotions, and advertisements of and related to XYZ's [sport] events which may include, among other things, product sampling, couponing, display booths, signage, public address announcements, in-game promotions, hospitality events and the rights to use and license the use of XYZ Marks. Such sponsorships are subject to the approval of XYZ.

2. **Signage**. ABCD shall have the exclusive rights to seek, negotiate and obtain agreements, including, without limitation, barter agreements as described in Section IX below, for securing sponsorships, promotions and advertisers, for all advertising space, not otherwise controlled by other third parties, on all designated [sport/market]-wide signage including, without limitation, the Fixed and/or rotating signage rights in the _______ Center and _______ Conference Pavilion; provided however, that such grant of exclusive rights under this subsection 2 shall not prevent XYZ from granting certain rights to [Management Company], L.P. or any successor manager under a certain Management Agreement dated _______, 20__. In the event any existing agreements between XYZ and any third parties for the

control of advertising space located in any of XYZ's [sport/team] facilities are not renewed, expire or terminate during the Term of this Agreement, XYZ shall make all such advertising space available to ABCD for its marketing and advertising sales hereunder.

3. **Game Sponsorship Packages**. In addition to the rights to secure multi-year and/or season long Corporate Sponsorships, ABCD shall have the exclusive rights to sell sponsorship packages of any mutually agreeable XYZ [sport/games] to include, without limitation, the following: (i) tickets to any sponsored Game, supplied by XYZ at no cost to ABCD, all of which shall be in a premium location with a view to their distribution by ABCD to a Game event sponsor; (ii) stadium public address announcements recognizing the Game event sponsor; (iii) exposure of a Game event sponsor through other mutually agreeable pre-game and half-time activities; (iv) the right to distribute, display and sample products or merchandise (including any coupons related thereto) of a Game event sponsor at a Game; (v) all rights to promote the Game event sponsorship on XYZ's [sport facility]; (vi) access to XYZ facilities for pre-game and post-game hospitality; (vii) Radio Network drop-in commercials; and (viii) access to all XYZ Marks in accordance with Section X and XI hereof. Notwithstanding the grant of such exclusive rights under this subsection 3, XYZ shall not be prohibited from granting certain rights to [Management Company], L.P. or any successor manager under a certain Management Agreement dated _______, 20__.

III. **PRODUCTION COVENANTS**. In connection with the Broadcast rights granted by XYZ and ABCD's option to organize a Radio Network, ABCD and XYZ mutually agree and covenant as follows:

A. **Broadcasts**. ABCD shall produce and broadcast all Game Broadcasts and related Coaches' Shows subject to (i) the terms and conditions contained in this Agreement; and (ii) XYZ, [LEAGUE] and FCC rules and regulations. ABCD will be responsible for the cost and format of any and all Broadcasts and Productions produced pursuant hereto.

B. **Radio Network Broadcasts**. In connection with the Radio Network, ABCD shall with the approval of XYZ (i) select radio stations to participate as affiliates in the Radio Network; (ii) be responsible for arranging affiliate contracts with such radio stations, Radio Network schedules, other Broadcast distribution outlets, and for all other Radio Network production elements including, without limitation, the necessary clearances to air broadcasts of the radio Productions on Radio Network stations; and (iii) use its best efforts to cause each Radio Network station to carry each [LEAGUE] sanctioned Game live in its Broadcast schedule in its entirety, unless preempted by emergency, unscheduled news interruptions, requirements of the Emergency Broadcast System, or regulatory requirements of the Federal Communications Commission.

C. **Talent**. ABCD and XYZ shall mutually agree on the play-by-play and color announcers to be used as over-the-air talent and as host(s) of all Productions produced by ABCD hereunder. ABCD shall be responsible for all compensation (including but not limited to related salary, union dues or withholding taxes or other taxes) of such talent and/or host(s).

D. **Coaches' Services**. Subject to Coach's availability and provided that it is not in violation of a Coach's agreement with XYZ (or any other agreement to which such Coach is a party to), for each Coach's Show, XYZ, at no cost to ABCD, shall: (i) cause its respective Coaches to provide their services for each Coach's Show produced by ABCD as the principal talent for such Coach's Show and including, without limitation, performance on the Coach's Show (whether live or recorded and in all retakes), participation in Production conferences, and personal appearances promoting such Coaches' Shows; (ii) prohibit its Coaches from participation in any other competitive radio programs and/or shows, as the principal talent for such programs, provided however, ABCD's exclusive rights hereunder shall not prohibit the Coaches from participating in news interviews by other Broadcasts. All other services of the Coaches to be provided to ABCD by XYZ shall be mutually agreed upon by ABCD and XYZ.

E. **Subcontracting**. ABCD, at its sole cost and expense, may subcontract Production responsibilities for any or all Broadcasts and Productions produced under this

Agreement provided that such subcontracting shall not relieve ABCD of any of its obligations hereunder.

F. **Access**. XYZ shall furnish ABCD, at no cost to ABCD, cards of admission and/or passes, if available, which enable employees of ABCD involved with any Broadcast to have free access to and egress from each Game site at all reasonable times before and after each Game, to prepare, record, broadcast each Game and related Coach's Show and to setup and remove any equipment. In conjunction with each Game, XYZ shall provide ABCD with adequate location of its equipment and personnel necessary to Broadcast the Game. If the permission of any third party is needed for the location of ABCD's equipment and/or personnel as provided in this paragraph, XYZ will use its reasonable efforts to obtain such permission. In addition thereto, XYZ agrees to provide ABCD, at no cost, with an adequate number of seats (coach class) on XYZ team planes or bus (as applicable) to enable employees of ABCD involved with Broadcasts to meet ABCD's Broadcast obligations for all away [sport games].

G. **Residuals**. XYZ shall own all rights in each Broadcast made pursuant hereto. In furtherance of XYZ's ownership rights, ABCD shall make appropriate copyright notice announcements during each Broadcast and shall affix appropriate copyright notices to all audio and video tapes and other forms of recordings or reproductions with respect thereto. Notwithstanding the foregoing, subject to XYZ's prior approval, ABCD shall have the right to use and license the use of any footage or audio recording of any Broadcast for promotional and newsworthy uses by ABCD or others contracting through ABCD or for any rebroadcast by ABCD or others contracting through ABCD; provided that (1) ABCD obtain the prior consent of XYZ; and (2) at all times XYZ shall own all right, title and interest in and to its archived Broadcasts.

H. **Reciprocal Rights for Away Games**. XYZ will secure for ABCD the rights to Broadcast all away or tournament [sport/games] in accordance with Conference, [LEAGUE] and FCC rules and regulations, unless ABCD shall stipulate to the contrary. In the event a rights fee is charged for any away or tournament Game, XYZ shall obtain the prior written approval of ABCD of such rights fee prior to any purchase thereof; provided, however, XYZ shall use its reasonable efforts to obtain such rights at no cost to

ABCD. Any rights fee approved by ABCD shall be its responsibility.

I. **Advertising Sales**. Except as expressly provided in this Agreement to the contrary, all advertising inventory and revenues from advertising sales relating to each Broadcast undertaken by ABCD shall be controlled and retained by ABCD to be utilized in the calculation of Royalties payable to XYZ pursuant to Section VII; provided that XYZ shall have the right to withhold certain inventory for XYZ's own advertising purposes as it deems necessary in its discretion. ABCD acknowledges and agrees that the advertising of alcoholic beverages on XYZ's [building] is prohibited.

J. **Clearances**. ABCD shall be responsible for obtaining all necessary clearances to air broadcasts live on radio stations in accordance with all applicable Conference, [LEAGUE] and FCC rules and regulations. Notwithstanding the foregoing, ABCD shall not incur any liability from its failure to obtain any clearance by reason of preemption by unscheduled news interruptions, requirements of the Emergency Broadcast System, regulatory requirements of the Federal Communications Commission, any pre-emption mutually approved by ABCD and XYZ or any other force majeure event described in this Agreement.

IV. **PUBLICATION COVENANTS**.

A. **Materials Supplied by XYZ**. XYZ shall supply to ABCD, editorial content material, black and white photographs, front cover materials, and meet other reasonable requests of ABCD for editorial resource materials for any publication produced and published by ABCD hereunder. XYZ's sports information director or his/her representative and other [sport/team] personnel will be available for consultation at all reasonable times.

B. **Program Composition**.

1. **Design**. ABCD and XYZ agree that the cover design and editorial/photographic Standing Material for any [sport/games] Programs produced by ABCD will be determined by XYZ prior to each season. During the Term of this Agreement, ABCD and XYZ will mutually agree no later than (month, date) for each [sport] season (as applicable) to a delivery schedule to

ABCD of the selected cover design and Standing Material.

2. **Change Pages; Program Deadlines**. XYZ shall have a mutually agreeable number of Change Pages in each Program published by ABCD hereunder. Change Pages to be used in the Programs for a given Game shall be delivered to ABCD, or ABCD's designated representative as follows: (i) features, rosters and photos shall be delivered no later than seven (7) business days preceding such Game and (ii) Today's Game, updated statistics and other final changes shall be delivered no later than three (3) business days preceding such Game. Changes or corrections at the Blue Line Stage shall be made promptly and at the sole expense of XYZ unless such changes are the result of an error by ABCD or its designated representative(s) in the reproduction of change information.

C. **Editorial Standards; Final Program Composition**. XYZ shall provide rough layouts of the Programs with final design mutually agreed upon by the parties. Final composition and page make-up shall be the responsibility of ABCD. High standards of editorial and advertising copy excellence shall be maintained, consistent with accepted levels of printing and media industries. Lack of quality due to photographic density, second generation negatives, and scheduled changes shall be held to a minimum, but when necessary, will be accepted as best available. ABCD shall be responsible for any and all reprints and shall bear the cost thereof, unless such reprint is caused by an act or omission of XYZ. If use of an outside printer is necessary, ABCD shall have the right to determine the area printer to be used in the final production of the Programs and will notify XYZ of that printer prior to use thereof. This paragraph applies to all advertisements and promotions to be included in the Programs, including all advertisements and promotions to be included in the programs from the sponsors referenced in paragraph V.E. of this Agreement.

D. **Inserts**. Inserts will not be used in any Program without approval of ABCD.

E. **Cooperation**. XYZ agrees to meet with ABCD's publishing staff, at least annually, to set dates by which copy for the Programs will be supplied to ABCD, and if copy is not timely supplied, ABCD will provide copy.

F. **Vendor Announcements**. XYZ will provide for two public announcements and two scoreboard announcements at each home game (as applicable) to promote vending sales.

G. **Program Storage Locations**. XYZ will make available dry, safe, convenient storage space to store the Programs to which ABCD shall have access at all times.

H. **Program Vendor**. In coordination with those rights granted to [Management Company], L.P. or its successor manager pursuant to a certain Management Agreement dated ___, 20__, ABCD will be the sole and exclusive publisher for XYZ's Program pursuant to this Agreement and shall be responsible for all publication operations. ABCD will also be responsible for arranging all contracts with vendors, suppliers, sponsors, media users and the like and all other production elements relative to all Game Programs.

I. **Other Programs; Roster Cards**. In the event ABCD reasonably determines that the publication of Roster Cards for any of XYZ's [sport/team] events not otherwise heretofore under contract with any third party is economically feasible, ABCD and XYZ shall mutually agree on the design and content of such Roster Cards. Any other Roster Cards published by ABCD pursuant to this Agreement shall meet high standards of advertising and print quality consistent with accepted levels of printing and media industries and shall be in accordance with all applicable rules and regulations of XYZ, the Conference and the [LEAGUE]. XYZ shall provide to ABCD such rules and regulations and all other information reasonably required by ABCD for inclusion in any Roster Cards in advance of publication deadlines reasonably determined by ABCD. If ABCD should decline to publish or produce any Roster Card or other publication requested by XYZ, XYZ may publish such Roster Card or other publication at its own cost; however, XYZ shall afford ABCD with an opportunity place sponsor logos or advertisements within such publications.

V. **COVERED ACTIVITIES COVENANTS AND WARRANTIES**. In connection with the rights granted by XYZ to ABCD to engage in the Covered Activities hereunder, XYZ and ABCD agree as follows:

A. **Covered Activities Duties**. ABCD shall use best efforts to: (i) advance XYZ's interest, (ii) obtain proper publicity of all Covered Activities, and (iii) secure suitable offers for purchases of or sponsorships involving any Covered Activity. The parties acknowledge that the Covered Activities undertaken by ABCD hereunder may have limited marketability, such that ABCD shall not incur any liability to XYZ from its inability to secure offers for purchases of sponsorships relating to any Covered Activity or from the failure of any Covered Activity to generate revenues. ABCD shall have no obligation to engage in Covered Activity upon its reasonable determination that a profitable market is lacking for the same.

B. **Inventory; Signage**. XYZ shall annually furnish ABCD with a written inventory indicating the [sport/team] facilities or other facilities as XYZ may request, and signage or other materials, such as posters or calendars, on which advertising space is available, as well as any other available rights relating to the Covered Activities. In addition thereto, XYZ shall be responsible for displaying, and maintaining any advertising, equipment, or signs in its [sport/team] facilities, arenas or stadiums secured by ABCD from advertisers and sponsors pursuant to this Agreement.

C. **Service of Head Coaches**. XYZ agrees to make available, without expense to ABCD, the reasonable services of its Coaches or other members of its [sport/team] for any promotional activity or advertising of and relating to XYZ's [sport team] which XYZ has approved in connection with any Covered Activity. ABCD shall furnish to XYZ, for its approval, a written description of the anticipated scope of the personal services of each Coach or personnel which ABCD projects will be necessary for the forthcoming promotion, endorsement and sponsorship programs related to any Covered Activity.

D. **Marketing to Existing Corporate Sponsors**. Subject to XYZ's Existing Corporate Sponsors, XYZ agrees that ABCD has the right to sell such Existing Corporate Sponsors media and other advertising rights associated with and related to the Productions and any and all Programs or other publications. All Existing Corporate Sponsors' agreements with XYZ shall be subject to this Agreement, including the right to Residual Royalties, only to the extent that ABCD negotiated new terms or renewal rights in addition to those set forth on Exhibit B attached hereto. For sponsorship agreements in addition to those Existing Corporate Sponsors listed on Exhibit B attached hereto, XYZ agrees to execute any documents reasonably deemed necessary by ABCD to renew such agreements and to otherwise take all necessary actions required of XYZ to fulfill and perform such sponsorships.

E. **Merchandising and Other Support**. In connection with the rights in and to the corporate sponsorship Covered Activities granted hereunder, XYZ will provide to ABCD the following:

1. **Sponsor Functions**. XYZ will host a sponsor dinner during the [sport] season to benefit any pre-approved corporate sponsors of XYZ's [sport/games] secured by ABCD under this Agreement. Corporate sponsors and other personnel associated with a corporate sponsorship or other promotional activities organized by ABCD to promote XYZ and its [sport/games] will be invited and provided with tickets as ABCD and XYZ shall mutually agree. The payment of all costs associated with all sponsor functions under this paragraph shall be mutually agreed upon in writing prior to any such function.

2. **Other Merchandising**. Subject to the Budget, XYZ will provide at to ABCD a reasonable number of autographed memorabilia items, media guides, team photos, and souvenirs for the benefit of any corporate sponsors secured by ABCD hereunder. XYZ will also provide to ABCD extra tickets at face value, parking passes and other amenities for promotional purposes when available.

F. **Tickets**. At no cost to ABCD and for its distribution to advertisers, sponsors or other entities, XYZ agrees to provide ABCD with ______________ (_______) complimentary season tickets, or such number of tickets as currently being used for servicing the existing base of XYZ sponsors, whichever is greater, to all XYZ regular home [sports games], all of which shall be located in seating areas to be mutually determined by ABCD and XYZ. ABCD shall have the right to purchase, at the face value price, at a minimum, the following: ______________ (_______) tickets to the first two (2) rounds of the [Playoff Tournament] in which XYZ [sports team] participates.

G. **Employment of Staff/XYZ Office Space**. Subject to the prior approval of XYZ, ABCD shall have full power and authority to employ, train, supervise, and discharge a general manager or other staff member, as may be required, to maintain an office for the general manager or other staff in its [State] offices. Any such employees hired by ABCD hereunder shall be on ABCD's payroll, and all wages or compensation provided to such employees, including the salary of the general manager, all costs associated with the operation of the office of the general manager, including the following: (i) mailings, postage and printing; (ii) salaries; and (iii) travel expenses, shall be a cost of ABCD's performance of this Agreement, subject to the Budget. XYZ shall provide at no cost to ABCD, reasonable office space at its [building] to be agreed upon by the parties and access to all necessary office machines, computers, telephones and similar necessary materials and equipment to properly operate an office for the purpose of ABCD's performance under this Agreement.

During the Term of this Agreement and for a period of one year after the expiration, termination or non-renewal of this Agreement, neither ABCD nor XYZ shall, directly or indirectly: (i) solicit, hire or seek to hire any of the personnel, employees or consultants of ABCD or XYZ, as applicable, in any capacity whatsoever nor induce or attempt to induce any personnel, employees or consultants of ABCD or XYZ, as applicable, to leave its employ to work for ABCD or XYZ, as applicable, or for any other person, firm, corporation or other business entity with whom the employee may be associated.

VI. **TERM**. Unless sooner terminated, this Agreement shall be in force and effect from the Effective Date through _______, 20__ and any renewal thereafter ("Term"). Unless this Agreement is terminated before its normal expiration date in accordance with the provisions hereof, XYZ shall have ___ (x) option(s) ("Option(s)") to extend this Agreement for a period of ___ years. XYZ shall exercise an Option providing written notice to Manager within 120 days prior to the expiration of the then-current Term.

Notwithstanding any obligation of XYZ in this Section VI, nothing in this Agreement shall be construed as prohibiting or diminishing XYZ's right to publicly bid the marketing rights granted pursuant to this Agreement.

A. **Early Termination Rights**. The terms of this agreement are subject to early termination by either party hereto upon the occurrence of any of the following events:

1. **Bankruptcy and Insolvency**. The filing by or against either party in any forum or jurisdiction of any petition, voluntary or involuntary, for relief in a court in bankruptcy for either adjudication of bankruptcy or for a reorganization or rearrangement under the bankruptcy laws, or an action for receivership of any nature or for an assignment for the benefit of such party's creditors.

2. **Dissolution**. The dissolution other than by merger or consolidation of either party for any reason where such party or successor shall not continue, without interruption, its business affairs.

3. **Loss of Permits**. The loss by either party of any license, permit or other evidence of the right and privilege of such party to conduct its business affairs which loss cannot be reasonably cured.

4. **Material Default**. The occurrence of any event of material default by either party which shall remain uncured for more than thirty (30) business days after written notice.

B. **Notice of Termination**. In the event of the applicability of the foregoing, the party having the option to terminate shall give written notice of its intent to elect early termination, and the defaulting party shall have thirty business days to correct the default. If the defaulting party fails to correct the alleged default, this Agreement shall terminate subject to the terms hereof.

C. **[LEAGUE] Sanction Termination Rights**. ABCD shall have the right, but not the obligation, upon at least fifteen business days' written notice, to terminate this Agreement if a [League Entity] imposes sanctions on XYZ's [sport/games] which results in an uncompleted Game schedule or in the cancellation of all of the scheduled Games for one or more years. In the event of termination by ABCD under this subparagraph, the parties shall have no liability to each other except for an accounting and distribution to XYZ of its Royalties, as defined in paragraph VIII(B), as contemplated hereunder which are realized prior to the date of such termination.

D. **Special Cancellation Privilege**. ABCD reserves the right to cancel this Agreement in the event that changes in the policies, rules and/or regulations of the

[LEAGUE], the Federal Communication Commission, or the Federal Trade Commission or other governmental agencies should necessitate such action to assure ABCD's conformity with those regulations; or, in the event of any material change in any agreement between XYZ and a third party would prohibit or limit rights granted by XYZ to ABCD hereunder. If ABCD elects to cancel this Agreement under the terms contained in this subparagraph, such cancellation would require thirty business days' written notice by ABCD in writing before the cancellation would take effect, absent a mutual, written agreement otherwise.

E. **XYZ Termination Rights**. XYZ will have the right to terminate the Agreement without liability, except for the ABCD's right to Royalties for the Contract Year during which the termination occurred as well as XYZ's obligation to pay Residual Royalties and Commissions, upon thirty (30) days advance notice if XYZ believes, in good faith that (i) its performance hereunder is or would result in a violation of a statute, rule or regulation of any governmental authority or professional association with jurisdiction over any party, or (ii) XYZ does not have adequate funds for XYZ to continue the Agreement, or (iii) ABCD has breached its obligations to comply with Executive Orders pursuant to Section XXII.L. below. Prior to issuing a notice of termination as set forth above, the parties shall use their reasonable efforts to amend the Agreement so that it no longer causes a violation.

F. **Reservation of Other Rights**. Notwithstanding any such termination hereunder, each party reserves all other rights and remedies hereunder and otherwise permitted by law that have accrued at the date of termination and does not waive any obligation of the other party by reason of the exercise of such termination option.

VII. **ROYALTIES**.

A. **Payment of Royalties**. In exchange for ABCD's performance of its responsibilities and obligations hereunder, XYZ shall pay Royalties to ABCD to the extent such Net Profits are received by XYZ. In an effort to maximize revenues for both parties, ABCD and XYZ shall agree on a Budget to be assumed by ABCD in the operation of XYZ [sport/team] sponsorship program for the remainder of the Term of this Agreement. The Budget shall be agreed to within thirty days of the execution of this Agreement and shall be annexed as a rider to this Agreement. Any expense or revenue not expressly assumed by ABCD shall remain an obligation or asset of XYZ. No additional expenses may be added to the Budget without the written consent of ABCD and XYZ's [sport/team] Director. Any shortfall in the revenues identified on the Budget during any Contract Year shall be deducted from XYZ's initial distribution of Net Profits. ABCD shall collect all revenues generated from XYZ [sport/team] sponsorship program during this Term. In the event that XYZ's [sport/team] sponsorship program should sustain a loss in any Contract Year, the loss shall be included into the Budget for the ensuing Contract Year. The Royalties earned during each Contract Year of this Agreement shall be distributed quarterly in arrears.

B. **Royalties Following Termination**. Upon the termination or expiration of this Agreement, ABCD shall no longer receive the Royalties as described above in Sections VII A. In lieu of such Royalties, ABCD shall receive Residual Royalties. ABCD's right to receive the Residual Royalty attributable to any such sponsorship agreement shall terminate upon the expiration, modification or renewal of such sponsorship agreement. XYZ shall remit payment of the Residual Royalties due to ABCD within thirty days of its receipt of any full or partial payment under the sponsorship agreements.

C. **Naming Rights Commissions**. In addition to the Royalties set forth above, ABCD shall be entitled to receive a commission of ______ percent (x%) ("Commission") on all revenues generated from the sale of the Naming Rights pursuant to any agreement that was executed during the Term of this Agreement as a direct result of ABCD's efforts. ABCD will have the right to collect the revenues from such Naming Rights and to disburse the revenues, less ABCD's Commission, to XYZ within thirty days of its receipt of any full or partial payment under the Naming Rights agreements. The right to the Commission shall survive the expiration or termination of this Agreement. ABCD's right to receive the Commission attributable to any such Naming Rights agreement shall terminate upon the expiration, modification or renewal of such Naming Rights agreement. In the event that any payment due under a Naming Rights agreement should be paid directly to XYZ, XYZ shall remit payment of the Commission due to ABCD within thirty days of its receipt of any full or partial payment under the Naming Rights agreements.

VIII. <u>**ACCOUNTING AND PAYMENT**</u>. ABCD shall provide an initial accounting settlement statement to XYZ showing the manner in which Royalties are calculated, together with a check for XYZ's distribution of Royalties collected by ABCD, if any, on or before the 30th day following the last day of each calendar quarter in each Contract Year during the Term of this Agreement. XYZ shall have the right, at its sole expense and upon reasonable notice at any time during any Contract Year, to audit all records of ABCD related to the revenues collected by ABCD in the performance of this Agreement. ABCD shall additionally provide written monthly reports to XYZ's Director of [sport] detailing sales progress, expenditures to date, financial forecasts, and comparison analysis to the Budget.

IX. <u>**BARTER AGREEMENTS**</u>. It is anticipated from time to time that there may be opportunities for promotions or sponsorships which can result in XYZ or ABCD receiving goods or services in kind to support its operations. As of the Effective Date of this Agreement, XYZ has existing barter agreements that generate [$xxx] in trade value according to the current contract values. XYZ shall retain [x]% of the revenues generated from the existing barter agreements, which are listed on <u>Exhibit C</u> attached to this Agreement. Any additional trade secured by ABCD, which is of direct value to XYZ [sport] Department, will count towards XYZ's share of profit with the prior approval of the [sport/team] Director. As mutually agreed by the parties, XYZ shall furnish to ABCD a list of those goods or services previously provided by vendors, a list of current vendors, an estimate of its future needs or requirements and other relevant information, including, any contract expiration dates. Any barter arrangement shall be subject to the prior approval of XYZ. The value assigned to any barter agreement under this paragraph shall be mutually agreed upon by ABCD and XYZ. If within any reasonable time the parties are unable to agree upon a value, then the value shall be determined in order of priority (i) by the price of the items as established by formal proposals or price quotations submitted to XYZ or ABCD in response to a request for competitive bids or (ii) by the price of such item based upon previous purchases of such items by XYZ or ABCD. The established value of any barter arrangement in excess of XYZ's current base shall then be used in the calculation of Royalties due XYZ hereunder and/or deducted from the total amount of the Rights Fees payable by ABCD under paragraph VII for any Contract Year in which such barter arrangement is received by XYZ or ABCD.

X. **LIKENESSES AND NAMES**. In connection with all of ABCD's activities conducted pursuant to this Agreement, XYZ hereby grants to ABCD the rights to use, display, exhibit and include the names, likenesses, audio and visual representations and biographical material (as applicable) of XYZ, the Games, and persons participating in and identified with the Games (including each Coach), in and for all of ABCD's Productions, Programs, and Covered Activities, including, without limitation, all of ABCD's broadcasts, publications, advertisements, promotional, sponsorship and marketing activities hereunder, provided that the same does not constitute an endorsement of any commercial products. Any promotional claim made by ABCD regarding any Broadcast, Production, publication or other sponsorship or promotional activity of ABCD hereunder shall not imply that XYZ, any Coach, any opposing team in any Game or their faculties, employees, or players recommend or endorse any advertised product. No athlete's name or picture shall be used for advertising so as to violate [LEAGUE], Conference or XYZ rules and regulations on the athlete's eligibility. To the extent that XYZ supplies or produces any publication or other material containing the names or likeness of any person for use by ABCD in connection with its responsibilities herein, XYZ warrants that it possesses the legal right and/or has secured the written authorization of such persons to utilize their names and likenesses.

XI. **XYZ'S NAME, TRADEMARKS AND LOGOS**. XYZ hereby grants to ABCD an exclusive worldwide license to use and to license the use of the Marks in connection with all of its activities conducted pursuant to this Agreement. Any marketing and/or use of XYZ's Mark shall be done in such a way as to preserve the integrity, character and dignity of XYZ and to advance XYZ's purpose of the maintenance of its [sport/games] consistent with the highest standards of competitive sports. Notwithstanding the foregoing, ABCD acknowledges and agrees that the foregoing rights shall not include the rights to engage in activities conducted by [Licensing Company] or any successor merchandise licensing company.

XII. **EFFORT AND COOPERATION; ADVERTISING INQUIRIES**. A member (or members) of ABCD's marketing staff in its [State] office shall be designated by ABCD as its "XYZ Marketing Team" and shall fully cooperate with XYZ to maintain and enhance the traditions and goals of XYZ. Except for inquiries from individuals directly resulting from XYZ's own efforts, XYZ shall refer all inquiries for advertising, promotions and sponsorships to ABCD and assist ABCD in advertising sales and/or promotional activities which involve (i) XYZ's Coaches and teams and/or (ii) the Productions, the Programs, other publications, any Covered Activities and corporate sponsorships. In connection herewith, XYZ shall furnish ABCD, upon ABCD's request, XYZ mailing lists of [sport/team] event season ticket holders, [sport/team] supporters, and XYZ vendors to be used by ABCD in its advertising and marketing efforts hereunder. XYZ will provide ABCD with access to key XYZ administration personnel for presentations by ABCD potential corporate sponsors. XYZ shall provide ABCD with introductions to its key XYZ former-players as determined by XYZ in its sole discretion.

XIII. **ADVERTISING POLICIES, STANDARDS**. ABCD will use commercially reasonable efforts to cause all advertising in and related to the Productions, Programs, other publications, Covered Activities and all corporate sponsorships, endorsements and other advertising associated with the Covered Activities to be in accordance with policies and regulations of XYZ, the Conference and the [LEAGUE]. XYZ agrees to provide ABCD with copies of all such policies and regulations on or before the execution of this Agreement and thereafter as reasonably requested by ABCD. Both parties understand that the presentation of commercial messages is subject to criticism and standards of good practice and each undertakes to assure that it will seek to maintain high quality in its respective presentation and be responsive to reasonable requests of the other party. ABCD will provide XYZ such logs of material related to the Productions as XYZ may request. Both parties acknowledge and agree that Conference, [LEAGUE] and opponent's rules, as well as regulations of the Federal Communications Commission or other government statutes or applicable laws may affect provisions of this Agreement and each party will undertake to abide by such rules and cooperate with the other to assure compliance.

XIV. **POWER AND AUTHORITY FOR CONTRACTS**. In connection with all services provided by ABCD pursuant to this Agreement, ABCD shall have the full power and authority to seek and negotiate all contracts relating to Covered Activities to the extent that such contracts (i) do not include XYZ as a signatory; (ii) do not extend beyond the Term or any renewal of this Agreement; (iii) do not violate any provision of [State] law applicable to XYZ; and (iv) include the Standard Contract Provisions. Any contract that extends beyond the Term or any renewal hereof must be executed and ratified in writing by XYZ. XYZ shall fully perform, or arrange for the performance of, all obligations of ABCD pursuant to the contract in the event of the expiration or termination of this Agreement provided that (A) such contract has been duly executed by both parties, and (B) XYZ's legal counsel has reviewed and approved of the form of such contract; and, for those contracts relating to Naming Rights, (C) XYZ's Board has authorized such agreement. ABCD shall also have the full power and authority to make all disbursements necessary to carry out its duties and obligations under this Agreement but only to the extent authorized hereunder.

XV. **FORCE MAJEURE**. If, due to an act of God, fire, lock out, strike, or other labor dispute, riot or civil disservice, act of government or governmental instrumentality (whether federal, state or local), failure of performance by common carrier, failure in whole or in part of technical facilities, or other causes beyond the control of a party hereto (expressly excluding financial inability), either party shall be unable to materially perform any or all of its duties or obligations hereunder, then such inability shall not be in default of this Agreement. In the event of force majeure, the non-performing party shall immediately notify the other party of such event causing the non-performance and if the non-performance continues for thirty consecutive days, then either party shall have the right to immediately terminate this Agreement upon written notice to the other party.

XVI. **REPRESENTATIONS AND WARRANTIES**.

A. **By XYZ**. XYZ represents, warrants and agrees that: (i) XYZ validly exists and possesses the power, right and authority to enter into and perform the terms of this Agreement; (ii) this Agreement by XYZ has been duly and validly executed and delivered by XYZ and constitutes a valid and binding obligation of XYZ enforceable against XYZ in accordance with its terms; (iii) the execution, delivery and performance of this Agreement by XYZ does not require the consent of any third party and does not violate, conflict with, result in a breach of, or create a default under the by-laws, charter or constitution of XYZ or violate any applicable law, judgment, order, injunction, decree, rule or regulation of any governmental agency or of the [LEAGUE] or constitute grounds for termination of, or result in the breach of, or constitute a default under any agreement, instrument, license or permit to which XYZ is either a party or is bound; (iv) any games for which sponsorships are being solicited have been or will be sanctioned by the [LEAGUE] at the time each game is played; (v) XYZ is the owner of all right, title and interest in and to the rights which are the subject of this Agreement and necessary to grant to ABCD the rights provided in this Agreement and to engage ABCD as its consultant in accordance with this Agreement; (vi) the exercise by ABCD of the powers granted to it by this Agreement will not infringe upon the rights of any person, firm or corporation or other entity; and (vii) except as disclosed to ABCD on Exhibits B and C attached hereto and incorporated herein, XYZ has not entered into any arrangement or agreement with any third party which will interfere or conflict with the rights granted to ABCD by this Agreement.

B. **By ABCD**. ABCD represents, warrants and agrees that: (i) ABCD is a corporation duly organized, validly existing and in good standing under the law of the State of ______ and has the corporate power and authority to enter into and perform this Agreement; (ii) all corporate action necessary to authorize the execution, delivery and performance of this Agreement by ABCD has been duly and properly taken, and upon the execution and delivery of this Agreement it will constitute a valid and binding obligation of ABCD enforceable in accordance with its terms: (iii) the execution, delivery and performance of this Agreement by ABCD does not require the consent of any third party and does not violate, conflict with, result in a breach of, or constitute a default under the Articles of Incorporation or By-Laws of ABCD, or any applicable law, judgment, order, injunction, decree, rule or regulation, of any governmental instrumentality, and does not constitute grounds for termination of or create a breach of, or constitute grounds for termination of any agreement, instrument, license or permit to which ABCD is now subject; (iv) ABCD will work closely with XYZ to assure XYZ of proper oversight of ABCD's activities under this Agreement; and (v) a senior member of ABCD's marketing staff shall oversee the marketing and promotional activities of ABCD hereunder and ABCD shall fully cooperate with XYZ to maintain and enhance the traditions and goals of XYZ.

XVII. **CONFIDENTIALITY OF TRADE SECRETS**. Subject to the conditions set forth in this Section XVII, all documents received by XYZ in connection with this Agreement shall be subject to [State] laws, including but not limited to [State] Code Chapter ___. ABCD and XYZ agree that ABCD's information regarding the financial status and performance of ABCD is not made available to the public ("ABCD Financial Information") and ABCD regards ABCD Financial Information as trade secrets within the meaning of [State] Code Section _______. ABCD will use its best efforts not to disclose such ABCD Financial Information to ABCD personnel unless there is a "need to know" in order to carry out this Agreement. ABCD agrees that it will not disclose to any outside party the amount of revenues paid to XYZ hereunder or under any other contracts, unless compelled to do so by law.

ABCD believes that ABCD Financial Information reveals financial, cost and other information regarding its business that is not available to the public and the disclosure of which would be damaging to ABCD if made available to its competitors. XYZ acknowledges and agrees that the disclosure of ABCD Financial Information would provide any competitor of ABCD with an unfair competitive advantage. To the extent that ABCD Financial Information is requested at any time by XYZ pursuant to the terms of this Agreement, ABCD shall be obligated to provide such ABCD Financial Information only upon the written acknowledgement and undertaking of XYZ that such ABCD Financial Information (i) constitutes trade secrets of ABCD, (ii) is confidential, and will be treated as such, and (iii) will not be disclosed to any person without the prior written agreement of ABCD or as directed by an order issued by a court of competent jurisdiction.

All sponsorship agreements or other documents containing ABCD Financial Information shall be made available for review by XYZ at any time upon request, but shall remain in the possession of ABCD at all times.

XVIII. **INDEMNIFICATION**.

A. **[Reserved]**

B. **Indemnification by ABCD**. ABCD covenants and agrees that it will indemnify, defend and hold harmless XYZ and its Board, officers, employees, agents and representatives from and against any and all liabilities, losses, claims, debts, obligations, judgments and expenses, of any third party arising out of any acts or omission of ABCD or the officers, agents, or employees of ABCD in the course of the performance or non-performance by ABCD of any provisions of this Agreement.

C. **Limitation of Liability**. The liability of XYZ hereunder shall be limited to contractual damages only. Notwithstanding anything to the contrary contained in this Agreement, in no event shall either party to this Agreement be obligated to indemnify the other party with respect to any indirect, incidental or consequential damages or for the lost profits, lost revenues of damage to goodwill or reputation.

XIX. **INSURANCE**.

A. **By ABCD**. ABCD agrees to obtain and maintain, throughout the term of this Agreement, general comprehensive liability insurance in the amount of ______ dollars ([$xxx]) combined single limit per occurrence for bodily injury, property damage and/or contractual liability. This insurance shall protect ABCD against any claims, demands, or causes of actions for damages, including attorneys' fees and costs, arising out of ABCD actions under this Agreement. This insurance shall name XYZ as an additional insured and this will not be cancelable until at least thirty days after written notice is given to XYZ. ABCD shall provide a certificate of insurance to XYZ evidencing the insurance coverage required hereunder upon execution of this Agreement and whenever requested by XYZ.

B. **By XYZ**. XYZ agrees to obtain and maintain throughout the term of this Agreement, general comprehensive liability insurance in the amount of ______ dollars ([$xxx]) combined single limit per occurrence for bodily injury, property damage and/or contractual liability. This insurance shall protect XYZ against any claims, demands, or causes of action or damages, including attorneys' fees and costs, arising out of or related to any [sport/team] events of XYZ held during the term hereof. This shall name ABCD as additional insureds and shall not be cancelled until at least thirty days after written notice is given to ABCD. XYZ shall provide a certificate of insurance to ABCD evidencing the insurance coverage required by it hereunder within thirty days from the execution of the Agreement and whenever requested by ABCD.

XX. **NOTICES**. All notices, claims, certificates, requests, demands and other communications hereunder shall be in writing and will deemed to have been given if delivered by hand; or mailed registered or certified mail, postage prepaid, return receipt requested; or any means of express mail with confirmed delivery as follows:

To ABCD: Name
Company
Address
Address
City, State Zip

To XYZ: Name
Company
Address
Address
City, State Zip

With a Copy to: Name
Company
Address
Address
City, State Zip

or to such other addresses as the person to whom notice is to be given may have previously furnished to the other in writing in a manner set forth above, provided that the notice of change of address shall be deemed given only upon receipt.

XXI. **RELATIONSHIP OF PARTIES**. ABCD shall perform its obligations hereunder as an independent contractor. All employees of ABCD remain employees of ABCD and are at all times under ABCD control and direction. Employees of XYZ shall remain at all times employees of XYZ and under XYZ's control and direction. This Agreement does not create a partnership, joint venture or any other relationship involving joint and several liability.

XXII. **MISCELLANEOUS PROVISIONS**.

A. **Nonexclusive Representation**. XYZ and ABCD mutually agree that ABCD and its subsidiaries, subsidiaries of a parent corporation and affiliated companies may provide similar services to other [sports teams], and/or other entities and may engage in other related businesses and ventures without limitation. Such representation shall not constitute a violation of ABCD's obligations hereunder.

B. **Assignment**. ABCD may not assign any or all of its rights or obligations under this Agreement without the prior written consent of XYZ.

C. **Choice of Law/Consent to Jurisdiction**. This Agreement shall be deemed to have been made in [State] and shall be governed by, construed and enforced in accordance with the law of the State of [State] without regard to its conflict of laws provisions. The parties agree that any dispute arising out of or related to this Agreement shall be brought in the appropriate state court or federal district court within the State of [State]; provided however, that first the parties agree that in the event any dispute, claim, or controversy of any kind or nature relating to this Agreement arises between the parties, the parties agree to meet and make a good faith effort to resolve the dispute. If the dispute is not resolved within thirty (30) days after the parties first met to resolve the dispute, and either party wishes to pursue the dispute further, that party will refer the dispute to non-binding mediation under the Commercial Mediation Rules of the American Arbitration Association ("AAA"). In no event may the mediation be initiated more than one year after the date a party first gave written notification of the dispute to the other party. A single mediator engaged in the practice of law, who is knowledgeable about media and marketing rights, will conduct the mediation under the then-current rules of the AAA. The mediation will be held in [City, State]. Nothing herein is intended to prevent either party from seeking any other remedy available at law including seeking redress in a court of competent jurisdiction. This provision shall survive the termination of this Agreement.

D. **Entire Agreement/Amendments**. This Agreement contains the entire understanding of the parties with respect to the subject matter. This Agreement supersedes all prior oral or written agreements and understandings between the parties with respect to its subject matter. Any condition to the parties' obligations hereunder may be waived with the mutual written consent of both parties.

E. **Headings**. The paragraph headings contained in this Agreement are for reference purposes only and will not affect in any way the meaning or interpretation of this Agreement.

F. **Waiver**. The failure at any time of any party to demand strict performance of another party or of any of the terms, covenants or conditions set forth in this Agreement shall not be construed as a continuing waiver or relinquishment thereof, and any party may, at anytime, demand strict and complete performance of any other party or such terms, covenants and conditions.

G. **Severability**. The unenforceability or invalidity of any provision of this Agreement shall not affect any other provision of this Agreement and this Agreement shall continue in full force and effect and be construed and enforced as if such provision had not been included.

H. **Authority**. Each party warrants and represents it has full right, power and authority to enter into this Agreement and make the covenants in this Agreement. The individuals executing and delivering this agreement have been duly authorized to do so and this Agreement is legally binding upon and enforceable against the parties hereto.

I. **Workers' Compensation**. ABCD certifies to XYZ that ABCD provides workers' compensation for all of its employees during the Term of this Agreement.

J. **Interpretation**. No provision of this Agreement shall be construed against or interpreted to the disadvantage of any party by any Court or other governmental or judicial authority by reason of any party having or being deemed to have drafted such provision.

K. **Campaign Contributions**. ABCD hereby certifies that all applicable parties listed in Division _______ of [State] Code Section _______ are in full compliance with Divisions _______.

L. **Conflicts of Interest and Ethics Compliance**. No personnel of ABCD or member of the governing body of any locality or other public official or employee of any such locality in which, or relating to which, the work under this Agreement is being carried out, and who exercise any functions or responsibilities in connection with the review or approval of this Agreement or carrying out of any such work, shall, prior to the completion of said work, voluntarily acquire any personal interest, direct or indirect, which is incompatible or in conflict with the discharge and fulfillment of his or her functions and responsibilities with respect to the carrying out of said work.

Any such person who acquires an incompatible or conflicting personal interest, on or after the effective date of this Agreement, or who involuntarily acquires any such incompatible or conflicting personal interest, shall immediately disclose his or her interest to XYZ in writing. Thereafter, he or she shall not participate in any action affecting the work under this Agreement, unless XYZ shall determine in its sole discretion that, in the light of the personal interest disclosed, his or her participation in any such action would not be contrary to the public interest.

ABCD represents, warrants, and certifies that it and its employees engaged in the administration or performance of this Agreement are knowledgeable of and understand [State] Ethics and Conflicts of Interest laws and Executive Order No. ______. In accordance with Executive Order No. ______, ABCD represents, warrants, and certifies that it and its employees and subcontractors shall not engage in discrimination against any employee or applicant for employment because of race, color, creed, religion, sexual orientation, national origin, sex, age, disability or Vietnam era veteran status. ABCD further represents, warrants, and certifies that neither ABCD nor any of its employees will do any act that is inconsistent with such laws and Executive Order. The Governor's Executive Orders may be found by accessing the following website: ______.

M. <u>**Findings for Recovery**</u>. Contractor warrants that it is not subject to an "unresolved" finding for recovery under [State] Code Section ___. If this warranty is found to be false, this Agreement is void *ab initio* and Contractor shall immediately repay to XYZ any funds paid under this Agreement.

IN WITNESS WHEREOF, the parties hereto have caused this Agreement to be executed by the duly authorized officer or agents on the date set forth below with an effective date being the date set forth on the first page of this Agreement.

XYZ ENTITY	**ABCD SPORTS MARKETING, INC.**
By:	By:
Name:	Name:
Title:	Title:
Date:	Date:

EXHIBIT 3

FOOD AND BEVERAGE AGREEMENT

This Food and Beverage Agreement (this "**Agreement**") is made as of the __ day of _______, 20__, by and between Food Services, L.P., a limited partnership organized under the laws of the State of [State] ("**FOOD SERVICES**"), and XYZ Entity, a ______________, organized under the laws of the State of ______________ ("**XYZ**").

RECITALS

WHEREAS, XYZ owns a multi-purpose sports and entertainment arena known as the _______ Center, consisting of approximately [xx,xxx] seats, and an attached conference center known as the _______ Conference Center, located in [City], [State] (collectively, the "**Facility**"); and

WHEREAS, FOOD SERVICES is in the business of managing and operating food, beverage, novelty and merchandise concessions services and catering services at indoor and outdoor single and multi-purpose facilities; and

WHEREAS, XYZ desires to grant to FOOD SERVICES the exclusive right and privilege to manage and operate the food, beverage, novelty and merchandise concessions services and catering services at the Facility; and

WHEREAS, FOOD SERVICES desires to accept the right and privilege to exclusively manage and operate such concessions and catering services at the Facility, subject to the terms and conditions contained herein.

NOW THEREFORE, for and in consideration of the foregoing, the mutual covenants and promises hereinafter set forth and other good and valuable consideration, the receipt and sufficiency of which is hereby acknowledged, the parties, intending to be legally bound, hereby agree as follows:

ARTICLE 1
DEFINITIONS

Capitalized terms used in this Agreement and not defined elsewhere in this Agreement shall have the following meanings:

"Base Fee" shall have the meaning given to such term in Section 3.1(a) hereof.

"Buyout Amount" shall have the meaning given to such term in Section 8.1(d) hereof.

"Buyout Payment" shall have the meaning given to such term in Section 8.1(a).

"Effective Date" shall have the meaning given to such term in Section 4.1 hereof.

"Equipment Monies" shall have the meaning given to such term in Section 8.1(b).

"Food and Beverage Areas" shall have the meaning given to such term in Section 2.1(b) hereof.

"Food and Beverage Sales" shall mean the sale of food and beverage items (as opposed to novelties, souvenirs and merchandise).

"Food and Beverage Services" shall mean the business of managing and providing (or causing to be provided) food, food products, candy, non-alcoholic and alcoholic beverages, novelties, souvenirs and merchandise in the concession areas, arena seating bowl, luxury boxes, restaurants, lounges, conference pavilion, banquet and conference rooms, catering areas, auxiliary gymnasium, office space, atrium, _______ Lounge and all other areas of the Facility.

"General Manager" shall have the meaning given to such term in Section 5.1(b) hereof.

"Gross Receipts" shall mean the total of all amounts received by FOOD SERVICES and any sub-contractors from the operation of the Food and Beverage Services, including any service charges and gratuities, whether such amounts are evidenced by cash, check, credit, charge account, exchange or otherwise, less only retail sales taxes and other direct taxes imposed upon receipts collected from the consumer. Gross Receipts shall include amounts received from the sale of goods at the Facility as well as amounts received from orders taken or received at the Facility (regardless of where such orders are filled).

"Incentive Fee" shall have the meaning given to such term in Section 3.1(a) hereof.

"Investment" shall have the meaning given to such term in Section 8.1(a) hereof.

"Losses" shall have the meaning given to such term in Section 11.1 hereof.

"Major Repair" shall mean the repair of any piece of equipment, structure or other item that costs, in the aggregate, in excess of _______________ dollars ($xxx).

"Management Fee" shall have the meaning given to such term in Section 3.1(a) hereof.

"Merchandise Sales" shall mean all non-edible souvenirs, novelties, articles of clothing and publications sold at the Facility.

"Monthly Accounting Period" shall mean each 4 or 5 week period during the Term ending on the last Wednesday of each month, except for the month of December, which shall end on December 31.

"Monthly Amortization Amount" shall have the meaning given to such term in Section 8.1(d) hereof.

"Net Loss" shall mean the amount by which Operating Expenses exceed Gross Receipts for the period in question.

"Net Profits" shall mean the amount by which Gross Receipts exceeds Operating Expenses for the period in question, provided that for purposes of calculating the Incentive Fee hereunder, the Monthly Amortization Amount shall *not* be included as an Operating Expenses in determining the Net Profits.

"Novelty Sales" shall mean the sale of novelties, souvenirs and merchandise (as opposed to food and beverage items).

"Operating Account" shall have the meaning given to such term in Section 10.1 hereof.

"Operating Expenses" shall mean (a) the cost to FOOD SERVICES of the sale of concession items and the performance of FOOD SERVICES' duties under this Agreement, including without limitation (i) personnel and payroll costs, including applicable taxes, benefits, relocation costs, and bonuses with respect to all on-site management, administrative staff, independent contractors, consultants and all other on-site employees, (ii) product costs, (iii) cost of permits and licenses, including without limitation the cost of securing all alcohol permits and licenses, (iv) all taxes paid by FOOD SERVICES hereunder on the sale of concession items, as described in Section 9.3 below, (v) equipment rental costs, (vi) cost of equipment repairs and maintenance performed by FOOD SERVICES or a contractor of FOOD SERVICES, (vii) insurance costs (which shall be allocated by FOOD SERVICES to the Facility in a reasonable and equitable fashion) and bonding costs, (viii) office supplies, printing costs and postage, (ix) telephone charges, (x) cost of utilities, (xi) cost of cleaning supplies and pest control, (xii) laundry costs, (xiii) armored car and other vehicle expenses, (xiv) legal, accounting and audit fees, (xv) cost of serviceware and paper supplies, (xvi) trash removal costs, (xvii) dues, subscriptions and membership fees, (xviii) travel, food and lodging costs, (xix) security expenses, (xx) computer costs, (xxi) uniform costs, (xxii) advertising and marketing costs, (xxiii) cost of ice, (xxiv) payments to sub-contractors engaged by FOOD SERVICES hereunder, (xxv) decorating costs, (xxvi) payroll processing expense, (xxvii) bank charges, (xxviii) temporary housing and relocation expense, (xxix) employment agency fees, (xxx) bad debt expense, (xxxi) any other miscellaneous expenses related to the foregoing, (xxxii) the Monthly Amortization Amount, and (b) the Base Fee. The parties specifically acknowledge that the term "Operating Expenses" shall *not* include any Start-Up Expenses, capital expenditures, debt service, and any expenses incurred in order to provide an initial inventory of food and beverage service ware and/or equipment, the cost and expenses for which (to the extent not purchased with the Investment) shall be borne solely by XYZ (or if paid for by FOOD SERVICES, shall be reimbursed to FOOD SERVICES by XYZ upon submission of invoice or otherwise as specifically set forth herein).

"Operating Year" shall have the meaning given to such term in Section 4.1 hereof.

"Shortfall" shall have the meaning given to such term in Section 10.2 hereof.

"Start-Up Expenses" shall mean all reasonable out-of-pocket expenses incurred by FOOD SERVICES in preparing to commence operations at the Facility, including, without limitation, travel costs, expenses related to staffing the Facility for the Food and Beverage Service prior to the first Facility event under this Agreement, obtaining liquor and other required licenses and permits, and otherwise preparing to provide Food and Beverage Service; provided that any out-of-pocket "Start-Up Expenses" in excess of $xxx shall require prior approval of Operator.

"Sub-Contractor Sales" shall mean any sales at or from the Facility from any third party sub-contractor of FOOD SERVICES.

"Term" shall have the meaning given to such term in Section 4.1 hereof.

ARTICLE 2
GRANT OF RIGHTS; SCOPE OF SERVICES

Section 2.1 Concession License.

(a) XYZ hereby grants to FOOD SERVICES the exclusive right and privilege to provide Food and Beverage Services at the Facility. FOOD SERVICES covenants and agrees to exercise the full Food and Beverage Service rights granted hereunder at all events in the Facility in such manner and with such number of personnel as are necessary to provide adequate supplies and service of the food, beverage and other products described herein to patrons of the Facility. XYZ agrees that it will not, without the prior written consent of FOOD SERVICES, grant to any party other than FOOD SERVICES or a sub-contractor mutually agreed by XYZ and FOOD SERVICES, the right to perform any Food and Beverage Services at or upon the Facility.

(b) In connection with the foregoing grant of exclusive rights, XYZ hereby licenses to FOOD SERVICES the concession stands, souvenir and gift shops, novelty stands, customer serving locations, food preparation areas, vendor commissaries, kitchen and warehouse facilities, and other areas related to the foregoing and/or reasonably required by FOOD SERVICES to perform the Food and Beverage Service at the Facility ("Food and Beverage Areas"), together with the improvements, equipment, and personal property upon or within such areas, along with the non-exclusive right to use the concourses, spectator seating areas, parking areas, common areas, loading areas, walkways, and other public areas of the Facility, solely for the purpose of providing Food and Beverage Services. FOOD SERVICES agrees to operate the Food and Beverage Areas with respect to all events at the Facility, during hours as may be reasonably requested by XYZ to adequately meet public demand.

ARTICLE 3
COMPENSATION; START-UP EXPENSES

Section 3.1 Fees.

(a) As consideration for the performance by FOOD SERVICES of its duties hereunder, XYZ shall pay FOOD SERVICES a fee each Operating Year equal to (a) ___ percent (x%) of Gross Receipts from Food and Beverage Sales, plus ___ percent (x%) of Gross Receipts from Novelty Sales (collectively, the "Base Fee"), plus (b) _______ percent (x%) of Net Profits (the "Incentive Fee"). The Base Fee plus the Incentive Fee are collectively referred to herein as (the "Management Fee"). The Management Fee shall be paid to FOOD SERVICES on a monthly basis as set forth in Section 3.1(b) below.

(b) On or about the twentieth (20th) day following the end of each Monthly Accounting Period, FOOD SERVICES shall remit to XYZ the Net Profits (if any) to which XYZ is entitled (after deducting from such Net Profits the Incentive Fee, any Shortfall advanced by FOOD SERVICES pursuant to Section 10.2 below, any receivables owed by XYZ to FOOD SERVICES, and any other amounts due to FOOD SERVICES hereunder) from such Monthly Accounting Period, together with the statements described in Section 10.3 below. The parties shall conduct a settlement within thirty (30) days of the end of each Operating Year at which each shall account to each other for any amounts that were underpaid or overpaid by the parties from such Operating Year. Any Net Losses under this Agreement shall be borne by XYZ, and FOOD SERVICES shall not share in any Net Losses.

(c) XYZ shall reimburse FOOD SERVICES for all Start-Up Expenses within thirty (30) days of submission by FOOD SERVICES of an invoice to XYZ for such expenses. Each such invoice shall include reasonable back-up documentation evidencing the incurrence of such expenses.

ARTICLE 4
TERM; TERMINATION

Section 4.1 Term. The term of this Agreement ("Term") shall be for ___ (x) years, beginning on _______, 20__ (the "Effective Date"), and, unless sooner terminated pursuant to the provisions of Section 4.2 below, ending on _______, 20__. Each twelve (12) month period during the Term commencing on the Effective Date and continuing on the anniversary of such date shall be referred to herein as an "Operating Year." Notwithstanding the above, if in any Operating Year, for any reason (including without limitation if due to the occurrence of a force majeure), less than _______ (x) XYZ [LEAGUE] [sport] games are held in the Facility, then FOOD SERVICES shall have the right (but not the obligation) to extend the Term of this Agreement for an additional one year period for each such affected Operating Year.

Section 4.2 Termination. This Agreement may be terminated (i) by either FOOD SERVICES or XYZ upon thirty (30) days written notice to the other, if the other party fails to perform or comply with any of the material terms, covenants, agreements or conditions hereof, and such failure is not cured during such thirty (30) day period, (ii) by either FOOD SERVICES or XYZ by written notice to the other upon the other being judged bankrupt or insolvent, or if any receiver or trustee of all or any part of the business property of the other shall be appointed and shall not be discharged within one hundred twenty (120) days after appointment, or if either such party shall make an assignment of its property for the benefit of creditors or shall file a voluntary petition in bankruptcy or insolvency, or shall apply for bankruptcy under the bankruptcy or insolvency laws now in force or hereinafter enacted, Federal, State or otherwise, or if such petition shall be filed against either party and shall not be dismissed within one hundred twenty (120) days after such filing, or (iii) as otherwise specifically provided for herein.

ARTICLE 5
PERSONNEL

Section 5.1 Generally.

(a) FOOD SERVICES shall employ, train and supervise personnel with appropriate qualifications and experience, in sufficient number to provide all the services appropriate for the duties of such party to be performed under this Agreement. All such personnel shall be employees, agents or independent contractors of FOOD SERVICES (or a subsidiary or affiliate thereof), as applicable, and not of XYZ. FOOD SERVICES shall select the number, function, qualifications, and compensation, including salary and benefits, of its employees and shall control the terms and conditions of employment relating to such employees. FOOD SERVICES agrees to use reasonable and prudent judgment in the selection and supervision of such personnel, and shall strive to employ persons who are courteous and efficient, and who will not use improper language or act in a loud or boisterous manner while performing duties at the Facility. FOOD SERVICES agrees that it will not discriminate against any employee or applicant for employment for work under this Agreement because of race, religion, color, sex, disability, national origin, ancestry, physical handicap, or age. Except as specifically set forth in Section 5.1(b) below, XYZ shall have no right to supervise or direct the hiring or firing of any such personnel.

(b) FOOD SERVICES shall employ as part of its personnel at the Facility an individual with managerial experience to serve as a full-time general manager of Food and Beverage Services ("General Manager"). Hiring of the General Manager by FOOD SERVICES shall require the prior approval of XYZ, which approval shall not be unreasonably withheld or delayed. The General Manager will have general supervisory responsibility for FOOD

SERVICES at the Facility and will be responsible for day-to-day operations of the Food and Beverage Services, supervision of FOOD SERVICES employees, and management and coordination of all activities associated with the Food and Beverage Services.

(c) FOOD SERVICES shall ensure that its non-management employees performing the duties of FOOD SERVICES at the Facility shall be neatly attired in clean, commercially-attractive uniforms which shall be subject to the approval of XYZ. FOOD SERVICES shall train all such employees so that they are aware of the high standards for cleanliness, courtesy and service required by FOOD SERVICES.

(d) All personnel engaged by FOOD SERVICES to work at the Facility shall be admitted to the Facility without payment of any admission fee, at an entrance to be designated by XYZ. All such personnel shall have the right to park at the Facility without charge in areas designated by XYZ.

Section 5.2 Non-Solicitation.

(a) During the Term and for a period of one (1) year after the end of the Term, XYZ and its affiliates shall not, without the prior written consent of FOOD SERVICES, solicit for employment by XYZ, or encourage to cease rendering services to FOOD SERVICES, any management-level employee of FOOD SERVICES with whom XYZ has had dealings by virtue of the engagement of FOOD SERVICES hereunder. In the event of a breach of this provision, FOOD SERVICES will be entitled (in addition to any other rights and remedies which FOOD SERVICES may have at law or in equity, including money damages) to equitable relief, including an injunction to enjoin and restrain XYZ from continuing such breach.

(b) During the Term and for a period of one (1) year after the end of the Term, FOOD SERVICES shall not, without the prior written consent of XYZ, solicit for employment by FOOD SERVICES, or encourage to cease rendering services to XYZ, any management-level employee of XYZ with whom FOOD SERVICES has had dealings by virtue of the engagement of FOOD SERVICES hereunder. In the event of a breach of this provision, XYZ will be entitled (in addition to any other rights and remedies which XYZ may have at law or in equity, including money damages) to equitable relief, including an injunction to enjoin and restrain FOOD SERVICES from continuing such breach.

ARTICLE 6
INVENTORY; EQUIPMENT; SPONSORSHIPS; UTILITIES

Section 6.1 Inventory. FOOD SERVICES shall order, stock, prepare, pay for and sell quality food, beverage and other concession and catering products. Consumables shall be first quality, wholesome and pure, and all food and beverage merchandise on hand shall be stored and handled with due regard for sanitation. FOOD SERVICES shall have sufficient amounts of product prepared and an inventory on the premises so as not to run out of product during an event at the Facility. During all events at the Facility, FOOD SERVICES shall post signs and provide menus displaying the prices of items offered for sale. Such signs and menus shall be subject to the reasonable approval of XYZ.

Section 6.2 Brands/Prices. The brands and price of all products sold by FOOD SERVICES shall be determined by FOOD SERVICES, subject to the reasonable approval of XYZ. Provided price, quality, market acceptability, service and other terms are generally competitive, FOOD SERVICES agrees to give preference to and feature at the Facility suppliers of products designated by XYZ who purchase advertising from XYZ (or, if applicable, an agent or licensee of XYZ) so long as the giving of such preference does not violate applicable laws, rules or regulations and the features of such product and terms of such transaction are reasonable (as determined by FOOD SERVICES in its sole discretion).

Section 6.3 Equipment. FOOD SERVICES shall have the right to use during the Term, all equipment owned or controlled by XYZ existing within the Food and Beverage Areas as of the date hereof and/or subsequently added by XYZ or FOOD SERVICES to such areas during the Term. XYZ represents that all such equipment is in good working order, and FOOD SERVICES agrees to exercise reasonable care when using such equipment, so as to avoid any damage to such equipment.

Section 6.4 Utilities. XYZ shall provide to FOOD SERVICES all utilities necessary for FOOD SERVICES' operation of the Food and Beverage Services (e.g., electricity, gas and water).

ARTICLE 7
MAINTENANCE

Section 7.1 Maintenance; Sanitation.

(a) FOOD SERVICES shall perform minor, routine servicing on all fixtures, equipment, furniture and other property installed, furnished or supplied by or for the benefit of FOOD SERVICES so that such items are kept in good order and repair. FOOD SERVICES shall further make all necessary repairs thereto, provided that any Major Repair or replacements of furniture, fixtures or equipment shall be paid for by XYZ.

(b) FOOD SERVICES will maintain the Food and Beverage Areas in a clean and neat condition by cleaning, on a day-to-day basis, the interiors of the Food and Beverage Areas and bars, concession stands and vending stations under its control at the Facility (and within a (5) feet perimeter of such stands and stations). Food Services shall further clean, as needed, the walls, windows, ceilings, light fixtures and equipment located within the Food and Beverage Areas. FOOD SERVICES shall deposit in receptacles provided by XYZ all waste, garbage and refuse which shall accumulate in the Food and Beverage Areas. FOOD SERVICES shall also provide extermination services as may be necessary for the Food and Beverage Areas.

(c) FOOD SERVICES shall comply with and observe all federal, state and local laws, ordinances and regulations as to sanitation and the purity of food and beverages or otherwise relating to its operations under this Agreement.

ARTICLE 8
INVESTMENT BY FOOD SERVICES

Section 8.1 Investment by FOOD SERVICES. Subject to the terms of this Article 8, FOOD SERVICES agrees to contribute up to (but not to exceed) ______________ dollars ($xxx) for use with respect to the Food and Beverage Areas or otherwise as described as follows:

(a) FOOD SERVICES agrees to pay to XYZ the amount of _______dollars ($xxx) (the "Buyout Payment") within _______ (x) days of the Effective Date for the purpose of enabling XYZ to satisfy its "buyout" obligation to Prior Food Service ("Prior Concessionaire") under its expiring concession agreement with the Prior Concessionaire. XYZ shall, upon receipt of the Buyout Payment from FOOD

SERVICES, pay the total buyout payment in the amount of $xxx to the Prior Concessionaire for such purpose.

(b) FOOD SERVICES agrees to invest up to (but not to exceed) ______ dollars ($xxx) ("Equipment Monies") at the Facility over the course of the Term for design services, leasehold improvements and/or capital equipment dedicated to the food and beverage Food and Beverage Services to be performed by FOOD SERVICES hereunder equipment (which shall include a cost equal to x% of the equipment purchased as an administrative fee for purchasing such equipment, on-site project management and FOOD SERVICES out-of-pocket expenses in connection therewith). The actual amount of Equipment Monies invested by FOOD SERVICES under this paragraph (b), aggregated with the Buyout Payment, is referred to herein as the "Investment." In the event additional amounts are required to satisfy XYZ's financial obligations to the Prior Concessionaire, complete the food and beverage facilities, or to provide equipment and/or smallwares so as to enable FOOD SERVICES to perform the Food and Beverage Services to a reasonable standard, XYZ shall be solely responsible for such amounts. XYZ and FOOD SERVICES shall mutually agree upon the specific equipment and improvements to be purchased or made with the Equipment Monies, as well as the location for such improvements or installation of such equipment.

(c) Once identified, the specific equipment and other related tangible personal property to be purchased with the Equipment Monies shall be set forth in a writing to be signed by the parties and updated by the parties from time to time as necessary to reflect any replacements or substitutions thereof. All equipment, improvements and other items purchased with the Equipment Monies, including any replacements or substitutions thereof, shall be owned by FOOD SERVICES until payment of the Buyout Amount (as described below), and XYZ agrees to execute such documents as FOOD SERVICES shall reasonably request evidencing FOOD SERVICES' ownership interest in such improvements and equipment, including financing statements. For the sake of clarity, nothing in this paragraph shall be construed as requiring FOOD SERVICES to replace any equipment or other personal property at its own cost.

(d) The Investment shall be amortized on a straight line basis over a ___ (x) year period (at the rate of x/x per month), commencing on the Effective Date. The monthly amortization amount ("Monthly Amortization Amount") shall be an Operating Expense. Upon the natural expiration of early termination (for any reason whatsoever, including without limitation if due to a breach, default or bankruptcy event by or affecting FOOD SERVICES) of this Agreement, XYZ shall immediately pay to FOOD SERVICES the unamortized amount of the Investment ("the Buyout Amount"). In the event that XYZ fails to repay FOOD SERVICES the Buyout Amount upon termination or expiration of this Agreement in accordance with the terms hereof, the Buyout Amount shall accrue interest at the rate of _______ percent (x%) per month, or the highest rate permitted by law, whichever is less, and FOOD SERVICES may, at its sole option, (a) continue to perform the Food and Beverage Services at the Facility and be paid for such services as provided hereunder, notwithstanding its receipt of any termination notice from XYZ or the expiration of this Agreement, and/or (b) peacefully reenter the Facility, with or without process of law, and remove in a commercially reasonable manner the improvements or equipment purchased with the Equipment Monies and retain or dispose of such improvements or equipment as FOOD SERVICES sees fit. In either event, FOOD SERVICES shall retain its right to receive the full Buyout Amount. XYZ covenants and agrees not to permit any liens or encumbrances to attach to the leasehold improvements and equipment purchased with the Equipment Monies, and hereby waives any right to attach any claim, lien, or attachment to such improvements or equipment. Once the Buyout Amount is paid to FOOD SERVICES, title to the equipment and improvements purchased with the Equipment Monies will become vested in XYZ, and FOOD SERVICES agrees to execute all necessary documents to evidence same. The rights of FOOD SERVICES set forth in this Section 8.1(c) shall be in addition to any other rights of FOOD SERVICES at law or in equity.

ARTICLE 9
LICENSES; ALCOHOLIC BEVERAGES; TAXES

Section 9.1 Permits and Licenses. FOOD SERVICES shall use reasonable commercial efforts to secure and maintain throughout the Term all licenses and permits necessary for the operation of the

Food and Beverage Services, including those required for the sale of alcoholic beverages at the Facility. XYZ shall cooperate with FOOD SERVICES in connection with filing applications for, and securing and maintaining in good standing, any and all licenses and permits and renewals thereof needed by FOOD SERVICES to fulfill its obligations hereunder. In the event that FOOD SERVICES is unable to secure or maintain the necessary licenses or permits to sell alcoholic beverages at the Facility for any reason, or if FOOD SERVICES is prevented or limited from selling alcoholic beverages at the Facility for any reason, at FOOD SERVICES' request the parties shall re-negotiate in good faith the economic terms of this Agreement so that the economic benefits provided to FOOD SERVICES hereunder are maintained. If, despite such good faith negotiations, the parties are unable to come to agreement on the revised economic terms of this Agreement, FOOD SERVICES may terminate this Agreement, without liability to FOOD SERVICES, upon thirty (30) days written notice to XYZ.

Section 9.2 Alcoholic Beverages. In connection with the sale of alcoholic beverages hereunder by FOOD SERVICES, FOOD SERVICES agrees to strictly comply with the laws of the State of [State] regarding the sale of such beverages to minors. FOOD SERVICES agrees to adopt an identification policy to verify the age of potential purchasers of alcoholic beverages. FOOD SERVICES further agrees that it will endeavor not to sell alcoholic beverages to customers who are visibly intoxicated. FOOD SERVICES will institute and conduct training programs for FOOD SERVICES employees at the Facility on the proper standards to use to avoid selling alcoholic beverages to customers who are or who appear to be intoxicated.

Section 9.3 Taxes. FOOD SERVICES shall collect and pay all taxes imposed upon the sale of concession items hereunder, as required by Federal, State or local law. FOOD SERVICES shall be responsible for and pay all social security, unemployment insurance, old age retirement and other federal and state taxes that are measured by the wages, salaries, or other remuneration paid to persons employed by FOOD SERVICES. XYZ shall be responsible for and hold FOOD SERVICES harmless from any and all possessory interest or leasehold taxes which may be levied or are in effect during the Term.

ARTICLE 10
OPERATING ACCOUNT; REPORTING

Section 10.1 Establishment of Operating Account. FOOD SERVICES shall establish and maintain, in its name, a separate commercial bank account for the Facility ("Operating Account") and shall deposit all Gross Receipts in such account.

Section 10.2 Payment of Expenses; Shortfall. FOOD SERVICES shall pay all Operating Expenses from the Gross Receipts generated under this Agreement. In the event at any time during the Term, Gross Receipts are insufficient to cover Operating Expenses (a "Shortfall"), FOOD SERVICES may at its option and in its sole discretion from time to time, either (a) advance its own funds to cover such Shortfall, in which case FOOD SERVICES shall be reimbursed from the first dollars otherwise due and owing to XYZ under Section 3.1 of this Agreement, or (b) notify XYZ of such Shortfall in which case XYZ shall be required, within two (2) business days of receiving such notice, to pay to FOOD SERVICES sufficient funds to cover such Shortfall until it is anticipated that no further Shortfall shall exist. Any amounts advanced by FOOD SERVICES under this Agreement towards a Shortfall shall accrue interest at the rate of Prime (as published from time to time in the _______ newspaper) plus _______ percent (x%), with such interest accruing from the date of the advancement. Any advances made by FOOD SERVICES that remain outstanding at the end of the Term shall be paid to FOOD SERVICES (together with accrued interest) within five (5) days of the end of the Term and, if not paid when due, shall continue to accrue interest until paid in full. FOOD SERVICES shall be entitled to offset any amounts owing to it by XYZ hereunder against any amounts otherwise payable to XYZ under this Agreement.

Section 10.3 Books and Records. FOOD SERVICES agrees to maintain separate and independent books and records, in accordance with generally accepted accounting principles, relating to its operations in connection with its management of the Food and Beverage Services, as applicable. Such books and records shall contain documentation regarding the deposit of all Gross Receipts in the Operating Account, and the incurrence by FOOD SERVICES of all Operating Expenses, including copies of invoices of all products and materials purchased by FOOD SERVICES hereunder, and copies of payroll summaries, deposit receipts and bank statements relating to the Operating Account. XYZ or its designee shall have the right to inspect such books and records from time to time upon reasonable notice during the ordinary business hours of FOOD SERVICES.

Section 10.4 Financial Reports. FOOD SERVICES shall provide to XYZ, within twenty (20) days following the end of each Monthly Accounting Period, financial reports regarding its provision of Food and Beverage Services during such Monthly Accounting Period, including a statement showing Gross Receipts and Operating Expenses for the applicable period. Additionally, FOOD SERVICES shall provide to XYZ, within twenty four (24) hours following each event at the Facility, a daily Gross Receipts report in a form to be mutually agreed upon.

Section 10.5 Audit. Not more than once each Operating Year, XYZ shall have the right, at its sole cost, to engage an independent third party to audit the books and records of FOOD SERVICES for the preceding twelve (12) month period, for the purpose of confirming that the amounts remitted by FOOD SERVICES to XYZ hereunder are the proper amounts due XYZ. Such audit shall be completed by XYZ or its representatives at FOOD SERVICES' corporate office, on reasonable advance notice to FOOD SERVICES, and on dates and times mutually agreed to by the parties. In the event such audit reveals any underpayment to XYZ, FOOD SERVICES shall promptly pay to XYZ the amount of such deficiency. If such audit reveals any overpayment to XYZ, XYZ shall promptly pay to FOOD SERVICES the amount of such overpayment.

ARTICLE 11
INDEMNIFICATION

Section 11.1 Indemnification by FOOD SERVICES. FOOD SERVICES agrees to defend, indemnify and hold harmless XYZ, its parents, subsidiaries and affiliates, and their respective successors and assigns, and all its agents, employees directors, officers and partners of the foregoing, against any claims, causes of action, costs, expenses (including reasonable attorneys' fees) liabilities, or damages (collectively, "Losses") suffered by such parties, arising out of or in connection with any (a) negligent act or omission, or intentional misconduct, on the part of FOOD SERVICES or any of its employees or agents in the performance of its obligations under this Agreement, or (b) breach by FOOD SERVICES of any of its representations, covenants or agreements made herein.

Section 11.2 Indemnification by XYZ. XYZ agrees to defend, indemnify and hold harmless FOOD SERVICES, its parents, subsidiaries and affiliates, and their respective successors and assigns, and all agents, employees, directors, officers and partners of the foregoing, against any Losses suffered by such parties, arising out of or in connection with (a) any negligent act or omission, or intentional misconduct, on the part of XYZ or any of its employees or agents in the performance of its obligations under this Agreement, (b) a breach by XYZ of any of its representations, covenants or agreements made herein, or (c) any construction, maintenance, operations or activities of or at the Facility, unless to the extent such Losses are caused by the negligence or intentional misconduct of FOOD SERVICES or its employees or agents.

Section 11.3 Conditions to Indemnification. Each party seeking indemnification shall give prompt written notice to the other party of each claim giving rise to an indemnification obligation under this Agreement (and in any event not more than 30 days after any third party litigation is commenced asserting the claim giving rise to an indemnification obligation hereunder), specifying the amount and nature of any such claim. The party seeking indemnification shall not settle or compromise any claim by a third party for which it is entitled to indemnification hereunder without the prior written consent of the indemnifying party, which consent shall not be unreasonably withheld. The party seeking indemnification shall cooperate in the indemnifying party's defense of such claim at the sole cost of the indemnifying party.

Section 11.4 Survival. The obligations of the parties contained in this Article 11 shall survive the termination or expiration of this Agreement and continue on indefinitely.

ARTICLE 12
INSURANCE

Section 12.1 Types and Amount of Coverage. FOOD SERVICES agrees to secure and maintain throughout the Term insurance coverage in the manner and amounts as set forth in Schedule I, attached hereto, and shall provide to XYZ promptly following the Effective Date a certificate or certificates of insurance evidencing such coverage.

Section 12.2 Rating; Additional Insureds. All insurance policies shall be issued by companies rated no less than A VIII in the most recent "Bests" insurance guide, and licensed in the State of [State] or as otherwise agreed by the parties, and shall be in such form and contain such provisions as are generally considered standard for the type of insurance involved. The commercial general liability policy to be obtained by FOOD SERVICES hereunder shall name XYZ as an additional insured.

ARTICLE 13
MISCELLANEOUS

Section 13.1 Authorization.

(a) FOOD SERVICES represents and warrants that it has the full right and legal authority to enter into this Agreement and to grant the rights and perform the obligations of FOOD SERVICES herein, and that, except as otherwise set forth herein, no third party consent or approval is required to grant such rights or perform such obligations hereunder.

(b) XYZ represents and warrants that it is XYZ of the Facility, and that it has the full right and legal authority to enter into this Agreement and to grant the rights and perform the obligations of XYZ herein, and that no other third party consent or approval is required to grant such rights or perform such obligations hereunder.

Section 13.2 Force Majeure. In the event that a party is prevented or delayed in the performance of any of its obligations under this Agreement (not including any payment obligation hereunder) due to circumstances beyond its control, including but not limited to, (a) fire, earthquake, hurricane, wind, flood, act of God, riot, or civil commotion occurring at the Facility, or (b) any law, ordinance, rule, regulation, or order of any public or military authority stemming from the existence of economic or energy controls, hostilities, war, or governmental law and regulation, or (c) labor dispute which results in a strike or work stoppage affecting the Facility or services described in this Agreement (each, a "*force majeure*" event), then, subject to Section 4.1 above, performance hereunder by the affected party shall be excused for the period of delay.

Section 13.3 Assignment. Neither party may assign this Agreement without the prior written consent of the other, which consent shall not be unreasonably withheld or delayed; however, FOOD SERVICES or XYZ may, without the prior written consent of the other, assign this Agreement and/or its rights and obligations hereunder (i) to any person or entity who succeeds (whether by merger, consolidation or sale of assets or equity or the like) to all or substantially all of the business and properties of such party, or (ii) in connection with a corporate restructuring, to any person who is an XYZ, parent, subsidiary or affiliate of such party, and who carries on the business of such party in substantially the same manner. Any assignee of FOOD SERVICES or XYZ pursuant to the preceding sentence must agree in writing to assume the assignor's obligations hereunder, in whole or in part (as applicable), in order for such assignment to become effective. This Agreement shall be binding on the parties' successors and permitted assigns.

Section 13.4 Notices. All notices required or permitted to be given pursuant to this Agreement shall be in writing and delivered personally or sent by registered or certified mail, return receipt requested, or by generally recognized, prepaid, overnight air courier services, to the address and individual set forth below. All such notices to either party shall be deemed to have been provided when delivered, if delivered personally, three (3) days after mailed, if sent by registered or certified mail, or the next business day, if sent by generally recognized, prepaid, overnight air courier services.

If to XYZ:	If to FOOD SERVICES:
XYZ Entity	Food Services, L.P.
______________________	______________________
______________________	______________________
Attn: ________________	Attn: ________________
With a copy to:	With a copy to:
______________________	______________________
______________________	______________________
Attn: ________________	Attn: ________________

The designation of the individuals to be so notified and the addresses of such parties set forth above may be changed from time to time by written notice to the other party in the manner set forth above.

Section 13.5 Severability. If a court of competent jurisdiction or an arbitrator determines that any term of this Agreement is invalid or unenforceable to any extent under applicable law, the remainder of this Agreement (and the application of this Agreement to other circumstances) shall not be affected thereby, and each remaining term shall be valid and enforceable to the fullest extent permitted by law.

Section 13.6 Prior Agreements. This Agreement (including the schedule(s) attached hereto) constitutes the entire agreement of the parties with respect to the subject matter hereof, and supersedes all prior and contemporaneous negotiations, correspondence, conversations, agreements, and understandings concerning the subject matter hereof. Accordingly, the parties agree that no deviation from the terms hereof shall be predicated upon any prior representations, agreements or understandings, whether oral or written.

Section 13.7 Governing Law. The Agreement is entered into under and pursuant to, and is to be construed and enforceable in accordance with, the laws of the State of [State], without regard to its conflict of laws principles.

Section 13.8 Amendments. Neither this Agreement nor any of its terms may be changed or modified, waived, or terminated (unless as otherwise provided hereunder) except by an instrument in writing signed by an authorized representative of the party against whom the enforcement of the change, waiver, or termination is sought.

Section 13.9 Waiver; Remedies. No failure or delay by a party hereto to insist on the strict performance of any term of this Agreement, or to exercise any right or remedy consequent to a breach thereof, shall constitute a waiver of any breach or any subsequent breach of such term. No waiver of any breach hereunder shall affect or alter the remaining terms of this Agreement, but each and every term of this Agreement shall continue in full force and effect with respect to any other then existing or subsequent breach thereof. The remedies provided in this Agreement are cumulative and not exclusive of the remedies provided by law or in equity.

Section 13.10 Relationship of Parties. FOOD SERVICES is engaged by XYZ hereunder as an independent contractor to perform the services described herein, and nothing contained in this Agreement shall be deemed to create, whether express or implied, a partnership, joint venture, employment, or agency relationship between XYZ and FOOD SERVICES, except as otherwise expressly set forth in this Agreement.

Section 13.11 Counterparts; Faxed or Emailed Signatures. This Agreement may be executed in counterparts, each of which shall constitute an original, and all of which together shall constitute one and the same document. This Agreement may be executed by the parties and transmitted by facsimile or electronic mail, and if so executed and transmitted, shall be effective as if the parties had delivered an executed original of this Agreement.

IN WITNESS WHEREOF, each party hereto has caused this Food and Beverage Agreement to be executed on behalf of such party by an authorized representative as of the date first set forth above.

XYZ ENTITY	FOOD SERVICES, L.P.
By: ____________	By: ____________
Name:	Name:
Its:	Its:

SCHEDULE I
INSURANCE

At all times during the Term of this Agreement, FOOD SERVICES shall maintain the following coverages, in the amounts set forth below:

Coverage	Amount
Commercial General Liability, including Products Coverage	$1,000,000 per occurrence
Excess Liability	$5,000,000 per occurrence and aggregate
Commercial Automobile Liability	$1,000,000 per accident
Workers Compensation	As required under law
Crime	$1,000,000
Liquor Liability (if applicable)	$1,000,000

Appendix B

A SUPPLEMENT TO "NEGOTIATING AND DRAFTING SPORTS VENUE AGREEMENTS"

TABLE OF CONTENTS

The Essential Facility Doctrine[1]

The common law "essential facility" doctrine is just one legal doctrine among many—such as those in antitrust law, property law, and contract law—that you will need to draft stadium leases that comply with the law and are "litigation-proof." In the beginning of the textbook, you will be negotiating the "Uses" provisions—describing permissible lessor and lessee uses of the premises—of a stadium lease. When negotiating and drafting "Uses," you will need to ensure that the covenants in your contract comply with the essential facility doctrine, or else your client may run into difficulties in the future. More specifically, the team's ability to secure exclusive use of the stadium will be limited by the doctrine.

When a team is about to lease a newly constructed facility designed for its play, it will likely seek to obtain a covenant that no other sports organizations—especially of the same professional sport—will be able to use that facility. It will also want to limit the ability of other sports or events to use the stadium to preserve the field and facility quality. Other parties—such as college teams or concert organizers—might seek to use the venue that is already leased by a team. When the lessee's demands for restrictions on third-party use, a third party who wants to use the facility, and a lessor who wants to generate additional rents by renting the space to a third party conflict, the essential facility doctrine applies.

In *Hecht v. Pro Football, Inc.*,[2] investors who unsuccessfully tried to acquire a team to participate in the upstart American Football League sued Pro Football Inc., the entity operating the Washington Redskins. The investors-plaintiffs claimed that a covenant in the defendant-team's lease of RFK Stadium—preventing the team from leasing the stadium to any other professional football team—violated the Sherman Antitrust Act. The Court, stating that the essential facility doctrine ought to apply to the case, described it as follows:

> The essential facility doctrine, also called the "bottleneck principle," states that, "where facilities cannot practicably be duplicated by would-be competitors, those in possession of them must allow them to be shared on fair terms. It is illegal restraint of trade to foreclose the scarce facility." . . . To be "essential" a facility need not be indispensable; it is sufficient if duplication of the facility would be economically infeasible and if denial of its use inflicts a severe handicap on potential market entrants. Necessarily, this principle

---

1 The information in this document has been adapted from Martin J. Greenberg & James T. Gray, SPORTS LAW PRACTICE (1998), 1280–1282.

2 570 F.2d 982, 985–86 (D.C. Cir.1977).

> must be carefully delimited; the antitrust laws do not require that an essential facility be shared if such sharing would be impractical or would inhibit defendant's ability to serve its customers adequately.[3]

Given that RFK was the only facility in the Washington D.C. area suitable for professional football games, the court reasoned that an instruction on the doctrine should have been presented to the jury and remanded the case.

Courts have not only applied the essential facilities doctrine to professional football stadiums, but also to professional basketball arenas. In *Fishman v. Estate of Wirtz*,[4] a prospective owner of the Chicago Bulls (seeking to negotiate a lease with the owner of Chicago Stadium) sued the owner of Chicago Stadium (who was also interested in purchasing the Bulls) when the Stadium owner refused to negotiate. The Seventh Circuit Court explained that the doctrine "imposes upon a firm controlling an essential facility—that is a facility that cannot reasonably be duplicated and to which access is necessary if one wishes to compete—the obligation to make that facility available to competitors on nondiscriminatory terms." Refusal to deal regarding an essential facility violates Section 2 of the Sherman Act because "control of an essential facility can 'extend monopoly power from one stage of production to another, and from one market into another.' "[5] The defendants in *Fishman* had violated antitrust laws because (1.) Chicago Stadium was not the only stadium available in the Chicago area and (2.) it could not feasibly be duplicated. Some of the facts on which the Court rested its legal conclusion were that Chicago Stadium had 6,500 more seats than the best alternative stadium, its locker rooms and lighting were significantly superior to any other stadium, it could charge higher prices without causing patrons to move to another facility, all the prospective buyers of the Bulls wanted to lease Chicago Stadium, and a new arena would cost an "economically unrealistic sum" of $19 million.

Overall, when delineating the acceptable "Uses" of a stadium and drafting covenants, bear in mind the consequences the application of the essential facility doctrine would have to your argument.

---

3 *Id.* at 992–93.

4 807 F.2d 520 (7th Circ. 1986).

5 *Id.* at 539 (quoting *MCI Communications Corp. v. American Tel. & Tel. Co.*, 708 F.2d at 1132 (7th Cir.1983)).

Negotiating Contracts: Basic Principles and Strategies[6]

Before you begin negotiating contracts on behalf of your clients in the sports industry, you might find it helpful to understand (1.) some of the basic principles and terminology used by negotiators and scholars alike to describe negotiations and (2.) how these principles and terms function in the sports contracting world. For some students, the former may be review.

I. "Formulating a Game Plan": Negotiation Considerations

Prior to meeting any party with which you are about to negotiate, regardless of the topics being negotiated, you should try to formulate a clear understanding of the goals of the parties, the nature of their businesses and interests, and the opportunities for value creation and conflict likely to arise.

A. *"Take the Shot or Pass the Ball?": Distributing and Creating Value*

Paramount in any negotiation is the tension between the desire for distributive gain and the opportunity for joint gains—distributing and creating value. For any negotiated agreement, both parties must believe that the negotiated outcome leaves them at least as well off as they would have been had there been no agreement. For any negotiated agreement that actually creates value, the parties must be better off than they would have been with any other negotiated outcome. To achieve these value gains, it is necessary for the parties to share information.[7] Without sharing information, it will be difficult for either side to find trades that might create value and potentially make both clients better off. But, if your own openness is not reciprocated, the other side may be able to exploit the information that you readily share. Skillful negotiations must balance between

---

[6] The materials in this packet have been synthesized and adapted from three influential texts on negotiation: Roger Fisher, William Ury, & Bruce Patton, GETTING TO YES (1981), Howard Raiffa, THE ART AND SCIENCE OF NEGOTIATION (1982), and Robert H. Mnookin, Scott R. Peppet, and Andrew S. Tulumello, BEYOND WINNING (2000). The goal of this packet is to familiarize you with basic concepts in the negotiation theory discourse so that you are cognizant of (a.) the strategies that best suit your personal negotiating style and (b.) the strategies those on the opposite side of the table are using. For more detailed information on the general principles described herein, consult the three sources listed above.

[7] The classic negotiator's tale used to illustrate this dilemma concerns two siblings who were both interested in the same orange. (For this course, you might want to instead imagine it is two offensive lineman looking to split a large hamburger.) After a heated discussion about who should get the orange, the two siblings decided to cut the orange into halves. Each sibling walked away with his half. One ate the fruit and threw away the peel; the other used the peel to add some zest to her cookies and threw away the meat. The moral: when negotiators fail to share information, they must squander a lot of value.

increasing their own slice of the pie and increasing the pie as a whole. When framing your demands, you may want to emphasize how the entire pie will increase to convince the other side that your proposal ought to be accepted. Creative solutions can be extremely useful for increasing the benefits that are expected to accrue to both sides.

There are four principal sources of value: (1.) differences between the parties, (2.) noncompetitive similarities, (3.) economies of scale and scope, and (4.) reducing transaction costs and dampening strategic opportunism.

1. *Differences Between the Parties.* Parties can use certain differences to achieve gains through trades. For instance, if the parties have different (a.) resources, (b.) relative valuations, (c.) forecasts, (d.) risk preferences, or (e.) time preferences, the parties can arrange contracts that exploit these differences and create value for both sides.[8] Consider the gains to be made from different forecasts. Suppose that an optimistic baseball club expects that the players it has assembled for next season will go to the World Series and are likely to win in six or seven games, whereas the team's pessimistic and recession-scathed advertising buyer, who is looking to renew its agreement for next season, believes that the team is unlikely to make it even as far as a championship series. The parties can create value by structuring the contract to reflect these differing forecasts. The team might agree to a flat advertising fee for the season, but increase the fee a great deal for each level of the playoffs the team reaches or each playoff game played. The team will be pleased that it projects to yield the extra advertising profits, and the advertiser will be pleased that it will have to pay a lower flat fee throughout the season in exchange for a higher contingent fee in the postseason.

2. *Noncompetitive Similarities.* Noncompetitive similarities are those interests that are not mutually exclusive, but rather overlap (though the parties may have different underlying motivations). A team and a city arranging to build a stadium may have noncompetitive similarities. The team will likely want to build a stadium that will attract fans and raise revenues. A city may want to attract a team so that it can help revitalize local businesses in the vicinity of

[8] For a more detailed description of these five differences, see Mnookin, et al., p. 14–15.

the stadium. Because both agree on these goals, the two parties may try to create a state-of-the-art stadium that will attract people both to the games and also to the surrounding area.

3. *Economies of Scale and Scope*. Economies of scale—gains from consolidation of production or consumption—can also create value. An auto parts maker and a car dealer seeking to advertise in a stadium may jointly approach a team. By combining resources, the two businesses might be able to create an advertisement that markets both their businesses at less cost than if they chose to purchase two separate advertisements.

   Economies of scope—gains from producing more than one good or service using the same basic resources—might also be useful for creating value. For example, imagine that when negotiating the "Uses" provision of a stadium lease, the City-Lessor argues that it wants a certain number of days for which to put its own events, but the Team-Lessee is worried about the potential damage to the field and facilities. The two parties could continue to haggle over rental price, or, a creative negotiator for the City might suggest that the team get a share of the revenues, free advertising opportunities, or some other benefit on the days of Lessor-events. This way, both parties might gain something on the days of Lessor-events.

4. *Reducing Transaction Costs and Dampening Strategic Opportunism*. By making the process of a negotiation less-time consuming, costly, and adversarial; reducing the risk that the parties will deceive each other; and aligning future incentives, the parties can create value for their clients. In complex deals, vast amounts of time and money can be wasted. There is no value for a lawyer to prolong a negotiation beyond what is necessary to secure a client's interests so long as the client is likely to have repeat business or other clients have matters awaiting.

B. "Calling an Audible": Asserting and Understanding Interests

The tension between distributing and creating value is not the only dynamic that affects negotiations. Related to this first tension is the tension between asserting one's own viewpoints and acknowledging the need of the other side. As an advocate for your client, you will need to persuasively assert your client's needs, goals, and point of view. But, to build consensus successfully, you will also need to understand the other party's needs, concerns, and interests. Communicate your interests concretely and be specific, when possible. Check to make sure each side understands the other's point of view. Misunderstandings cannot only lead to conflicts but also to vague or ambiguous drafting.

When a contract is vague or ambiguous, courts may apply the "forthright negotiator principle."[9] Recently invoked by a Delaware Court to resolve a contract dispute regarding the availability of specific performance in a contract, the forthright negotiator principle, as applied in situations where contract language is unclear, requires that "the Court considers the evidence of what one party subjectively 'believed the obligator to be, coupled with evidence of what one party knew or should have known of such belief.' In other words, the forthright negotiator principle provides that, in cases where the extrinsic evidence does not lead to a single, commonly held understanding of a contract's meaning, a court may consider the subjective understanding of one party that has been objectively manifested and is known or should be known by the other party." In essence, this means that when negotiating, clear communication is essential. Otherwise, if a contract's terms are not clear, and one party expressed its belief regarding a term, the other party, knowing that belief, will be held to that interpretation of the contract.

C. *"Studying the Game Tapes": Preparing for the Negotiation*

Before you can assert your own needs, however, you will need to prepare for the negotiation. To prepare, you should first identify the issues and think about the interests of both sides. With careful thought, you will know your own interests and can make a tentative list of the other side's interests. Be sure to prioritize your own interests and anticipate how the other side will prioritize their own. This requires more than a superficial understanding of the narrow issue. Think carefully about the business at hand. Is there anything unique about the city in which I am planning to lease a stadium, such as nearby public roads next to which I can sell valuable advertising space? Are there any unique aspects to a sponsor's business that can be used in the sponsorship agreement? Are there non-monetary trades that can be made? How might reputational factors affect the

---

9 See *United Rentals, Inc. v. RAM Holdings, Inc.*, 937 A.2d 810 (Del. Ch. 2007). Though his principle is rarely invoked, the Delaware court's willingness to apply it is important, given the number of corporations incorporated in Delaware. This may also be a consideration when negotiating the governing law provision of a deal.

deal, such as placing a premium on sponsors that are "blue chip" and "family friendly"? Next, think about the various value-creating opportunities, described above, that might arise. Before you enter the negotiating room, try to improve your best alternative to a negotiated agreement as much as possible and get an accurate measure of your reservation value. This will give real "teeth" to your threat to walk away from the deal if the other side is being difficult. Finally, establish an "ambitious but realistic aspiration level," one that will enable you to claim as much of the surplus in the negotiation range (or ZOPA, described below) as possible.

To understand how to properly prepare for a negotiating session, it is necessary to side step for a minute to discuss what is meant by the "best alternative to a negotiated agreement" (BATNA), and some other concepts you might have heard before: "zone of possible agreement" (ZOPA), "no possible agreement" (NOPA), "reservation deal," "must haves," "nice to haves," and "throwaways."

BATNA. The BATNA is the standard against which any proposed agreement should be measured. It is the only standard which can protect you from accepting terms that are too unfavorable and from rejecting terms it would be in your interest to accept. Rather than focusing on a "bottom line," focus on the counterfactual of what your options are if you do not agree to the deal. Potential purchasers of sports franchises have weak BATNAs; there are only a limited number of franchises up for sale. As such, sellers often have a great deal of negotiating leverage because they know that their product—a professional sports team—is very unique. By contrast, teams that are considering sponsorships deals with a credit card service will have a more robust set of BATNAs; if VISA is being difficult, the team can always try to negotiate with MasterCard. Be wary, though, of being overly optimistic and assuming that you have too many other choices, especially when the economy is fluctuating. Further, be sure to identify and isolate the best single "alternative," and do not mistakenly aggregate all possible alternatives when comparing your BATNA to the negotiated deal.

ZOPA. The ZOPA is the range of possible deals between either side's BATNAs. Within this zone, either side would be better off reaching a deal than not. In a situation with a buyer and seller, if the buyer's BATNA is higher than the seller's BATNA, the range between these two values is the ZOPA. By contrast, if the buyer's BATNA is lower than the seller's BATNA, there is no ZOPA. This situation is also known as a NOPA.

NOPA. In a NOPA, no agreement is possible. Think carefully about whether what you are demanding is necessary if it is within the other party's range of NOPAs.

Reservation deal. The reservation deal is analogous to a reservation price in a simply buy-sell situation. The reservation deal should be your BATNA if there are other alternatives available. If not, you will have to think carefully about the minimum deal terms you require.

Must haves. Must haves are deal terms that your client insists upon. Prioritize these when negotiating. Consider the order in which you choose to present your must haves, as opposed to other terms that are less important. Each negotiation will necessitate a reconsideration of strategy. In some instances, you will want to present your "must haves" first. In others, you might want to intersperse your "must haves" with your "nice to haves" and your "throwaways." Other times, you will want to negotiate simpler terms first, and then reach your "must haves" once a cordial atmosphere has been established. The particular strategy you choose will depend on your personal style and the dynamics/economics of the deal at hand.

Nice to haves. "Nice to haves" are deal terms within the ZOPA that shift surplus one way or the other. These are lower in priority than your "must haves," but can affect how satisfied your client is with the ultimate deal.

Throwaways. "Throwaways" are points that are ultimately less important to you, but that you will nevertheless negotiate, either because these terms are important to the other party or because you can use them as leverage. Consider how aggressively or passively you want to negotiate these terms and how to strategically use these terms for leverage when negotiating.

Now that you are conversant in the basics of negotiation terminology, you are ready to prepare for the actual negotiation. Here is a "checklist" of things to do for any negotiation:

1. *Preparing for Negotiations*: Be sure you know your client's needs, and consider what will happen if no deal is consummated. Search diligently for competing and substitute alternatives, and find your BATNA. Assess your reservation price/deal terms before and after each round of negotiations, and consider how the "sunk costs"—time spent gathering information and negotiating—affect your reservation price/deal terms as the negotiating progress. Gather your arguments for the negotiations, combining facts, data, arguments, and rationalizations. Once you have properly assessed your client, move to assessing the other side's interests and needs and speculating about their alternatives.

Having information about both sides is not enough. You need to think about how you will use this information in the negotiation process. How open should you be? How open/trustworthy is other party? You might want to consider the use of a Confidentiality Agreement, if appropriate. Can the negotiations be done in stages, or should you raise all the issues at once? Consider the tone you will use to discuss the issues and how forceful you want to be. If you had the option to choose any venue, which would you choose? The environment can make a substantial difference in how the parties approach the negotiations. Finally, before entering into negotiations, determine what your "ideal" deal (or range of deals) would be. How do various "gives" and "gets" interact? Keeping all the moving parts of the deal in order can be difficult, so organization and preparation are essential.

2. *Opening Gambits*: Both which party presents the first offer and the substance of that party's first offer is important to establishing the negotiations. The first offer made has an "anchoring effect"; it influences the other party's perception of their own reservation deal and anchors the other party's thinking about the value of the deal. Furthermore, beware of opening with an extreme offer in your favor (whether it be a low-ball price of what a presenting sponsor company is willing to pay or a very high price of what the team demands from their presenting sponsor). Extreme offers have two negative potential effects: (1.) they damage the tone of the negotiation and the collegiality between the parties, and (2.) they force the parties to make disproportionately large concessions.

   If the other side opens with an extreme offer, gauge your reaction. Instead of spending effort discussing the extreme offer, thereby locking you into a dissatisfactory starting position, reset the parameters of the discussion. You might want to start discussing a different issue, or, instead of countering with a modified form of the other party's offer, present your own offer. Before presenting your counteroffer, consider what the midpoint between the original offer and the counteroffer are, as this is a natural focal point for the negotiations. Compare with the midpoint with your aspiration level and reservation price/deal terms, and adjust accordingly.

Finally, consider carefully the words you choose to use. Instead of saying what you "must" get, thereby signaling your reservation price/deal terms, say what you would "like" to get. If your client is not present, you can also use the powerful phrase, "I'll have to check with my client," if you need more time to strategize or consider your answer.

3. *The Negotiation Dance*: Consider how you want to make concessions. As discussed above, decide if you want to alternate your "must have" provisions with your "throwaway" positions. This might give the impression that both sides are equals in the "gives" and "gets." Or, consider presenting your "throwaways" first, so the other side may be more conciliatory when you raise your "must haves." These strategies are context specific, depending upon the personalities and items at the table. Moreover, developing a specific pattern can work against you at times if you and the other party will be "repeat players" and have an ongoing relationship. If you develop a "tell" for what the more or less important deal terms are, the other party can use this to its advantage. Therefore, you should be mindful that every negotiation is different, and adjust your approach as needed.[10]

   During the negotiations, be sure to reassess your perceptions and your aspirations based upon what the other party says. Again, due to the number of "moving parts" in complex deals, you will have to have a thorough understanding of how the terms work together. And, of course, communication and clarification of misunderstandings is paramount prior to memorializing the final version of the agreement. Still, do not merely take the other side's statements at face value. Think critically about their statements, and question the assumptions under which they are operating. For example, when negotiating a stadium lease and considering how to divide revenues, perhaps the lessor's expectations of concession sales differ from the lessee's, in which case you need to reconcile these two estimates.

---

10 Mark McCormack, ON NEGOTIATION, p. 81.

II. "The Playbook": Negotiating Tactics

When negotiating, you are faced with two primary strategic considerations: (1.) What's the best agreement that I can reasonably hope to get, and (2.) can we make a deal here at all? When deciding what steps to take, each party must consider the other's possible reaction. To color the other party's view of one's own position, one might mislead the other party about one's best alternative, e.g. by pretending to have another offer on the table or by understanding one's interest in a product by "low-balling" the other side. These tactics might "backfire," however. If a seller does not have another offer, and the buyer finds out, it will completely undermine the seller's bargaining hand. Similarly, if a buyer "low balls" a seller, a seller might think the buyer is not serious and therefore is reluctant to invest the time to negotiate a purchase and sale.

A. *"Unnecessary Roughness?": Hard Bargaining Tactics*

Some negotiations might employ "hard bargaining" tactics. When using these tactics, there are often high costs and substantial risks. One might alienate, offend, or simply rile the other side. But, the following list of ten common hard-bargaining tactics is useful for knowing when such strategies are being used against you and might come in handy when dealing with a particularly aggressive opponent.

1. *Extreme claims followed by small, slow concessions*: Aiming high (or low) and conceding slowly. This tactic protects the user from giving away too much surplus[11] at the start, but at the cost of potentially lessening the chance of making a deal and inviting protracted haggling.

2. *Commitment tactics*: Committing to a course of action that ties one's hands, thus forcing the other side to accommodate; limiting one's freedom of action in order to influence the other side's view of what agreements are possible. To be effective, a commitment must seem "binding, credible, visible, and irreversible."

3. *Take it or leave it offers*: Stating that one's offer is non-negotiable—that the negotiation will end if it is not accepted. Like commitment strategies the risk is that no deal will be consummated. Imagine that when negotiating an extension to a lease, the team that is responsible for repairs, maintenance and additions

[11] Surplus is amount above a party's reservation value within the negotiating range. For instance, if I am willing to sell my team for $900 million, and you are willing to buy it for $1.1 billion, I reap a $200 million surplus by selling it to you at your reservation purchase price.

demands that the lessor contribute monies to make the stadium "state of the art," or else the team will leave the city.

4. *Inviting unreciprocated offers*: Asking the offerer to bid against himself. Instead of meeting an offer with a specific counter, the hard bargainer indicates that the first offer is insufficient and requests a better offer.
5. *Flinch*: Piling one demand on top of another until the other side makes a sign that the demands have reached their breaking point.
6. *Personal insults and feather ruffling*: Attacking the other side's insecurities, flustering the other side, and otherwise gaining psychological advantage.
7. *Bluffing, puffing and lying*: Trying to influence the other side's perception of what would be acceptable by exaggerating or misrepresenting facts.
8. *Threats and warnings*: Promising drastic consequences if one's demands are not met.
9. *Belittling the other party's alternatives*: Trying to influence the other side's reservation value by basing their BATNA. E.g. "You don't really want Mark Cuban to buy your team, do you?"
10. *Good cop, bad cop*: Designating one person in a two-negotiator team as a reasonable person who is supposedly trying to help the other side out, while the other negotiator adopts a tough, abrasive manner and pushes for concessions.

B. "Staying Inbounds": Problem Solving Tactics and Principled Negotiation

While you will want to tailor negotiation style to suit your own personality, your style, regardless of the specific form it takes, should be aimed at "principled negotiation". "Principled negotiation" follows four tenets: (1.) separate the people from the problem; (2.) focus on interests, not positions; (3.) generate a variety of possibilities before deciding what to do; and (4.) insist that the result be based on some objective standard.

1. *Separate the people from the problem*. Given that you will be in a 12-week seminar, working in two-person groups, it is especially important to work together as opposed to in a consistently combative manner. A working relationship where trust, understanding,

respect, and friendship are built up over time can make each new negotiation smoother and more efficient. Try to constrain emotions, even with hard-bargainers, and instead refocus on the issue at hand. You don't want your own personality or ego to interfere with your client's goals. Similarly, if you have a particularly difficult or aggressive client, you may want to strategize when the client should be in the room and when instead you should negotiate for potential packages that you can then present to the client for approval. If you think the other side is asking for something unreasonable, ask them why they desire a particular item and goal they hope it will serve. Restate what you think the other side is saying to ensure that you are hearing correctly. Avoid conversations about trust and self-interest, and focus on principles and fairness.

2. *Focus on interests, not positions*. Instead of focusing on positions, or specific outcomes each side wants, focus instead on interests, or the reasons you want things. This will facilitate creative problem solving by avoiding "locking" the parties in to particular positions, and instead opening the door for a variety of solutions to satisfy each side's interests. When trying to identify the other sides interests, resources, and capabilities, ask the following questions: "what is important to you?"; "why?"; "why not?"; "what else?"; "what could be wrong with. . . ?". When asking these questions, you can tweak your earlier assessment about the other side. If the other side puts forth a position, instead of attacking it, look behind it to see what interests the other side is trying to protect. When expressing your own interests and ideas, invite criticism and advice instead of immediately trying to defend them. Let the other side explain to you why you are wrong, rather than trying to justify why you are right.

3. *Generate a variety of possibilities before deciding what to do.* Once you identify your own and the other side's interests work to generate options. Only after you have generated an initial set should you try to compare and evaluate them. By generating options first and evaluating them later, one can expand the sphere of creative solutions without immediately rejecting ideas.

4. *Insist that the result be based on objective criteria.* When possible, try to find some standard, such as market value for stadium rent, expert opinion on the value of a sports franchise, custom, or law. This way, neither party will have to give in to the other, and the deal can eliminate the subjective tastes that can be used to hold up a deal.

III. "The Championship": Memorializing a Deal Document

Now that you have identified what you are looking for and have gathered information, you will need to determine how to use the deal document to reflect what you have negotiated for and what you cannot negotiate for. We will cover the specific provisions of deal documents from week to week.

Generally, you can use deal terms to shift risk and obligations back and forth and to affect deal certainty. The basic components of an agreement are representations and warranties, covenants, conditions, and remedies.

Representations—statements about existing facts—and warranties—promises about future facts—describe the business or product and shift risk between the parties. As the cornerstone of the agreement, reps and warranties are typically negotiated first. These terms can also be used to engage in due diligence. If you are asking the other party to rep to something, and the other party is uncomfortable making the rep, this should raise a red flag and prompt more questioning (or a more generous indemnification). The scope of reps and warranties reflect both parties' bargaining power and deal economics: the attractiveness of price, the prospect of competing purchasers, and the availability of market substitutes.

Parties will negotiate over whether or not the reps and warranties ought to be qualified by "knowledge" or "materiality." With respect to knowledge, you can qualify reps and warranties to "actual knowledge," "actual knowledge after reasonable inquiry," or "constructive knowledge." You also have various options when qualifying by "materiality." You can try to define "material" at a set dollar amount, or use various baskets, thresholds and deductibles in the indemnity. Using the term "Material Adverse Effect" or "Material Adverse Change," which you will have to define in the agreement, to qualify terms will ensure that small problems do not violate the rep or warranty. Rather, a "Material Adverse Effect" or "Material Adverse Change" is something that affects a fundamental aspect of the business in a durational-significant manner.

Parties can also negotiate by tinkering with language in the reps and warranties. Stating that a company "is in compliance" is different from saying, "is, and has been, in compliance with all laws." The former permits closing down a business that has violated some laws, whereas the latter leaves the seller on the hook.

Covenants are promises to perform or refrain from performing certain actions. For instance, if annual governmental filings are necessary for a stadium, the lessee may covenant to complete such filings. Covenants will also describe the level of efforts required, whether they are "best efforts," "reasonable efforts," "reasonable best efforts," "commercially reasonable efforts," or any permutation you can think of. Parties can also haggle over whether things must be done "immediately," "promptly," or "within a reasonable period."

Conditions are statements that, if false, give parties the option to walk away from the deal. The conditions lack substance. Their force is in the power they give parties to walk away if left unsatisfied.

Finally, remedies can be tailored to suit the needs of the parties, such as a purchase price adjustment if some of the representations and warranties are not true. Still, when drafting a contract, some things will remain incomplete because it is impossible to conceive of the full range of risks in a deal or all future contingencies.

Overall, the goal of this seminar is to help you find your negotiating style and learn how to draft various complicated deal documents in the sports industry, thereby preparing you to work in the legal world.

An Introduction to Agreement Structure, Recitals, and Definitions

Complex deal documents have many parts, and your responsibility as a lawyer not only includes drafting all those parts, but also understanding how those parts work together and what obligations they create for your client. Failure to do so could have serious repercussions for the rights and remedies available to your client. Thus, this guide is designed to familiarize you with the provisions that typically appear in agreement and to explain the purpose and structure of the recitals and definitions of an agreement. In subsequent weeks, we will discuss the other portions of agreements more in depth.

Agreements typically start with a **title page** that states the type of agreement, who the agreement is between, and the date of the agreement. For instance, the first page of a lease might read:

AGREEMENT OF LEASE

between

CITY OF CAMBRIDGE

as Lessor

and

SPORTSTEAM, LLC

as Lessee.

Dated as of January 14, 2016[12]

The title page serves the obvious purpose of identifying the subject matter of the agreement and the parties. It can be useful to include such a page when a deal requires the signing of multiple agreements or when the parties sign multiple agreements of the same type, but one party differs in each agreement.

For agreements with many provisions, the next part of the agreement is a **Table of Contents**. The Table should list the Article and Section numbers, along with the titles of these provisions, and the corresponding page numbers on which they appear.

Following the table of contents, come the first three substantive portions of an agreement. These portions identify the agreement, explain its purpose, and state that the parties agree to the provisions that follow.

---

12 Use the form "Dated January 14, 2016" when the parties reach and sign the agreement on the same day. Use the form "Dated as of January 14, 2016" when the parties reach an agreement on the as of date but do not actually sign until a later date. This can be an important distinction in some cases. For instance, if representations and warranties and covenants are included, they are effective upon the "as of" date, not the date the contract is signed. To indicate the signing date, you can put the date in the signature block. But see *Sweetman v. Strescom Indus., Inc.*, 389 A.2d 1322 (Del. Super. Ct. 1978) (holding that putting two different dates in the preamble/title page and under the signature block creates ambiguity regarding the effective date).

Alternatively, you can include a provision on the signature page that says, "To evidence the parties' agreement to this agreement's provisions, the parties have executed and delivered this agreement on [signing date] but as of the [date set forth on the titlepage/preamble]."

Do not put a future date in the title page/preamble. Rather, if you want the agreement to be effective following the signing date, include an "Effective Date" provision in the agreement.

The **preamble** identifies the contract by setting forth the name of the agreement, the parties, and the date the parties signed the contract. When naming the parties, you should conform that you are using the correct legal name of an entity by checking its organizational document. After the entity's name, state what type of entity it is and its jurisdiction of organization.[13] For example, the preamble to the lease agreement described above might read:

> This LEASE[14] is made and entered into as of this 14th day of January, 2016, by and[15] between[16] THE CITY OF CAMBRIDGE, a municipal corporation of the State of Massachusetts (the "Landlord"), and SPORTSTEAM, LLC, a Delaware limited liability company (the "Tenant").[17]

The preamble is followed by the **recitals**. The recitals are a series of clauses that describe the background of the contract and why the parties are entering into it. The recitals do not provide rights or remedies and are not enforceable unless explicitly incorporated, but they do provide a short and specific summary of the purpose of the agreement and clarify the parties' intent.[18] These are particularly useful if the parties want to inform interested third parties about an agreement's purpose or if the specific agreement is part of a broader deal. If recitals and other "operative provisions" are inconsistent, but recitals are clear and the operative part is ambiguous, then the

---

13 This is typically important if you are dealing with the subsidiary of a parent entity with the same name as the parent entity, but organized in a different state. More critical than accuracy in the preamble, though, is accuracy in the reps and warranties.

14 Instead of using all capital letters, you can also put the name of the agreement in normal upper- and lowercase letters and in bold. *See* Howard Darmstadter, HEREOF, THEREOF, AND EVERYWHEREOF, A CONTRARIAN GUIDE TO LEGAL DRAFTING 80 (ABA 2002).

15 The words "by and" are redundant of "between," but have conventionally been included anyway.

16 There is disagreement in the legal community about whether to use "among" if there are more than two parties to an agreement. According to THE OXFORD ENGLISH DICTIONARY, "between" is correct whenever two or more parties are in a direct reciprocal relation with each other. By contrast, "among" should be used to express a less direct relationship with a group. The convention, though, is to use "among" when there are more than two parties to an agreement.

17 If you have more than one tenant as party to this agreement, you can list the parties as "SPORTSTEAM, LLC, and Team Owner (individually, a "Tenant" and collectively, the "Tenants").

18 In the famous contracts case *Wood v. Lucy, Duff Gordon*, the court used the recitals to interpret the contract. The contract between Lady Duff-Gordon and Wood included a promise that Lady Duff-Gordon granted Wood an exclusive license to market her designs, but did not include a return promise from Wood to use his best efforts to do so. Justice Cardozo held that the contract included an implied promise, based partly on the text of the recitals.

recitals will govern the construction.[19] Recitals to a lease agreement might read:

> Whereas, Landlord is the owner of that certain real property more particularly described in Exhibit A hereto (the "Real Property") which is located at the intersection of Main Street and State Highway 100 in the City of Cambridge, Massachusetts; and
>
> Whereas, Landlord intends to construct a certain baseball facility and related improvements (the "Ballpark") and surface parking lots immediately adjacent to the Ballpark (the "Parking," and together with the Ballpark, the "Facility") on the Real Property (the "Facility" and the "Real Property" are the "Premises"); and
>
> Whereas, Landlord also intends to construct on the Premises a park and ride facility that will be dedicated to public transportation, together with necessary public access to the Premises; and. . .

Generally, it's best to keep the recitals short, and include only as much as is necessary for the intended audience.

At the end of the recitals is the **statement of consideration**. Traditionally, this followed the introduction "NOW, THEREFORE," but can also be written as "Accordingly, the parties agree. . . " The statement of consideration for the recitals above might read: "Now, therefore, for and in consideration of the foregoing premises and the terms, conditions, covenants, and undertakings contained in this Lease, the Landlord and the Tenant mutually agree as follows. . . " After the preamble, recitals, and statement of consideration end, the first article begins.

Though **definitions** can be elsewhere in an agreement, they are often inserted near the beginning as the first article[20] and are listed in alphabetical order. Definitions provide a shorthand way of referring to complex concepts and ensure that the same concept is said the same way throughout an agreement. They can be used to (1.) expand or limit the dictionary meaning of a word; (2.) clarify the meaning of a word or phrase (e.g. Business Day); (3.) resolve the meaning of an ambiguous word; (4.) explain the meaning of a technical word or phrase; (5.) express a concept that is specific to a transaction; (6.) list all the things to which a word or phrase refers;

---

19 *Jamison v. Franklin Life Ins. Co.*, 136 P.2d 265, 269 (Ariz. 1943) (citations omitted).

20 Alternatively, you can define the term the first time the term appears in the agreement, in its context; however, it might be more difficult to unambiguously define terms if you use this approach.

and (7.) explain the meaning of a word or phrase. Once you have created definitions, you will have a set of **defined terms** that you can use throughout the agreement. It is important to craft the definitions precisely, and, once a term is defined, to use the defined term—designated as such because it will start with a capital letter—consistently throughout. During Week 1, if you say that "Advertising" means such and such signage, then the term cannot include anything else; that definition is both complete and exclusive. If you say "Advertising" includes such and such signage, your definition leaves open the possibility that there are other things, which you did not explicitly list, that are part of the definition. Finally, you might also say "Advertising" excludes such and such signage, to describe what is not included in your definition. One important definition you will draft during Week 2 is the definition of a "force majeure" in a Stadium Lease.

Oftentimes, defined terms can have other ordinary uses. For instance, "Parking" might be a defined term in a lease agreement referring to a specific lot or area. When referring to, and only when referring to that specific lot or area should the defined, capital "P", Parking is inserted. When referring to parking that is not the specific lot, such as in the clause, "additional parking will be available for playoff games. . . ", the defined term should not be used.

The number of years that the contract will govern the parties' relationship, or the **term**, typically follows thereafter. Your term provision should state how long the original term of the contract is, the effective date of the agreement, and, if there are any options to renew, what such options are or where they are located elsewhere in the agreement.

The "meat" of the agreement will follow these introductory, foundational provisions. Of course, depending on the type of agreement, the composition of these portions will differ. Representations and warranties are common to most agreements, though their scope, importance, and placement will differ from deal to deal. Covenants, describing what the parties agree to do to and the level of efforts required, are also common to agreements. For instance, a **lease** might include articles on "Acquisition and Construction of the Project," "Rent," "Expenses Relating to Landlord Events," "Security," "Repairs and Maintenance," "Alterations and Capital Improvements," and "Financial Reports and Records." **Sponsorship agreements** might include the following articles: "Sponsorship Rights," which includes a description of the sponsorship rights, state who is responsible for the presentation and approval of the advertising copy, and state who is responsible for maintaining the signage; "Fees and Payment;" "Package Changes;" and "Copyright and Trademark."

"Endgame provisions," describing the end of the parties' contractual relationship, typically follow the articles setting forth the descriptive sections of what good or service is the subject of the contract. **Indemnification** (and **survival** of the indemnification terms), **termination**, **events of default**, manner of **amendment**, **limitation of liability**, and compulsory **mediation** or **arbitration** upon the advent of a dispute is described.

The final provisions of an agreement are commonly known as "boilerplate." This moniker can be misleading to the extent it suggests that these provisions are immutable or negligible. Rather, boilerplate ought to be considered as so important that it warrants inclusion in nearly every agreement, and lawyers should be careful to tailor the terms to the needs of a particular agreement. Typical "boilerplate" provisions are **Force Majeure**, **Assignment**, **Governing Law**, **Notice**, **Merger**, **Counterparts**, **Waiver**, **Severability**, **Authority**, and **Captions**.

Finally, agreements end with **signature blocks** so that the agreement can be signed by those with the requisite authority to bind the parties.

It is important to remember that the basic building blocks of agreements described above are not self-contained. Rather, they work together in important, and often complicated, ways. Be careful to synchronize the various sections. For instance, the "Events of Default" should match "Remedies" available for the various types of default to ensure that in a particular circumstance, your client can seek the specific relief it desires. Now, go forth and draft your own agreement!

An Introduction to Naming Rights Agreements and Intellectual Property

Next, you will attempt to draft a Naming Rights Agreement between a sports franchise and a company. Naming Rights Agreements—generally speaking, an agreement that grants an entity the right to give a sport's stadium a name (and, to receive related benefits) in exchange for monetary payments over a period of time—have become quite a lucrative revenue source for teams and a method of relatively inexpensive advertising for companies. If a company's name is already in an NFL stadium, it need not dole out huge sums of money for Super Bowl advertising. Rather, it benefits from consistent visual and auditory exposure during the "big game" at no additional charge. Naming Rights Agreements, as alluded to above, are typically accompanied by a slew of other benefits for the company, such as pouring rights for PepsiCo at the Pepsi Center in Denver or the now-famously defunct Enron's exclusive agreement to be the energy provider for the Astros' Enron Field.

I. Naming Rights Agreements

After the preamble, recitals, and definitions that typically begin all agreements,[21] Naming Rights Agreements begin with a grant of the naming rights from the franchise to the company and a description of what the grant includes. This grant also typically states if the grant is exclusive or categorically exclusive, the naming sponsor's right to approve or veto other potential sponsors, and the right to approve the advertising plan. NFL and MLB franchises usually have their own venues, while NHL and NBA teams usually share venues, and consequently, split the revenues and other rights from the grant of naming rights. If, as is normally done nowadays, the agreement also confers other benefits on the company—luxury suites, playoff tickets, etc.—the parties may enumerate these benefits here or in a separate exhibit.

The agreement will next go on to describe the term of the agreement, and any options for renewal or rights of first refusal. The description of the options may be accompanied by a description of how either party can renew the term, e.g. in writing by a specified date.

Of course, a critical term of the agreement will outline the payment or fees. The payments might be a lump sum, installments that increase uniformly or fluctuate, or some other permutation. The agreement might provide for the amount, timing, and method of payments.

Depending on the parties' preferences, the naming rights agreement might warrant the creation of a new, joint logo. Regardless, the parties will want the right to use one another's logos. The agreement will likely provide the team with the right to use the company's trademarks for advertising and promotion, subject to the company's approval. The agreement might also provide for similar rights to the team's logo to the company. This provision of the agreement might read:

> **Development of Arena Mark and Arena Graphic Logo.** The parties agree that the Franchise shall develop, at the Franchise's expense, the Arena Mark and the Arena Graphic Logo, provided that the final design of the Arena Mark and Arena Graphic Logo shall be subject to the approval of Naming Rights Holder, which approval shall not be unreasonably withheld, delayed or conditioned.

---

21 *See* An Introduction to Agreement Structure, Recitals, and Definitions.

Since the parties are using one another's marks, and the use of the mark reflects on the reputation of the parties, they might also demand that such use be of a certain quality. For instance, the company might require that all team-related merchandise with its logo or the joint stadium logo be of high quality and free from all defects. Or, the team may require that the company not use the mark in a manner that "is contrary to public morals or which has been found to be deceptive or misleading, or which reflects unfavorably on the good name, goodwill, reputation or image of the Team." The agreement may also give the company the right in connection with the promotion of games or other events to produce its own event-related merchandise bearing its trademark, the trademark of the event, and the logo of the stadium. In the interest of preserving the quality of the mark, the parties may specify the ability of each party to license the logo as well. This, of course, will be related to who "owns" the mark.

If there is a change of control at either party, the parties will likely have to modify the contractual terms. Naming Rights Agreements will provide for the time period within which such amendments must be made, the attendant approval rights, and who is responsible for spearheading the changes. The parties might also consider changing the exclusivity/categorical exclusivity provision in the event that the company's business changes. For example, assume that Gillette expands the scope of its business from razors and other shaving related products to bath soaps, body washes, lotions, and other grooming products from men. In this case, a company like Axe may become a competitor. The naming company may want to preserve the right to modify the definition of "Competitor" or "Direct Competitor" in the event of such a change.

At this point in the agreement, the parties may include a section on representations and warranties. The "reps and warranties" might certify that:

- The entity operating the team has the right, power and authority to enter into the agreement,
- That the entity is duly organized and in good standing,
- That no additional consents are required,
- That the team has a valid lease for the stadium, and
- That there are no league rules that would impair the company's rights under the agreement.

The scope and import of reps and warranties will be covered in greater detail next week.

The indemnification provision will typically contain cross-indemnification provisions that effectively make each party responsible for claims or liabilities incurred by that party (and its affiliates, heirs, assigns, etc.) as a result of conduct under the agreement or its breach. The company might require indemnity for any claims for infringement by a third party, any breaches of the team's obligations, any claims raised by event attendees, or any claims by people who argue that are not paid for services in relation to game day productions. The team, by contrast, might require indemnity for breach of obligations under the agreement and the company's use of the intellectual property.

To pay at least part of the indemnity, the parties might also require one another to carry insurance. The parties may be required to carry insurance covering personal injury, death, property damage, contractual obligations, product liability protection, worker's compensation, and any other insurance necessary to protect the parties.

As with stadium leases, the "force majeure," or other events that limit the company's anticipated exposure, might also be addressed in the agreement. Parties may discuss what happens in the event of a strike/lockout, or any other event that affects the value of the agreement in a material manner.

Naming rights agreements may explicitly state that the parties are not joint venturers, and therefore, neither part has the authority or right to incur obligations for the other or to commit or bind the other.[22]

Finally, as in any other agreement, the Naming Rights Agreement will explain the parties' rights and remedies upon termination, including what happens to any trademarks or service marks produced. The Agreement might also have a dispute resolution section and a limitation of liability. The parties may also want to include a "Confidentiality" provision, that prohibits each party from disclosing the terms and conditions of the agreement.

II. Intellectual Property: Trademarks, Trade Names, Service Marks and Logos

Naming Rights Agreements, obviously, involve significant intellectual property. Below is a brief overview of broad classifications of intellectual property, and how each plays a role in the Naming Rights Agreement.

---

[22] This might be especially important for state-owned entities. In 1995, the Georgia state attorney general claimed that the sponsorship agreement between McDonald's and Georgia Tech University violated the state Constitution, which prohibited the state becoming a joint owner with a private organization.

Trademarks. A trademark, as defined in the Lanham Act, is ". . . any word, name, symbol, or device, or any combination thereof adopted and used by a manufacturer or merchant to identify his goods and distinguish them from those of others."[23] Unlike copyrights—which after a specified period[24] become part of the public domain—a trademark may be in the public domain before it is selected by a person/business to represent that business or product, or rather, before it becomes a trademark. The trademark owner gets a property right in the trademark.

The Lanham Act protects trademark owners from unauthorized uses that are likely to cause confusion, to cause mistake, or to deceive.[25] The robustness of the trademark—and the level of protection afforded to it—varies depending upon the uniqueness of the mark. A mark that is very unique will get greater protection, while a mark that is weaker, also known as a "suggestive mark," will get narrower protection.

Some trademarks may have difficulty even getting narrow protection. "Generic terms" that fail to distinguish one good from another are never granted trademark status because they only generally describe the class of product, and do not identify the specific product.[26] Similarly, descriptive marks, such as geographic terms (e.g. Pitt) or terms of a general nature (e.g. Musicfest), will not be protected unless there is a secondary meaning that distinguishes the product. Showing the following elements can prove secondary meaning: (1.) the amount and type of advertising; (2.) the volume of sales; (3.) the length and manner of use; (4.) direct consumer testimony, or (5.) consumer surveys.[27] Whichever party bears the responsibility for creating the trademark should expect to spend time and money not only filing the trademark application, but also ensuring that the trademark is robust enough to qualify for protection.

If a party has to pursue a potential trademark infringer, the court will apply the "likelihood of confusion" test, an eight-factor test designed to determine if the allegedly infringing mark will create

---

23 Lanham Trademark Act, 15 U.S.C. § 1127.

24 This time period of a copyright differs depending upon whether the work was published or unpublished, with or without notice, renewed or not, and the prevailing copyright law at the time of publication. For works created today, the copyright lasts for 70 years from the death of the author or 95 years from creation if the author is a corporate entity.

25 15 U.S.C. § 1114(1)(a).

26 *University of Georgia Athletic Ass'n v. Laite*, 756 F.2d 1535, 1540 (11th Cir.1985).

27 For an example of cases involving "secondary meaning" disputes, see *University of Pittsburgh v. Champion Products, Inc.*, 566 F. Supp. 711 (D. Pa. 1983), *American Basketball Association v. AMF Voit, Inc.*. 358 F. Supp. 981 (D. N.Y. 1973).

consumer confusion as to the origin of the product. The eight elements of the test are: (1.) the strength of the mark, (2.) the degree of similarity between the two marks, (3.) the proximity of the products, (4.) the likelihood that the prior owner will bridge the gap, (5.) actual confusion, (6.) the defendant's good faith in adopting its own mark, (7.) the quality of the defendant's mark, and (8.) the sophistication of the buyers.

Trade names. A trade name is the name a business uses for commercial purposes. The trade name may be, but need not be, registered as a trademark. Trade names are protected to the extent that another business in the same jurisdiction cannot use the same trade name in particular circumstances. To prevent such conflicting uses, trade names must be registered with the state. But, don't assume that the protections afforded to trademarks apply to trade names upon registration of a trade name.

Service marks. While trademarks apply to products, the term service mark is used to distinguish marks that apply to services. According to the Lanham Act, a service mark is "any word, name, symbol or device, or any combination thereof (1.) used by a person, or (2.) which a person has a bona fide intention to use in commerce and applies to register on the principal register established by this Chapter, to identify and distinguish the services of one person, including a unique service, from the services of others and to indicate the source of the services, even if that source is unknown." For example, a company like 1-800-Flowers might put their mark on their trucks, but not on the flowers themselves. Service marks are also registered with the USPTO and are protectable to the extent of trademarks. Whereas trademarks need to be used in goods to count as in commerce, service marks need only be used in advertising to warrant protection. Corporate naming rights sponsors register their service under the class "education and entertainment."

The registered service marks of corporate naming rights sponsors characteristically consist of their previously established marks plus the term "Field," "Stadium," "Park," or "Center." Some examples are:

a. BUSCH STADIUM, "providing a sporting and entertainment facility for the enjoyment of others," owned by Anheuser-Busch, Inc.;

b. ENRON FIELD, "Providing Stadium Facilities for Sports and Entertainment; Arranging and Conducting Athletic Competitions; Providing Entertainment in the Nature of Sporting Events and Related Activities," owned by the Enron Corp.;

c. UNITED CENTER, "entertainment services; namely providing and leasing stadium facilities for sporting events. . . ," owned by United Airlines, Inc.;

d. INVESCO FIELD AT MILE HIGH, "Providing Facilities for Sporting Events, Namely Football Games and Soccer Matches. . . " owned by Amvescap PLC Company United Kingdom;

e. PACIFIC BELL PARK, "Entertainment Services in the Nature of Baseball Exhibitions," owned by Pacific Telesis Group (Nevada Corp.);

f. PEPSI CENTER, "Operation of a Sports, Entertainment, Convention and Exhibition Arena, and Production of Sports and Entertainment Events for Public Exhibition and Television and Radio Broadcast," PepsiCo, Inc. (North Carolina Corp.)

Logos. A logotype, or logo, is a graphical symbol created for an individual company or product. Logos are designed to communicate quickly by virtue of being a distinctive and easily recognizable symbol. Logos often include a special typeface or font used to spell out the company name or initials. They also tend to include specific colors and graphical shapes. Perhaps the simplest logo is the Nike "swoosh," that is immediately associated with the sports apparel company's brand. Logos can be protected as trademarks/service marks, and all the above rules regarding trademarks/service marks apply to logos.

Naming Rights Agreements should specify who is responsible for creating and preserving IP, the permissible uses of the IP, and who is the owner of the rights during and after the term of the agreement.

Breach, Termination, and Remedies

Contractual relationships end for a variety of reasons, such as the expiration of the term, the assignment of contractual rights, or breach of the agreement. Endgame provisions—breach, termination, and remedies—establish the circumstances under which the parties' relationship ends and the mechanics of what happens at that point and whether the parties have continuing obligations.

Upon the expiration of a contractual term, typically one or more of the following things come into effect: (1.) termination of the parties' rights and obligations, (2.) obligations return the parties to the status quo before the contract, (3.) substantive obligations that continue, or (4.) exit strategies. For instance, if at the end of the term of a concessions contract, the concessionaire returns to the team the equipment it was leasing, the team may return a security deposit it held on the items. The parties may have continuing obligations to keep the term of the deal confidential.

The relationship, of course, does not always end amicably. Contractual relationships may also terminate under one of the following circumstances:

- Misrepresentation
- Breach of warranty
- Breach of covenant
- Failure to satisfy a condition
- Cross-default
- Force majeure event
- Violation of law
- Failure to obtain government or agency approval
- Death
- Business dispute
- Change of control
- Bankruptcy

To figure out how each of these things might affect the contract you draft, go through the contract section by section and ask yourself what would happen if the representation or warranty is not true, if the covenant is breached, if a party fails to perform, etc. Consider whether the contract should provide the defaulting party with notice and an opportunity to cure the default, i.e. fix the problem without penalty. Contracts that provide such opportunities for cure may distinguish "defaults" from "events of default." A default happens upon the breach, but before the notice/grace period. If the party fails to cure, then it may turn into an "event of default," and the non-breaching party will have the right to exercise remedies.

When deciding the appropriate remedy, analyze whether the contract should provide different remedies for different termination events. In certain circumstances, the parties may want to compel alternative dispute resolution; in others, they may want to preserve the right to go to court. Alternatively, the parties could arrange for a liquidated damages provision.

Endgame provisions are a series of "if/then" propositions, taking the form that "if X event happens, then the consequence is Y." The consequences may be an obligation to perform and pay some penalty, the grant of discretionary authority to terminate the contract to the non-breaching party, or a declaration that the contract has terminated.

Below are samples of endgame provisions from some food and beverage agreements:

> 14.2 **Termination**. This Agreement may be terminated prior to the expiration of the initial term by prior written notice to the other party as follows:
>
> > 14.2.1 By either party upon written notice of termination if the other party breaches any material term or condition of this Agreement and fails to cure that breach within thirty (30) days after receiving written notice stating the nature of the breach and the non-breaching party's intent to terminate; or
> >
> > 14.2.2 By either party, effective immediately, if the other party should become the subject of any voluntary or involuntary bankruptcy, receivership, or other insolvency proceedings or make an assignment or other arrangement for the benefit of its creditors, or if such other party should be nationalized or have any of its material assets expropriated; or
> >
> > 14.2.3 By Team, effective immediately, if there should occur any materials change in the management, ownership, control, sales personnel, sales and marketing capability, or financial condition of Concessionaire; or
> >
> > 14.2.4 By Team, effective immediately, if any law or regulation should become adopted or in effect in the Territory that would restrict Team's termination rights or otherwise invalidate any provisions hereof; or
> >
> > 14.2.5 By Team, effective immediately, if Concessionaire should violate the terms of Section 2.7[28] above or Section 16.3[29] below; or

---

28 **No Conflicts**. Concessionaire represents and warrants that, as of the Effective Date, it is not involved, directly or indirectly, in any activities involving products which compete or have the potential to compete with the products, including but not limited to the distribution of competing product lines ("Competing Activities"). Concessionaire agrees that it shall not enter into any Competing Activities in the Territory during the term of this Agreement and for a period of five (5) years afterward. If Concessionaire becomes involved in any Competing Activities, Concessionaire shall promptly inform Team of such involvement, and Team shall have, in addition to all other remedies to which it may be entitled, the right to terminate this Agreement without liability at any time thereafter pursuant to Section 14.2.

29 16.3 Assignment. Concessionaire may not transfer or assign any of its rights or obligations under this Agreement without the prior written consent of Team. Team

14.2.6 By Team, effective immediately, in accordance with provisions of Sections 15.3 or 15.5; or

14.2.7 By Team, effective immediately, if Concessionaire knowingly makes any false or untrue statements or representations to Team herein or in the performance of its obligations hereunder.

* * *

a) Termination upon Default. Either party may terminate this Agreement immediately upon the occurrence of an event of default by the other party. The following shall constitute events of default under this Agreement:

i) Breach by either party of its obligations under this Agreement, which such breach shall not be remedied within thirty (30) days after receipt by the breaching party of written notice thereof from the other party; provided however, if such breach is as a result of software errors or malfunctions, the cure period shall be sixty (60) days from receipt of written notice and SEAVISION shall provide RCCL with a written plan and timetable to remedy such software problem within fifteen (15) days of receipt of written notice of such breach; or

ii) The making by either party of any statement, representation or warranty in this Agreement or in any document furnished or to be furnished to the other party in connection herewith which shall prove to be knowingly or recklessly untrue or incorrect in any material respect, when made; or

iii) Either party (A) applying for or consenting to the appointment of a receiver, trustee or liquidator of all or a substantial part of its assets; (B) being unable or failing to pay or admitting in writing its inability or failure to pay its debts as they mature; (C) making a general assignment for the benefits of creditors; (D) being adjudicated a bankrupt or insolvent or being dissolved; (E) filing a petition in

---

may freely transfer or assign its rights or obligations under this Agreement without the prior written consent of the Concessionaire. Subject to the foregoing, this Agreement will be binding upon and inure to the benefit of the parties hereto, their successors and assigns.

bankruptcy or for reorganization or for an arrangement pursuant to a bankruptcy act or any insolvency law; or (F) filing an answer admitting the material allegation of, or consenting to, or defaulting in answering a petition filed against it, in any bankruptcy, reorganization or insolvency proceeding.

(b) Rights and Remedies. Termination of this Agreement upon an event of default shall be without prejudice to any other rights and remedies available to the terminating party.

Notice how the termination provisions rely heavily upon references to other sections, requiring careful attention to how the various portions of the agreement will work together.

Covenants, Efforts Requirements, and Conditions

This guide introduces you to two important provisions of an agreement: covenants and conditions. Covenants are promises to do particular things, while conditions are requirements that must be satisfied for the deal to close—if there is a lapse between signing and closing—or for the contractual relationship to continue throughout the term.

I. Covenants: "But I promise you one thing. A lot of good will come out of this. You have never seen any player in the entire country play as hard as I will play the rest of the season, and you'll never see someone push the rest of the team as hard as I will push everybody the rest of the season. And you'll never see a team play harder than we will the rest of this season."[30]

Covenants are promises by a party to do something related to the deal. Covenants might either exist between the signing and closing of an agreement, or could extend beyond the effective date of an agreement. For example, if government approval is necessary for signage adjacent to a highway, the sports franchise might covenant to get the government approval. Or, in a Naming Rights Agreement, a team might covenant to get its players to appear at an event for the sponsor company or the party responsible for pursuing infringers will covenant to pursue third parties who infringe on trademarks or service marks.

---

30 Tim Tebow, Florida quarterback, after the Gator's loss to Ole Miss. Glenn Guilbeau, " 'Tear-bow' tugged at the heart, then sparked run to SEC title game," *THENEWSTAR.com*, Dec. 6, 2008.

Typical covenants in naming rights agreements are promises to:

- Obtain third party consents,
- Obtain approvals from government entities,
- Elicit publicity, erect and maintain signage,
- Cause others to use the venue's new name
- Pursue infringers, and
- Use the new logo.

To obligate a party to perform, use the word "shall." Instead of stating what your client has a right to, e.g. to have five players appear at the company picnic, state what the other party shall do, e.g. use best efforts to have five players appear at the company picnic. The latter is clearer. Use either "shall not" or a negative subject followed by "may" (e.g. "neither party may") to obligate a party not to do something. To the fullest extent possible, try to use the active voice. This will help clearly identify the party obligated by the covenant, and avoid language that illogically binds third parties/nonparties to do something.

Unlike other deal documents, which have a separate covenants section, in the Naming Rights Agreement the covenants are woven into other provisions. As a lawyer, it is important to scan the agreement and ensure you are aware of all your client's obligations before and beyond closing. For instance, in the article granting the naming rights, the parties may include language that states:

> "the Team shall use commercially reasonable efforts during the Term to (i) cause any and all announcements relating to the Arena or an Arena Event to refer to the Arena as "Company Center;" (ii) identify the Arena as "Company Center" in all official documents, press releases, and Naming Rights Inventory; (iii) cause others (including, without limitation, news media, sports teams, service providers, advertisers promoters and sponsors) to identify the Arena as "Company Center" (provided that any failure of such parties to refer to the Arena as the Company Center shall not be considered a breach of this Agreement); and (iv) use the Arena Graphic Logo and Arena Mark consistent with the provisions of this Agreement. Team shall use commercially reasonable efforts to include in all contracts (including leases and use agreements) involving the use of the Arena for any Arena Event open to the public or for the provision of services in connection with an Arena Event open to the public, which is entered into after the Naming Rights Effective Date, a requirement to refer to and identify

the Arena as "Company Client" in all promotional, advertising and other material disseminated to the public by or on their behalf."

A. *Efforts Requirements: "Just Do It."*

Not all covenants are "flat" or unqualified, but rather covenants typically state the level of efforts that must be used, such as "reasonable efforts," "best efforts," "commercially reasonable efforts," or some other term. The level of efforts actually required can become even more complicated if the parties include a term like "reasonable best." As an alternative to using "efforts" qualifiers, the parties could also specify precisely the steps that should be taken, e.g. go to the necessary state office and file an application for the requisite approval. The parties may also include requirements for how soon a covenant must be completed, such as "immediately," "promptly," "within a reasonable period," or "within X days/business days." "Immediately" means "as soon as can be done." "Promptly" is a less onerous obligation." And, "within a reasonable time" is more vague has been subject to much litigation.

What the various "efforts" qualifiers mean, however, is more complicated.[31] Here is an excerpt from an article on efforts:

> "Even though these differing standards are used frequently by contracting parties in almost all types of commercial agreements, they are not well-tested in the courts. Indeed while some general principles can be gleaned as to how a "best efforts" standard might be interpreted by a court, there is by no means any settled law as to precisely what these two words really mean. Moreover, we are not aware of any case that interprets "commercially reasonable efforts," or even "reasonable best efforts" as distinct, less stringent standards than "best efforts." The few cases that have analyzed a contracting party's behavior in light of a "reasonable best efforts" clause often simply ignore the word "reasonable" and interpret the provision as a "best efforts" standard, rather than some lesser performance standard. And while common sense would suggest that a single contract, where one section requires "commercially reasonable efforts," another requires "reasonable best efforts" and a third requires "best efforts" would be construed as imposing differing, and progressively more

---

31 The information in this paragraph has been adapted from Paul S. Bird, "Private Equity M&A: Current Topics," 1339 PLI Corp.11 (Oct.–Dec. 2002). The law of this varies a great deal from state to state, and it would be wise for the parties to check the law in a particular state and to choose their governing law appropriately before using various efforts qualifiers.

onerous, performance standards, there is no clear guidance as to how a court would interpret such a contract. . .

Courts have generally interpreted "best efforts" and similar clauses as creating an obligation to act reasonably and in good faith under the applicable circumstances. As a result, the clause has generally been held to have different meanings in different commercial contexts. For example, an agreement of a licensee to use its best efforts to sell a licensor's products will be measured differently from a covenant by an LBO fund to use its "best efforts" to raise financing to consummate an acquisition. As one New York case put it, the clause "necessarily takes it's meaning from the circumstances." Perma Research & Development v. Singer Co. (308 F.Supp. 743, 748 (S.D.N.Y. 1970)) Courts frequently look outside the four corners of a contract to find appropriate standards to interpret a "best efforts" clause in a particular context. These outside sources can include testimony from industry experts, and possibly even testimony about the promising party's behavior in similar transactions in the past.

Most of the case law interpreting best efforts provisions has arisen in the context of a licensee or distributor being accused of not using its "best efforts" to make sales of the licensor's, or principal's, products. Few cases involve transactions similar to the ones private equity funds enter into on a regular basis. Nevertheless, there are a few cases that are instructive for private equity and other M&A professionals.

The leading case is *Bloor v. Falstaff Brewing Corp.* (601 F.2d 609 (2d Cir.1979)). The context of Bloor will be relatively familiar to private equity professionals. It involved a dispute over an earn-out. Falstaff Brewing Corp. had purchased Ballantine Ale from Bloor, and had agreed to pay Bloor a percentage of the profits on sales of Ballantine for a certain period of time following the closing. Falstaff agreed in the acquisition agreement to use its "best efforts" to maintain a high sales volume for Ballantine during the period, so as to maximize the value of the earn-out to Bloor. When the sales volume of Ballantine began to slip following the closing, Falstaff did little to stop the slide. Instead, it focused on its other, more profitable business lines, and Bloor sued, alleging that Falstaff was not using its "best efforts" to maintain a high sales volume of Ballantine, as promised in the agreement. The Second

Circuit agreed that Falstaff's neglect was a violation of the "best efforts" clause. It stated that while a duty of best efforts "does not strip the promising party of a right to give reasonable consideration to its own interests," it did impose an obligation to act with good faith in light of one's own capabilities or, at least to "perform as well as the average prudent comparable performer."

In *In Re Valuevision International, Inc. Securities Litigation* (896 F.Supp. 434 (E.D.Pa. 1995)), Valuevision had entered into a merger agreement with National Media Corporation pursuant to which it would acquire National Media in a tender offer followed by a back-end merger. The acquisition was contingent on Valuevision obtaining requisite financing. Not surprisingly, the agreement also contained a covenant, whereby Valuevision agreed to use its "reasonable best efforts" to obtain the necessary financing. In the tender offer documents, along with press releases, the reasonable best efforts covenant was emphasized as one of several reasons that shareholders of National Media should tender their shares. When Valuevision eventually terminated the merger agreement because it found the debt markets too expensive, tendering shareholders and other purchasers of National Media stock sued Valuevision, alleging that they had been materially misled about Valuevision's commitment to consummate the transaction. The Pennsylvania district court refused to dismiss the complaint, finding that a "reasonable investor" could conclude that the covenant to use reasonable best efforts to obtain financing suggested a "strong willingness to conclude financing arrangements without imposing any limitation on the type of financing [Valuevision] would accept."

Two points about this case are worth emphasizing. The first is that the court did not appear to give any weight to the use of the word "reasonable" before "best efforts" in the covenants, and examined the case as if "best efforts" had been the standard.

Second, while the case does provide some rare insight into how a court might interpret covenants to obtain financing, this was not a contract law case. The court's obvious desire to protect the public stockholders of National Media does not necessarily bear on how that—or any other—court would have ruled in a lawsuit between the two sophisticated contracting parties. One can easily imagine the stockholders' lawyer arguing that while the parties to the merger agreement may have understood that Valuevision was not going to accept any and all terms for its acquisition financing, public stockholders not represented by counsel would not necessarily draw the same inference from a "reasonable best efforts" clause. Nevertheless, the case is at least an important reminder as to the necessity of adequate public disclosure and possibly also an important potential precedent in judicial interpretations of covenants to obtain financing in a transaction involving public stockholders.

The 1998 New York Supreme Court case, *Showtime Networks, Inc. v. Comsat Video Enterprises, Inc.* (reported in the August 10, 1998 New York Law Journal), on the other hand, plainly demonstrates the potentially open ended nature of a "best efforts" undertaking, at least in certain circumstances. In *Showtime*, the court was called upon to interpret Comsat's obligations to use "best efforts" and "reasonable business efforts" to promote Showtime's programming in various ways ("best efforts" was to be used in signing up new customers). Comsat had allegedly failed to do so, arguing that it had no obligation to take actions that would cause it to sustain disproportionately large losses.

The court was not sympathetic, refusing to grant Comsat summary judgment on the breach of contract claim. It held that whether "best efforts" or "reasonable business efforts" had been used was a question of fact to be determined by a jury, and that Comsat's argument that it could not be obligated to incur substantial losses was not convincing. It wrote: "difficulty of performance occasioned [*56] only by financial difficulties, even to the extent of insolvency, does not excuse performance of the contract," and "the cost of providing the Showtime programming and its unprofitability does not excuse [Comsat's] performance of this provision." While this case falls outside of the vast majority of cases interpreting "best efforts" and similar clauses, it nonetheless demonstrates the potential risks posed by agreeing to these clauses, and has accordingly made lawyers very reluctant to agree to them in practice. . .

One should not conclude with confidence that a "best efforts" clause will be interpreted as akin to a guarantee, or a near guarantee, of performance. Accordingly, if you want to require your counterparty to produce a particular commercial result, you should impose a flat obligation to do so, rather than agreeing to a performance obligation qualified by "best efforts" or some similar standard.

Don't assume it won't be deemed a Guarantee of Performance. On the other hand, in light of the Showtime case described above, one also should not assume that a "best efforts" clause will not be interpreted as similar to a guarantee, or a near guarantee, of performance, at least in some circumstances. Accordingly, while it may sometimes be beneficial to be the recipient of a "best efforts" undertaking, particularly in circumstances where the other party refuses to agree to a flat obligation and where it is otherwise impractical to spell out the nature of the other party's performance obligation with more precision, it is ill-advised to provide one unless you are prepared to be held to a very high level of performance. This is particularly true in the private equity arena given the dearth of case law interpreting "best efforts" or similar clauses in the context of obtaining financing, avoiding UBTI and other commercial contexts where these clauses are frequently used by private equity sponsors.

Use the lower standards—but be careful. Given the uncertainty associated with "best efforts" clauses, it is often tempting to utilize some seemingly lesser variation thereof, like "reasonable best efforts," or "commercially reasonable efforts," as a compromise formulation. But while these alternative standards would appear to create less stringent performance obligations than a "best efforts" undertaking, the absence of helpful case law interpreting distinctions among these differing standards makes it difficult to be certain that these distinctions would be recognized by a court. . . Still, in many circumstances, these alternative lesser formulations will probably be the most practical means for parties to reach agreement on the scope of these types of performance obligations.

Define what you mean—where appropriate. The best way to create more certainty as to how a "best efforts" or similar clause would be interpreted by a court is for the parties themselves to specify what they mean, to the greatest extent practicable. For example, it may make sense in some deals to provide that an established private equity sponsor's obligation to use its "reasonable best efforts" to obtain financing for a transaction will be deemed satisfied if the sponsor exercises a level of effort comparable to effort it has

> exercised in obtaining financing for a transaction will be deemed satisfied if the sponsor exercises a level of effort comparable to effort it has exercised in obtaining financing in similar transactions in the past. Similarly, it may be desirable to make clear that a sponsor's obligation to use its "best efforts" to avoid causing its limited partners to recognize UBTI will be deemed satisfied if the sponsor exercises the same level of effort in this regard as is customarily exercised by similarly situated sponsors. Another approach along these lines is to specifically include or exclude certain actions from a particular performance undertaking, such as specifying that a buyer's obligation to use "reasonable commercial efforts" to obtain third-party consents in connection with a closing will not require it to pay any consent fees (perhaps above a certain nominal level). Whether these kinds of refinements are appropriate for individual transactions will of course depend on the circumstances of each deal, including the relative negotiating leverage and sophistication of the parties and other tactical considerations. But any decision to forego them should be made with a recognition of the inherent imprecision associated with the mere use of a "best efforts" or similar standard to establish the scope of a performance obligation.

Overall it is important to use your creativity to draft language that is precise and to bear in mind the general practices and understandings in the industry for which you are drafting the agreement.

II. Conditions: "Winning isn't everything, but wanting to win is."[32]

Conditions describe the circumstances under which the parties do not need to proceed with the deal if the conditions are unsatisfied or provide remedies for their breach. Unlike covenants they do not require the parties to *do* anything; rather, the conditions merely specify what the "state of the world" must be for the deal to be in good standing. Furthermore, there is no requirement that the conditions agreed to by the parties be reasonable or qualified by materiality, though courts tend to interpret ambiguous contractual language as requiring only substantial compliance or satisfaction.[33] Courts disfavor conditions because they result in the forfeiture of a right.

---

[32] Vince Lombardi.

[33] See *e.g., Jungmann & Co. v. Atterbury Bros. Inc.*, 249 N.Y. 119 (1928).

If your client must satisfy the condition, draft it so that the client can satisfy it easily. If the other party must satisfy the condition, consider how difficult it should be in the context of the transaction. To signal a condition, use words such as "if/then," "must," "when," "subject to," "provided that if," "conditioned upon," and "upon." When drafting, use "must" with another verb in one of three ways: (1.) must + be, to indicate a fact that must exist on the closing date; (2.) must + have + the past tense of a verb, to indicate something that someone must have cause to happen to happen after the signing date but no later than the closing date; (3.) must have need + the past tense of a verb, to indicate that the issue is an action, not the actor; this is the passive version of use. Finally, state the consequences for the failure to satisfy a condition.

Like covenants, conditions are likely to be woven through the Naming Rights Agreement, as opposed to occupying their own section. A condition of the agreement might be that no material adverse effect has occurred to the business, that no force majeure event has occurred, that the fees have been paid on time, or that the parties maintain the confidentiality of the deal terms.

With respect to a future name change, the parties might agree—as the Jacksonville Jaguars and Alltel did in their naming rights agreements—as follows:

> 6. **Future Name Change**.
>
> (a) Naming Sponsor agrees that it shall have no right to change the Stadium Name except as provided herein. During the term of this Agreement, Naming Sponsor shall have the right to cause the name of the Stadium to be changed once in compliance with all terms of this Section 6. In order to change the name of the Stadium, Naming Sponsor shall notify Team and City that it desires to change the name of the Stadium and disclose the new name. Team and City shall approve the new name if the following conditions are satisfied:
>
> (i) The new name may only be the brand name under which Naming Sponsor, or its successor in interest, actively markets the Designated Products, or a significant portion thereof, then being marketed by Naming Sponsor or its successor in interest.
>
> (ii) The new name does not violate any NFL rule or policy then in effect and is not a name that

could not be a sponsor of Team under NFL rules then in effect.

(iii) Unless Team specifically consents, the new name cannot violate any documented material advertising or sponsorship policy of Team then in effect. For example, Team has a policy in effect that it will not accept tobacco advertising.

(iv) The new name cannot be obscene or of a nature which would seriously offend the reasonable sensibilities of the public at large, or which would seriously disparage or place in serious disrepute the City or Team.

(v) The new name cannot be such as to confer the impression of an association or affiliation with a metropolitan area in the United States having a population of more than 100,000 (other than Jacksonville).

(vi) Unless Team specifically consents, the new name may not include the name or trade-name of a major competitor to the then-current Team sponsors in the categories of banking, automobiles, beer, soda, health and hospital services or local television.

(b) If all of the conditions of Section 6(a) above are satisfied, Team and City agree that they will consent to the change of the name of the Stadium. Team and City agree to evidence their consent in writing, within forty five (45) days of the satisfaction of the above conditions. City agrees to promptly submit all necessary requests for the approval of all governmental agencies whose approval is necessary at such time.

Note that if the conditions regarding the new name are not satisfied, the Team cannot change the name to the new name.

Presenting Sponsorship Agreements: What to Include in the Sponsorship Package

In many ways, Presenting Sponsorship Agreements are similar to Naming Rights Agreements; in both cases, a company is buying an advertising package associated with a venue. Now that you have drafted a Naming Rights Agreement for a particular stadium, it is important to draft the Presenting Sponsorship Agreement for that same stadium in a way that does not conflict with the benefits granted under the Naming Rights Agreement, but still exploits the opportunities to generate revenue to the fullest extent possible.

In exchange for a fee, the "presenting sponsor" gets recognition as just that—the presenting sponsor of events/games that the team holds. The Milwaukee Brewers recently named the Potawatimo Bingo Casino as its presenting sponsor, giving the Casino signage throughout the ballpark, local advertising and marketing rights on radio and print material, sponsorship on regular season game tickets and additional collateral materials. The partnership will be called "Milwaukee Brewers Baseball presented by Potawatomi Bingo Casino." Hierarchically, the presenting sponsor is less prominent than the naming rights sponsors—whose name is presumably mentioned any time the stadium is mentioned, e.g. for the Brewers, Miller Park—but more prominent than other, "second-tier" sponsors.

The presenting sponsor's benefit package varies from deal to deal. The presenting sponsor will be interested in garnering the exclusive right to promote its product or serve it at an event, and may also seek recognition as the "official" supplier of a particular product or service to a team. For instance, pursuant to the terms of a five-year sponsorship deal, Office Max earned the right to be called the official supplier of office products/supplies to the Cleveland Browns. W.B. Mason is the official office supplier of the Boston Red Sox, and the St. Petersburg Times is the official newspaper of the Tampa Bay Rays. The sponsor may also seek to sell the official product at the stadium. In Coca-Cola's sponsorship deal with the Tampa Bay Buccaneers, the soft-drink provider secured the right to have its logo occupy 90 percent of the surface of each cup, relegating the team logo to 10 percent or less of each cup.

Presenting sponsors will, of course, also seek signage in the stadium. The placement of this signage is limited only by the creativity of the parties, and their aesthetic concerns. Issues such as the number of signs, the placement of signs, and distance from other sponsor signs might be addressed in the contract. Sponsorship agreements may include rights to signage in areas such as rotating signs on the stadium structure, gate signage, "adsleeves" on turnstile arms, or "stall tactics" in restroom stalls. The most lucrative signage is in places where the broadcast camera hits, followed by the area near the scoreboard. Teams can also sell "virtual advertising" visible only to television or Internet viewers.

Moreover, presenting sponsors need not limit their exposure to signage, but can also seek other forms of advertising and promotion. For example, the presenting sponsor can seek the following benefits:

- mention in print advertising, team newsletter, or on the team's website;
- the right to have events designated as presented by the sponsor;
- use of the sponsor's name/trademark on promotional materials, such as stationary and brochures;
- the right to be named in press releases;
- the right to have its name in programs, press guides, yearbooks and similar materials;
- the right to have its name appear on tickets, booklets, and pocket schedules;
- the right to have its name/logo on team uniforms or other clothing;
- the right to offer promotional events, such as fan contests and giveaways;
- use of the product in prize packages;
- a license to use the stadium logo in advertising; and
- the right to exposure at practice facilities.

Another creative benefit the presenting sponsor can earn is a mention when it donates an amount of money for every touchdown scored or homerun hit. Presenting sponsors might also seek a stake in the team itself, as American West did with the Arizona Diamondbacks.

As part of its presenting sponsorship package, the presenting sponsor may seek perks for company members. Presenting sponsors could push for a luxury suite in a prime location, tickets to regular and post-season games, parking passes, a special "VIP day," player appearances, and special corporate events at the park.

Aside from the presenting sponsor's benefits, the Presenting Sponsorship Agreement will describe the following:

(1.) *Events of Termination*: What happens if there is a breach of the agreement? What if a party files for bankruptcy or is accused of legal or moral wrongdoing? What if there is a strike/lockout, as in *Nashville Hockey League*?

(2.) *Right of First Negotiation*: If the presenting sponsor has one, it will likely commence shortly before the end of the term, and will be preceded by a quiet period.

(3.) *Right of First Refusal*: What the "triggering event" is, such as a third party offer in writing, whether the current presenting sponsor has the right to match, and whether there is an exception not to have to match terms that cannot be matched in a commercially reasonable way.

(4.) *Post Expiration/Post Termination Rights*: How long the sell off period for signature/licensed products is, whether it applies to products on hand or already ordered from the factory, whether there is a right (or obligation) to exhaust promotional materials, and the applicable time limit.

(5.) *Other*: Such as representations and warranties, confidentiality, and assignability (consider the NASCAR-Nextel dispute).

Assignment and Anti-Assignment

You have already studied and drafted covenants. But what do these covenants create? They create, in the party who is the promisee of the covenant, a right. An assignment transfers those rights to a third party. Consider a simple example. If a sponsor covenants to pay a team for the sponsorship rights and benefits, the team can assign the receipt of those payments to someone else. In this example, the team is the "assignor," the new recipient of the payments is the "assignee," and the sponsor is the "non-assigning party." Once the team assigns its rights, it no longer has a right to payment. Rather, the third party has that right, and the sponsor has a duty to perform in the third party's favor.

By contrast, under the simple arrangement described above, the third party has no duty to perform in favor of the sponsor, as the team did not delegate its performance contemporaneously with the assignment. A party delegates its performance when it appoints someone else to perform in its place. The party who delegates its performance is the "delegating party," the party to whom it delegated its performance is the "delegate," and the other party is the "non-delegating party." Upon delegation, the performance refers not only to duties, but also to conditions. Recall from your contracts course that not all duties are delegable, such as those that are personal in nature or require unique skills.

Anti-assignment provisions prohibit a party from assigning its rights under a contract. Parties insert these provisions to prevent assignments that would materially change the non-assigning party's duties or materially increase its risks. In addition, parties pair them with anti-delegation provisions. Drafting an enforceable anti-assignment provision is not easy. The UCC renders ineffective any anti-assignment provisions subject to the UCC. If the UCC is inapplicable, a court might still invalidate the provision in the tradition of judicial hostility towards anti-assignment provisions because of the view that they restrain commerce. When drafting an anti-assignment provision, you should state specifically that the prohibition applies to "an assignment of rights under the agreement." If the prohibition only extends to "the assignment of the agreement," a court is likely to interpret the provision as an anti-delegation provision—which are generally enforceable and can be drafted in a straightforward manner—instead.[34] To create an anti-assignment provision that renders an assignment void, you must take away not only the right to assign, but also the power to assign. To do this, the contract must prohibit the assignment of rights under the contract and declare that any purported assignment is void.

Below are some sample clauses:

> Neither party shall assign or otherwise transfer any of its rights, interests or obligations under this Agreement (Contract) to a third party [without the prior written consent of the other party] [which shall not be unreasonably withheld].
>
> Licensee may assign the Agreement to an entity that acquires all or substantially all of Licensee's assets. In the event Licensee wishes to make an assignment to one of these competitors, Licensee will request such assignment in writing to Licensor and the parties will negotiate whether such assignment is appropriate.
>
> Neither this Agreement nor any rights or obligations hereunder may be assigned or transferred by either party to any other person or entity, voluntarily or by operation of law, without the advance written consent of the other party; provided, however, that Sponsor may assign this Agreement to an affiliate. If Sponsor makes such an assignment, it shall remain liable for all payment obligations to Team hereunder.
>
> Assignment. This Agreement shall be binding upon and inure to the benefit of each party's respective successors and lawful assigns; provided, however, that Sponsor may not assign (by operation of law or otherwise) this Agreement, in whole or in part, without the prior written approval of Team. For purposes of the foregoing, an assignment shall be deemed to include, without limitation, a merger of

---

[34] Restatement (Second) of Contracts, § 322(1).

> Sponsor with another party, whether or not Sponsor is the surviving entity, or the acquisition of direct or indirect control of management through one or a series of transactions. Any attempted assignment by Sponsor in violation of this Section shall be void and shall entitle Team to terminate this Agreement immediately upon written notice to Sponsor.

Note the options for approval in the various assignment clauses, and the amount of discretion you can provide for that approval. Further note the deemed assignment in the event of a merger in the clause above.

Finally, what does the phrase "successors and lawful assigns" mean? The language is actually quite controversial and its effect is unclear. The general understanding is that this language eliminates the need of an express assumption in the event of assignment, binding the assignment perform as it is also a delegate, and restates the common law that a non-assigning party must give the benefit of its performance to the assignee. Some courts have held, however, that assignment does not bind an assignee merely because of the presence of a "successor and assigns" provision. Other cases have held that the provision demonstrates that the parties intended that the contract rights be assignable and performance obligations be delegable. Check the law in the state whose law governs the contract if you choose to include this language.

Media and Broadcasting Rights Agreements: The Nexus of Intellectual Property, Antitrust, and Administrative Law

Though the negotiating and drafting skills you have been honing throughout the semester are carrying forward from week-to-week, the substantive law working amidst these skills are changing. This week's broadcasting agreement is more deeply intertwined with copyright law, as opposed to the trademark law explored last week. Antitrust law would apply to the actions of leagues seeking to exploit the media rights from all the games, but for the immunity granted through the federal Sports Broadcasting Act of 1961. The Federal Communications Commission (FCC) has jurisdiction to regulate part of the broadcasting universe, and federal and state laws heavily regulate the cable operators on which the games are televised.

I. Copyright Protection of Broadcasts

Copyright law, codified in title 17 of the U.S. Code, protects "original works of authorship" that are fixed in a tangible form of expression. The following categories of works are copyrightable:

1. literary works
2. musical works, including any accompanying words
3. dramatic works, including any accompanying music
4. pantomimes and choreographic works
5. pictorial, graphic, and sculptural works
6. motion pictures and other audiovisual works
7. sound recordings
8. architectural works

A copyrightable work, such as the televised or radio broadcast of a sports game, is protected immediately upon creation. The right vests in the author or creator of the work, or in the employer if the work is a "work for hire." For instance, while the person recording a radio broadcast or the broadcaster is the "author" or "joint author" of the sound recording, this work is created for the employer. NFL broadcasts are accompanied by the warning, "This telecast is copyrighted by the NFL for the private use of our audience. Any other use of this telecast or any pictures, descriptions, or accounts of the game without the NFL's consent is prohibited."

Copyright holders have the right to do the following:

- To reproduce the work in copies or phonorecords;
- To prepare derivative works based upon the work;
- To distribute copies or phonorecords of the work to the public by sale or other transfer of ownership, or by rental, lease, or lending;
- To perform the work publicly, in the case of literary, musical, dramatic, and choreographic works, pantomimes, and motion pictures and other audiovisual works;
- To display the work publicly, in the case of literary, musical, dramatic, and choreographic works, pantomimes, and pictorial, graphic, or sculptural works, including the individual images of a motion picture or other audiovisual work; and
- In the case of sound recordings, to perform the work publicly by means of a digital audio transmission.

Therefore, who ultimately owns a copyrighted work can dictate how that work is used in the future, and importantly, appropriate the revenue earned from future uses. The owner can assign or license his or her rights, and can take on or delegate the pursuit of infringers.

MLB, who owns the copyright to all its game broadcasts, considered suing the makers of the Sling Box, which has the ability to record content and allow the viewer to shift the time and place of viewing. The NFL raised similar complaints about TiVo, and notoriously threatened a church with litigation over a Super Bowl Party at which the church was showing the game, allegedly an infringing "public performance."

II. The Sports Broadcasting Act

Just how did MLB and the NFL come to own, and have the right to ink lucrative broadcasting deals, all their games? The answer lies in the 1961 Sports Broadcasting Act, codified at 15 U.S.C. 1291. The statute, enacted in reaction to the Supreme Court's decision holding that the NFL's pooling agreement to broadcast games with CBS violated antitrust laws, reads:

> The antitrust laws, as defined in section 1 of the Act of October 15, 1914, as amended (38 Stat. 730) [15 U.S.C. 12], or in the Federal Trade Commission Act, as amended (38 Stat. 717) [15 U.S.C. 41 et seq.], shall not apply to any joint agreement by or among persons engaging in or conducting the organized professional team sports of football, baseball, basketball, or hockey, by which any league or clubs participating in professional football, baseball, basketball, or hockey contests sells or otherwise transfers all or any part of the rights of such league's member clubs in the sponsored telecasting of the games of football, baseball, basketball, or hockey, as the case may be, engaged in or conducted by such clubs. In addition, such laws shall not apply to a joint agreement by which the member clubs of two or more professional football leagues, which are exempt from income tax under section 501(c)(6) of the Internal Revenue Code of 1986 [26 U.S.C. 501(c)(6)], combine their operations in expanded single league so exempt from income tax, if such agreement increases rather than decreases the number of professional football clubs so operating, and the provisions of which are directly relevant thereto.

Interest in the Act was revived after the NFL announced the creation of the NFL Network, which is shown in many fewer homes than the channels on which games were previously broadcast. Senator Arlen Specter raised complaints that the NFL's antitrust exemption ought to be revoked. In 2011, the NFL announced nine-year extensions to the broadcast television deals with CBS, NBC, FOX, and Disney worth $27 billion, which are set to expire following the 2022 season. Additionally, DirecTV pays $1 billion annually for the right to carry

NFL Sunday Ticket.[35] Finally, CBS pays over $300 million annually for the rights to eight Thursday night games, with the NFL-owned property NFL Network broadcasting an additional eight games on Thursday and Saturday nights.

FOX Sports and Turner Broadcasting System (TBS) paid for the rights to Major League Baseball broadcasts through 2021 and worth a combined $12.4 billion. Under the deal, TBS retain the rights to air one LCS, two Division Series, one Wild Card game and afternoon games on the final 13 Sundays of the regular season, and Fox retains the rights to the World Series, the All-Star Game, one LCS, two Division Series, one Wild Card game and double the previous amount of regular season national window games.[36]

NBA games are played on a variety of networks. For the 2008–2009 season, ABC has the right to air 30 regular season games, TNT paid for the 52 games, including the season opener, ESPN and ESPN2 have the right to multiple games, and NBA TV can broadcast 96 games. According to an article on the TNT and ABC deals, signed in 2007, "The NBA's new television contracts with ESPN/ABC and TNT include rights to technologies that have yet to invented, an indication of the importance the deals place on newer forms of media."[37] ESPN/ABC and TNT will each be able to simulcast and offer video on-demand for games that air on its networks. These deals extend through the 2015–2016 season. In return for the broadcast rights, the NBA will receive about $930 million a year, an increase of more than 20 percent from the previous average of $767 million.

III. The FCC

Depending on who is broadcasting the games, the broadcasts may come under the purview of the FCC. While states have jurisdiction over intrastate communications, the FCC, created by the Communications Act of 1934, has jurisdiction over interstate and international communications, i.e. television, radio, wire, satellite, and cable in all of the 50 State and U.S. territories.[38] The "Media Bureau" of the FCC regulates AM, FM radio and television broadcast stations, as well as cable televisions and satellite services. With the advent of Internet communications, the FCC adopted an internal policy in 2005. Of the five commissioners who serve on the FCC, one is designated as the Chairman after presidential nomination for the role. As an agency, the FCC has the power to create federal

---

35 Starting with the 2016 season, DirecTV will begin paying $1.5 billion annually under the eight-year extension.

36 *See* Newman, Mark. "MLB Reaches Eight-Year TV Agreement with Fox, Turner," *MLB PRESS RELEASE,* Oct. 2, 2012, http://m.mlb.com/news/article/39362362/.

37 http://www.usatoday.com/sports/basketball/2007-06-27-3096131424_x.htm.

38 www.fcc.gov/aboutus.

regulations. The Commission is responsible to Congress, and must hold a monthly meeting that is open to the public. Procedural requirements for the agency are outlined in the Administrative Procedure Act, and govern the steps of the FCC rulemaking process: notice, comment, reply comments, decision with explanation, and appeals. The decisions and rules must be justified to withstand judicial review.

Any viewer of sports games is familiar with the blue screen that appears from time to time when turning on a game, a result of the "Sports Blackout Rule." Historically, according to the FCC, the "Sports Blackout Rule protected the holder of the exclusive distribution rights to a local sports event (i.e. a sports team). The sports blackout rule was only applied if a local TV broadcast station was not carrying the local sporting event. Therefore, if a local TV broadcast station did not have permission to carry the local game, then no other broadcaster's signal displaying the game could be shown in the protected local blackout zone." In September 2014, the FCC repealed its sport blackout rules.

Representations and Warranties

Like covenants and conditions, representations and warranties are important building blocks of agreements. As can be seen from *Sportschannel Assoc. v. Sterling Mets, L.P.*, these terms can play an important role in litigation regarding media rights.[39]

Representations—or a statement about a past or current fact—and warranties—promises about future facts—help paint a picture of the parties and the status of the various components of the deal. In the NFL's "Interactive Media Rights Agreement" with America Online, CBS Broadcasting, and Sportsline.com, Sportsline.com represented and warranted that:

> "SportsLine owns or has the legal and valid right to use and to license to the other Parties as contemplated herein all Content (other than the NFL Content), including without limitation the SportsLine Materials and the Coding, used on or in connection with the NFL Sites;

[39] Representations and warranties also played an important role in *C.B.C. Distribution and Marketing, Inc. v. Major League Baseball Advanced Media*, 505 F.3d 818 (8th Cir.2007). In *C.B.C.*, the court found the provision in which the Player's Association stated it "is the sole and exclusive holder of all right, title and interest" in and to the names and playing statistics of virtually all Major League Baseball players to be a warranty that the MLBPA had violated. The court found the Players Association's express warranty of title in and to the players' information a material breach of contract. Consequently, CBC was relieved of its obligations under the agreement and the Players Association could no longer enforce the no-use and no-challenge provisions of the 2002 license agreement.

> SportsLine is and shall be in compliance with any and all applicable laws with respect to its performance or obligations under this Agreement, including without limitation, laws and regulations applicable to contests and sweepstakes;
>
> All Content on the NFL Sites and all Promotional Content (excluding AOL Frames, other AOL Intellectual Property and the NFL Content) does not and shall not infringe on or violate any copyright, trademark, U.S. patent, rights of publicity or privacy, or any other third party intellectual property right, including any musical performance or other music-related right; and
>
> All Content contained within the Customized Site (other than AOL Frames or other AOL Intellectual Property and the NFL Content) and all Promo Content, Promotional Materials and all Licensed Content does not and will not violate the terms of this Agreement, including without limitation, the AOL Carriage Terms or AOL Terms of Service."

In the same deal, the NFL, acting through NFL Enterprises, Inc., represented and warranted that:

> "NFLE is and shall be in compliance with any and all applicable laws with respect to its performance or obligations under this Agreement;
>
> NFLE owns or has the legal and valid right to use and to license to the other Parties as contemplated herein NFL Content licensed hereby . . . and the NFL Content does not and shall not infringe on or violate any copyright, trademark, U.S. patent, rights of publicity or privacy, or other third party intellectual property rights including without limitation any music performance or other music-related rights; provided that the Parties agree and acknowledge that in respect of audio broadcasts feeds provided to the Interactive Parties for their own use, pursuant to Section 8 hereof, additional fees may be required to be paid to the licensors of such audio broadcast feeds for residuals or other rights;
>
> NFLE has full power and authority to grant the licenses to perform the obligations required of its affiliates, including NFLP and NFL Productions, pursuant to this Agreement;
>
> No NFL Content licensed hereunder contains or refers in any manner to any textual, pictorial, video, audio or other

> matter that is, by reasonably prevailing community standards, lewd, obscene, libelous, offensive, inappropriate or unsuitable, and nothing contained in or referred to in such NFL Content conflicts with or violates any applicable laws or regulations (including those relating to contests, sweepstakes or similar promotions), or otherwise facilitates the commission of any local state or federal crime or any immoral or offensive act."

Note that the representations and warranties can be stated in the positive, "the Company has the authority to enter into this transaction, and in the negative, 'No NFL Content conflicts with or violates any applicable laws.' "

If the representations and warranties are not true at the time made, then the party to whom the representation or warranty was being made has a claim for damages. This claim is typically linked to the indemnity. As a result, the party making the representations and warranties has an interest in limiting the scope of the representations and warranties made and in qualifying them. (We will revisit the representations and warranties in more detail when we discuss the purchase and sale of a sports franchise. The deal documents will have more extensive representations and warranties.)

A representation or warranty can be qualified by either a "knowledge" or a "materiality" qualifier. For example, when licensing IP rights, the licensor might state with respect to the legality of its IP rights, "There is no litigation pending, and, to the best of the licensor's knowledge, threatened against the licensor's copyright/trademark." Before inserting a knowledge qualifier, ask yourself (a.) is it appropriate, and (b.) to whose knowledge? The use (or absence) of knowledge qualifiers allocates risk for its falsity between the parties. Moreover, if a party is insisting upon a qualifier or is otherwise hesitant to make a representation or warranty serves a "due diligence" function of smoking out potential parties that the other party may not have forthrightly explained.

Knowledge itself can be qualified by "actual" or "constructive," and "after reasonable/due inquiry." For instance, with respect to the representation above, the licensor may say that it has no way of actually knowing if a third party is threatening litigation, and therefore it cannot give a "flat" representation. The licensee might reply that the representation is about putting the risk of threatened litigation on the licensor, not about what the licensor can or cannot know.

Materiality limitations depend heavily on the context. The parties might try to specify a dollar level of an item or problem necessary to result in a representation being false, but given the incompleteness of contracts, there are advantages to using the admittedly more nebulous term material. Be cautious when inserting material, as where it is placed in the clause affects the meaning of the term. It is different to say that the "material IP licenses are in good standing," and the "IP licenses are in material compliance with applicable law." Some provisions that are never qualified by materiality are representations as to due organization, capitalization, and authority to do the transaction.

Finally, choice of language, even apart from the addition of qualifiers, is extremely important. If a party represents that "is and has been" in compliance with all laws, it is liable for both the present and the past, whereas saying it "is" in compliance with all laws only holds it liable for its present state. Keep this and the considerations above in mind when drafting these clauses.

Alternative Dispute Resolution

Alternative dispute resolution (ADR) is less noisy and less expensive than litigation to resolve disputes that arise under agreements. As a result, alternative dispute resolution has greatly expanded over the last several years to include many areas in addition to the traditional commercial dispute in the form of arbitration, and mediation has become an important first step in the dispute resolution process. Unlike litigation, these alternative procedures do not automatically create public or binding decisions.

Mediators act as neutrals to reconcile the parties differences before proceeding to arbitration or litigation. Mediators preside over an informal and non-adversarial process to encourage and assist in resolution. Decision-making authority rests with the parties, not the mediator. The mediator assists the parties in identifying issues, fostering joint problem solving, exploring settlement alternatives, and in other ways consistent with these activities.

Arbitrators act as neutral third parties to hear the evidence and decide the case. Arbitration can be binding or non-binding, but the ultimate decision rests with the arbitrator, not the parties. Therefore, it is important to establish a process for selecting the arbitrator and to determine whether there will be one arbitrator or a panel. The parties should pick a person with expertise in the industry. Courts are extremely deferential toward arbitrated decisions, reflecting a judicial preference and respect for ADR.

ADR clauses should address the following points:

- Mediation prior to Arbitration
- Issues Subject to Arbitration
- Agreement to Arbitrate
- Rules and Arbitral Body
- Entry of Judgment
- Language
- Location
- Substantive and Procedural Law
- Number of Arbitrators
- Form of Award
- Interim Relief
- Limitations of Damages
- Confidentiality
- Attorney's fees

The Metropolitan Corporate Counsel has issued the following tips:

> ***Drafting to Avoid Disputes over Arbitrability***
>
> One of the most vexing and wasteful experiences in arbitration is being subjected to ancillary litigation regarding what is or is not arbitrable. Because the question of "arbitrability" is almost always for a court to decide, [2] a party that wishes to delay final adjudication of the merits can initiate litigation regarding the arbitrability of the controversy at hand. Such disputes can add months, even years to the process, before ever reaching the merits. Moreover, these disputes could result in arbitration proceedings over the objection of a party on the issue of arbitrability, only to be followed by a motion to vacate by the losing party, on those very same grounds. This, again, can add years to any final resolution of a dispute and create uncertainty regarding the effect of any award. Accordingly, the best practice is to be as clear as possible about what is or is not arbitrable in the ADR Provision itself.
>
> The simplest way to do this is to draft an arbitration clause as broadly as possible. Courts have held the following language to encompass virtually every conceivable dispute between parties: "Any controversy or claim arising out of or relating to this contract, or the breach thereof, shall be

settled by an arbitration administered by the American Arbitration Association." While there is nothing to prevent an adversary from bringing an action seeking to foreclose arbitration of a particular claim on the grounds that it exceeds the scope of the arbitration clause, such attempts will most likely fail, and, indeed, most practitioners will avoid such frivolous arguments given the clarity of the case law on this issue.

On the other hand, some practitioners have sought to increase certainty regarding what is or is not arbitrable by crafting ADR Provisions with subject matter exclusions, such as "Any controversy or claim arising out of or relating to this contract, or the breach thereof, except for disputes involving [intellectual property or tax obligations or torts, etc.] shall be settled by arbitration." While it may seem that these types of clauses create more certainty as to arbitrability, the opposite is often true. A savvy adversary can litigate not only what is or is not arbitrable, but can do so on the theory that dispute categories such as "intellectual property" or "tax obligations" are susceptible to different meanings and are often completely and inextricably intertwined with claims that are clearly arbitrable (usually an underlying breach of contract). Thus, rather than clarifying the issues, carve-out provisions may create even more confusing issues with the consequence being months or even years of tangential and expensive litigation over arbitrability.

If parties are going to choose arbitration as the dispute resolution mechanism, resolving all categories of disputes arising under the subject contract is usually the best option, and parties should, therefore, employ the broadest possible ADR Provision, and, indeed, the standard clause suggested by the AAA. Courts are familiar with it, there are reams of case law interpreting it, and it is almost certain that what starts out in arbitration will remain there.

Drafting to Limit Disputes over the Type and Scope of Permissible Discovery and Motion Practice

Along with arbitrability disputes, some of the most problematic and costly aspects of arbitration concern disputes over discovery and permissible motion practice. These disputes also often become the subject of wasteful ancillary proceedings, whether in front of an arbitration panel or a court. Unfortunately, the AAA Commercial Arbitration Rules and Mediation Procedures (the "AAA

Rules") are virtually silent regarding discovery, stating merely that at the request of a party, the arbitrator may direct the production of documents or the identification of witnesses to be called. [3]

Accordingly, arbitration can spawn even more discovery disputes than traditional litigation if the scope of discovery is not specifically delineated. For example, simple questions concerning party discovery (e.g., document demands, interrogatories, depositions, and experts) can result in interminable delays as panels listen to arguments concerning the need for or opposition to requested discovery. In litigation, however, the applicable federal or state procedural rules usually provide quick and clear-cut answers.

Even more difficult are questions concerning non-party discovery. [4] While a discussion of non-party discovery in aid of arbitration is beyond the scope of this article, it is important to note that failure of parties to agree in advance on the scope of non-party discovery could result in extremely lengthy detours as parties engage in motions and appeals before courts, and perhaps in multiple jurisdictions. Even in cases where parties agree on the need for non-party discovery, numerous procedural problems can arise since permissibility of pre-hearing non-party discovery remains unsettled. For example, in the *ImClone v. Waksal* arbitration, while the parties themselves had no dispute over the need for non-party discovery, numerous motions and appeals erupted when the non-parties objected. Such a thorny issue would not have been present in traditional litigation, where the scope of permissible non-party discovery is more clearly defined.

It is highly recommended, therefore, that parties explicitly outline the scope of discovery in their ADR Provision. While it may be difficult to predict exactly what discovery may be necessary should a future dispute arise, the parties' choice to arbitrate rather than litigate should indicate that the process needs to be streamlined. To that end, parties need to best estimate the financial and legal implications of any disputes that may arise and use that to inform how much discovery is necessary.

In a potentially complex dispute, for example, it might be advisable to provide for depositions and to specify a reasonable number that will be allowed in the ADR Provision. Since the AAA Rules do not provide the right to depositions, failure to set forth such rights in the ADR Provision creates a risk that such discovery will be prohibited. Moreover, if the potential dispute is likely to require expert testimony—as in the case of a complex intellectual property or securities dispute—then the right to utilize expert witnesses and take discovery of them should be set forth in the ADR Provision.

Indeed, the exchange of documents, the use of interrogatories, and any other discovery devices should be specified. Remember, should there come a time when such discovery becomes unnecessary, the parties can choose to forego it. If the parties fail to provide for wanted discovery mechanisms, however, they risk losing the opportunity to obtain potentially valuable discovery at the whim of the arbitrator.

Additionally, if parties feel that motion practice, specifically dispositive motions, might be appropriate, it is imperative that they cover this in the ADR Provision and specify the type, timing, and procedure thereof (including whether there are rights to reply, etc.). For example, the AAA Commercial Arbitration Rules do not provide for dispositive motion practice. In fact, some practitioners have argued that since the AAA Employment Arbitration Rules do provide for dispositive motions, [5] the absence of such provision in the Commercial Rules evinces the AAA's intent to exclude such procedures from commercial arbitrations.

Drafting Forum, Claim and Remedy Provisions

Most parties and practitioners already include choice of law and venue selection language in their ADR Provisions (and they should be specific about this), but forum selection is sometimes overlooked. As important as it is to be careful in drafting the ADR Provisions as they relate to arbitrability and discovery and motion procedures, forum selection can be equally important and can influence how particular issues and disputes are resolved. Parties should pay particular attention to what, if any, rules and procedures the forum has in place. For instance, the AAA maintains an active administrative function, while the Institute for Conflict Prevention & Resolution ("CPR") leaves administration of the arbitration to the arbitrators themselves. Further differences become apparent when the specific rules enforced by the forum are examined.

This can be of paramount importance when parties attempt to agree on the manner in which disputes may be brought in arbitration. Parties may desire to exclude class treatment or consolidation or joinder of claims. Forum rules (and choice of law) can play a significant role here. Where the AAA has rules governing arbitrations of class claims, the CPR does not.

Further, parties may wish to attempt to exclude punitive damages or statutorily prescribed damages (such as multiplied damages) from the authority conveyed to the arbitrator. Such remedy waivers need to be explicit and should be consistent with the rules of the forum selected.

Conclusion

Parties need to carefully examine their goals in drafting ADR Provisions and need to remember that arbitration was designed to be a more efficient and economic process than litigation. If that remains a goal of the parties, the ADR Provision should be drafted with efficiency in mind and with an eye towards avoiding non-merits-based disputes. On the other hand, the more that parties attempt to make arbitration look like litigation by building in all of the procedural rights and protections afforded by state and federal court rules and procedures, the less efficient and cost-effective it will be. [6]

Endnotes:

[2] See *First Options v. Kaplan, 514 U.S. 938 (1995).*

[3] See *AAA Rules, R. 21.*

[4] See *ImClone v. Waksal, 22 A.D.3d 387, 802 N.Y.S.2d 653 (1st Dep't 2005).*

[5] See *AAA Employment Arbitration Rules and Mediation Procedures, R. 27.*

[6] Some practitioners have made the choice that arbitration is simply not an effective alternative to litigation, no matter how well drafted the ADR Provision is, and to that end have come up with a new alternative—the "modified litigation clause"—engaging in litigation but with contractual limits on the scope of the court proceedings, such as waivers of certain types of motions, limited discovery (particularly e-discovery), and fee-shifting provisions, all of which are intended to combine the desired benefits of arbitration—namely a streamlined proceeding—with the certainty that the well-established state and

federal rules of procedure provide. See Fishman, Eric, "When Arbitration Makes Matters Worse," Legal Times, *October 23, 2006, Vol. XXIX, No. 43.*

The ABA issued the following "checklist" for drafting ADR provisions:

1. Specify the type and combinations of ADR desired. Select number and type of ADR steps
   a. Mediation only
   b. Arbitration only
   c. Negotiation and arbitration
   d. Mediation and arbitration
   e. Negotiation, mediation and arbitration
2. Good faith, face-to-face negotiation
   a. Between same players
   b. Escalate above players with stake in outcome to "big picture" executive (recommended approach)
   c. Require authority to bind (minimum is reachable decision maker). This step slows process down (Is time an issue?)
3. Mediation by neutral third party
   a. Always a good idea, and successful a majority of the time
   b. Require authority to bind (minimum is reachable decision maker)
   c. This step slows process down (Is time an issue?)
4. Arbitration
   a. Binding (preferred)
   b. Nonbinding (operates to give both sides a view of how a court may decide the issues and facilitates settlement, but may give losing party idea of how to improve arguments. Risky, time consuming, added expense)
5. Other alternatives (for example, mini-trial with mock judge and jury)
6. Provide whether mediation may continue even though arbitration has begun

7. Specify size and skillset of ADR panel—One mediator (allow mediator expert help in complex or multi-party cases)
   a. One arbitrator (quicker process, less expense)
   b. Three arbitrators (preferred for big $$$ or complex matters)
      - Decisions by majority, more consensus decision making
      - Broader experience base applied to decisions
      - Slower process, more expensive
8. Specify neutral's required skillset and background
   a. Lawyer
   b. Former judge
   c. Non-lawyer professional (for example, accountant, architect, engineer)
   d. Knowledge of specific law areas of jurisdiction's law
   e. Knowledge of type of specific business or industry
   f. Educational background or licenses
   g. ADR neutral training and experience
9. Name specific neutral or panel list from which neutral must be drawn
10. Specify location of ADR proceedings
    a. Specific city, state
    b. Specific site (party, ADR entity or neutral)
    c. Specific only site-selection process (for example, the neutral selects)
    d. Allow claimant to select convenient or dispute-related site
11. Specify scope of issues and parties subject to ADR
    a. All-inclusive (use magic words "all disputes arising out of or relating to")
    b. All-inclusive with carve-outs, e.g., subject-matter carve-outs (for example, patent disputes) or claim value carve-outs (matters within small claims

court jurisdiction or determined by arbitrator to be above a specified $$$ amount)

c. Only specific issues subject to ADR

d. Only signatory parties can/must adjudicate disputes in ADR

e. Permit/require additional third-party beneficiaries (for example, suppliers, affiliates) to adjudicated disputes in ADR

f. Expressly prohibit joinder of disputes or parties from other contracts (that is, prohibit creation of class actions)

g. Include claims arising under prior or related contracts (address impact of superseding contract in ADR and merger clauses)

h. Make all disputed subject to ADR even if arises from prior contract, or

i. Only disputes arising out of or related to new contract

j. Specify who determines arbitrability and scope questions

k. Absent contract provision, the court determines threshold questions of arbitrability and scope

l. Specify that arbitrator determines all threshold issues of arbitrability and scope (preferred)

12. Specify who determines applicability of statutes of limitations and issue preclusion

    a. Court (absent contract provision court determines issue)

    b. Arbitrator (preferred)

    c. Specify that arbitrator determines all issues of contract validity

13. Specify applicable substantive law

    a. Specify that Federal Arbitration Act governs and enforces the ADR obligation and that state law, excluding its choice of law and its ADR law, governs all other substantive matters (preferred, if contract involves interstate commerce), or

    b. Specify state ADR law and state substantive law

14. Provide for specific limitations periods that apply to disputes
    a. Provide for application of state law statutes of limitation, allow parties to seek injunctive relief in court to preserve claims; or
    b. Provide for tolling of state statutes of limitations on notice of dispute; or
    c. Provide for special limitations for adjudicating disputes and specify that state statutes do not apply
15. Provide that arbitrator must follow applicable legal privileges (for example, lawyer-client and work-product privilege)
16. Be sure to conform boilerplate provisions in contract, for example, choice of law with the choice of law language in the ADR provision
17. Specify applicable ADR procedural rules
    a. Allow neutral panel to determine all procedures, or
    b. Include most procedures in ADR provision by incorporating ADR entity rules:
        - Non-administered (for example, CPR commercial arbitration rules)
        - Administered (for example, AAA commercial arbitration rules)
        - Special sector rules of an ADR entity (for example, AAA construction, AAA complex commercial), and
        - Allow neutral panel to provide for any other required procedure
        - Provide that ADR contract provisions supplement and override conflicting ADR entity rules
    c. Provide for an application of all or specific federal or state rules of procedure
18. Provide for application of federal or state rules of evidence

19. Specify permitted type of hearing
    a. Oral hearing before arbitrator for presentation of evidence required
    b. Permit telephonic or electronic proceedings (or portions of proceedings)
    c. Permit resolution of dispute by arbitrator based on written submissions and documents
20. Provide specific time limits for each ADR step and for the issuance of an arbitration decision and award
    a. Provide arbitrator power to conduct proceedings and render award when party refuses to participate or cooperate,
    b. Specify arbitrator obligations and restrictions,
    c. Specify any desired limits of arbitrator discretion,
    d. Always specify that arbitrator must follow dictates of agreement,
    e. Provide whether arbitrator must apply applicable substantive law to dispute,
    f. Specify permitted scope of review of ADR award,
    g. Permit only that provided by applicable federal or state ADR statute,
    h. Expressly provide that arbitration award is not reviewable for error of law by arbitrator, only manifest disregard of the law,
    i. Create private review panel (for example, three-person panel to review entire decision and award or only for errors of law), or
    j. Grant courts right to review beyond applicable statute (for example, right to review for errors of settled law) (this is dangerous and unsettled ground)
21. Specify extent of confidentiality
    a. Confidentiality of existence and nature of the dispute
    b. Confidentiality of information provided or statements made in prior ADR step
    c. Confidentiality of information provided or statements made in arbitration

d. Confidentiality of the reasoned decision and/or the award

e. Confidentiality of the disclosures, statements, decision or award in any other subsequent litigation proceedings regarding same dispute

f. Specify whether proceedings may be transcribed or recorded

g. Specify permitted scope and methods of discovery

22. Adopt ADR entity rules concerning discovery

a. Adopt ADR entity rules concerning discovery with specific additions or overriding exceptions, or

b. Adopt civil discovery rules with or without specific additions or exceptions

c. Exclude civil discovery rules with exception, for example, provisions for third-party subpoenas and extraterritorial party subpoenas

d. Provide that arbitrator shall determine all issues regarding the scope and types (for example, depositions) of permitted discovery

e. Specifically provide in detail for the scope and type of discovery that will be permitted, with administration by the arbitrator (for example, no depositions, no interrogatories, no party-issued subpoenas (arbitrator-issued only), mandatory pre-hearing meetings for sharing of documents and lists of potential witnesses)

23. Specify type, timing and confirmation of award

a. Rely on ADR entity procedural rules

b. Require written, reasoned decision and award

c. Permit only bare award (no reasoned basis for award)

d. Specifically permit arbitrator to resolve issues by summary judgment, that is, based on documents without oral testimony from witnesses found to be irrelevant by arbitrator

e. Provide for confirmation and entry of arbitrator's award in any court of competent jurisdiction

f. Provide whether the decision and award may be given res judicata effect in subsequent proceeding between the parties

g. Specify relief available from arbitrator and court

h. Be silent on the issue of relief (rely on decisional law)

i. Specify that arbitrator may provide for any relief available at law or equity and not otherwise lawfully restricted by parties' agreement, for example giving effect to contract's limited warranty and limitations of liability provisions

j. Provide for specific limitations on the scope of relief the arbitrator may award, for example, no punitive damages, no attorney's fees, no consequential damages, no specific performance, only monetary relief (no injunctions)

k. Permit arbitrator to issue injunctive relief, including requiring party to seek dissolution of court injunctions that conflict with ADR process or relief awarded

24. Expressly make taking dispute to court rather than submitting it to the required ADR process a breach of contract for which arbitrator must grant relief and attorney's fees

a. Provide for party absorption of own attorney's fees, costs and ADR fees

b. Provide for award of attorney's fees and costs to prevailing party

c. Provide for sharing of mediator and arbitrator fees and ADR fees

d. Provide for arbitrator allocation of all or some of the ADR fees (for example, loser pays)

e. Allow parties to seek injunctive relief in court solely to preserve status quo or to preserve statutes of limitations

25. Miscellaneous considerations

a. Specify precise process for and timing of initiation of each step of ADR

b. Method (for example, written demand or notice)

   c. Set time limits for each step

26. Specify scope of disputes subject to particular ADR proceeding
    a. Only those disputes specifically set forth in the demand and the other party's response to that particular demand, or
    b. Require joinder of all known outstanding disputes and waiver of disputes not expressly joined or set forth in written demand
27. Specify that each separate dispute (if not waived) must go through all ADR steps (no skipping steps, no surprise disputes)
28. Specify what happens when one party fails to pay fees of administering ADR entity or neutral
    a. Allow other party to pay to permit ADR to continue administration, or
    b. Provide what happens in the event of failure to pay

Now that you know what to look for, consider the following sample clauses below, before going to draft your own provision.

American Arbitration Associations Suggested Clauses:

Arbitration

Any controversy or claim arising out of or relating to this contract, or the breach thereof, shall be settled by arbitration administered by the American Arbitration Association in accordance with its Commercial [or other] Arbitration Rules [including the Optional Rules for Emergency Measures of Protection], and judgment on the award rendered by the arbitrator(s) may be entered in any court having jurisdiction thereof.

Mediation Preceding Arbitration

If a dispute arises out of or relates to this contract, or the breach thereof, and if the dispute cannot be settled through negotiation, the parties agree first to try in good faith to settle the dispute by mediation administered by the American Arbitration Association under its Commercial Mediation Procedures before resorting to arbitration, litigation, or some other dispute resolution procedure. If they do not reach such solution within a period of 60 days, then, upon notice by either party to the other, all disputes, claims, questions, or differences shall be finally settled by arbitration administered by the

American Arbitration Association in accordance with the provisions of its Commercial Arbitration Rules.

Other Samples:

Negotiation

The parties shall attempt in good faith to resolve any dispute arising out of or relating to this agreement promptly by negotiation. The negotiations will be conducted by the [title] of [Party 1] and the [title] of [Party 2]. If the dispute has not been resolved by negotiation within [45] days after notification of the dispute, then the parties shall. . .

Mediation

If a dispute arises out of or relates to this contract, or the breach thereof, the parties agree first to try in good faith to settle the dispute by mediation under the Commercial Mediation Rules of the American Arbitration Association.

If matter is not resolved within 30 days, the dispute will be resolved under the arbitration provisions below.

Arbitration

Issues Subject to Arbitration: Any controversy or claim arising out of or relating to this contract, or the breach thereof, will be settled by arbitration.

Issues not Subject to Arbitration: The following issues will not be subject to arbitration. . .

Arbitral Body: The arbitration will be administered by [the American Arbitration Association].

Applicable Rules: The rules applicable to the arbitration proceedings will be the ______________ rules.

**A number of arbitral bodies are available (AAA, CPR, ICC, WIPO, UNCITRAL, etc.). When you select one be familiar with the rules!

Binding Decision: Decisions of the arbitrator will be binding on the parties and judgment on the award rendered by the arbitrator may be entered in any court having jurisdiction thereof.

Form of Decision: All awards will be in writing and shall state the reasoning on which the award rests.

Law to be Applied: In rendering the award, the arbitrator shall determine the rights and obligations of the parties according to the substantive and procedural laws of [state].

Venue: The arbitration will be conducted in the city of __________, in [country].

**Consider logistics—transportation, accommodations, costs, convenience of witnesses, etc.

Number of Arbitrators: The number of arbitrators will be ['one', 'three']

Selection of Arbitrators: Default Rules position or Agree to an arbitrator up front or each party selects one and the two arbitrators select the third.

Qualifications: The arbitrator will be a retired judge of the [specify] Court. Or the arbitrator must be [a member of the _____ state bar] actively engaged in the practice of law with expertise in the process of deciding disputes and interpreting contracts in [the particular field of law involving the potential controversy].

Evidence: The arbitrator will be the judge of the relevance and materiality of the evidence offered, and conformity to legal rules of evidence shall not be necessary. Or the arbitrator will apply the _____ rules of evidence.

Discovery: At request of party or discretion of the arbitrator, . . . arbitrator may direct (i) production of documents and other information, and (ii) identification of any witnesses to be called.

Other Discovery that may be specified: Scope of document discovery (All documents relating to subject matter, Documents to be relied by parties in proceedings, Documents exchanged with third parties, Documents in the control of a party); Scope of witness discovery (Provide list of witnesses including experts with summary of anticipated testimony, Make witnesses available for deposition, Deposition by written questions, Interviews of employees, Audits of books and records, Inspection of premises).

The arbitrator may take whatever interim measures he or she deems necessary, including relief and measures for the protection or conservation of property and disposition of perishable goods.

A request for interim measures addressed by a party to a judicial authority shall not be deemed incompatible with the agreement to arbitrate or a waiver of the right to arbitrate.

The arbitrator may issue such orders for interim relief as may be deemed necessary to safeguard the property that is the subject matter of the arbitration, to preserve evidence, and/or to protect trade secrets or other proprietary information that might be disclosed during the arbitration. . .

A request for interim measures will only be addressed to the arbitrator in accordance with the AAA Optional Rules for Emergency Measures of Protection.

Attorney's Fees: The arbitrator may award reasonable attorneys fees to the prevailing party.

Drafting Concert Agreements for Sport Venues

I. Introduction

Sports venues are a major source of entertainment in cities all across the world. While their primary function is to host athletic competitions, venues often put on special events such as concerts and music festivals to generate additional revenue. One of the most fundamental determinations to make is who is entitled to enter into agreements with third-parties for the production of a special non-athletic event under the stadium lease agreement. In all properly executed stadium lease agreements[40], you will find a provision pertaining to the right to host events at the venue. Sometimes this right is shared by the landlord and the lessee, but more times than not it is held exclusively by one party. Once this fundamental determination has been made, there are particular aspects to concert agreements that are unique and require special consideration.

Concert agreements present numerous potential problems that most other sports-venue agreements typically avoid. The agreements often involve the venue, individual artists or groups, and/or a music management company that handles the touring of one or many artists at a time. Concert agreements typically include provisions concerning the basic aspects of the event, the advertisement and promotion of the event, licensing of the artist's name and likeness, obligations and limitations of the artist(s), and how the revenue from the event will be shared. The agreements will also include force majeure provisions, as well as lay out the rights, duties, and obligations of the venue (i.e., limiting the use of cameras and other devices by patrons to record the event). This chapter looks closely at these provisions, discusses the typical negotiation positions of the parties, and provides a likely ZOPA for each of the negotiated terms.

II. Fundamental Aspects of the Event

A. *The Stage, Equipment, and Support Staff*

While the details surrounding the stage, equipment, and other basic elements of the concert may not be the first area of the agreement negotiated, it is an appropriate place to start this chapter's discussion of concert agreements and the like. Questions that will need to be answered include: Where will the stage be located? Where will vendors be able to sell merchandise? Who is responsible for supplying

[40] *See* Peter A. Carfagna, NEGOTIATING AND DRAFTING SPORTS VENUE AGREEMENTS 16–34 (2016) (discussing the essential terms and considerations to drafting and negotiating the stadium lease agreement).

the support staff needed to set up and take down all of the equipment for the performance? Who is responsible for supplying the various forms of equipment? Will the artist or management company have approval rights for the different aspects that affect the performance (i.e., stage placement, logistics, etc.)? These, among others, are questions that will need to be addressed when drafting a concert agreement.

B. *Supporting Acts*

Concerts often consist of performances by multiple artists. Therefore, the finalized agreement should establish if the event consists of performances by multiple artists and which party has the right or obligation to secure other artists for the event. If the concert is part of a multiple-venue tour involving a predetermined set of artists, this provision will be of little importance. However, if the venue is contracting with an individual artist or group, the agreement must set forth who maintains the right to select the supporting acts. The other party will often like to reserve the right to approve or disapprove any supporting act.

Agreements with supporting acts will likely be less convoluted than the agreement entered into with the main artist or group, but this is not always the case. The supporting acts may also have special requests or needs that must be addressed in the agreement. Agreements with supporting acts will often be much easier to negotiate and draft if the major aspects of the event have been addressed in the agreement with the primary artist. Nevertheless, many of the topics discussed in this chapter will apply to all artists to perform at the concert.

C. *Rights, Duties, and Obligations of the Venue*

There are particular tasks involved with putting on a concert event that the venue is typically responsible for overseeing. Some of these responsibilities include advertising and promoting the concert, selling tickets, staffing the event, and satisfying artists' specific needs. Furthermore, the venue may be responsible for limiting the likelihood of unauthorized reproduction of the performance. Each of these responsibilities should be addressed in the agreement to prevent any possible disputes.

D. *Advertisement, Promotion, and Sales*

Venues will often be responsible for the advertisement and promotion of the concert. However, it is unlikely that the venue will be able to make, in its sole discretion, all of the decisions as to the advertisement and promotion of the event. First and foremost, the venue will want to use the artist's name, image and likeness in the promotion of the event. Therefore, the venue will need to secure from the artist the right to use such, which must be explicitly stated in the finalized agreement or subsequent addendum. Venues will also want this provision to grant the right to use the "artist's name, image, likeness, and any other promotional materials in all promotions, advertising or other activities used to increase attendance at the event." However, depending on the caliber of the artist at the event, the artist is likely to require that the venue receive prior written consent before any advertisement or promotional activity uses the artist's intellectual property.

E. *Recordings of the Event*

While concerts are sometimes recorded and used in albums, more often than not the concert will not be recorded for later use. If the latter is the case, the venue's level of responsibility in limiting the unauthorized recording of a performance will likely be an issue. Some artists encourage audience members to take photographs and video recordings, others are apathetic, and some are strongly against any form of replicating their performance. Regardless of which category the artist falls under, the agreement should specify what level of effort, if any, must be taken to limit fans from taking pictures or video during the performance. If the artist does not object to fans participating in such acts, then the agreement should clearly absolve the venue from any liability for copyright or trademark infringement due to fans recording the event. However, if the artist does not wish to have any aspect of the performance duplicated, the agreement will need to state what level of effort must be taken by the venue to prevent unauthorized recordings. An artist adamantly against any form of reproduction will likely want the venue to guarantee that no such activities will take place and to be responsible for limiting the use of technological devices during the performance. However, the venue will likely be unwilling to make such a guarantee since the technological advancements in the past decade have resulted in everyone having a digital camera and video recorder in their pocket through their cell phone. Therefore, the likely result of negotiations in instances where the artist wants such a guarantee will be that the venue be required to put forth "reasonable" or "best efforts" in limiting attendees from duplicating the performance through such methods.

F. *Miscellaneous*

Some artists also have particular requests that may need to be satisfied by the venue before or after their performance. These may include a list of particular foods or drinks, access to particular areas of the venue, or particular needs when it comes to security or transportation. The artist will undoubtedly make these types of demands well known to the venue. However, the venue must make sure that it does not succumb to so many of the artist's demands that the performance of such tasks become overly difficult, which subsequently increases the risk of breaching the agreement or causing some other form of dispute between the artist and the venue.

The venue is typically responsible for hiring security and developing a security strategy, but the artist or management company sometimes holds this obligation. Different genres of music and artists have fan bases that require various levels of security (i.e., an extremely popular artist's concert may require a more extensive security detail due to the number of fans likely to be present). Local governments may also express concerns about safety at the venue and surrounding area in particular instances. Such concerns may lead to difficulty in securing necessary permits for the concerts production. Venues should develop a security strategy that adequately protects the interest of everyone involved based upon the type of concert or event. The details surrounding the security strategy may or may not be included in the finalized agreement, but the venue's obligation to provide such will likely be a material term of the agreement.[41]

III. Rights, Duties, and Obligations of the Artist

A. *Compensation*

There are two basic methods in which artists are compensated for their performance, and once again, this often depends on the caliber of the talent being contracted with. The first model is typically reserved for higher-caliber talent and involves a "guaranteed" payment to be made to the artist prior to the event. This method often pays the artist a deposit on the effective date of the agreement (or some other specified date), with the balance to be paid prior to the performance. Under this method, artists will likely receive payment of their revenue percentage after the conclusion of the performance. The second model, typically involved in agreements with lesser-known artists, is where the venue withholds payment of the artist's fee until the performance has been successfully completed. Artists

---

41 Consider *Platinum Links Entertainment v. Atlantic City Surf Professional Baseball Club, Inc.*, 2006 WL 1459986 (D.N.J. May 23, 2006). In *Platinum Links*, litigation ensued after the operators of minor league baseball stadium cancelled a concert because of security concerns expressed by the Atlantic City Police Department ("ACPD"). The concert was ultimately held, but Plaintiff entertainment company claimed that it suffered monetary damages as a result of decreased attendance which was caused by the cancellation announcement. *Platinum Links* demonstrates an example of a concert where there was a need for a higher level of security at the venue, as well as a breakdown in communication between the parties. The parties may have been able to present the concert without interruption, thereby avoiding litigation, had the parties communicated better and developed a security strategy that was sufficient to protect the interests of attendees, as well as the surrounding community.

being paid under the second model may or may not receive a portion of certain revenue streams in addition to the "base" fee for the performance. Revenue sharing arrangements are discussed in detail within the section entitled *Revenue* that follows.

Agreements that pay artists according to the first method often set forth the various payment requirements on a separate page that itemizes the various amounts and times that particular payments are to be made to the artist. See Exhibit 1 for a sample agreement detailing this type of payment method. A clear and unambiguous statement of all fees to be paid to the artist, as well as the division of the various revenue streams, will allow for an easy interpretation of how the revenues from the concert will be distributed amongst the parties. Another circumstance that should be memorialized into the agreement is whether any deposits that have been paid to the artist will be refunded if the artist cancels the concert.[42]

Less convoluted payment arrangements that follow the second method can often be seamlessly included through a single provision of the agreement that states the amount and time payment will be tendered. If the artist is to be paid upon the conclusion of the performance, the drafter must be careful in his or her wording so as to alleviate the possibility of disputes. Problems of interpretation may arise if the venue is only obligated to pay the artist upon "successful completion of the performance." Consider an artist that has completed 75% of his performance who, through his own negligence, suddenly falls off the stage and is unable to finish the performance due to injury. Has the artist successfully completed the performance? If this kind of language is used in the agreement, an explanation of what constitutes a "successful completion" of the performance might be helpful in settling any possible disputes.

B. Other Performances

As stated before, playing host to concerts can be a very profitable endeavor if executed properly. However, the venue must take very calculated steps to ensure that it maximizes its earning potential. One way for a venue to help ensure it maximizes attendance at its venue is to limit the ability of the artist to perform in the surrounding area for a period of time before and after the date of the event. By doing so, the venue ensures that it will not lose potential patrons to other venues located within a reasonable distance. The artist may or may not agree to such a term without receiving something in return

---

42 *See Milan Music, Inc. v. Emmel Communications Booking Inc.*, 829 N.Y.S.2d 485 (N.Y. App. Div. 2007) (Concert promoter was precluded from bringing a breach of contract action based on rescission of contract for concert when the cancellation of concert was memorialized in two separate writings, and the booking agent promptly refunded to promoter the deposit for the concert.).

(i.e., greater percentage of revenue, higher guaranteed pay, etc.). However, the venue will likely have more to lose if it fails to give the artist a bigger piece of the pie and the attendance of the event falls due to the agreement lacking such a restriction.

C. *Personal Appearances*

Whether the artist will be making personal appearances at local radio or television stations is another term of the agreement that will likely be negotiated. The venue may want the artist to appear at one or more of these media outlets to garner interest in the event and increase attendance. However, the artist may be unwilling or unable to make such appearances for any number of reasons. Nevertheless, if the artist is willing to make such appearances, the agreement should state with particularity the number of appearances that will be required, the process for scheduling such appearances (i.e., who will schedule the appearances), and if the artist has approval rights over when and where he will appear. An alternative to particularly stating "the way appearances shall be made would be to state in the agreement that the artist shall be required to make himself reasonably available for personal appearances on television or radio stations for "x" number of days prior to the concert." However, always be leery of using the language "reasonably available" in agreements because of the lack of certainty as to the standard that the artist will be held to. Nevertheless, using this language is sometimes unavoidable and may be the only option the parties have when trying to secure personal appearances by the artist. The parties may wish to consider the possible alternatives to having an artist make personal appearances that can be achieved through the use of modern technology in circumstances where the artist's tour schedule renders "in-person" appearances for the promotion of the event impractical or impossible.

IV. Revenue

To avoid any possible disputes, the agreement must specifically state how the revenue generated from the event will be shared. How the revenue is divided is closely tied into which party is responsible for selling various merchandise and concession items. There are three basic revenue streams that are pertinent to almost all concert agreements: (1) tickets; (2) concessions/alcohol; and (3) merchandise.

A. *Ticket Sales*

In addition to generating revenue through sponsorship agreements, profit from ticket sales is one of the initial revenue streams for concert events. The price of concert tickets varies depending on various factors, which include the number of artists performing and the popularity of the talent. The circumstances surrounding the concert can also affect how the prices of the tickets are determined. If the venue has secured lesser-known talent that has not participated in the planning and preparation of the event, the venue will likely be the party charged with developing a price structure for the concert tickets. However, if the venue is contracting with an artist or a company handling a tour of artists that are performing in multiple cities, it is likely that both parties will be involved in the determination of the pricing structure of tickets.

As previously stated, a price structure for the tickets will need to be developed and the agreement will likely state the number of tickets that will be sold at each price point. When developing the pricing structure, the parties must decide whether there will be different prices for seats in various locations of the venue or if all tickets to the concert will be identically priced. Making this determination often turns on the various factors (including, but not limited to): the type of venue, the amount of the venue being used, the type of concert, etc. For example, music festivals that involve numerous acts throughout the course of the day, where patrons are encouraged to move freely about the venue, often have flat rate ticket pricing. Whereas if a concert involves one or a few artists, and is held at an arena where everyone has assigned seats, the concert would likely have a variable pricing structure. Furthermore, the price and sale of luxury suites to the concert should also be negotiated so as to prevent any possible dispute over the allocation of the revenue from such sales. The venue may wish to "carve out" the luxury suite revenues from the ticket revenues to be shared with the artist so as to increase the venue's profits.

B. Concessions/Alcohol

Concessions and alcohol revenue is almost always retained entirely by the venue and is possibly the next largest income stream after ticket sales. The venue typically retains this income stream because it is almost always the venue that is responsible for securing concessionaires and other venders to distribute these goods. Therefore, the details of the concessions and alcohol sales will not always make it into the final written agreement. However, there are various issues that arise in planning where, when, how, and how much of these types of goods will be sold. The venue must make careful considerations in its plan of distribution to maximize the potential income from these sales. The venue will also need to consider whether or not it is limited to using particular vendors due to its pre-existing agreements with sponsors and concessionaires. If it is, then there is likely little leeway in providing different foods and beverages than would typically be provided at the venue. However, if the venue is not constricted by its pre-existing agreements, it could contract with different concessions and alcohol providers for the concert. Agreements between the venue and the concessionaires and alcohol providers for the concert would need to specify that the contractual relationship is for this event only and not bind the venue to an agreement that may conflict with any pre-existing or future agreements.

C. Merchandise

The sale of merchandise at the concert is another very important aspect of the agreement. The agreement should state who is permitted to sell merchandise on behalf of the artist at the event and the percentage of the profits to be given to each party. The artist may wish to retain the majority, if not all, of the merchandise revenues. The venue does not have much leverage when it comes to capturing a large portion of this revenue stream because the merchandise typically bears the name, image, and/or likeness of the artist. However, the venue may still be able to receive a piece of the merchandise revenues, even if it is a minor portion. The venue will sometimes "give" the artist this revenue stream as an incentive to perform at the event if the artist is a lesser-known talent and is receiving a lower fee. However, the merchandise sales at the event for a more popular artist is likely to be a significant revenue stream and the venue will likely wish to receive a percentage of the sales.

V. Force Majeure

Neither party wants to suffer due to inclement weather or unforeseeable occurrences that render the performance impossible, unfeasible, or unsafe. Situations that often fall into this category include, but are not limited to: inclement weather, municipal acts or regulations of local public authorities, delay of transportation services, war, or other emergencies. However, the caliber of the artist to perform is often the determining factor as to whether the venue will be required to pay the agreed upon compensation for performing. Popular artists often require that the agreed upon compensation be paid to them regardless of inclement weather that renders performance impossible, unfeasible, or unsafe. In this situation, the venue may be able to slightly limit its liability by requiring that the artist be "ready, willing, and able" to perform in order to receive the agreed upon compensation. Furthermore, popular artists will likely want to retain their compensation in the event that the artist or members of the artist's band become sick or injured, which subsequently requires the event to be cancelled.[43] Depending on how

43 In *Druyan v. Jagger*, 508 F.Supp.2d 228 (S.D.N.Y. 2007), a holder of a concert ticket brought a class action against the Rolling Stones' lead singer, Mick Jagger, an online ticket selling agency, and the concert promoter, asserting claims for breach of contract, fraud, prima facie tort, negligence, and violation of truth in advertising

strong a position the artist takes on this issue, the venue may only be able to curtail this limitation on the artist's obligation to perform by requiring that the missed performance not result from the artist's or his/her representative's negligence.

As discussed above, lesser-known artists are often paid upon "successful completion" of the performance. However, the artist should push to have a force majeure clause included into the final agreement to prevent the venue from withholding payment if an unforeseeable event occurs before or during the performance that makes it impossible for the artist to perform or continue to perform.

VI. Limiting Liability

A mutual release is typically included in concert agreements to limit each party from being held liable for the acts or negligence of the other party. The venue and the artist alike would like to limit themselves from any liability for negligent acts or omissions of the other party. Consider an artist that uses pyrotechnics as a part of his show. A venue may agree an artist's use of such stage tactics insofar that the artist agrees to indemnify and hold the venue harmless if a member of the crew or audience is injured by their use. Contrarily, the artist will likely wish to be indemnified by the venue from claims surrounding injuries by audience members caused by the venue's negligent maintenance of the facility or any other possible claim arising out of the venue's negligence. Another provision aimed at limiting the liability of the parties is an "Insurance Clause" that requires either one or both parties to carry a minimum level of insurance to cover damages that may occur at or as a result of the event. Regardless of how the parties structure the agreement, the goal of the parties should be to prevent the parties from being held liable for damages that they should not be responsible for or could have otherwise been avoided had the proper precautions been taken.

HYPOTHETICAL EXERCISES

Negotiating and Drafting a Concert Agreement Between a Sports Venue and a Worldwide Music Tour

A. Assume that the NBA is currently experiencing a lockout, which has caused a significant drop in revenues for Madison Square Garden ("MSG"). In order to generate additional revenue, MSG is seeking a major musical talent for a concert event.

---

statutes, based on allegations that the defendants intentionally withheld timely notice of postponement of a concert, causing plaintiff and other ticketholders to incur expenses for travel, food, alternative entertainment. *See also Spence v. Marley*, 1992 WL 122878 (E.D.P.A. 1992) (court found artist liable to concert promoter for $207,830 as a result of the artist's last minute cancellation of multiple performances).

1. The seating capacity for concerts at MSG is 20,000 and MSG hopes that the concert will be a "sell out" event. However, due to the fact that the event is being held on such short-notice, MSG wishes to employ an aggressive marketing strategy to increase awareness of the event, including, but not limited to: an appearance by the headlining artist on a major network's morning television show, regional television commercials, utilization of social media outlets, and radio appearances by the headlining artist and opening acts.

2. MSG has pre-existing agreements with concessionaires and alcohol vendors with predetermined revenue sharing.

B. Lady DaDa has just commenced a worldwide tour called The Elegant Ball Tour (the "Tour"). However, the Tour has not yet secured a venue in New York, NY for the third leg of the North American tour. After first touring in Boston, MA, and Philadelphia, PA, the Tour has three consecutive days that it wishes to perform in New York City, preferably at the same venue. The Tour has multiple opening acts that will perform before the headline performance by Lady DaDa. These artists change throughout the course of the tour, but the same opening artists would perform on all three days of the New York City tour stop.

C. Assume that MSG does not have any scheduling conflicts for the three days proffered by the Tour, but does have a NHL game scheduled for the afternoon following the last performance. This short span of time requires MSG to hire double the amount of staff and doubles its typical cost to transition the arena. Be sure to address *all* facts in the drafting exercise.

D. Students should split into groups of four, with two members representing MSG and two members representing The Tour.

E. In light of the foregoing "drafting tips" and possible ZOPA's set forth in this chapter, negotiate and draft the following clauses using the Exhibit 1 "Template Agreement" found hereafter as a guide.

1. <u>Rights and Obligations of the Parties</u>

    a. Address the issue of advertising and promotion of the Tour's performances to take place at MSG. Who will be responsible for advertisement and promotion? If MSG is responsible, address the issue of the use of Lady DaDa or other Tour performers' name, image, and likeness.

b. Assume that Lady DaDa wants to eliminate any possibility of audio, photo, or video reproduction of any of the performances to take place at MSG.

c. Does the Tour have any specific requirements for its artists (i.e., particular number of suites for performers and their bands to relax before and after the show, etc.)?

d. Will Lady DaDa or any other Tour performers be required to make personal, radio, or television appearances to promote the show? Keep in mind that the Tour has a very busy concert schedule that may make personal appearances difficult.

2. Revenue and Other Payments

a. What type of fee schedule will the agreement set forth? Address whether the Tour will receive an initial fee and, if so, the amount of the initial fee?

b. How will the revenue be distributed? Assume that the Tour has all of the necessary equipment and staff to sell merchandise at the event.

c. Assume that MSG has all of the contracts in place and a full staff capable of servicing the concession stands and serving alcohol.

d. Address the issue of variable ticket pricing and how the revenue from ticket sales will be shared amongst the parties.

3. Force Majeure

a. Draft a clause that governs performance or existence of the agreement in the event of unforeseeable force majeure events that interfere with the ability of the parties' duties under the agreement.

b. Since there are multiple artists to be performing at the event, is one artist's failure to perform a breach of the agreement or is it covered under the force majeure clause?

c. In general, please be sure to draft each clause to ensure that it is "litigation proof" and "execution ready" for your clients to sign.

Litigation Hypothetical

A. In this hypothetical litigation exercise, assume the following breaches of the Template Agreement have occurred:

1. Lady DaDa is claiming that she is "too tired" from all the stops on the Tour. As a result, she is developing a

"sore throat" that will prevent her from performing at her highest level at MSG.

2. Lady DaDa wants to go on a shopping spree in New York City pre-performance that will prevent her from rehearsing before the show.

3. MSG has (arguably) failed to provide Lady DaDa with a "first-class" dressing room, per Lady DaDa's Agent.

4. MSG's stage is slightly higher off the ground and shorter in width than required by the Agreement. Lady DaDa's Agent now claims, without her having rehearsed on the stage, that she is afraid of falling off the stage and hurting herself.

5. Assume finally, that Lady DaDa does, in fact, take the stage, but is inebriated after her shopping spree. Assume further that she does, in fact, also fall off the stage near the end of an (uninspired) performance and damages her vocal cords in so doing.

B. In this fact pattern, please consider the following questions:

1. What rights, remedies and liabilities fall upon Lady DaDa and/or MSG?

2. How would you revise the Template Agreement to cover all of the eventualities created by the Litigation Hypothetical?

C. Break up into groups of four to so revise the Template Agreement.

AGREEMENT FOR CONCERT ENGAGEMENT

between

LADY DADA dba ELEGANT BALL TOUR, INC.

and

MADISON SQUARE GARDEN

as Lessee.

Dated as of January 14, 2016

Lady DaDa DBA Elegant Ball Tour, Inc.
Lady DaDa "Elegant Ball Tour" 2015–2016
Agreement for Concert Engagement

This Contract for the personal services of musicians / artists on the engagement described herein (the "Agreement") has been made this date, January 3, 2016, by and between LADY DADA dba ELEGANT BALL TOUR, INC. (may also be referred to as "Artist" or "Performer") and MADISON SQUARE GARDEN (hereinafter referred to as "Purchaser"). If is understood and mutually agreed that the PURCHASER engages the ARTIST to perform the following engagement upon all the terms and conditions hereinafter set forth.

The parties hereto acknowledge that the following additional terms and conditions are incorporated in and make a part of the Agreement between the parties hereto.

Artist	Lady Dada	**Doors Open**	6:00 PM
Date of Show	February 23–25, 2016	**Showtime**	8:00 PM
Other Acts	TBD	**Performance**	9:45 PM
		Set Length	140+ Minutes
		Curfew	Midnight
Venue	Madison Square Garden 4 Penn Plaza New York, NY 10121	**Announcement Date** **On Sale Date**	January 31, 2016 February 5, 2016
Terms	$250,000 Guarantee Plus 50% Over $500,000 Net Door Receipts Purchaser to provide first class sound and lights to meet Artist's approval		

Deposit Required	$200,000		
Deposit Due Date	January 27, 2016 Balance is payable to Artist or Artist's authorized representative immediately prior to the performance.		
Sellable Capacity	20,000		
	3,500	Lower Reserved	$150.00
	6,500	Lower Bowl	$100.00
	3,000	Upper Reserved	$85.00
	3,500	General Admission	$75.00
Tax	6.25%		
Gross After Tax	$1,827,925		

As part of show security, all parties agree that all patrons, including backstage guests, will be subjected to security personnel who may perform pat downs and bag searches, or use handheld wand metal detectors.

Artists will not be held responsible for building damages unless damage arises out of any negligent and intentional acts or omissions by the producer/artist, its agents, employees, or representatives.

Bob Sugar
c/o Elegant Ball Tour, Inc.
Tour Manager

x__________________________

199 W. 57th St #6
New York, NY 10019

James Dougan
c/o Madison Square Garden
Special Events Coordinator

x__________________________

4 Penn Plaza, Suite 21
New York, NY 10121

Lady DaDa DBA Elegant Ball Tour, Inc.
Lady DaDa "Elegant Ball Tour" 2015–2016 Rider

In regard to the Engagement at Madison Square Garden, New York, NY, on February 23, 24, and 25 of 2016, this Letter of Agreement sets forth additional terms and conditions regarding the Engagement and is hereby made part of the Agreement dated January 3, 2016, between Lady DaDa dba Elegant Ball Tour, Inc. (may also be referred to as "Artist"), and Madison Square Garden (hereinafter "Purchaser").

DEFINITIONS

"Engagement" shall mean the time from which Artist arrives at the Venue prior to the first Performance on February 23, 2016, until Artist and its representatives have removed any and all of their equipment and relinquished their occupation of any part of the Venue in connection with the performances associated with the Elegant Ball Tour 2015–2016.

"Featured Artist" shall mean Lady Dada in her sole capacity as a musical performer.

"Net Ticket Sales Revenue" shall mean the gross revenue generated from the sale of tickets to each Performance during the Engagement minus any Show Costs incurred by Purchaser in its performance of its duties under this Agreement.

"Performance" shall mean the time period beginning when the general public has been granted admittance to the Venue on for that day's schedule concert until the Featured Artist has concluded the concert performance that evening and the general public has begun exiting the venue. This Agreement calls for three (3) Performances to occur during the course of the Engagement.

"Show Cost" shall mean a cost incurred by the Purchaser in furtherance of its duties under the Agreement, which shall be deducted from the gross revenue from ticket sales before the Net Ticket Sales Revenue is divided amongst the parties pursuant to the terms of this Agreement. All costs to be classified as Show Costs must be expressly stated in this Agreement or subsequently agreed upon in writing by both parties.

"Supporting Artist" or "Supporting Artists" shall mean the musical artists obtained to perform during each Performance of the Engagement, but shall not include Lady Dada herself or any band members.

"Venue" shall mean Madison Square Garden, and is used herein to reference the physical facility itself, not the corporate entity that is a party to this Agreement. Any and all references to the corporate entity shall be made using the term "Purchaser."

ARTICLE I. PAYMENT TO ARTIST AND REVENUE DIVISION

Section 1.1. Ticket Sales

Purchaser shall pay to Artist fifty percent (50%) of the Net Ticket Sales Revenue upon conclusion of the Engagement.

Section 1.2. Billing, Advertising, and Publicity

Advertising and publicity materials (including, but not limited to, Lady Dada and Elegant Ball Tour logos, photos, radio & television commercials, flyers, and posters) not provided by Artist need to be approved in advance in writing by Artist.

Section 1.3. Merchandise

Artist shall have the exclusive right to sell Artist souvenir programs, photographs, records and any and all types of merchandise including, but not limited to, articles of clothing (i.e., T-shirts, hats, etc.), posters, stickers, etc., on the premises of the place(s) of performance by Purchaser subject however to concessionaire's requirements, if any. Artist shall retain seventy-five percent (75%) of the gross revenue from all of its merchandise sales and twenty-five percent (25%) shall be paid to Purchaser.

Section 1.4. Concessions

Purchaser shall provide beverages and food in concessions at the venue from the time the gates open until a time that it, in its sole discretion, desires to conclude the sale of such goods. The staffing and operation of concession stands shall be the sole responsibility of Purchaser and Purchaser shall retain one hundred (100%) of the revenue generated from the sale of food and beverages at these locations.

ARTICLE II. RIGHTS, DUTIES, AND OBLIGATIONS OF PURCHASER

Section 2.1. Reproduction of the Performance

Purchaser shall not record, broadcast, televise, photograph or otherwise reproduce the visual and/or audio performances hereunder, or any part thereof. Purchaser shall use its best efforts to prevent any unauthorized duplication of the performances by members of the audience, staff, or individuals otherwise exposed to the performances.

Section 2.2. Right to Likeness; Grant/Reservation of Right

Artist's name or likeness may not be used as an endorsement of any product or services nor in connection with any commercial tie-up without Artist's prior written consent. Artist hereby retains all rights not expressly granted herein.

Section 2.3. Seating Area

Purchaser shall provide Artist with a detailed diagram of the seating area before tickets go on sale; no seats may be sold past (towards the stage) the line of the security barricade, and the diagram of the seating showing tickets to be put on sale must be approved in writing in advance by Artist. Obstructed view seating shall not be acceptable.

Section 2.4. Stage

At its sole expense, Purchaser shall furnish the stage, stage lighting, sound and power for the Performance, and Purchaser shall provide all stagehands required to assist the setup for and conduct of the Performance and takedown after the conclusion of the performances. The stage shall be constructed according to the following requirements:

(A) The stage must be at least sixty (60) feet wide and forty (40) feet deep, plus wings on both stage left and stage right, with a height between four (4) and five (5) feet, and a clearance to the ceiling of at least thirty (30) feet.

(B) All staging must not have any lip, rough edges, or nails sticking through which may cause injury to Artist or crew.

Section 2.5. Barricades

Purchaser shall supply, as a show cost, wall-style (not bike-rack style) barricades acceptable to Artist, placed between three (3) and six (6) feet in front of the stage, including wings. The front row of the audience should not be less than three (3) feet nor more than six (6) feet from the stage.

Section 2.6. Electrician

Purchaser shall provide as a show cost an electrician at the venue from the time the equipment for the performance is being unloaded until the time that the equipment has been completely disassembled after the conclusion of the performance.

Section 2.7. Sound Provided by Purchaser

Purchaser agrees to provide all necessary audio equipment specified herein, or as amended by Artist's Production Manager, as a Show Cost. All components shall be at the complete disposal of Artist and Artist reserves the right to reject any equipment deemed "not suitable" or "sub-standard" for live performance.

Section 2.8. Lights Provided by Purchaser

Purchaser agrees to provide all necessary sound equipment specified herein, or as provided by Artist's Production Manager, as a Show Cost. Complete details of the entire lighting system must be provided by Artist a minimum of thirty (30) days prior to the date the performance is scheduled to take place. Please see "Optimum Detailed Lighting Plot" (not attached as a part of this Example Agreement). The lighting system provided by Purchaser must include all necessary cable and rigging to make a complete and show-ready lighting system as per Artist's provided lighting design plot.

Section 2.9. Electricity Provided by Purchaser (Alice Cooper #30)

Purchaser agrees to provide and pay for as a Show Cost sufficient power for the Performance.

Section 2.10. Security

(A) Purchaser, as a Show Cost, shall supply adequate, able-bodied, easily identifiable and uniformly dressed security personnel for the audience area and all entrances and exits to the backstage area, as well as the dressing room area.

(B) Purchaser bears all financial and legal responsibility for losses caused or contributed to by reason of inadequate security, except for those losses caused or contributed to by the negligence of Artist or its representatives.

(C) Purchaser shall provide a security guard to be positioned at Artist's tour bus at all times that the bus is parked at the venue.

(D) Purchaser shall provide security guards to be positioned at the doors of the dressing rooms of all of the performers and their bands.

(E) Purchaser shall provide one security guard at the foot of any stairs leading to the stage from fifteen (15) minutes before until fifteen (15) minutes after each Performance.

Section 2.11. Catering

Purchaser shall provide a catering area supplied with the following prior to 10 AM on each day of the Engagement:

(A) Coffee, tea, & cold drinks, including non-carbonated spring water, soft-drinks, Gatorade, & fresh fruit juices, plus sugar, milk, lemon, honey, artificial sweetener, cups, spoons & napkins, etc.

(B) A hot lunch must be provided, for at least twenty-five (25) persons, including the beverages listed above, plus sandwiches, deli tray, soup, egg salad, tuna or chicken salad, cheese, bread & rolls, hamburgers, ketchup, mustard, mayonnaise, fresh fruit, low-fat cottage cheese. The hot lunch must include a main course for vegetarians as well as a meat-based main course.

(C) A hot dinner must be provided, for at least forty (40) persons, including the beverages listed above, plus the following: Fresh salad bar with low calorie/low fat dressings and oil and vinegar; fresh vegetables; a main course (including two of the following: fresh fish and/or fresh chicken and/or beef, plus one vegetarian main course option); hot pasta; wine; dessert; bread & rolls; soup; as well as all beverages listed above. Dinner should be a full sit-down service, buffet-style—not "plated" or "waiter service." No plastic/paper plates, or plastic utensils should be used for dinner. Linen tablecloths and napkins should be used. Dinner should be approved by Artist or its authorized agent prior to arrival.

Section 2.12. Advertisement and Promotion

Purchaser shall be responsible for the advertisement and promotion of the Engagement and any and all costs associated with such advertisement and promotion shall be considered a Show Cost and therefore deducted from the gross ticket sales revenue prior to the division of the engagement proceeds.

Section 2.13. Other Performances

Other than the already scheduled performances in Boston, MA, and Philadelphia, PA, Artist shall not schedule any performance within two hundred (200) miles of the Venue for forty-five (45) days prior to and forty-five (45) days following the Engagement.

ARTICLE III. RIGHTS, DUTIES, AND OBLIGATIONS OF ARTIST

Section 3.1. Tickets Provided to Artist

Purchaser shall provide Artist with fifty (50) complimentary tickets for each performance, in the highest ticket price, but not in the first twenty rows. Tickets should be contiguous groups of at least 8 tickets together. Tickets shall be provided to Artist by 3 PM on the date of the performance.

Section 3.2. Controlling Authority

Artist shall have the sole and exclusive control over the production, presentation and performance of the engagement hereunder including but not limited to the details, means and methods of the performance of the performing artists hereunder and Artist shall have the sole right or may see fit to designate and change at any time the performing personnel.

Section 3.3. Publicity/Promotion

Purchaser may not commit Artist to any interviews, photo sessions, "meet & greets," or any other promotional activities without Artist's prior written consent.

Section 3.4. Length of Performance

Each Performance hereunder is approximately one hundred eighty (140) minutes, including encores, which will be performed when deemed appropriate by Artist. Purchaser shall insure that the Performance will not be interrupted by local curfews, building policies, or any similar cause.

Section 3.5. Rehearsal and Sound Check

(A) Purchaser shall make the Venue, complete with all staging and structures used during the Performance, available to Artist no less than five (5) hours prior to the first Performance of the Engagement for rehearsal. Artist shall not be responsible for any damages incurred by Purchaser as a result of a delay in the Performance if Purchaser fails to provide the Artist with the Venue for rehearsal purposes pursuant to this paragraph.

(B) A minimum of two (2) hours is required for sound check prior to each Performance. No audience shall be allowed to enter the venue until Artist has completed sound check.

Section 3.6. Pre-Recorded Music

Artist shall provide all pre-recorded music to be played before and after each Performance, including any intermissions during the Performance.

Section 3.7. Dressing Rooms

(A) Purchaser shall provide Artist with six (6) dressing rooms are required—one (1) for Featured Artist, three (3) for Supporting Artists, one (1) for the band members, one (1) for the Tour's crew. Each dressing room must be in the same building as the stage, include sufficient room for wardrobe and instruments, electrical outlets, and each must have couches, mirrors, private restroom, and private shower. Purchaser shall provide and pay for at his sole expense heaters or air conditioners necessary to maintain temperatures between 65 and 75 degrees Fahrenheit. Each dressing room must have seating for a minimum of eight (8) persons. Chairs must be comfortable and cushioned or upholstered, not folding chairs. Featured Artist's personal dressing room should have an upholstered couch, a coffee table, and must be in FIRST-CLASS condition.

(B) The dressing rooms must be lockable and Purchaser shall provide Artist's production manager with keys, which shall be returned after the conclusion of the Engagement. Access to dressing rooms shall be restricted to Artist personnel and their authorized guests only.

(C) There must be access between the dressing rooms and the stage without entering the audience area or being seen by the audience.

(D) Artist's guests, with appropriate passes, must have access to a backstage hospitality area within five (5) minutes of the conclusion of each Performance. Access will be at the discretion of Artist personnel only.

Section 3.8. Production Office

Purchaser shall provide Artist with a production office, made available upon the arrival of Artist at the Venue at the beginning of the Engagement, which should contain adequate workspace, lighting, and chairs. The production office should contain a minimum of two (2) direct dial push button telephones and two (2) lines with long distance access and one (1) venue extension phone, and must have high speed (broadband) Internet access. All relevant telephone numbers should be provided to Artist's tour and production manager at least seven (7) days prior to the engagement.

Section 3.9. Supporting Acts

Artist shall have the sole authority to select the artists to perform as Supporting Artists for the Engagement. Artist shall inform Purchaser of the Supporting Artists thirty (30) days prior to the Engagement.

ARTICLE IV. TERMINATION

Section 4.1. Breach by Purchaser

In the event Purchaser refuses or neglects to provide any of the items to perform any of its obligations herein stated, as amended, and/or fails to make any of the payments as provided herein, Artist shall have the right to refuse to perform this contract, shall retain any amounts theretofore paid to Artist by Purchaser, and Purchaser shall remain liable to Purchaser for the agreed price herein set forth. In addition, if, on or before the date of any scheduled performance, Purchaser has failed, neglected, or refused to perform any contract with any other performer for any other engagement, or if the financial standing or credit of Purchaser makes it impossible to make such payment forthwith, Artist shall have the right to cancel this engagement by notice to Purchaser to that effect, and to retain any amounts theretofore paid to Artist by Purchaser and Purchaser shall remain liable to Artist for the agreed price herein set forth.

Section 4.2. Sickness, Accident, and Force Majeure

In the event of sickness or of accident to Artist, or if a performance is prevented, rendered impossible by any Acts of God, act or regulation of any public authority or bureau, civil tumult, strike, epidemic, interruption or delay of transportation services, war conditions, or emergencies or any other similar or dissimilar cause beyond the control of Purchaser, it is undertook and agreed that there shall be no claim for damages by Purchaser and Artist's obligations as to such performance shall be deemed waived. In the event of such non-performance for any of the reasons stated in this paragraph, if Artist is ready, present, willing and able to perform, Purchaser shall pay the full compensation hereunder, otherwise, the monies (if any) advanced to Artist hereunder, shall be returned on a pro-rata basis. Provided Artist is ready, present, willing and able to perform at designated date and time, Artist's obligations hereunder are subject to detention or prevention by sickness, inability to perform, accident, means of transportation, Acts of God, riots, strikes, labor difficulties, epidemics, any act or order of any public authority or any other cause, similar or dissimilar beyond Artist's difficulties, epidemics, any act or order of any public authority or any other cause, similar or dissimilar beyond Artist's control.

Section 4.3. Inclement Weather

Inclement weather rendering performance impossible, unfeasible or unsafe shall not be deemed a force majeure event and payment of the agreed upon compensation shall be made notwithstanding, provided Artist is present, ready, willing and able to perform. If Purchaser and Artist disagree as to whether rendition of performance(s) is impossible, not feasible or unsafe because of inclement weather, Artist's joint determination with Purchaser as to performance shall prevail.

Section 4.4. Purchaser's Right to Terminate

Unless stipulated to the contrary in writing, Artist agrees that Purchaser may cancel the engagement hereunder without liability by giving the Artist notice thereof at least thirty (30) days prior to the commencement date of the engagement hereunder. If the Purchaser cancels this Agreement pursuant to this paragraph, Purchaser shall reimburse Artist for all reasonable expenses incurred from promoting the performances to have been made under this Agreement and Purchaser shall not be entitled to a refund of any deposit already paid to Artist.

Section 4.5. Artist's Right to Terminate

Artist shall also have the right to terminate this Agreement without liability in the event Purchaser fails to sign and return this Contract within ten (10) days. Unless stipulated to the contrary in writing, Purchaser agrees that Artist may cancel the engagement hereunder without liability by giving the Purchaser notice thereof at least thirty (30) days prior to the commencement date of the engagement hereunder. If Artist terminates this Agreement pursuant to this paragraph, Artist shall reimburse Purchaser for all reasonable expenses incurred from promoting the performances to have been made under this Agreement and Artist shall return any deposit received from Purchaser pursuant to this Agreement within seven (7) days.

Section 4.6. Dispute Resolution

Any claim or dispute arising out of or relating to this Agreement or the breach thereof shall be settled by arbitration in accordance with the rules and regulations then obtaining of the American Arbitration Association governing panels. The parties hereto agree to be bound by the award of such arbitration and judgment upon the award rendered by the arbitrators may be entered in any court have jurisdiction thereof.

ARTICLE V. LIMITATION OF LIABILITY

Section 5.1. Insurance

Purchaser agrees to provide at least two (2) weeks prior to the performance, a certificate of insurance as evidence of comprehensive general liability insurance in the amount required by the venue, but, in no event, with a limit less than Two Million Dollars U.S. ($2,000,000), for bodily injury and property damage, with both Elegant Ball Tour, Inc. and Lady Dada added to said policy as additionally-named insured

Section 5.2. Mutual Indemnification and Release

The Purchaser and Artist agree, to the fullest extent permitted by law, to mutually indemnify and hold harmless the other party, its officers, directors, agents and employees against any and all damages, liabilities or costs, including reasonable attorney's fees and defense costs to the extent they are proximately caused by its negligent or intentionally wrongful performance of services under this Agreement. Neither the Purchaser nor the Artist, however, shall be obligated to indemnify the other party in any manner whatsoever for the other party's negligence.

Section 5.3. Damage by Others

Artist shall not be responsible for damage or injury to any patrons or the venue or any fixtures or personal property therein caused by fans or any other persons other than members of Artist's band or the band of any Supporting Act, unless such damage was the result of negligence on behalf of the Artist or its representatives. Purchaser shall indemnify and hold Artist harmless from any third-party claims concerning the foregoing (as provided above), and no claim, deduction, or offset shall be made by Purchaser in respect of same.

ARTICLE VI. GENERAL PROVISIONS

Section 5.1. Applicable Law; Conflict in Laws

Ohio law shall control all conflicts arising out of this agreement, except as set forth below. Nothing in this agreement shall require the commission of any act contrary to law or to any rules or regulations of any union guild or similar body having jurisdiction over the services and personnel to be furnished by the Purchaser to Artist hereunder. If there is any conflict between any provision of this Agreement and any law, rule or regulation, such law, rule or regulation shall prevail and this Agreement shall be curtailed, modified, limited onto to the extent necessary to eliminate such conflict. Artist agrees to comply with all relevant regulations and requirements of any union(s) that may have jurisdiction over any of the said materials, facilities and personnel to be furnished by Purchaser.

Section 5.2. Entire Agreement

This Agreement constitutes the enter agreement between the parties with respect to any matter referenced herein and supersedes any and all other prior writings and oral negotiations. The terms of this Agreement shall prevail over any inconsistent provision in any other contract document appurtenant hereto, including appendixes to this Agreement.

Section 5.3. Modification

This Agreement may only be modified in writing and signed by the parties in interest at the time of such modification.

Section 5.4. Notices

Any notices, documents, correspondence or other communications concerning this Agreement may be provided by personal delivery, facsimile or certified mail and shall be addressed as set forth below. Such communication shall be deemed served or delivered: (a) at the time of delivery if such communication is sent by personal delivery; (b) at the time of transmission if such communication is sent by facsimile; and (c) 48 hours after deposit in the U.S. Mail as reflected by the official U.S. postmark if such communication is sent through regular United States mail.

IF TO ARTIST	IF TO PURCHASER
Elegant Ball Tour, Inc.	Madison Square Garden
199 W 57th St #6	4 Penn Plaza, Suite 21
New York, NY 10019	New York, NY 10121
Attn: Bob Sugar	Attn: James Dougan
Tour Manager	Special Events Coordinator

Section 5.5. Assignment

This contract (a) cannot be assigned or transferred without the written consent of PURCHASER, (b) contains the sole and complete understanding of the parties hereto and (c) may not be amended, supplemented, varied or discharged, except by an instrument in writing signed by both parties. The validity, construction, and effect of this contract shall be governed by the laws of the Ingham Co, MI apply and prevail, regardless of the place or performance, per Accepted Offer. AS AMENDED AND TOGETHER WITH ACCEPTED OFFER, THE PERSON EXECUTING THIS AGREEMENT ON PURCHASER'S BEHALF WARRANTS HIS/HER AUTHORITY TO DO SO. The terms "PUCHASER" and "ARTIST" as used herein shall include and apply to the singular, the plural and to all genders, and any authorized representatives thereof.

Section 5.6. Interpretation; Authority for Inconsistencies

In the event of any inconsistency between the provisions of this contract and the provisions of any riders, addenda, exhibits or any other attachments hereto, the parties agree that the provisions, as amended and executed by both parties, shall control.

Section 5.7. Severability

If any provision of this Agreement is determined by a court of competent jurisdiction to be unenforceable in any circumstance, such determination shall not affect the validity or enforceability of the remaining terms and provisions hereof or of the offending provision in any other circumstance.

Section 5.8. Artist's Status as Independent Contractor

It is agreed that Artist signs this Contract as an independent contractor and not as an employee of Purchaser. This contract shall not, in any way be construed so as to create a partnership, or any kind of joint undertaking or venture between the parties hereto, nor make Purchaser liable in whole or in part for any obligation that may be incurred by Artist in Artist's carrying out any of the provisions hereof or otherwise, unless explicitly stated in this Agreement or subsequently agreed to in writing.

IN WITNESS WHEREOF, the parties have executed this Contract for Personal Services.

ARTIST	PURCHASER
Elegant Ball Tour, Inc.	Madison Square Garden
Bob Sugar	James Dougan
Tour Manager	Special Events Coordinator
x____________________	x____________________
Date __________	Date __________

For guidance on both of the Hypotheticals above, please see the "Exemplar" Student Group response in the Teacher's Manual that accompanies this supplement.

Negotiating and Drafting Sports-Venue Celebrity Softball Games

I. Introduction

Star-studded celebrity sports event fundraisers have seen massive growth and popularity in recent years. From celebrity golf tournaments to celebrity softball games, each year these events prove to be more star-studded and bigger than the last. Fans jump at the chance to see A-List sports celebrities even if they are not competing in their traditional sports setting. Beyond the opportunity to see A-List sports superstars competing out of their everyday sports setting lies the opportunity to raise significant donations for various charitable organizations and purposes. However, the charities alone are not the only individuals to benefit. With hosting any celebrity sports event lies the opportunity for venue owners and franchises to gain positive publicity and additional revenues from these non-traditional events. In particular, this Study Guide will explore the necessary agreements and terms involved in the context of a celebrity softball game.

II. Fundamental Aspects of the Event

A. *Stadium and Facilities*

Location of the celebrity softball game is a pivotal consideration. As in the previous Study Guide concerning Concert Agreements, one of the main questions involved in the planning of a celebrity softball game is: where will the event be located? However, in the context of a celebrity softball game, the venue selection is likely to be more limited. The Event Holder will need to secure a venue properly equipped with baseball or softball facilities. While Major League Baseball stadiums are an option, the Event Holder will most likely find a stadium with a smaller capacity and great availability, such as a minor league or college baseball stadium, to be preferable. This option will not only provide a more intimate atmosphere depending on the projected attendance, but will also have more reasonable operational costs.

Once a particular venue is agreed upon, there are various considerations between the Venue Owner and Event Holder to be negotiated in regard to the facilities. Questions that will need to be answered include: What areas of the stadium will be made available to the Participants and for what duration? What facilities may the Event Holder have to sell or use (e.g. raise donations by selling luxury boxes)? What areas and facilities will the Venue Owner retain rights to?

The Agreement will need to answer these questions with specificity and also grant access to the field, dugouts, locker rooms, common areas, and parking lot(s) for the duration of the celebrity softball game. Other areas such as clubhouses, luxury boxes, and VIP areas will likely be split between the Parties with the Venue Owner retaining rights to designated home areas and the Event Holder being granted designated visitor areas.

B. *Event Timeline*

The Venue Owner must ensure that the celebrity softball game does not conflict with the regular use of the stadium, including pre-season, in-season, and post-season games. The Venue Owner will be more apt to agree to the use of the stadium during the off-season. However, the Event Holder must negotiate a date with the availability of the celebrity participants in mind. Thus, the interests in securing a date to mutually benefit all individuals involved may be difficult. However, because the success of the event depends on the attendance of the sports superstars, the event will likely be scheduled during the majority of the participant's off-season. Therefore, the Venue Owner should incorporate a detailed Event Schedule to ensure the celebrity softball game does not conflict with its home team's games.

C. *Ensuring a Headliner and Participants*

The key to a successful celebrity sports event is securing an A-List sports superstar to headline the event. Venue Owners may prefer a local celebrity to increase attention to the event in the area. However, depending on the player's level of popularity, a national superstar may be better for the Event Holder to reach appearances by other top notch athletes. In any event, the headlining celebrity should appeal to the venue's demographic. If the Event Holder is given the right to select the headlining superstar, the Venue Owner may want to reserve the right to mutually agree upon other participants. Also, the likelihood of increasing participants may depend on the charitable cause. While the Event Holder will likely have already established the major charity for the event to benefit, the Venue Owner may want to negotiate that other smaller local charities benefit as well.

The finalized agreement between the parties should establish answers to questions such as: Who will be responsible for procuring and ensuring the appearance of the "headliner" and/or celebrity participants? How many sports superstars must be obtained and commit to appear, and by what date? Is there a certain scope to be defined that the participant must meet (i.e. NFL football player or any professional sport, current or retired, national or local, etc.)? The Venue Owner will also want to acknowledge within the Agreement that the Event Holder has, in conjunction with the guarantee of participation, secured the publicity rights to these individuals' name, image, and likeness for the purpose of promoting the celebrity softball event.

III. Rights, Duties, and Obligations of the Venue

A. Venue Rental Fee

Generally, the rental of a facility may only be procured by paying a negotiated or fixed rental fee. However, given the nature of a charitable fundraiser, many Venue Owners are likely to waive this standard fee and negotiate to obtain revenue elsewhere, as will be discussed hereafter. The benefits of charitable tax deductions, positive publicity, establishing connections within the professional sports world, and the ability to gain additional revenues from a non-traditional event at the facility outweighs the minimal loss incurred by the Venue Owner in waiving the venue rental fee. Additionally, the Event Holder can gain a significant bargaining chip in negotiations regarding sources of revenue and rights within the agreement with a guarantee for greater success and attraction.

IV. Rights, Duties, and Obligations of the Event Holder

A. Event Production Expenses

Various production expenses are involved in hosting any event at a stadium facility. When drafting, the Venue Owner should consider costs it may incur to run its facility for the celebrity softball event such as utilities, field maintenance, venue maintenance, staff, security, garbage, etc. The Venue Owner will likely request the Event Holder reimburse some, if not all, of these production expenses so that it does not sustain a deficit from hosting the event. The Event Holder will likely agree to pay said costs, so long as the Venue Owner agrees to other expenses such as participant uniforms and/or reserving sole rights to event merchandise or other revenue producing sources to be used for donations. However, the Venue Owner may offer to pay for additional expenses if a certain number of personal appearances by A-list celebrities, to be defined, are obtained and guaranteed by the Event Holder prior to an agreed upon date. Alternatively, the Venue Owner may negotiate that any of the production expenses may be conditional on the appearance of the participants.

B. Participant Expenses

Hosting a celebrity softball game is not an easy feat. The procurement of superstar athletes to participate in the event often involves persuading the athlete to attend by reimbursing many of his/her expenses. The parties should establish within the agreement who will be responsible for travel and airline costs, hotel accommodations, transportation, meals, and any other expense the professional athlete may request to be reimbursed. It is important to note that each of these expenses must be defined with specificity as to limit each to a certain scope. For example, the duration of the participant's hotel stay, the star grade of the hotel, the hotel's proximity to the event facility, and room inclusions, such as Internet, room service, and telephone calls, should be noted within.

C. *Cancellations by Participants*

Let's face it—sometimes sports superstars fail to meet expectations, including guaranteed attendance at a charity event. Therefore, it is crucial to include within the agreement whom should bear the risk of loss should a headliner, or other advertised participant, fail to appear. While many of those in attendance purchase tickets to a celebrity softball event to support a charitable cause, a number of fans and donors will not be shy to request a refund of their ticket value if the event ceases to exist or the event fails to include the celebrity participants who have been promoted to the public via the event advertisements. The Venue Owner will want the Event Holder to absolve all liability given their level of involvement and interest in obtaining the headliner and/or participant for the event. The Event Holder will likely want to carve out that they are not responsible for a failed appearance due to force majure, as defined by the agreement. Outside of this limited circumstance, the Event Holder will likely be responsible for refund requests of patrons for the celebrity softball event.

V. Revenue

A. *Ticket Sales*

Ticket sales to any event are a prime source of revenue. Because of the Venue Owner's likelihood to waive sources of revenue it generally obtains (i.e. venue rental fee), ticket sales remain a point of negotiation. The Venue Owner will request that the Event Holder pay all local and state taxes on ticket sales in conjunction with the event. Additionally, the Venue Owner may want to obtain a percentage of the revenues gained on such sales. The Event Holder will probably agree to pay such taxes, so long as they retain all ticket revenues from the game. However, the agreement should define who will have the right to sell the tickets to the celebrity softball event.

Furthermore, as similar to Concert Agreements, the parties will need to determine a pricing structure of tickets. Because of the baseball stadium setting, the pricing structure will likely follow different prices for seats in various locations of the facility. This pricing structure should define the number of the various levels of seats to be sold, including luxury suites, grandstands, baseline, upper-level deck, etc., and the corresponding rates. A coded map of the stadium with the corresponding areas and prices may be incorporated as an instructive exhibit to the agreement. The Venue Owner may want to negotiate to reserve a certain number of "complimentary tickets" to the celebrity softball game to provide to its regular baseball season ticket holders or within the franchise.

B. Sponsorships

A major funder of charitable events comes from those willing to sponsor the event itself. The Event Holder will want to retain all proceeds from the sponsors to cover the costs of holding the event and pledging the remaining funds towards its donative amount. However, the Venue Owner is likely to have local sponsors that the Event Holder may only procure with through the Venue Owner's communications and assistance. The Venue Owner will probably reach out to these potential sponsorship avenues to support the event so long as the Event Holder is willing to fund any costs incurred in doing so and/or split the net proceeds from the obtained sponsorship. The Event Holder may want to negotiate to reserve a Presenting Sponsor whose name is affiliated and incorporated with the charitable event. If the Venue Owner agrees to such provision, this option should prohibit any direct competitors to those already established in exclusivity with the Venue. The list of those holding exclusive rights in the stadium should be incorporated therein and attached as an exhibit to the agreement, including a definition of each sponsor's category it represents. Additionally, the Venue Owner may want to reserve the right to pre-approve sponsors the Event Holder obtains. While the Event Holder is likely to agree to this term, the agreement should establish that approval is not to be "unreasonably withheld" by the Venue Owner.

VI. Limiting Liability

A. Participant Release of Liability

The participants in such celebrity fundraising events have generally risen to stardom because of their athletic abilities within their respective professional sports setting. Thus, a potential problem presented is with injuries and accidents that may occur during the event. Participants risk having a negative effect on their skill and livelihood should a worst-case scenario injury occur during the event. Both the Event Holder and the Venue Owner will be in agreement that the participants sign an Individual Waiver of Liability where both are absolved of all liability of any injuries confirming that the participants are acknowledging and agreeing to "play at their own risk."

B. *Insurance*

It is inevitable—bad, unforeseen events can occur. Use of an indemnification clause can operate to prearrange who shall bear the costs of which liabilities.[44] Neither party wants to be liable for the negligence or acts of the other party. Thus, both the Venue Owner and the Event Holder will likely negotiate for mutual cross-indemnification provisions within the Agreement. Furthermore, each will benefit by requiring proof of insurance and a request to be named an as an additional insured party on the insurance policy. Please refer to the beginning of Appendix B on Premises Liability for a more in-depth discussion of such issues, provisions, considerations, and negotiation of these terms.

HYPOTHETICAL EXERCISE

Negotiating and Drafting a Celebrity Softball Game and Venue Rental Agreement

A. Imagine that NFL Superstar, Marquan Sinch ("Sinch"), has seen a surge in popularity since his winning Super Bowl performance in the 2014 season. Not only is Sinch an A-List sports celebrity, but he is also known in the league as one of the NFL's most charitable players. Sinch has decided to work with T.D. Makers Worldwide, LLC to hold the first ever "Marquan Sinch Celebrity Softball Tournament" (the "Softball Game") to generate awareness and donations for charitable causes.

B. Assume that the Ocean County Seagulls (the "Seagulls"), a minor league baseball team, plays at and owns Pacific Park, a venue in a suburban city close in proximity to Sinch's NFL Team's stadium. This is the only baseball stadium in the area.

   1. The venue has a seating capacity of approximately 10,000 seats.

   2. The playing field is natural grass, and there are three (3) home Seagulls games starting the day after of the celebrity softball event.

   3. Additionally, the facility offers luxury suites, home and visitor dugouts, locker rooms, two parking lots, a VIP grandstand, and two clubhouses.

C. Students should split into groups of four, with two members representing the Seagulls and two members representing the Softball Game.

---

[44] *See* Peter A. Carfagna, NEGOTIATING AND DRAFTING SPORTS VENUE AGREEMENTS 9–10 (2016) (discussing the essential terms and considerations to drafting and negotiating insurance and indemnification provisions).

D. Each subgroup should consider how they would negotiate and draft the following clauses.

1. Facilities

   a. Address the issue of what areas in Pacific Park are made available to whom. Additionally, consider any scheduling restrictions that may apply to the various designated areas usage.

2. Participants

   a. As stated above, assume Sinch has already agreed to be the headliner for the celebrity softball game. Negotiate and draft a clause guaranteeing his participation in the event including a grant for the parties to use his publicity rights in conjunction with the event.

   b. Address what party shall procure other participants. Is there a specific scope to what participants should be obtained?

   c. Address who is to bear the risk of loss if Sinch or other participants fail to attend. Is this clause limited to specific circumstances? Does the non-liable party have any available remedies?

3. Waiver and Release from Liability

   a. Assume the celebrity softball event's procurement of Sinch as a headliner has led to the guaranteed appearances from many of his NFL teammates. In particular, franchise quarterback, Randy Wilson, jumped at the chance to display his talents as a former baseball player while supporting a charitable cause.

   b. Assume that during his participation in the event, Randy Wilson was present on second base as both celebrity teams were tied in the bottom of the 9th inning. His next teammate up to the plate, Richard Sherbert, hit a line drive to right field and Randy Wilson eagerly circles toward home plate. While sliding into the home headfirst, the opposing team's catcher, G.G. Natt, goes for an aggressive tag out play. As a result, Randy Wilson suffers a severe injury to his elbow which will hold him out of NFL play for the majority of the season.

   c. Does Randy Wilson have a claim against the Seagulls for his injury? What about T.D. Makers Worldwide as the Event Holders?

d. Draft a clause that holds the Seagulls harmless from any liabilities arising from the above-described incident.

4. Mutual Indemnification and Insurance

a. Assume the Venue Owner is potentially liable for Wilson's injury, due to the Venue Owner's (alleged) negligent failure to provide a field that is "suitable for use," which arguably gets around the Waiver that Wilson would have signed.

b. Assume there was an intent to harm by GG Natt, the catcher who hurt Wilson.

c. Address if the Waiver protects the Venue Owner or the Event Holder if such events occurred? How would the mutual insurances and indemnification clauses respond if both parties are found to be "comparatively" at fault for Wilson's injury?

5. Playing Field

a. Assume the Venue Owner must provide a Playing Field that is "suitable for use as a Celebrity Softball Game" in the reasonable discretion of the Event Holder. There will be a "pre-approval" walkthrough by the Event Holder of the Facility, after which the Event Holder waives any right to make a claim/counterclaim versus the Venue Owner unless the Venue Owner engages in "gross negligence" or "intentional wrongdoing" in finally setting up the Field.

b. Assume Wilson gets hurt, and that the Venue Owner's Groundskeeper "negligently" leaves the lip of home plate tipped up, and that Wilson's sliding into that tip of the plate contributes to his injury, which is otherwise caused by GG Natt being "intentional" about injuring Wilson, as he slides into home.

c. Will a well-drafted "Limitation of Liability Clause" hold up between the Venue Owner and the Event Holder, in that case of catastrophic damage to Wilson's career, current/future endorsements, etc.?

Please see the Teacher's Manual for an "Exemplar" Student Group response to this Hypothetical.

Urging Stadium Owners and Venue Managers to Start Rethinking Reasonable Foreseeability in Premises Liability

I. Introduction

Tragic incidents occurring at stadiums that result in serious injury or death to spectators make for unwanted headlines from media outlets and even greater undesired potential litigation. As a result, stadium safety is becoming a topic of great concern. The primary types of incidents that lead to spectator injuries are: (1) fans falling over railings or down escalators; (2) fan violence occurring inside the stadium and at parking lots outside the stadium; and (3) objects leaving the field of play (i.e. foul balls and pucks). Although they are not as common, fireworks accidents are also a concern and will be discussed herein. The issue of stadium safety is gaining continued exposure, and this Chapter should serve as a reminder and update to everyone on the legal principles and related issues surrounding premise liability for stadium owners and venue managers.

II. Brief Conclusion

It would be prudent for stadium owners to start rethinking what is and is not reasonably foreseeable and consider ways to prevent those potential dangers in order to avoid potential future liability. Stadium safety continues to garner media attention, thus owners must realize the potential for courts to alter their stance of reasonable foreseeability particularly in the face of a sympathetic plaintiff.

III. Premises Liability Law

Premise liability laws potentially make owners or possessors of premises responsible for injuries suffered by people that are present on the premise. Thus, premise liability imposes a duty of care on these owners or possessors of premises to protect people that enter onto their property. Different standards of care apply to different types of people that enter onto the owner's premises. Sports spectators are considered business invitees. Often times this is a position agreed on by both the plaintiff and the defendant in injury cases.[45] This means stadium owners owe a reasonable duty of care to the spectators entering the premises. Furthermore, the business invitee rule extends to areas outside of the stands.[46] Under a reasonable duty of care standard, stadium owners have an obligation to inspect the premises for hazards, remove and repair dangerous conditions to make the facility reasonably safe, and to warn those on

---

[45] *Teixiera v. New Britain Baseball Club, Inc.*, 2006 WL 2413839, *2 (Superior Ct Conn. Jud. Dist. New Britain, 2006).

[46] *Maisonave v. Newark Bears Professional Baseball Club, Inc.*, 185 N.J. 70, 85 (N.J. 2005).

the premises of any hidden dangers that are reasonably foreseeable.[47] Moreover, under a reasonable duty of care standard, "stadium owners are not insurers of safety, however, they must exercise reasonable care for anything that threatens or could potentially threaten an invite with an unreasonable risk of harm."[48] In other words, the mere occurrence of an accident by itself does not give rise to negligence. Thus, a plaintiff will have to show that the stadium owner breached the above-mentioned duty of care in order to recover.

A. *Reasonable Foreseeability*

The key distinction in virtually all litigation turns on whether the incident was reasonably foreseeable. A voluntary participant in a sporting or entertainment pursuit consents to the risk of those injury-causing events which are known, apparent or reasonably foreseeable consequences of the participation.[49] The scope of reasonable foreseeability is when the action of spectators are so likely based on past experience that a reasonably attentive landowner should have taken steps to prevent or reduce the risk of harm that might result.[50] However, an event will not be reasonably foreseeable if there is a superseding act. For example, criminal acts by third parties are generally considered to be superseding acts that are not reasonably foreseeable. Ordinarily, the duty of a landowner is to respond reasonably to situations occurring on the premises because, as a matter of public policy, owners should not be expected to assume that others disobey the law.[51] However, it is important to keep in mind that some jurisdictions have ruled criminal acts to be foreseeable when evidence of prior crimes is present. In determining foreseeability, the courts weigh the evidence of prior crimes by using five factors: 1) proximity, 2) publicity, 3) recency, 4) frequency, and 5) similarity.[52] Comment f to Restatement of Torts § 344 provides an excellent illustration:

> He may, however, know or have reason to know, from past experience, that there is a likelihood of conduct on the part of third persons on general which is likely to endanger the

---

47 Restatement (Second) of Torts § 343 (1965).

48 Peter Prigge, "Stow Lawsuit Could Have Significant Impact on MLB Franchises and Stadium Liability," *SPORTS LAW 101* (Jan. 31, 2012), http://www.sportsmedia101.com/sportslaw/2012/01/31/stow-lawsuit-could-have-significant-impact-on-mlb-franchises-and-stadium-liability/.

49 *Minho Hahn v. Town of West Haverstraw, NY*, 2014 WL 1613032, *1 (2nd Cir.2014) *quoting Turcotte v. Fell*, 68 N.Y.2d 432, 439 (NY, 1986).

50 Peter Prigge, "Stow Lawsuit Could Have Significant Impact on MLB Franchises and Stadium Liability," *SPORTS LAW 101* (Jan. 31, 2012), http://www.sportsmedia101.com/sportslaw/2012/01/31/stow-lawsuit-could-have-significant-impact-on-mlb-franchises-and-stadium-liability/.

51 *MacDonald v. PKT, Inc.* 464 Mich. 322, 337 (Mich. 2001).

52 62 AM. JUR. (Second) Premises Liability § 47.

> safety of the visitor, even though he has no reason to expect it on the part of any particular individual. If the place or character of his business, or his past experience, is such that he should reasonably anticipate careless or criminal conduct on the part of third persons, either generally or at some particular time, he may be under a duty to take precautions against it, and to provide a reasonably sufficient number of servants to afford a reasonable protection.[53]

1. *Crowd Control*

The reasonable duty of care also imposes a duty on the stadium owner to deal with crowd control, which may be imposed where there is inadequate crowd management.[54] Owners have a duty to exercise reasonable care to prevent injury on its premises when the owner has the opportunity to control the conduct giving rise to the injury and the owner is reasonably aware he or she needs to control the conduct.[55] An interesting issue venue operators are beginning to face is the degree to which a heightened atmosphere created by an excited crowd increases foreseeability, resulting in a greater duty for more effective crowd control. Two cases, both involving New York law, may help us understand what the law truly demands. In *Rotz*, the plaintiff sued the City of New York for injuries sustained during a stampede which erupted during a Diana Ross concert held in Central Park.[56] The Court here noted that the plaintiffs generally would not be able to bring a claim that was predicated upon insufficient police protection.[57] However, the plaintiffs would be able to bring a claim predicated on the City's negligence as owner and operator of the park. [58] The Court here determined the duty owed as owner operator includes the obligation to provide an adequate degree of supervision of the spectators invited into the event.[59] Furthermore, the Court went on to dismiss defendant's summary judgment motion holding that a jury could find that a riot or stampede would be reasonably foreseeable in the absence of proper crowd control.[60]

---

53 Restatement (Second) of Torts § 344 cmt. f (1965).

54 *See Rotz v. City of New York*, 143 A.D.2d 301 (1st Dept. 1988) (holding New York City liable as owner/operator of venue for injuries to spectator as a result of ineffective crowd management).

55 Restatement (Second) of Torts § 343 (1965).

56 Robert Kelner & Gail Kelner, "Crowds, Violence, and Tort Liability," Kelner & Kelner (2015), http://www.kelnerlaw.com/pages/crowds-violence-and-tort-liability.

57 *Id.*

58 *Id.*

59 *Id.*

60 *Id.*

In a separate and opposite case, however, the Court granted summary judgment to the defendant where the plaintiff was injured when she was allegedly pushed down a very crowded stairway as she and others were exiting the circus.[61] Here the Court stated "where a plaintiff's negligence claim is premised on the theory that his or her injuries were caused by overcrowding and inadequate crowd control, the plaintiff must establish that he was unable to find a place of safety or that his free movement was restricted due to the alleged overcrowding conditions."[62] Put very simply, insufficient evidence was presented to suggest the plaintiff's movement was unduly restricted or that she was unable to find safety; therefore, summary judgment was granted for the defendant.[63] The concept of heightened foreseeability will continue to be talked about here but also keep in mind the potential repercussions in future cases.[64]

In assessing liability of stadium owners in crowd violence cases, ordinarily the criminal acts of third parties are considered superseding causes sufficient to exonerate a stadium owner's liability. However, criminal conduct by a third party has not always been found to be a superseding cause. In *Ventrone v. Ha Di Corporation*, a security guard was injured at the hands of angered guests not allowed to enter a New Year's party that was filled beyond its capacity.[65] The court noted that:

> The fact that the third person's acts may constitute criminal conduct does not necessarily make them a superseding cause as a matter of law and to the contrary, intervening criminal acts may still give rise to liability.[66]

In refusing to grant the defendant's motion to dismiss, the court concluded that it could not be determined as a matter of law that the assault on the security guard was unforeseeable and could indeed be the consequences of the defendant's conduct in overselling the event.[67] The Bryan Stow case discussed later in this Chapter will provide an even more recent and clearer example of how teams can still be liable despite criminal actions.

---

61 *Palmieri v. Ringling Bros. and Barnum and Bailey Combined Shows Inc.*, 237 A.D.2d 589 (2nd. Dept. 1997).

62 *Id.*

63 *Id.*

64 *See e.g.* Patrick Cooley, "Body of Cory Barron found in Lorain County Landfill," *CLEVELAND.com* (July 22, 2014) http://www.cleveland.com/metro/index.ssf/2014/07/body_of_cory_barron_found_in_l.html (discussing man who went missing at a concert at Progressive Field and was later found dead in a landfill).

65 Robert Kelner & Gail Kelner, "Crowds, Violence, and Tort Liability," Kelner & Kelner (2015), http://www.kelnerlaw.com/pages/crowds-violence-and-tort-liability.

66 *Id.*

67 *Id.*

Violence amongst fans before and during sporting events is certainly not a new phenomenon; however, some would say that the problem has gotten exponentially worse over the recent years. In the wake of the Bryan Stow incident, California proposed legislation known as the "Improving Personal Safety at Stadiums Act" that would create a ban list that would prohibit violent fans from being permitted to attend professional games for five years.[68] Under the proposed bill, the fan's picture and name are sent to stadiums and ticket vendors and any attempt to violate the ban could result in an additional five to twenty-five years.[69] Like California, the NFL has instituted a program where it places undercover police officers in opposing teams' gear in an attempt to catch fans that subject visiting team's fans to mistreatment.[70] However, unlike the California proposed bill, the NFL does not prohibit unruly fans from attending future games if the fans simply pass a four-hour online course and a code of conduct exam.[71]

2. *Building Codes*

The International Building Code calls for 42-inch railings at the base of isles, but only a 26-inch front of foxed seating, regardless of the potential fall distance.[72] The 26-inch minimum height standard was codified in 1929 and sets the safety standard for all types of venues.[73] In premise liability law, code compliance is evidence of reasonableness. As such, the 26-inch standard, codified in 1929, was designed mainly for theaters and symphony halls with its primary focus on preserving site line to the stage. This was at a time when large-scale sports stadiums were an unfamiliar phenomenon. Thus as stadium safety continues to gain media exposure, combined with the recent emergence of billion dollar stadiums, stadium owners may potentially be no longer able to rely on code compliance as evidence of reasonableness since the standards arguably need to be revised to conform to modern facilities.

3. *Weather Conditions*

In the wake of the lighting incident before a Columbus Crew soccer game, it is perhaps prudent to look into what potential liability can

---

68 Assembly Bill No. 2464, California Legislative Info. (Sept. 7, 2012), *available at*: http://leginfo.legislature.ca.gov/faces/billNavClient.xhtml?bill_id=201120120AB2464.

69 *Id.*

70 Mike Florio, "Unruly fans must pass code-of-conduct exam to return to games," *NBC SPORTS* (April 15, 2012), http://profootballtalk.nbcsports.com/2012/04/15/unruly-fans-must-pass-code-of-conduct-exam-to-return-to-games.

71 *Id.*

72 Paul Lavigne, "Fans Split on Stadium Safety Changes," *ESPN* (Aug. 27, 2011), http://espn.go.com/espn/otl/story/_/id/6899698/mlb-stadium-deaths-officials-raising-railings-some-fans-disagree-changes.

73 *Id.*

come from this or similar incidents.[74] In *Sall v. T's, Inc.*,[75] the court ruled that the golf course owed a duty of care to protect golfers from the harm caused by lightning strikes on its golf course. The golf course voluntarily assumed the duty by employing a policy or procedures for monitoring the weather to protect patrons in the event of threatening inclement weather and by sounding an air horn to warn golfers on the course of approaching severe weather. The golfers relied on golf course to warn them of lightning. Therefore summary judgment for the defendants was denied in order to determine if the golf course was negligently performing its duty to monitor weather conditions and warn its patrons.[76] The general rule appears to be that if injury or damage results from an act of God and, concurrently, an act of negligence committed by a responsible person, such person cannot escape liability if the injury or damage would not have occurred except for that person's failure to exercise due care.[77] However, for example the Supreme Court of Ohio has stated, "while it has long been the rule of law in Ohio that a defendant cannot be held liable for an act of God which causes injury to the plaintiff, it has also long been the rule of law that if proper care and diligence on a defendant's part would have avoided the act, it is not excusable as the act of God."[78]

Finally, in regards to foreseeability, where a party whose duty it is to protect others from injury seeks to use "Act of God" as a defense against liability for injury or damage to such others, the defense is available only if the force of nature causing the injury or damage was not within the realm of ordinary human experience and could not have been foreseen or prevented by the use of due care. Since so many professional outdoor stadiums track for inclement weather, those operators must make sure to warn patrons in the event of a storm. Nevertheless one could argue Acts of God liability is fairly narrow since negligence also has to be the proximate cause of the injury.

B. Open and Obvious Danger Rule

A caveat to the reasonable foreseeability rule is the open and obvious danger rule. Under the open and obvious danger rule, an owner of land is not liable to invitees if the nature of the potential danger on

---

74 "Lightning Strikes Columbus Crew fan: game against Dallas postponed," *ASSOCIATED PRESS* (June 28, 2014), http://www.cleveland.com/sports/index.ssf/2014/06/lightning_strikes_columbus_cre.html.

75 *Sall v. T's, Inc.*, 281 Kan. 1355 (2006).

76 *Id.*

77 Jane Draper, "Personal injury or property damage caused by lightning as basis of tort liability," 46 A.L.R.4th 1170.

78 *Bier v. New Philadelphia*, 11 Ohio St 3d 134 (1984).

the property is open and obvious.[79] The rationale is that the open and obvious nature of the danger acts as a warning to the invitee and he is expected to recognize the potential danger and guard against it.[80] However, when special conditions make an open and obvious risk unreasonably dangerous, the owner has a duty to take reasonable precautions to mitigate the unreasonable risk.[81] The *Tang* case, which will be discussed, is a nice illustration of how courts will not impose liability on stadium owners where the danger was open and obvious.

However, even when a danger is open and obvious, there are two exceptions to the rule that could be relevant in cases against stadium owners.

1. The Distraction Exception

The open and obvious danger rule does not apply if the landowner has the reason to know that the invitee's attention was distracted, resulting in the invitee failing to discover the open and obvious danger or forgetting about the danger and failing to protect against the danger. To prevail under the distraction exception, a plaintiff will have to show that a stadium owner should have expected that something on the property would cause a careful person to become distracted. Simply saying that a person was not paying attention is not sufficient; a condition on the property must cause the person to not pay attention to his surroundings. For example, in one case, a football stadium invitee brought a negligence action against Park District alleging he was pushed over the railing of the exit ramps while exiting the stadium in extreme crowd conditions. The court ruled that even if such danger could be considered open and obvious, the obviousness of the risk did not absolve the park district from all responsibility because: (1) plaintiff had the major distraction of crowding such that his movements were literally controlled by the force of the crowd, and this type of frustration would cause an invitee's attention to be distracted; and (2) Park District was aware that at every game some fans proceeded to jump over the open air railings to escape the crowds, despite the risk.[82] However in another case where a spectator was distracted by a mascot's antics and was hit by a foul ball, the court denied plaintiff recovery because she had been warned about foul balls and could have avoided it if she was

---

79 Mohit Khare, "Foul Ball! The Need to Alter Current Liability Standards for Spectator Injuries at Sporting Events," 12 Tex. Rev. Ent. & Sports L. 91, 96 (2010).

80 *Id.* at 97.

81 Walter Champion, Fundamentals of Sports Law § 7:4.

82 *Boll v. Chicago Park Dist.*, 249 Ill App 3d 952 (1st Dist 1991).

paying attention.[83] This exception is important to keep in mind not only in planning the entertainment aspect of sporting events but also in dealing with the practical realities of the crowd.

2. *Deliberate-Encounter Exception*

The open and obvious rule also does not apply if the landowner has reason to expect that the invitee will proceed to encounter an open and obvious danger because, to a reasonable person in the invitee's position, the advantage of doing so outweighs the apparent risk. Furthermore, as with the distraction exception, the focus of the deliberate-encounter exception is on what the stadium owner anticipates or reasonably should anticipate the spectator will do. However no cases were found in the sports context in which this argument was made. Furthermore, even in the non-sports cases this argument was largely unsuccessful. Nevertheless the exception itself does exist in the law and at the very least stadium owners should be aware of it.

3. *The Baseball Rule and Its Relation to the Open and Obvious Danger Concept*

Stadium owners have a duty to mitigate unreasonably dangerous risks. However, the baseball rule limits negligence liability for owners who screen in the most dangerous areas of the parks, usually behind home plate and areas where fans may reasonably expect to need extra protection. [84] In all other areas of the ballpark, invitees assume the risk of injury from foul balls and flying bats, which are considered open and obvious dangers inherent in the game of baseball.[85] The rule limits liability to areas of the stands that pose an unreasonable risk, regardless of whether the risk is open and obvious.[86] It affords the owners some protection to liability, but only to certain sections of the stadiums because applying the rule to the entire stadium would convert the reasonable protection for owners to immunity by eliminating liability for foreseeable and preventable injuries to spectators.[87]

This is particularly evident by the New Jersey Supreme Court's holding in *Maisonave v. Newark Bears Professional Baseball Club, Inc.*[88] stating the standard of care for areas of a baseball stadium

---

83 *Harting v. Dayton Dragons Professional Baseball Club, L.L.C.*, 171 Ohio App. 3d 319 (2nd Dist. 2007).

84 James Juliano & Alison Healey, "Update: ballpark liability and the baseball rule," *LEGALLY SPEAKING* (Winter 2009–10), http://www.legallyspeakingonline.com/archive_winter09-10_update.html.

85 *Id.*

86 2005 No. 127 Premises Liability Alert 1.

87 *Id.*

88 *Maisonave v. Newark Bears Prof'l Baseball Club, Inc.*, 881 A.2d 700 (2005).

outside of the stands is not the baseball rule but, in fact, the business invitee rule.[89] In that case, a foul ball hit a spectator in the face as he was at the concession cart on the concourse of the stadium.[90] The court limited the application of the baseball rule to the stands of the ballpark, which was defined as the stairs that fans use to access their seats and to areas immediately adjacent designated solely to viewing the game.[91] The rationale was that stadium owners and venue managers are the ones in the best position to determine which areas of the stadium are the most dangerous giving them a duty to identify those areas and to take preventive measures to ensure fan safety to a reasonable extent.[92]

Under the baseball rule, courts generally hold a home team not to be liable to a spectator who is injured by certain inherent risks assumed with watching the game. "[I]t is not possible for baseball players to play the game without occasionally sending balls or bats into the stands," nor is it possible for a spectator to be protected against such risks without altering play or fan experience.[93] However, the *Coomer v. Kansas City Royals* case looked to answer the question: are other baseball related fan experiences covered under the baseball rule? On September 8, 2009, John Coomer, a Royals fan who had attended approximately 175 games in the past, decided to move from his assigned seat to an area behind the visitor dugout since attendance was low that day.[94] During the customary "Hot Dog Toss" in between innings, Coomer was struck in the eye by a hot dog thrown by Sluggerrr, the Royals mascot, causing Coomer's retina to detach.[95] Coomer brought suit for negligence and battery against the Royals.[96] The Court found the key issue of this case to be whether the incident causing Coomer's injury "involved some aspect of the game which is inevitable or unavoidable in the actual playing of the game."[97]

While mascots and customary entertainment is often found at a baseball game, the court ruled that Sluggerrr's hotdog toss was "not an inherent, inevitable or unavoidable part of watching a baseball

---

89 2005 No. 127 Premises Liability Alert 1.

90 *Id.*

91 *Id.*

92 *Id.*

93 Scott A. Andresen, "When a Wiener Can Make a Team a Loser: The Coomer v. Kansas City Royals Case," *SPORTS LITIGATION ALERT*, vol. 11 issue 14 (Aug. 8, 2014).

94 R. Douglas Manning, Ph.D., "Royal Pain: Flying hot dogs not a risk inherent in baseball (in Missouri)," *SPORTS LITIGATION ALERT*, vol. 11 issue 14 (Aug. 8, 2014).

95 *Id.*

96 Scott A. Andresen, "When a Wiener Can Make a Team a Loser: The Coomer v. Kansas City Royals Case," *SPORTS LITIGATION ALERT*, vol. 11 issue 14 (Aug. 8, 2014).

97 *Id.*

game."[98] Instead of being injured by a baseball or bat entering the stands, Coomer was hit by an object, a flying hot dog, totally disconnected from the actual playing of the game. A mascot and the team responsible for the mascot still owe its fans a duty of reasonable care in conducting such activities whether it be a hot dog toss or shooting t-shirts from an air gun. Thus, the question of whether Sluggerrr's eye injuring hot dog toss was negligent was deemed to be a question of fact for a jury to decided, as the court carved this mascot's injury as an act not afforded protection of the baseball rule.[99]

It should also be noted that the baseball rule has also been applied to the sport of hockey which, next to baseball, is the second most likely sporting event to be injured at.[100] Take the case of *Verneris v. Wang*, where a hockey puck struck a spectator.[101] Here, the issue was whether the baseball rule should also be applied to hockey.[102] The court ruled that the baseball rule should apply, and the owner met his duty by placing a higher wall of Plexiglas and protective netting over most dangerous area of stadium, the area behind goals and adequately warning spectators of the danger of errant pucks through disclaimers on tickets and an announcement over the public announcement system.[103]

While the baseball rule is currently the majority rule in jurisdictions it is important to recognize the minority jurisdictions and the possible changing of views. In the case of *Rountree v. Boise Baseball, LLC.*,[104] plaintiff lost an eye after being struck by a foul ball while attending a Boise Hawks game. At the time of incident, Rountree was eating in the Executive Club, an area at the very end of the third base line.[105] The entrance to the Executive Club had no warnings regarding the dangers of being struck by foul balls and Rountree claimed he never read the back of his ticket prior to the injury. The ticket contained the following language: "THE HOLDER ASSUMES

---

98 Scott A. Andresen, "When a Wiener Can Make a Team a Loser: The Coomer v. Kansas City Royals Case," *SPORTS LITIGATION ALERT*, vol. 11 issue 14 (Aug. 8, 2014).

99 R. Douglas Manning, Ph.D., "Royal Pain: Flying hot dogs not a risk inherent in baseball (in Missouri)," *SPORTS LITIGATION ALERT*, vol. 11 issue 14 (Aug. 8, 2014).

100 Leigh Augustine, "Who is Responsible when Spectators are Injured while Attending Professional Sporting Events?," http://www.law.du.edu/documents/sports-and-entertainment-law-journal/issues/05/05-Augustine.pdf.

101 *Verneris v. Wang*, No. CV075014070, 2010 WL 1546049 (Conn. Super. Ct. Mar. 19, 2010).

102 *Id.*

103 *Id.*

104 Rountree v. Boise Baseball, LLC, 154 Idaho 167 (2013).

105 James C. Kozlowski, "Majority 'Baseball Rule' Limits Spectator Liability," *LAW REVIEW* 5 (May 2013), *available at* http://cehdclass.gmu.edu/jkozlows/lawarts/05MAY13.pdf.

ALL RISK AND DANGERS INCIDENTAL TO THE GAME OF BASEBALL INCLUDING SPECIFICALLY (BUT NOT EXCLUSIVELY) THE DANGER OF BEING INJURED BY THROWN OR BATTED BALLS."[106] The Idaho Supreme Court would go on to affirm the decision of the district court which had refused to adopt the baseball rule. Rountree's lawsuit was, allowed to proceed to trial. At trial, the jury applied general legal principles governing a landowner's liability for negligence to determine whether Boise Baseball was responsible for Rountree's injury.[107] Rountree also claimed that the baseball rule was being rapidly abandoned.[108] Although rapidly may be an exaggeration it is still plausible to think a jurisdiction may likewise refuse to apply the baseball rule in the near future.

C. *Spectator Fall Cases and Railing Height*

As mention earlier, ordinarily compliance with the applicable building codes is evidence of reasonableness. However, given the age of these building codes it is prudent to ask if the standards for railing heights are still reasonable today. Certainly the fact that many stadiums choose to raise their railing heights in the wake of incidents could tell us that the code is not as reasonable as it once was. Do the exceptions to the open and obvious rule apply to railing heights, and how does one strike to perfect balance between optimal safety and preservation of the sight lines to the field? These appear to be the main issues related to railing heights. Amazingly even fans that happen to be friends or family members of the deceased as a result of falling are split on whether the railing heights should be raised.[109] Since 2003, there have been more than two-dozen cases of fans falling at stadiums across the United States according to the Institute for the Study of Sports Incidents. However, even the experts say this does not mean stadiums are unsafe.[110] Nevertheless litigation is almost inevitable in the wake of one of these tragic incidents so knowledge of precedent is essential particularly given the apparent frequency of these incidents.[111]

---

[106] *Id.*

[107] *Id.* at 8.

[108] *Id.* at 6.

[109] Lavigne, "Fans Split on Stadium Safety Changes," *ESPN* (Aug. 27, 2011), http://espn.go.com/espn/otl/story/_/id/6899698/mlb-stadium-deaths-officials-raising-railings-some-fans-disagree-changes.

[110] Nancy Armour, "There's no way to totally prevent deadly falls at stadiums," *THE ASSOCIATED PRESS* (Aug. 14, 2013), http://www.sltrib.com/sltrib/sports/56733317-77/homer-safety-stadiums-death.html.csp.

[111] Madison Hartman, et. al., "Man Falls from Citi Field Party City deck before Mets-Giants game," *NEW YORK DAILY NEWS* (Aug. 2, 2014), http://www.nydailynews.com/sports/baseball/mets/fan-falls-party-city-deck-mets-game-witnesses-article-1.1889843.

D. *Shannon Stone Case*

On July 7, 2011, as his six-year old son watched, Shannon Stone fell to his death when he reached over a 33-inch railing (higher than the minimum required height) and lost his balance while attempting to catch a ball tossed by center fielder Josh Hamilton.[112] Stone was 6'3" and the 33-inch railing came to just below his waist.[113] After the incident the Rangers conducted an investigation and decided to implement several safety measures including raising the railing heights despite already being in compliance with the codes.[114] Not only did the Stone family not threaten litigation, they did not even want players to stop throwing balls into the stands.[115] The Stone family felt that the Rangers were not at fault and believed the incident was a complete accident.[116]

E. *Tang v. AEG*

On November 21, 2010, Lucas Tang, a two-year-old boy, fell 27 feet from a skybox at the Staples Center during a Laker's game.[117] Tang made his way over to the barrier as his family was reviewing pictures on a digital camera.[118] Tang's parents filed suit claiming AEG's negligence in the design of the skybox and that no posted warning signs created an unreasonable and dangerous condition.[119] However, the superior court dismissed the case and held that the arena operator was not responsible for the toddler's death. The judge ruled that the stadium operator had no duty to supervise the child and said the onus was on the parents to supervise the child.[120] The court found that it was not foreseeable that Mr. Tang and Ms. Nguyen would place Lucas in an open and obviously dangerous situation by putting

---

112 Stephan Hawkins, "Rangers Fan Dies After Falling Out of Stands During Game," *HUFFINGTON POST* (Sept. 6, 2011), http://www.huffingtonpost.com/2011/07/07 rangers-fan-dies_n_892943.html.

113 Paula Lavigne, "Fans Split on Stadium Safety Changes," *ESPN* (Aug. 27, 2011), http://espn.go.com/espn/otl/story/_/id/6899698/mlb-stadium-deaths-officials-raising-railings-some-fans-disagree-changes.

114 Nancy Armour, "There's no way to totally prevent deadly falls at stadiums," *THE ASSOCIATED PRESS* (Aug. 14, 2013), http://www.sltrib.com/sltrib/sports/56733317-77/homer-safety-stadiums-death.html.csp.

115 Sean Gregory, "The Rangers' Best Move: How Texas Remembers Shannon Stone," *TIME* (Oct. 21, 2011), http://keepingscore.blogs.time.com/2011/10/21/the-rangers-best-move-how-texas-remembers-shannon-stone/.

116 *Id.*

117 Frank Snepp & Colleen Williams, "New Details in Staples Toddle Death," *NBC L.A.* (Nov. 11, 2011), http://www.nbclosangeles.com/news/local/Staples-Center-Toddler-Death-AEG-Lakers-NBA-133705873.html.

118 *Id.*

119 "Judge Dismisses Lawsuit in Child's Death at Staples Center," *KTLA NEWS* (July 2, 2012), http://articles.orlandosentinel.com/2012-07-02/news/ktla-lakers-boy-falls_1_lucas-tang-luxury-box-aeg.

120 *Id.*

him on the beverage bar where it was easily foreseeable that he could climb over the tempered glass and fall.[121] However, on appeal AEG was replaced by L.A. Arena because this subsidiary of AEG owns and manages the Staples Center.[122] The Appeals court refused to dismiss the claim against L.A. Arena, sending the case back to trial. The court found that it was reasonably foreseeable that patrons such as the Tang family would view the shelf as something to stand on, and that someone falling from the height at Staples Center would be injured or killed. Thus, L.A. Arena had a duty to prevent people from misusing the shelf by using a taller glass barrier, or at least by placing warning signs instructing patrons not to sit or stand on the shelf. As a result, the case will proceed with the full trial previously denied to the Estate of Lucas Tang by the lower court.[123]

F. Mayfield v. Oklahoma State University

On December 9, 2011, Charlotte Mayfield, who was 66 years old, was attending her grandson's high school football game at Oklahoma State University's Boone Pickens Stadium.[124] While walking up to her seat, Charlotte slipped and fell backwards and subsequently died of head injuries sustained during the fall.[125] Charlotte's husband claimed that Oklahoma State demonstrated negligence in failing to maintain a safe environment for guests at the stadium. More specifically, he claimed the graduated size of the steps, lack of handrails, and uniform color of the steps contributed to the death of his wife.[126] The school's main argument for dismissal was that Oklahoma State has sovereign immunity from prosecution when participants in athletic contests are injured; however, the judge overruled the motion to dismiss the case, saying the main issue will be whether or not the school was negligent.[127]

---

[121] Denisse Salazar, "Lawsuit Dismissed in tot's fall at Lakers game," *THE ORANGE COUNTY REGISTER* (Aug. 21, 2013), http://www.ocregister.com/articles/lucas-361725-court-beverage.html.

[122] John T. Wolohan, "Death Sparks Lawsuit Over Codes, Staples Center Design," *ATHLETIC BUSINESS* (June 2014), http://www.athleticbusiness.com/civil-actions/child-death-lawsuit-cites-building-code-violations-design-defects.html.

[123] *Id.*

[124] Silas Allen, "Man Sues Oklahoma State University over Wife's Fatal Fall at Boone Pickens Stadium," *NEWSOK* (Oct. 10, 2012), http://newsok.com/man-sues-oklahoma-state-univeristy-over-wifes-fatal-fall-at-boone-pickens-stadium/article/3717672.

[125] *Id.*

[126] *Id.*

[127] Russell Hixson, "Judge overrules motion to dismiss Oklahoma State fall victim lawsuit," http://www.stwnewspress.com/local/x2056573554/Judge-overrules-motion-to-dismiss-Oklahoma-State-fall-victim-lawsuit.

IV. Spectator Fall Cases Contributed by Acts of the Injured Party

An important issue presented by these cases is whether excessive consumption of alcohol by the injured party is an intervening act or is reasonably foreseeable. This is because stadium owners have and continue to allow individuals into the facility even after they have consumed alcohol and/or drugs although many teams reserve the right to deny admission if the fan is already visibly intoxicated before entering the stadium.[128] Nevertheless the issue still exists as to whether a plaintiff could argue that a stadium owner owes a duty to protect them from reasonably foreseeable dangers once they have entered the facility despite maybe showing some signs of intoxication.

Furthermore, there is the issue of liability when stadium owners and/or vendors allow spectators to over consume alcohol at the game. From a liability standpoint, vendors should also be mindful of who and how much they serve. Liquor service liability, also known as dram shop liability, varies from state to state but generally holds the parties overseeing the sale of alcohol accountable if they serve a visibly-intoxicated patron who then causes or sustains injuries as a result of their intoxication.[129] At sporting events, alcohol vendors are typically owned and operated by the host team, meaning they may be potentially liable for deaths and injuries. However, every incident is different. Accidents will be appropriately investigated to determine if any negligence occurred by the team or vendor.[130]

A. *Isaac Grubb's Fall at the Georgia Dome*

On August 31, 2012, Isaac Grubb, a 20-year-old, fell 35 feet to his death over a 33-inch railing at the Georgia Dome.[131] Grubb, who authorities say was drinking before the game, but not during the game, fell while cheering for Tennessee's second touchdown.[132] The exact cause of the accident is still being investigated as the preliminary autopsy tested negative for drugs and alcohol, which is contrary to the police report.[133] However, the preliminary screen

---

128 http://www.brownsgab.com/2011/10/07/cleveland-browns-announce-new-rules-for-game-attendees/.

129 Nadeem Bezar, "Staying Safe at the Game: Sporting Events and Alcohol Liability," http://kolsbygordon.com/attorney-blogs/staying-safe-at-the-game-sporting-events-and-alcohol-liability/.

130 *Id.*

131 Maria White, "Fan Dies After Fall at Football Game," http://www.cnn.com/2012/09/01/us/georgia-fan-dies/index.html.

132 *Id.*

133 Jim Matheny, "Autopsy Obtained for Georgia Dome Fatal Fall Victim," *WBIR* (Oct. 1, 2012), http://archive.wbir.com/news/article/236905/2/Autopsy-obtained-for-Georgia-Dome-fatal-fall-victim.

cannot give a conclusive determination and further blood tests would be needed to truly determine if he was intoxicated or not.[134]

B. Jonathon Kelly's Fall at Reliant Stadium

On August 30, 2012, Jonathon Kelly, a 25-year-old man, fell to his death when trying to slide down the outside of the escalator's handrail at Reliant Stadium.[135] The escalator was immediately closed until technicians had the opportunity to inspect and make sure none of the equipment was faulty.[136] The final investigation did not conclude faulty equipment but rather stated that the death was an accident caused by him simply losing balance.[137] However, the final important caveat is that the medical examiner concluded that his BAC was .16 which is twice the legal limit.[138]

C. Robert Seamans' Fall at Coors Field

On May 24, 2011, Robert Seamans, a 27-year-old man, was attending a Rockies game at Coors Field when he died as a result of falling some 20 feet while trying to slide down a stair railing.[139] The autopsy report showed that a mix of drugs and alcohol played a significant part in his death.[140] Specifically, the report showed that Seamans had marijuana in his system and a BAC of .19. [141] Unlike Kelly, Seamans death did not prompt any kind of special review of the safety of Coors field.

D. Violence Cases and Crowd Control

The criminal acts of third parties and their ability to be reasonably foreseeable has become a key issue. The underlying sub-issue in the following cases appears to be to what degree a heightened atmosphere created by an excited crowd may increase foreseeability for crowd control? Also, to what extent do deficiencies in the stadium security make the stadium owners liable? An *Outside the Lines* piece by ESPN proposed the idea that stadium owners should have a duty

---

[134] *Id.*

[135] Maggie Hendricks, "25-year-old Jonathan Kelly Falls to His Death at Houston Texans Game," *YAHOO SPORTS* (Aug. 31, 2012), http://sports.yahoo.com/blogs/shutdown-corner/fan-falls-death-houston-texans-game-140708071--nfl.html.

[136] Chris Baldwin, "Dead fan fell three levels at Reliant Stadium: Details on 25-year-old victim's night at Texans game," *CULTURE MAP HOUSTON* (Aug. 31, 2012), http://houston.culturemap.com/news/sports/08-31-12-dead-fan-fell-three-stories-at-reliant-stadium-details-on-25-year-old-victims-night-at-texans-game/.

[137] "Man who Fell to Death at Texans Game at Reliant Stadium was Legally Drunk," *ABC HOUSTON* (Sept. 25, 2012), http://abc13.com/archive/8824687/.

[138] *Id.*

[139] Josh Hamilton, "Alcohol, drugs factored in fan's fatal fall," *ESPN* (Aug. 1, 2011), http://espn.go.com/mlb/story/_/id/6824651/alcohol-drugs-factored-fatal-fall-fan-coors-field/.

[140] *Id.*

[141] *Id.*

to people as they exit the stadium because of excessive alcohol sales during the game.[142] Furthermore, in the event of a sympathetic plaintiff, the stadium owners may be the only feasible party that can afford to pay the damages caused by an unable or unknown third party.

E. *Iacono v. MSG Holdings*

In this case, the plaintiff, a professional photographer, was injured while taking photographs during a boxing event as a riot broke out.[143] He argued that the owner was negligent for failing to provide reasonable security and in preventing the riot.[144] The basis of plaintiff's argument was that the venue operator was aware of the animosity between the two fighter's camps and still failed to implement reasonable security measures.[145] The New York Supreme Court denied the defendant's motion for summary judgment stating that in the absence of adequate crowd control, a jury could find it reasonably foreseeable that a riot could ensue in the heightened atmosphere of this boxing match, which is already predicated upon violence.[146]

F. *Bryan Stow Case*

On March 31, 2011, Brian Stow, a 42-year-old Giants fan, was beaten into a coma by two Dodgers' fans in the parking lot outside of Dodgers Stadium following the opening day game. As a result, Stow suffered significant brain damage.[147] Stow filed suit against the Dodgers claiming they were negligent in the lack of security in the parking lot or by the pickup area for taxis combined with inadequate lighting presenting a perfect opportunity to commit a variety of crimes. Additionally, Stow argued that the Dodgers' security should've escorted him to a taxi.[148] Stow's family sued former Dodgers owner Frank McCourt and the Dodgers organization claiming McCourt's lavish lifestyle and messy divorce as reasons why the Dodgers failed to provide adequate security detail.[149] The complaint also cited the

---

142 *Fan Violence*, ESPN Outside the Lines (Oct. 14, 2012), http://www.youtube.com/watch?v=EDAk4EVBNHg.

143 *Iacano v. MSG Holdings*, 2005 WL 1645480 (2005).

144 Robert Kelner & Gail Kelner, "Crowds, Violence, and Tort Liability," Kelner & Kelner (2015), http://www.kelnerlaw.com/pages/crowds-violence-and-tort-liability.

145 *Id.*

146 *Id.*

147 "Bryan Stow Progressing at Rehab," *ESPN* (Oct. 14, 2011), http://espn.go.com/mlb/story/_/id/7100232/beaten-san-francisco-giants-fan-bryan-stow-making-progress-amid-rehab.

148 "Bryan Stow Lawsuit: Stow's Family Sues Frank McCourt, Los Angeles Dodgers," *HUFFINGTON POST* (May 24, 2011), http://www.huffingtonpost.com/2011/05/24/bryan-stow-lawsuit-stows-_n_866376.html.

149 *Id.*

Dodgers' poor track record for securing the stadium, not only through the exposure of criminal acts but also the poor response times particularly in Stow's case where it was 10 to 15 minutes.[150] As Stow's attorney described, "Dodger Stadium got to a place where it was a total mess, there was a culture of violence and beer sales were off the charts."[151] However, the Dodgers insisted that responsibility for the beating in a parking lot belonged to Dodgers fans Louie Sanchez and Marvin Norwood, who later pleaded guilty to charges filed in the attack but also presented testimony that Stow's BAC was .18 percent.[152]

When the dust settled, the jury agreed that the Dodgers did not provide adequate security and ordered that the Dodgers pay roughly $14 million of the $18 million in damages awarded to Bryan Stow for lost earnings, medical expenses, pain and mental suffering.[153] The rest of the damages were assessed to the attackers, but interestingly enough Frank McCourt was absolved of all liability despite holding the Dodgers negligent.[154] However even after the incident and before the verdict, the Dodgers hired a consultant to develop a security blueprint for the stadium and its parking lots.[155] The L.A. County Supervisor also called for stricter limits on the sales of alcohol at Dodger Stadium and chastised the Dodgers lack of security.[156] As a result, the Dodgers and Los Angeles police increased their security at games, including adding more patrols and undercover officers wearing rival team jerseys.[157]

G. *The San Francisco 49ers and Oakland Raiders Brawl*

On August 20, 2011, during an annual preseason game between the San Francisco 49ers and Oakland Raiders, several fights broke out between fans that resulted in at least two shootings and one serious

---

150 *Id.*

151 "Bryan Stow jury mulling verdict," *ESPN* (June 26, 2014), http://espn.go.com/los-angeles/mlb/story/_/id/11140464/san-francisco-giants-fan-bryan-stow-seeks-least-372-million-damages-los-angeles-dodgers-trial-goes-jury?

152 *Id.*

153 "Stow jury absolves Frank McCourt," *ESPN* (July 10, 2014), http://espn.go.com/los-angeles/mlb/story/_/id/11196081/jury-finds-los-angeles-dodgers-negligent-beating-san-francisco-giants-fan-bryan-stow-absolves-owner-frank-mccourt?ex_cid=null.

154 *Id.*

155 Bill Shaikin, "Dodgers hire former police chief Bratton to come up with security plan," *LOS ANGELES TIMES*, April 6, 2011, http://articles.latimes.com/2011/apr/06/sports/la-sp-0407-dodgers-security-20110407.

156 "L.A. County supervisor wants curbs on alcohol sales, more security at Dodger Stadium," *LOS ANGELES TIMES*, http://latimesblogs.latimes.com/lanow/2011/04/official-wants-curbs-on-alcohol-sales-more-security-at-dodger-stadium.html.

157 "Jury finds Dodgers negligent in Bryan Stow beating, absolves Frank McCourt," *LOS ANGELES DAILY NEWS*, http://www.dailynews.com/general-news/2014 0709/jury-finds-dodgers-negligent-in-bryan-stow-beating-absolves-frank-mccourt.

beating.[158] A man that was beaten unconscious and the friend that was shot four times trying to rescue him sued the NFL, the 49ers, and the security company for negligence in failing to provide a safe atmosphere and failing to "proactively create an environment that was free from fighting, taunting, or threatening remarks or gestures and gang activity."[159] To show that the owners foresaw the violence, the plaintiffs cited warnings over the years, from the 49ers management to its players to not bring their families to the Raiders games.[160] Plaintiff first sued the team in San Francisco Superior Court in November 2011, a few months after the attack. He then filed a separate, nearly identical suit in California federal court in June 2013, adding the team's co-chairman John York as a defendant. Plaintiff voluntarily dismissed the state case two months later; however, the district court judge quickly dismissed the federal suit last October, finding he lacked jurisdiction because both Plaintiff and some of the team's owners are California residents. Plaintiff filed a new case in state court and also asked the court to set aside the dismissal of the 2011 suit.[161]

Although these procedural problems have stopped the case from making as much head way, it certainly seems plausible that a well pleaded case in the proper jurisdiction with evidence describing owner's knowledge of a significant risk could be very problematic.

V. Spectator Injuries Through Objects Leaving the Field of Play

Injuries as a result of flying objects are by far the most common injury to occur while watching a sporting event. One study found that during 127 National Hockey League games, pucks injured 122 people, 90 of which required stitches, and 57 of which required transport to a hospital emergency room. Another study found that injuries to Major League Baseball fans from foul balls occur at a rate of 35.1 injuries per million spectator visits.[162] Fortunately, for the owners these types of incidents are overwhelmingly decided in favor

---

158 "2 Shot, 1 Beaten At 49ers-Raiders Game," http://espn.go.com/los-angeles/mlb/story/_/id/11196081/jury-finds-los-angeles-dodgers-negligent-beating-san-francisco-giants-fan-bryan-stow-absolves-owner-frank-mccourt?ex_cid=null.

159 "Fan Sues NFL, 49ers for negligence following fan violence at Candlestick Park," *BUSINESS INSIDER*, http://www.businessinsider.com/fans-sue-nfl-49ers-for-negligence-following-fan-violence-at-candlestick-park-2012-8.

160 Mike Florio, "Fans Sue NFL, 49ers over injuries from beating, shooting," *NBC SPORTS* (Aug. 24, 2012), http://profootballtalk.nbcsports.com/2012/08/24/fans-sue-nfl-49ers-over-injuries-from-beating-shooting/.

161 Beth Winegarner, "49ers Say Fan Filed Gunshot Liability Suit Too Late," *LAW 360* (Feb. 25, 2014), http://www.law360.com/articles/513234/49ers-say-fan-filed-gun shot-liability-suit-too-late.

162 Leigh Augustine, "Who is Responsible when Spectators are Injured while Attending Professional Sporting Events," at 1.

of the stadium owners.[163] In order for an injured spectator succeed in a suit they must prove that the owner breached their limited duty of care and that the spectator did not assume the risk, both of which are powerful impediments to overcome.[164] The courts are increasingly broad in their definitions of what constitutes common or inherent risks of the game, and it does not seem to matter whether the injuries happened in pre-game warm-ups or during the actual game. Courts will find no duty exists in either instance. Further, if the state adopts a non-liability statute, the question of negligence and duty owed to the spectator will not make it very far.[165] When spectators attend professional sporting events, they assume the risks of the inherent dangers of the event including pucks, balls, bats or tires and other objects inherent to the game which may come off the playing field and cause bodily injury of even death, unless the venue owner/operator severely deviates from their duty of care.[166] The following cases from *Inadequate Protection of Spectator at Sporting Event*[167] should thoroughly demonstrate this point.

A. *Hobby v. City of Durham*

Ballpark was not liable in negligence for injuries that spectator sustained when she was hit by a foul ball, which occurred when ball bounced over stadium roof and hit her from behind. Ballpark provided a screened seating section, and it thus discharged its duty to spectator even if that screen did not protect her from injury. Spectator accepted common hazard incident to the game by choosing not to sit behind the protective netting, but instead electing to sit in a seat with some exposure to the risks of the game.[168]

B. *Rosenfeld v. Hudson Valley Stadium Corp.*

Spectator, who was struck by a foul ball while seated in a picnic area located within a minor league baseball stadium, failed to allege that she was struck in the area behind home plate or that the screening was not sufficient to provide adequate protection for as many spectators as may reasonably be expected to desire such seating in

---

[163] *See* "Woman hit in face by foul ball loses case against Ind. Independent league team," *WASHINGTON EXAMINER* (July 2, 2014), http://m.washingtonexaminer.com/woman-hit-in-face-by-foul-ball-loses-case-against-ind.-independent-league-team/article/feed/2146283.

[164] Matthew Ludden, *Take Me Out to the Ballgame. . .But Bring A Helmet: Reforming the "Baseball Rule" in Light of Recent Fan Injuries at Baseball Stadiums*, 24 Marq. Sports L. Rev. 123, 128–29 (Fall 2013).

[165] Leigh Augustine, "Who is Responsible when Spectators are Injured while Attending Professional Sporting Events," at 11.

[166] *Id.* at 12.

[167] Christopher Hall, "Inadequate Protection of Spectator at Sporting Event," *45 AM. JUR. PROOF OF FACTS 2D 407.*

[168] *Hobby v. City of Durham*, 569 S.E.2d 1 (2002).

the course of an ordinary game, as required to state a personal injury cause of action against stadium owner and stadium lessee.[169]

C. *Schneider v. American Hockey and Ice Skating Center, Inc.*

Hockey rink operator has a limited duty to provide a protected area for spectators who choose not to be exposed to the risk posed by flying pucks and to screen any spectator area that is subject to a high risk of injury from flying pucks. The critical circumstance that determines scope of the duty of an operator of a baseball field or hockey rink is that most spectators prefer to sit where they can have unobstructed view of the game and are willing to expose themselves to the risks posed by flying balls or pucks to obtain that view. It is not unreasonable to accommodate this preference, so long as the sports facility operator provides sufficient screened seats for those spectators who may be reasonably expected to request protected seats and also screens any seats that pose an unduly high risk of injury from flying balls or pucks.[170]

D. *Injury or Property Damage from Fireworks Displays*

In this modern age of sports, teams often implement pyrotechnics in the presentation of their team, in the celebration of score or victory, and in hosting an elaborate show after the game. Furthermore pyrotechnic displays have not only become more common at the professional level but now are also seen as early as the high school level.[171] The concerns regarding fireworks are fairly obvious as misfiring, fires, or falling debris can cause substantial personal injury and property damage.[172] With the significant risk present during pyrotechnics displays it is important that stadium owners understand the potential liability that can come in the wake of an accident. The courts have reached opposing conclusions, depending on the facts, as to whether nongovernmental operators of public fireworks displays causing injuries to spectators were or could be found liable under common-law principles for negligence. The courts often discussed whether spectators were placed too close or there was inadequate room for the apparatus, whether the firing apparatus was defective, whether the mortars were properly aimed, and whether the

---

169 *Rosenfeld v. Hudson Valley Stadium Corp.*, 885 N.Y.S.2d 338 (2009).

170 *Schneider v. Am. Hockey And Ice Skating Ctr., Inc.*, 777 A.2d 380 (App. Div. 2001).

171 Brian McDowell, "CHS Football still fireworks-free zone," *THE CHANUTE TRIBUNE* (Sept. 11, 2014), http://www.chanute.com/news/article_115dd514-3a05-11e4-bbc7-001a4bcf6878.html.

172 *See* Tom Kisken, "Fireworks Accidents Spark Debate Over Dazzling Displays," *VENTURA COUNTY STAR* (Sept. 14, 2013), http://www.huffingtonpost.com/2013/07/15/fireworks-accidents-debate_n_3593295.html.

firing was done in a hurried manner.[173] However the government may also be the promoter of a fireworks display, and thus courts have generally held that governmental operators or promoters of public fireworks displays could not be found liable at common law for injuries to spectators based on principles of government tort immunity.[174]

Regarding potential tort claims, there are competing theories on whether strict liability or negligence standards should be applied. Under your typical negligence claim, liability must be predicated upon the proof of negligence. The producer of a public fireworks exhibition has a duty to use the care and prudence of a reasonably prudent and intelligent man in providing a reasonably safe place for spectators and in protecting them from unnecessary risks of harm. Although, the mere happening of an accident at such an exhibition is not proof of negligence, and negligence will not be presumed.[175] Thus, a person who put on a public fireworks display in a reasonably safe area under the proper supervision could not be held liable for injuries sustained by certain spectators due to latent defects in the fireworks themselves.[176] For example, Ohio follows this negligence standard, and a defendant is generally not liable for injuries caused as a result of a fireworks display unless the negligence results in a foreseeable injury to the plaintiff.[177]

However in jurisdictions where absolute or strict liability is the standard, no proof of negligence is needed. Strict liability is imposed for ultra-hazardous or abnormally dangerous products or activities and, in the sports context, is only really seen for explosions/pyrotechnics and wild animal mascots.[178] An example of a state that considers fireworks to be abnormally dangerous is the state of Washington. In *Klein v. Pyrodyne Corp.*, the court found the fireworks company strictly liable and ordered them to pay all damages caused by the fireworks display regardless of whether or not they were caused by negligence.[179]

Regardless of what standard is applied, before a large public fireworks display can commence, the stadium owners must first

---

173 Jay M. Zitter, *Common Law Liability for Injury Caused by Fireworks or Firecracker*, 21 A.L.R.6th 81, § 2 (2007).

174 *Id.*

175 *Haddon v. Lotito*, 399 Pa. 521, 525 (1960).

176 *Id.*

177 *Self v. American Legion Post No. 389*, 29 Ohio App.2d 189, 192 (4th Dist. 1972). *See also* § 10:52. Dangerous instrumentalities-Fireworks, Baldwin's Oh. Prac. Tort L. § 10:52 (2d ed.).

178 Adam Epstein, "Teaching Torts with Sports," *JOURNAL OF LEGAL STUDIES EDUCATION*, vol. 28.1, p. 140 (2011).

179 *Klein v. Pyrodyne Corp.*, 117 Wash.2d 1, 18 (Wash. 1991) *En Banc*.

obtain a permit in their governing county. These permit applications not only contain information regarding when the display will take place and who will operate the fireworks but also generally contain proof of insurance and proof that the fireworks operator is licensed in that jurisdiction. Aside from being required by state law, it would also be wise to contractually require the fireworks company to obtain a commercial general liability policy that will cover potential accidents and tort liability. Provided the company adheres to the policy and the jurisdiction mandated safety procedures, the insurance company will be unable to deny coverage in the event of a misfiring.[180] The following case law further illustrates the steps/precautions stadium owners should take regarding their fireworks displays. Since sports stadiums are often owned by the city and leased by the team and fireworks are conducted by independent contractors, several government and non-government entities are involved. The first two cases illustrate the city's potential liability and next two focus more on the team's liability based on their relationship with the fireworks contractor.

E. Costello By & Through Costello v. Pittsburgh Athletic Co.

Here, spectators at a baseball game were injured when a rocket landed in the stands during a postgame fireworks display.[181] The court held that the city was entitled to summary judgment on the ground of sovereign immunity.[182] The plaintiffs contended that the claim against the city fell within an exception for the care, custody, or control of real property. However, the stadium was not under the care, custody, or possession of the city, but rather a stadium authority was the owner of the real property, and the authority, the baseball club, and a management company had custody and control of the stadium.[183] The court rejected the argument that since the authority was created and funded by the city and its board appointed by the mayor, and that as a creature of the city its possession and control established the city's possession and control and maintained that the city and authority were separate entities.[184] The plaintiffs also argued that the stadium was under the city's custody and control because the city fire department inspected and approved the fireworks and permitted the display to go on. The court responded that these averments amounted to no more than a failure to properly inspect or supervise, and that would not satisfy the real property

180 *T.H.E. Ins. Co. v. Chicago Fireworks Mfg. Co.*, 311 Ill.App.3d 73, 79 (1st Dist. 1999).

181 *Costello By & Through Costello v. Pittsburgh Athletic Co.*, 652 F. Supp. 1579 (W.D. Pa. 1987).

182 *Id.*

183 *Id.* at 1580.

184 *Id.*

exception.[185] To accept the plaintiffs' theory of control would make the city potentially liable under the real property exception each time it conducted an inspection, the court concluded.[186]

F. McLellan v. City of Chicago Heights

In this case, spectators were injured at a fireworks display and brought a negligence action against the city. The injured spectators claimed that the city allowed them to sit too close to the launching site. The court held, however, that the city was immune from liability due to the provisions of the Tort Immunity Act.[187] In effect, crowd control and traffic management at this celebration constituted police functions that barred the spectators' claims. Additionally, the court found that it was irrelevant that firemen, not policemen, set up and manned the barricade at the event, as immunity attaches to "police services," not police departments, and it mattered not whether fireworks display was ultra-hazardous activity, as Act does not distinguish between theories of tort liability.[188] However, simply because the city was immune from liability does not mean that it was not negligent. A private promoter would not have been granted this same immunity so obviously if the city were to conduct/operate the fireworks show any plaintiff would have more difficulty succeeding in a suit.

G. Miller v. Westcor Ltd. Partnership

Here, the plaintiffs were injured as a result of a misfiring of an independent contractor's fireworks display at a mall and brought an action against both the mall and independent contractor to recover for injuries sustained.[189] The court held that the mall, as a landowner, was vicariously liable for the negligence of its independent contractor. The court explained that as a general rule, the possessor of land is not liable for the negligence of an independent contractor hired to conduct some activity on the land absent some independent negligence on the part of the possessor, since the possessor has no control over the contractor's methods of operation.[190] However, the court cautioned that a landowner is nevertheless liable for inherently dangerous activities conducted on the land by the independent contractor, even if the work could be done without a risk of harm to others and does not involve a high degree of risk of such harm, where the risk can be recognized in advance and the risk is

---

185 *Id.*

186 *Id.*

187 *McLellan v. City of Chicago Heights*, 61 F.3d 577, 578 (7th Cir.1995).

188 *Id.*

189 *Miller v. Westcor Ltd. P'ship*, 171 Ariz. 387 (Ct. App. 1991).

190 *Id.* at 390.

either inherent in or normally expected in doing the task, as when the work involves the use of instrumentalities, such as fire or high explosives, which require constant attention and skillful management in order that they may not be harmful to others.[191] The court reasoned that public fireworks displays are inherently dangerous within such exception, and it thus ruled that the mall could be held liable since the fireworks display presented a special danger to others that could not be eliminated. The court explained that this was so since any time a person ignites aerial shells or rockets with the intention of sending them aloft to explode in the presence of large crowds of people, a high risk of serious personal injury or property damage is created because of the possibility that a shell or rocket will malfunction or be misdirected. The court added that the mall was the one primarily benefiting by the fireworks display as it received all of the benefits, including goodwill among the local community.[192]

It is important to note in this case that the court considered fireworks to be inherently dangerous and thus made an exception. However in jurisdictions where fireworks are not considered inherently dangerous activities, the duty of care can be delegated to the independent contractor and thus a stadium owner will not be liable for the negligence of the independent contractor.[193] Furthermore it is inconclusive as to whether comparative negligence or assumption of the risk will provide stadium owners with a defense against claims.[194]

H. *Esposito v. New Britain Baseball Club, Inc.*

Here, a minor league baseball stadium had weekly fireworks displays which the court determined to be a private nuisance.[195] The actions of the owner of the professional minor league baseball team, fireworks display company, and city which owned and leased stadium and granted fireworks permit, in holding fireworks shows at the conclusion of each Friday night baseball home game from April through August constituted a private nuisance; because the fireworks substantially and unreasonably interfered with neighbors' use and enjoyment of their homes and with their families' lives during such time. The severity of the interference outweighed benefits of the interfering use which was, fundamentally, a profit

---

191 *Id.* at 391.

192 *Id.* at 394.

193 *See Cadena v. Chicago Fireworks Mfg. Co.*, 297 Ill.App.3d 945 (1st Dist. 1998) (holding displaying of fireworks not be an ultra-hazardous activity).

194 Jay M. Zitter, *Common Law Liability for Injury Caused by Fireworks or Firecracker*, 21 A.L.R.6th 81, § 21–22 (2007).

195 *Esposito v. New Britain Baseball Club, Inc.*, 49 Conn. Supp. 509 (2005).

making enterprise that provided entertainment.[196] More specifically, it was the excessive sound level that the residents complained about. The plaintiffs were given injunctive relief which reduced the fireworks shows to just once a month. Also, each plaintiff was awarded $100 for his or her discomfort.[197]

Although here the consequences may have been relatively insignificant to the stadium owners, it nevertheless highlights an important fact which is that stadium fireworks can constitute a legal nuisance. And more importantly, once they have been labeled a nuisance, a stadium owner can become liable for any damage caused by the nuisance.

VI. Conclusion

It would be highly prudent for stadium owners to start rethinking what is or is not reasonably foreseeable based upon the concepts and cases mentioned here. Furthermore, stadium owner should find ways to diminish the potential dangers in order to diminish the chances of litigation. Stadium safety is garnering unprecedented attention in our modern age and with this increased attention courts could alter their view and find more things reasonably foreseeable, especially in the event of a sympathetic plaintiff. Owners and operators of stadiums should be on the alert in order to know what measures need to be taken and to plan accordingly in the event a tragic accident does occur.

A. Advice

Limiting Liability for Falls and Other Injuries

1. Consider increasing the rail heights above the minimum standards in areas that pose the greatest risk of injuries from falling.
2. Place warning signs and make PA announcements that tell fans not to lean or reach out over the railings.
3. Place some kind of netting or safety measure so that in the event of a fall the spectator's injuries are minimized.
4. Instruct players to only throw balls sufficiently deep into stands to insure people are not tempted to reach over.

---

196 *Id.* at 526.

197 *Id.* at 528–29.

5. Teach team mascot's safety procedures for crowd interaction such as making eye contact with fans and throwing items into the crowd at an arc.

Limiting Liability for Violence and Crowd Control

1. Install a phone number for fans to call or text in order to report unruly behavior and make sure fans are aware of this service, and advertise said phone number on tickets, scoreboards, signs, etc.
2. Instruct your vendors to not sell to patrons who are visibly intoxicated and cease all alcohol sales sufficiently before the game is over.
3. Place undercover officers and security officials in normal or opposing team gear to catch unruly fans.
4. Properly evaluate your security measures perhaps by using outside consultation and increase or fix security issues in the needed areas.
5. Designate a safe area of the stadium where security officials can escort fans to a taxi or to their vehicle if needed.
6. Impose stricter penalties or require conduct classes for fans caught behaving in an unruly or utterly inappropriate manner.

Limiting Liability for Flying Objects and Fireworks

1. Print "Assumption of Risk" disclosures on the back of all tickets and on programs so that every fan is aware of the terms.
2. Place warning signs and make PA announcements telling fans to look out for flying objects.
3. Inspect all danger area fences routinely to ensure there is no deficiency and thus staying under the protection of the baseball rule.
4. Evaluate and possibly remodel the stadium to minimize or eliminate the possibility of flying objects reaching standing areas where fans are less likely to be watching the game.
5. Learn the governing rules on fireworks liability in your jurisdiction to see if absolute or strict liability is the standard.
6. If you operate in a strict liability jurisdiction, have only the government officials and city fire department

personnel operate pyrotechnics as they will likely have immunity. If you operate under a negligence jurisdiction, delegate the duty of care to the independent contractor so they will be solely responsible for negligent acts.

Table of Cases